THE FOG
OF PEACE

THE FOG
OF PEACE

A Memoir of International
Peacekeeping in the 21st Century

JEAN-MARIE GUÉHENNO

BROOKINGS INSTITUTION PRESS
Washington, D.C.

Copyright © 2015
THE BROOKINGS INSTITUTION
1775 Massachusetts Avenue, N.W., Washington, D.C. 20036
www.brookings.edu

The Brookings Institution is a private nonprofit organization devoted to research, education, and publication on important issues of domestic and foreign policy. Its principal purpose is to bring the highest quality independent research and analysis to bear on current and emerging policy problems. Interpretations or conclusions in Brookings publications should be understood to be solely those of the authors.

Library of Congress Cataloging-in-Publication data
Guéhenno, Jean-Marie, 1949–
    The fog of peace : a memoir of international peacekeeping in the 21st century / Jean-Marie Guéhenno.
        pages   cm
    Includes bibliographical references and index.
        ISBN 978-0-8157-2636-4 (hardcover : alk. paper) — ISBN 978-0-8157-2630-2 (pbk. : alk. paper) —   ISBN 978-0-8157-2631-9 (ebook : alk. paper) 1. Peacekeeping forces—History—21st century. 2. Wars—History—21st century. I. Title.
    JZ6374.G84 2015
        327.1'72—dc23   2014047637
9 8 7 6 5 4 3 2 1

Printed on acid-free paper

Typeset in Minion and Univers Condensed

Composition by R. Lynn Rivenbark
Macon, Georgia

To the millions of desperate people whose lives have been
shattered by war and to the peacekeepers who,
against all odds,
risk their lives to help them escape from hell

Contents

The decade that started with the momentous elections in Poland, followed by the collapse of the Berlin Wall, the unification of Germany, and the demise of the Soviet Union, had an optimistic beginning for those who had lived in the richest parts of the world. For many years, some of us had felt slightly uncomfortable that our wealth and security apparently were not transferable. In Europe, there was a sense that the immense waste of the cold war was ending and that the hopes that had existed in 1945, and then were dashed by the divisions of the cold war, could now be realized. Nation states would come together in a "new world order," and the states would serve their people instead of sometimes being their jailers. Even more radically, borders would stop being walls behind which governments could commit the worst abuses.

The fall of the Berlin Wall was just the beginning. In 1991, for the first time in the history of the United Nations, the Security Council intervened directly against an oppressive government, adopting Resolution 688 insisting that "Iraq allow immediate access by international humanitarian organizations to all those in need of assistance." At the time, this was read by Western nongovernmental organizations (NGOs) as demonstrating a growing sense of solidarity that was chipping at traditional notions of sovereignty: Borders could not be a barrier when people were dying. The fact that the resolution reiterated "the commitment of all Member States to the sovereignty, territorial integrity and political independence of Iraq" and noted that the violence against the Kurds had cross-border impact and was therefore a threat to international peace and security, was seen as a tactical concession to dying traditions of state sovereignty.

What a difference ten years can make. In the spring of 1999, the picture of the world had become much fuzzier. NATO was conducting a seventy-eight-day bombing campaign over Kosovo to stop the violence of Slobodan Milošević, but that campaign had not been sanctioned by a resolution of the Security Council. The sense of hope and unity that had briefly existed in the immediate aftermath of the fall of the Berlin Wall had been shattered by a series of failures: first, the long breakup of Yugoslavia and the inability of the international community to stop the violence that accompanied it; second, the collapse of the international humanitarian relief effort in Somalia after U.S. soldiers were killed in Mogadishu and international forces quickly ran away; and third, the genocide in Rwanda, and the passivity of the international community, which mastered the will to deploy troops to evacuate rich Westerners but not to protect poor Africans.

The arrival of the twenty-first century, and the hype that accompanied it as the big cities of the world outdid each other to celebrate the new millennium, was a time of uncertainty and doubts, but not of despair. The post–cold war world had not produced the "end of history," as Francis Fukuyama had optimistically predicted, nor had it spelled the "end of democracy" and of the nation state, as I had, a bit glibly, announced in a small book published in 1993, when I was challenging the optimism of the early 1990s. In 2000 the world was all shades of grey.

That is the time when I joined the United Nations to become the head of its peacekeeping department. I was going to turn fifty, and at the time I did not know if I would again be operationally involved in international affairs. I had held interesting positions in the French Ministry of Foreign Affairs. As the head of policy planning in the early 1990s, I had done my best to convince French leaders that the fall of the Berlin Wall was an opportunity, not a threat, and that strengthening European institutions should not be conceived as a way to contain a unified Germany but as a means for Europe to keep its relevance in a world where the end of the East-West divide spelled the end of the centrality of Europe. But my present job was quite removed from the challenges of the post–cold war era. I was a senior sitting judge in France's highest financial court, one of its oldest institutions, the Cour des Comptes. It had been created by Napoleon in 1807, but its origins went back to the Middle Ages. And indeed, on solemn occasions, I would put on a long black silk robe adorned with white lace, and make various bows following a ritual that has not changed much since the seventeenth century. I had stayed involved in international affairs, attending conferences, chairing a French defense institute, teaching, and writing articles and books. I had become a commentator, and could have written a guide book on the best conference places of the world. I was trying to make an intellectual difference, but I was not sure I would. How many political scientists are remembered a century after they have written and commented on current events?

As a child of the baby boom, I witnessed the momentous transformation of France in the postwar decades. But my life was infinitely easier than that of my parents, and most important, I never experienced war. War was an abstraction in the peaceful Western Europe of the 1950s and 1960s, and the bomb sirens that blew every first Thursday of the month to test the systems were a quaint reminder that there had been other periods in the history of Europe. The only time when I had a vague sense that this nice world could unravel was during the Cuban missile crisis. But most of the time, I had a protected and privileged life. I was immersed in a world of writers and free spirits who cared about ideas, not money, and that made schoolwork effortless. With that family background, I should have become a professor, or I could have remained a sitting judge with a beautiful black silk robe. But I did not want to.

Throughout the 1990s, I had been reflecting on the historical experience of the twentieth century, which had had such a defining role for my parents. We usually learn the wrong lessons of history, and fight the last war. The generation of my father was broken by the experience of World War I. The world powers of the time stumbled into a war they expected to be quick and clean but that turned out to be long and dirty. And when new threats emerged in the 1930s, the fear of stumbling into another devastating war led many European intellectuals to pacifism and contributed to the initial weak response to Hitler. My father was ambivalent. He was a strong antifascist and distanced himself from some of his pacifist friends. But it was not until World War II broke out that he realized, as did my mother (the two had not yet met), that peace is not always an absolute goal, and that sometimes freedom is worth a fight. My father was wary of military power, wary of force, wary of the advice of generals.

Working on East-West relations and nuclear deterrence in the 1980s, I had developed a very different view of the world. Just as my father's view had been shaped by World War I, mine was shaped by World War II. What World War II had shown was that weakness was never a good response to force. Force had to be met by force. Since war supposedly had become too destructive to be waged, the abstract conceptual game of nuclear deterrence had been invented. I admired the writings of Tom Schelling, and as a young expert I was thrilled to attend meetings with Albert Wohlstetter, whom I considered to be one of the most brilliant strategic analysts of our time. I had a hawkish position when the Soviet Union invaded Afghanistan, and I felt closer to the group of American analysts who would later become the "neocons," such as Paul Wolfowitz—whose intellectual curiosity I have always admired—than to détente peaceniks. I was happy to play a minor role in encouraging the French government to give support to the mujahedin in Afghanistan even before the United States launched a huge program that would eventually contribute to the withdrawal of Soviet forces but also would help build up the Taliban. For me the collapse of the Soviet Union vindicated such hard-nose policies. My view of the world was "Kissingerian," shaped by big powers in a strategic game where local factors have little relevance. In 1989–90 my world was still one of dangerously big ideas.

As the post–cold war world unfolded, I began to suspect that this view of the world was too neat and clear-cut. It assumed too much control on the part of governments and states. It ignored human passions and the frailty of many states. I became more and more suspicious of traditional state institutions, which I saw as gradually bypassed by new, nongovernmental actors: corporations, non-profit organizations, rebel movements, and also new transnational institutions like the European Commission. My cold war worldview had also assumed too much moral clarity. As children of World War II and of the cold war, my cohorts and I did not have the doubts of the generation that followed World War I. We thought we had a clear moral compass. We knew what was good and what was evil. Although there had been circumstances in which we had to bend our principles to strategic expediency, which sometimes had meant supporting dictators during the cold war, we never envisaged that the world could be so messy that there could be conflicting goals that were equally good. It was one thing to accept that sometimes the ends justified the means, even if the means were questionable. It was quite another to find out that good ends might be in conflict with each other—that, for instance, the legitimate desire of a human community to run its own affairs could conflict with the legitimate desire for peace and stability, or that the admirable desire of some to show solidarity to human beings at risk might be perceived as a threat by others, and not only by nasty dictators. Good intentions might not always produce good results.

In many ways, such questions should have kept me away from the United Nations and peacekeeping. I had written a book expressing my skepticism about the continued relevance of nation states. How could I work for an organization composed of nation states? How could part of my job be to help consolidate fragile states? I had growing doubts about the capacity of major nations to come together coherently, and I would have as my boss the Security Council. I questioned the clarity of moral goals in the world of international politics, and I would become a self-righteous international civil servant working for the good of humankind.

In addition, I had no direct work experience with the United Nations. Once, when I was the head of the French policy planning staff and was passing through New York, the French mission had given me a pass to have access to the small room where the Security Council holds its private consultations, a room where I would spend so much time in later years. I have no recollection of the topic that was then being discussed, but I remember vividly my surprise, and—if I may say—my disappointment. I had expected some solemn and orderly chamber, and what I saw was a cramped little space, with not enough seats for all the people present. The ambassadors were huddled around the table, but they did not look like my idea of ambassadors. The whole place looked more like one of those small auction rooms I used to visit in Paris, or worse, like some kind of clandestine parlor where card players

ambiguous environment of peacekeeping

play unauthorized games. It did not look like the keystone of the international system. So much for my first personal experience of the United Nations.

When, in early 2000, the French government put me on the shortlist of candidates submitted to Secretary General Kofi Annan for the position of under secretary general in charge of peacekeeping, I was not at all sure that the combination of diplomatic, military, and management experience that I would bring to the job would outweigh my lack of UN experience. But I certainly wanted the job more than my competitors because I saw it as a unique opportunity to change my life by having for the first time the opportunity to change the lives of others. That intuition was right, but I had no idea of the magnitude of the personal challenges I would have to face. As I was preparing for the interviews in New York, I wanted to compensate for my lack of direct UN experience by absorbing all the information I could. I read the reports on Srebrenica and on Rwanda; I read the publications on peacekeeping. I read painfully boring reports produced by the bureaucracy of the UN—reports in which everything said is factually correct and yet where nothing really stimulates fresh thinking. I am not sure that I have really been able to change that. I read the more accessible book by William Shawcross, *Deliver Us from Evil*, to get a better understanding of the man who might be my future boss, Kofi Annan. All that reading prepared me well for the interviews that I went through, along with the other candidates, in May 2000. I had acquired an intellectual idea of peacekeeping, and I was sufficiently well-informed of the tragedies of the 1990s to understand the ever-looming dangers of peacekeeping.

As I was interviewing for the job, a severe crisis almost brought down the peacekeeping mission in Sierra Leone. A peace agreement had been broken by the Revolutionary United Front (RUF), a cruel rebel faction that had made a habit of chopping off arms of members of rival groups. Hundreds of peacekeepers, who had not been prepared for the challenge, had been taken hostage. I felt sorry for my predecessor, Bernard Miyet, a French diplomat. I spoke to him as one does to a gravely ill person, with a mix of visible concern, to show sympathy, and fake optimism, to be reassuring. He laughed at my concerned look and showed an optimism that did not sound fake; he told me that he had just spoken to the press, and that everything would be fine. He suggested that this was just one day in the life of peacekeeping. And one had to take it in stride. I wondered at the time whether I was the right person for the job, or whether my judgment was right. In that particular case, my predecessor was right. Although two key troop contributors—India and Jordan—eventually pulled out, the mission, after a daring operation conducted by Indian troops and with the help of British Special Forces, did recover. The hostages were freed, Pakistani troops replaced Indian troops, and Sierra Leone eventually became a success story.

What I did not see, and the optimistic character of Bernard Miyet did not help me there, is that the way in which the international community, the Security Council, and the Secretariat of the United Nations interact puts a unique responsibility on the secretary general of the United Nations and the under secretary general for peacekeeping. I would have to learn through experience that an international civil servant has a lot of company when success comes, but is a very lonely person in times of trouble.

I did not know, in those crisp sunny days of May 2000, that I would spend eight years of my life in the position I was interviewing for—the longest commitment of my career—and that those eight years would be, in some ways, eight years of solitude.

Why do I write today? Peacekeeping is an enormous managerial challenge, which has some lessons for all sorts of unrelated activities; as a particularly risky activity, it is a never-ending exercise in risk management and decisionmaking in an environment of uncertainty. As an activity that brings together very different national and professional cultures, it is an exercise in building a team and mobilizing very diverse human beings for a common goal. There were many days of crisis during those eight years, many days that were just like the one in May 2000, another day in the life of peacekeeping. Why not just smile like my predecessor and let others find out for themselves? I actually believe that I may have gained a few insights that could be of interest not just to those who are engaged in peacekeeping—and their number has been continuously growing since 2000—but also to those who want to operate effectively in a world that is being redefined by the conflicting forces of globalization and fragmentation. The study of disease helps one understand a healthy body, and the study of societies that have broken up can give us some insights into how to keep societies together. It is becoming more and more evident that one of the key strategic challenges of the next twenty years actually will be how to help keep societies together, how to prevent state failure and its potentially devastating consequences.

As the international community reflects on two decades of interventions in the lives of others, and wonders whether it was worth it, the mood is very different from the one that prevailed at the beginning of the millennium. Liberal interventionists as well as neocons now have self-doubts, and in many countries public opinion is turning inward, wary of foreign adventures that look too difficult and too uncertain. The temptation is great to prefer the safety of home to the hazards of an unpredictable and maybe unmanageable world.

This book is an attempt to chart a course that eschews reckless intervention-ism as well as an emerging parochialism. No course of action—or inaction—is without dangers, and the prudent interventionism that I advocate will, from time to time, fail. But it is better to fail after having tried than to fail for not having tried.

The book I have decided to write is very different from the one I would have wanted to write in 2000. Not just for the obvious reason that I could not, as I was starting in my new job, formulate the questions the way I can today. The more essential difference is that I strongly believe today that I should try to tell a personal experience, that general lessons are of no relevance if they are not grounded in the specifics of a unique situation. I do not want today to be a commentator on peacekeeping but rather to convey all the uncertainties, the flaws, the false hopes, the wrong assumptions, the unnecessary fears, the fog of real action.

Before I became the head of peacekeeping, I had a reputation as an intel-lectual rather than as an operator. I never thought that being characterized as an intellectual should be taken as an insult, although I knew that it usually does not help a career to be called an intellectual or a thinker. It suggests that you cannot operate but does not guarantee that you really can think. Having had to become an operator, I have not lost my respect for thinking, but I do believe that a lot of the "thinking" that goes on is useless for operators. The most useless way to pretend to help is to offer detailed, specific solutions, or recipes. There are dozens of political science books that look like "how to" books. They do not have the texture of life and therefore fall off the hand. Operators do not read much. They do not have the time. I, who was an avid reader, read much less during those eight years than I used to. And the more operational I became, the less interested I was in operational books. I would rather read memoirs, history books, or real philosophy. What I needed was the fraternal companionship of other actors before me who had had to deal with confusion, grapple with the unknown, and yet had made decisions. What I also needed was the solidity of true abstraction and the harmony of good visual art (music does not do it for me; I can hardly sing the French national anthem). What I needed was, in times of difficulty, the distance of the mind.

The unfortunate truth is, however, that when you are immersed in action, you mostly live on the intellectual capital you acquired beforehand; you draw on it. You may be accumulating, in some corner of your brain, new patterns, new chains of thinking that will eventually help you, but you are not really aware of it, and you certainly do not have the time to reflect on it.

When I now reflect on what helped me most, I find it is not the knowledge that the bureaucrats who determine how to conduct an interview in the UN would characterize as "directly relevant." What I knew about specific crisis situations, or about institutional procedures, would be quickly outdated, often insufficient, while a well-drafted note could tell me all I needed to know. What helped me, what I would not find in any note, was the philosophical and ethical framework I had acquired in my classical studies. What helped me was the historical experience of my parents, and the questions that it raised.

As the head of peacekeeping, a person whose job description includes trying to establish a relationship with a lot of unsavory characters, I had to answer in a very practical way the question that so dominated the twentieth century: How far should one go to ensure peace? And who are we to decide for others when to compromise and when not to compromise? I found that peacekeeping, far from being a cynical enterprise aimed at preserving peace at any price, can be successful only if it is understood as a highly moral enterprise. One needs a reliable compass to navigate through the fog of peace. And I found that an enterprise becomes moral not because it is a fight against evil, but because it has to consider conflicting goods, and lesser evils, and make choices. It is those dilemmas that make peacekeeping an ethical enterprise. It is those dilemmas that I would like to share with the reader.

[handwritten notes:]

peace keeping → only sucessful when considered a moral enterprise

becomes moral ent. when considers conflicting goods/lesser evils to make choices

THE FOG
OF PEACE

one
AFGHANISTAN
9/11 and the War on Terror

September 11, 2001, started in New York as a particularly beautiful September day: there was not a single cloud, the air was transparent, and the light was crisp. I was less than three weeks away from the first anniversary of my joining the United Nations and had no sense of the momentous global changes that would be set in motion by the tragic events of the day. In his acceptance speech for the Nobel Peace Prize in Oslo three months later, Kofi Annan would say of September 11, with some flourish: "We have entered the third millennium through a gate of fire." The historic importance of events is not always immediately perceived, but September 11 was almost immediately understood as the beginning of a new era.

I wrote in my notebook on the 12th of September: "This is as important as the Berlin Wall; it will change the relationship of the United States with the rest of the world." To many of us, it was clear that the world had changed radically, but the direction it would take was unclear. The French ambassador to the United Nations, Jean-David Lévitte, was among those who immediately understood how critical it was to encourage the United States not to take a solitary path, but on the contrary to turn to the rest of world and to the United Nations for solidarity and support. As the French daily *Le Monde* put it in a banner headline on September 12: "We are All Americans." Lévitte pushed hard for the quick adoption, just one day after the attack, of a wide-ranging resolution. The political intention was obvious, and I agreed with it: everybody expected the Bush administration to take action after such a devastating and humiliating blow, but it was important that the U.S. actions not challenge the post–World War II legal order.

However, the casual way in which the Security Council radically broadened the right of self-defense enshrined in the charter of the United Nations was worrying. Resolution 1368 recognized the right of member states to combat terrorism "by all means," identifying as legitimate targets "those responsible for aiding supporting, or harboring the perpetrators, organizers and sponsors," and inviting member states "to suppress terrorist acts, including by increased cooperation," which meant that they could also act individually. We were moving away from the clarity of inter-state conflict, in which the right of self-defense had been restrictively defined so that use of force by a country without the explicit authorization of the Security Council would be the exception. What the Security Council was in effect doing was granting a member state—in this case the United States, but other countries could later avail themselves of the precedent—the right to launch strikes inside another country with which it was not at war, solely because it was deemed to "harbor terrorists," and that was enough to assert the right of self-defense. Sergei Lavrov, who would later become the foreign minister of Russia, but in 2001 was still the Russian ambassador to the UN, wryly noted that the council had dropped the word "lawful" when affirming its determination to combat threats to international peace and security caused by terrorist acts. A sort of panic had in effect seized the world, but there was no conceptual framework ready for this new situation in which the central role of states as the guardians of law was being challenged. The balance between when a state can choose unilaterally to use force and when it must pursue a more collective process involving the Security Council had changed.

The ground for this evolution had been prepared during the Clinton administration, when in the summer of 1998 the United States launched cruise missiles against targets in Afghanistan and in Sudan, in response to the bombing of American embassies in Africa. But the operations that were launched in November 2001 against the Taliban regime were of a different order of magnitude. The Bush administration, probably encouraged by British diplomacy, formally informed the president of the Security Council of the actions taken, but no mention of the United Nations was to be found in the letter simultaneously sent to Congress. There was also an ominous mention in the U.S. letter to the Security Council of "other organizations and States" that possibly could be targeted. That did not go unnoticed in the Arab world. The circumstances under which use of force in self-defense could be considered had been dramatically expanded: the international community would be informed, but it was the sovereign decision of the United States to determine when, where, and how it would wage what was beginning to be called the "war on terror."

The way President Bush defined the fight against the terrorists of September 11 was to have a profound impact on the way the United States saw itself and was seen by the rest of the world. There was a fleeting moment, illustrated by the quick adoption of the UN resolution, during which the whole world seemed to come together in a genuine, even if superficial, show of sympathy. French president Jacques Chirac, who would later be described as public enemy number one of the United States during the run-up to the Iraq war, was genuinely moved when he arrived in New York a few days later as the first foreign head of state to visit the still-smoldering ruins of the World Trade Center. He met Kofi Annan for lunch immediately afterward. This would be the first of many occasions where I saw the French president and the secretary general together. Their relations were always cordial, even though France had been a staunch supporter of Annan's predecessor Boutros Boutros-Ghali and probably had been initially suspicious of a candidate so strongly pushed by the United States. But France is generally supportive of the United Nations—where its permanent seat on the Security Council gives it more clout than it might otherwise have in world affairs—and it quickly understood that Kofi Annan would be a good partner. At a personal level, it was clear that the two men had a mutual liking, as they recognized in each other a real humanity, an interest in people. But they could not be more different: an understated African aristocrat and a populist French politician, a feline sprinter and a boxer with a heavy frame.

Chirac was happy that there was a broad consensus on the fight against terrorism and insisted that it should be a collective fight. "There was no alternative to the United Nations in the fight against terrorism," he said. He had come to New York from Washington and described George Bush as a "man with an open mind," and Colin Powell as a "wise man." Vice President Dick Cheney had not spoken much, but "what he had said was reasonable," and "Condoleezza Rice had not opened her mouth." He confirmed what I had concluded from the resolution, that the United States would not go to the Security Council before taking action, but he added: "It does not really matter; it is a detail for technicians." The bitter discussion about Iraq that started a year later was to show that those details did matter, and that one of the great achievements of the post–World War II period was under threat: at risk was a common, albeit limited, understanding of international law with respect to the use of force.

This legal issue that was being so lightly brushed aside pointed to a more fundamental question: Would September 11 bring the world together, or on the contrary, pull it further apart? The United States, in contrast to most other nations on earth, had never been exposed to an attack on its homeland during the last century, except for Pearl Harbor, but Hawaii was not yet a state of the Union at the time. For the first time since the War of 1812, the United

States felt truly vulnerable to foreign attack, which is the common lot of most nations around the world. Americans had "lost their innocence" as Chris Patten, the European commissioner for external relations and a sharp mind, would tell me a couple of weeks later in Brussels. Would that sense of shared vulnerability bring greater proximity and solidarity—and the rest of the world seemed to be ready for that—or would it, on the contrary, push a wounded country into a more assertive nationalism driven by fear, and create more divisions in a world already fractured by enormous differences in wealth? Kofi Annan, a few weeks later in his Nobel speech in Oslo, would try to encourage the United States and the world to take the first path. He said:

> If today, after the horror of the eleventh of September, we see better, and we see further—we will realize that humanity is indivisible. New threats make no distinction between races, nations or regions. A new insecurity has entered every mind, regardless of wealth or status. A deeper awareness of the bonds that bind us all—in pain as in prosperity—has gripped young and old.

Unfortunately, President Bush's famous declaration that "either you are with us, or you are with the terrorists"[1] became an excuse not to try to understand what kind of world could make such extreme violence possible. Trying to understand became conflated with trying to excuse. And those who did seek an understanding often seemed to suggest a kind of symmetry that could only be perceived as a cruel insult to the thousands of victims who had died on September 11. When I read "The Algebra of Infinite Justice," an article written by an Indian writer I usually admired, Arundhati Roy, I was at times profoundly shocked, at times in agreement. I admired her when she wrote:

> America's grief at what happened has been immense and immensely public. It would be grotesque to expect it to calibrate or modulate its anguish. However, it will be a pity if, instead of using this as an opportunity to try to understand why September 11 happened, Americans use it as an opportunity to usurp the whole world's sorrow to mourn and avenge only their own. Because then it falls to the rest of us to ask the hard questions and say the harsh things. And for our pains, for our bad timing, we will be disliked, ignored and perhaps eventually silenced.

---

1. President Bush first used the declaration in an address to Congress on September 20, 2001; see "Address Before a Joint Session of the Congress on the United States Response to the Terrorist Attacks of September 11," September 20, 2011, American Presidency Project (www.presidency.ucsb.edu/ws/index.php?pid=64731&st=&st1=).

I was shocked when she wrote, "The message [of the attacks] may have been written by Bin Laden (who knows?) and delivered by his couriers, but it could well have been signed by the ghosts of the victims of America's old wars." But I thought she was largely right to warn:

> The U.S. government, and no doubt governments all over the world, will use the climate of war as an excuse to curtail civil liberties, deny free speech, lay off workers, harass ethnic and religious minorities, cut back on public spending and divert huge amounts of money to the defense industry. To what purpose? . . . Terrorism as a phenomenon may never go away. But if it is to be contained, the first step is for America to at least acknowledge that it shares the planet with other nations, with other human beings who, even if they are not on TV, have loves and griefs and stories and songs and sorrows and, for heaven's sake, rights. Instead, when Donald Rumsfeld, the U.S. defense secretary, was asked what he would call a victory in America's new war, he said that if he could convince the world that Americans must be allowed to continue with their way of life, he would consider it a victory.

I could not accept the violence of her tone, the disingenuous way in which she seemed to equate the decision to kill with the benign neglect of human suffering that wealth usually produces. She established an unfair symmetry between the nihilistic violence of September 11, which had killed thousands, and the nihilistic materialism of a Western civilization driven by money and success, which does not make the choice of evil, which does not wittingly kill but has little understanding for the misery of millions. But she rightly understood that at the heart of the fractures of our world was a tragic lack of imagination and empathy, a juxtaposition of self-righteous, closed communities reflecting the absence of a genuine human community. I felt that for the United Nations, it was a defining moment. I wrote a long note to Kofi Annan, in which I tried to find the right tone.

My starting point was that a "global community" remains elusive and that "people are now more scared by globalization and its threatening diversity. They feel dependent more than they feel empowered. They want to assert what makes their community different and unique and long for the comfort of a homogeneous community in which familiarity breeds security; they want a limited horizon, not a borderless world. Hence, the paradox of growing parochialism in the age of globalization." I continued, "In the permanent tradeoff between the opportunities of openness and the safety of a closed community, the closed community has won. More 'gated communities,' metaphoric or real, are coming." I then turned to the attacks of September 11:

The abyss of hatred revealed by the attack is not confined to a few "mad" terrorists. It is shared by tens of thousands, and condoned by tens of millions of people, who deeply resent what they perceive as Western hubris and moral bankruptcy, and who denounce the gap between the functional and economic integration of the world, and its moral vacuity. . . . The liberal consensus now under attack was a convenient one: it posited that the world, if left to its own devices, is largely self-balancing. . . . This was indeed a morally and politically expedient analysis: it reconciled ethics and efficiency (self-interest produced the best society); it did not put too many demands on the rich and powerful (especially the U.S., whose power, in that non-political view of the world, was subsumed in the anonymous power of the "Market"); it shifted the burden of efforts on the developing world, which had to mend its ways. . . . It reflected the latest triumph of the age of Enlightenment and of the United States, as its most concrete expression. Its rejection by radical Islamists, but also by the religious right in the U.S. as well as by unreconstructed leftists is a rejection of a functional view of the world, and the affirmation that values rather than interests govern societies and bring human beings together. Ethics and ideas are back as the dominant force in Human history. This can bring progress as well as disaster: historically, ideas have been much greater killers than greed.

I never sent the note, and I was certainly right not to. When I read it eight years later, as the global economic crisis provided a bookend to the first decade of the twenty-first century, it took a different meaning. But I am glad I did not send it: this was the work of an abstract French intellectual who had not yet quite become a practical operator. As a piece of advice, the note was useless. The United Nations and its secretary general, in a world of nation states, can do little to shape national perceptions. Empathy between different nations cannot be prescribed; it has to come from within, from national leaders who do not take the easy route of self-righteous nationalism. Other leaders in the United States and Europe might have seized the moment to foster that empathy, to change the discourse on justice, and bring the world closer together. The politics of solidarity rather than the politics of fear could have prevailed. But Kofi Annan could not go much further than the exhortations of his Nobel lecture. His priority had to be the more immediate implications of September 11 on the conduct of international relations, and Afghanistan was to be the first test.

Almost immediately after the attacks, it became clear that al Qaeda was the organization responsible, and that Afghanistan was the safe haven of al Qaeda.

Until then, the United States had been more concerned about so-called rogue states than failing states. September 11 signaled that failing states could actually be more dangerous than rogue states. Nonstate actors could almost take over a state, as had happened in Afghanistan, without being subject to the checks and balances provided by traditional power politics. The world was discovering that the old structures of states were being destroyed by globalization much faster than new ones could be built. It was soon obvious that the government of the United States would respond, to avenge its humiliation and to send a clear message to all governments on the planet that they were responsible for what happened on the land they were expected to control, and that no government, no matter how fragile, could distance itself from nonstate actors using its territory. The traditional order in which states are the ultimate guardians of a world order had to be reestablished. The Bush administration could have—and in my view should have—tried diplomacy and pressed the Taliban to abandon bin Laden. It chose force instead and decided that the Taliban state had to be toppled. This fateful decision was the logical outcome of the posture that the international community had taken when it decided to break all relations with the Taliban regime and refused to recognize its authority over Afghanistan, although the Taliban came to have effective control over most of the country. This political isolation, which had been challenged only by Pakistan, Saudi Arabia, and the United Arab Emirates, probably contributed to the weakening of state structures and to its association with a criminal terrorist organization. We still wanted an international order based on the sovereign responsibility of states, but we were willing to pretend that a state with which we had a fundamental difference did not exist. It is remarkable that more than ten years after September 11, we have not really overcome that contradiction.

Two days before the attacks in the United States, Ahmad Shah Massoud, the most respected Afghan leader fighting the Taliban, had been assassinated in his stronghold by Taliban agents. At the time, the war for control of Afghanistan was continuing, and the Taliban were winning. While their ethnic base was in the Pashtun south, their program was not an ethnic one, and since capturing Kabul in 1996 they had gradually taken control of the whole country, including the mainly Tadjik and Uzbek northern regions. Only a small part of the country remained under the control of warlords and other forces.

Subsequent U.S. support of the Northern Alliance—a loose coalition of non-Pashtun ethnic groups from the northern part of the country—radically changed the course of the war. In a few weeks starting in early October 2001, the combination of a ground offensive by the Northern Alliance, CIA intelligence, and a powerful U.S. air campaign routed the Taliban. From the moment the air campaign started, on an autumn Sunday, the outcome of the Afghan war was not in doubt, although the speed at which "victory" was achieved was a surprise, as it would be in Iraq in early 2003. In both cases, the international community overestimated the difficulty of the military campaign and underestimated the challenges of political stabilization. What is remarkable, looking back on those fateful weeks at the end of 2001, is how early some of the fundamental issues that dominate today's debate on Afghanistan were identified, while at the same time major mistakes, for which we now pay a heavy price, nevertheless were also made.

A week after September 11, Hubert Védrine, the socialist French foreign minister who was accompanying President Jacques Chirac, had lunch at the United Nations with Kofi Annan and myself. At this meeting he was already wondering whether Pakistan had the capacity and political will to act effectively in the fight against terrorism. I do not know if he had the opportunity to make his case to American officials, but in the intervening years, it has become abundantly clear that Pakistan, for which the issue of Kashmir remains a unifying national cause and a useful rationale for a big army, has great difficulties fighting the same terrorist cells that have launched operations in the Indian-occupied part of Kashmir. The fact that the Northern Alliance had Indian support increased the concern in Islamabad that Pakistan would lose what some of its generals have called "strategic depth," that it would be squeezed between a hostile India and a hostile Afghanistan. After all, Pakistan intelligence services (the Inter-Services Intelligence or ISI) had handled as partners of the CIA some of the Pashtun factions that had fought the Soviets, like the Hezb-e-Islami of Gulbuddin Hekmatyar, which later joined the Taliban. And many Pakistanis felt that an Afghanistan driven by a religious ideology—as the Taliban were—would be less of a threat to the territorial integrity of Pakistan than an Afghanistan driven by nationalism: Pakistan has fought Balush and Pashtun nationalism for decades and has had only limited control over its border with Afghanistan. Encouraging tribal leaders to have a religious rather than a national agenda remained a more attractive option for many Pakistanis.

In the fall of 2001, however, when the United States asked Pakistan to break ties with the Taliban and support the U.S. campaign, General Pervez Musharraf, Pakistan's president, had no choice but to oblige. Nevertheless, as early as October 12, 2001, the first demonstrations against the American campaign took place in Pakistan. They were limited in scope and did not cause too much concern at the time. But they were a signal. I was amazed, a few years later, during one of my visits to Islamabad, to witness the depth of anti-American sentiment not just among lay people but among an elite that sends its children to the United States for their college education. It looked as if some members of the Pakistani upper class resented U.S. policies all the more because they knew they had no choice but to support them, and they would be doomed if the policies failed.

As the U.S. campaign started, the prestige of Kofi Annan was at its highest. After September 11, he had found the right words to express his compassion for the United States in a moment of national tragedy, and the U.S. government was making friendly gestures toward the UN. More than half a billion dollars in arrears owed by the United States were paid quickly. Kofi Annan suspected early on that after the U.S. campaign, a UN operation would be required. A journalist had mentioned that possibility in an article in the *Guardian*, and U.S. officials already were hinting at a possible UN role in Afghanistan. When I called Annan to congratulate him on his Nobel Prize, the conversation quickly turned to Afghanistan: Would it be like Somalia? Would the UN be caught in a fight between Afghan factions? What was the risk that the victory of one group over another would be wrapped in a UN flag, while Iran and Pakistan vied for influence and control? This was the first time on my watch that a new peacekeeping operation was being considered, and I was focused on the many different ways in which things could go badly wrong. I had not directly experienced Yugoslavia, Somalia, and Rwanda, but my initial reactions to the first major challenge of my tenure were shaped by the reports and analyses I had read on the tragedies of the 1990s, when UN peacekeeping was cast as a bystander to genocide in Europe and Africa. I would later acquire more direct experience, and possibly more confidence, but for better or worse I would never depart from that initial caution, for which I have sometimes been criticized.

Debating Options for a Security Force

The first important meeting on Afghanistan with the United States took place in mid-October 2001 at the UN. Kofi Annan asked Lakhdar Brahimi, a respected Algerian diplomat, to be the point person for the UN on Afghanistan. The U.S. delegation was led by John Negroponte, the American ambassador to the UN, and included Richard Haass, who was then the head of policy planning at the State Department. I had known Haass for many years and I admired his capacity for bringing intellectual clarity to complex issues without oversimplifying them. Richard was among the first to speak, according to my notes of the meeting. He explained that his mandate was to think about the future of Afghanistan: "We are not trying to remake Afghanistan, but in Afghanistan, even the most limited thing is ambitious." He added: "We need to do enough now so that we do not have to do it again in three years." How right he was, and how different our actions were to be from that aspiration to get it right. Interestingly, the discussion that took place stands the test of time on the strategic issues.

Haass outlined an approach that, if it had been followed, might have led to a very different Afghanistan. But as head of policy planning, he was not making policy, just recommending an ideal course of action. My own experiences in France at the end of the cold war, when I was running the French planning staff and was often in disagreement with the dominant policy, should have taught me that there can be a wide gap between the recommendations of a planning staff and government policy. Haass remarkably said: "We need to have an Afghan entity, even transitional, up and running. We want a broad government. We have to be careful not to ostracize Taliban rank and file. The problem is with Mullah Omar and his lieutenants. But you cannot exclude Taliban and attract the Pashtu. Certainly, the military campaign and the appeal of money can help rally former supporters of Mullah Omar."

The same openness and flexibility was apparent when the discussion moved to the broader strategic picture. Haass was supportive of the so-called 6+2, a group that included Iran, China, Pakistan, Tadjikistan, Turkmenistan, and Uzbekistan, as well as the United States and Russia; but he wanted to complement it with a broader group, "the friends of Afghanistan," to bring in countries and organizations that would contribute to the reconstruction effort, like Japan, the European Union, and India. Kofi Annan, in response to Haass, confirmed that Brahimi would quickly deploy to the region and visit Pakistan and Iran. He stressed how a UN role could be crucial for those two countries. Both countries would want a friendly regime in Kabul. He gently suggested to his U.S. interlocutors—some of whom might not be very inclined to engage with Iran—that it was important not to give the impression that only Pakistan mattered. "We will have to do quite a bit of work with Iran," he said, "and the Iranians are eager to cooperate." He then added that the Northern Alliance was deeply divided and that "it was good that the United States was not in favor of the Northern Alliance entering Kabul." This was Kofi Annan's subtle way of encouraging a policy line that was far from unanimously supported in the U.S. government. He knew that for some, especially in the Pentagon, the Northern Alliance was a useful proxy that had made it possible for Washington to wage a war on the cheap, and that the temptation now was just to hand over Afghanistan to the Northern Alliance. By mentioning the divisions within the Northern Alliance, and thus hinting at the Iranian connections, Annan was arguing a case without appearing to argue too much. I saw him do that many times, delicately letting his interlocutors draw their own conclusions, rather than hammering a point like a litigator.

Haass got it, and first reassured the secretary general that indeed several channels were opened with the Iranians and that the discussions were "businesslike." He noted that the Pakistanis were saying the right things, but their intelligence people had to be reined in. He then addressed the main issue that Kofi Annan had so delicately tackled: "We are happy that the Northern Alliance is not rushing into Kabul, but eventually, they will move in. It is not a question of if but when. . . . Keeping them out forever is impossible, although some say that it is plausible that they hold back for a long time." The message was clear, but Kofi Annan reminded Haass that the Northern Alliance was a collection of minorities, and "there are risks of killings." Haass replied, a little defensively, "We will do our best so that they say the right thing and not do the wrong things." Brahimi, who had remained silent until then, spoke up: "The players have no confidence in each other, and they may all rush and do the wrong things." Brahimi, who was aware that convincing the United States to prevent the Northern Alliance from entering Kabul was probably a lost battle, then moved to the diplomatic level. "We must do everything we can to prevent such misunderstandings, and create a minimum level of trust. It is important that Iran trust the U.S. If you use the UN, that will reassure the parties, especially when it comes to building an Afghan entity. One needs to talk through one channel."

To enter or not to enter Kabul: this was the question for the Northern Alliance. After the meeting, Brahimi told me that some of the followers of Massoud were wise, and they saw how entering Kabul might have a negative impact and break the delicate balance that was needed for stability in Afghanistan. But the Iranians were extremely worried about the intentions of the Pakistanis, and therefore actively pushing the Northern Alliance to enter Kabul.

This was probably the most crucial issue, but in the end necessity rather than reason made the decision. Everybody agreed that it would be good to keep Kabul as a city that did not belong to any particular group and embodied the impartiality of the new government of Afghanistan. But Kabul could not be left in a vacuum, and there were no takers in the international community to fill that vacuum, as became clear from the brief discussion on the kind of force that could be deployed that took place at the end of the meeting with the U.S. delegation. Three options were considered, each with its drawbacks:

A multinational force—an ad hoc coalition not under the command of the UN—would be the most effective, but where would volunteers be found?

Turkey had been mentioned, but so far there was no offer. The second option was a national Afghan force composed of different Afghan groups, but what would be its cohesiveness? The last option was a force of blue helmets—under the command of the UN—but it would take three to five months to deploy. None of the three options had much reality, and we were all deluding ourselves, as is often the case when there is no attractive solution but nobody is prepared for the humiliation of admitting it. The UN option, in particular, did not address the immediate needs in Kabul; moreover, Kofi Annan knew the dangers of inserting a weak UN force in the midst of warring parties; as the head of peacekeeping at the time of Srebrenica, he certainly remembered only too well that it could lead to tragic failure.

The discussions that took place in late 2001 leading up to a planned Afghan peace conference were quite revealing of the ambiguities and limits of international commitments. More than a dozen years later, the relative disarray of international policies on Afghanistan is the price we now pay for our initial lack of strategic and moral clarity. Neville Chamberlain, the British prime minister before World War II, famously described Czechoslovakia as "that faraway country of which we know little." In late 2001 most of us in the West knew even less about Afghanistan, which was much further away, and there was no serious discussion on the military goals, the "war aims," that were pursued in Afghanistan. I remember the sharp exchange that took place, early on, at a luncheon offered in honor of the foreign minister of Pakistan: the Pakistanis complained that the international coalition had "acquiesced" to the entry into Kabul of the Northern Alliance, and that it could have disastrous consequences; Rwanda and massive killings were even mentioned. Sir Jeremy Greenstock, the British ambassador, always precise and to the point, retorted that the coalition was not in Afghanistan on the basis of a mandate of the Security Council but "of another article of the [UN] Charter" (Article 51, the right to self-defense). He was indeed right: the war was the response to the attack of September 11, and it had been launched to oust the Taliban and to chase al Qaeda, not to broker a nice and fair deal among all Afghans. The U.S. military did not seem to have much interest in what would happen once the Taliban had fallen. The way the victory would be handled, and the implications for future national reconciliation, was of little concern, since for many in the Bush administration the enemies were not prisoners of war but "terrorists." When, in November 2001, we were informed that 15,000 Taliban wanted to surrender to the Northern Alliance in Kunduz, and that there was a great risk of massive human rights abuse and possibly killings, Kofi Annan informed the International Committee of the Red Cross (ICRC) and raised the issue with the five permanent members of the Security Council, but he did not elicit much interest among the "P5."

The Russians would prove to be among the least inclined to contemplate any accommodation with the Taliban, on the battlefield or in politics. When President Vladimir Putin met with Kofi Annan in November, he clearly stated Russian support for Northern Alliance leader Burhanuddin Rabbani, the "head of an internationally recognized country." Burhanuddin Rabbani had been president of Afghanistan from 1992 until he was ousted by the Taliban in 1996, after which he had become the nominal head of the Northern Alliance. Putin added that the international community only had to "save face" for Musharraf, and he made clear that any participation of the Taliban was "out of the question." Russia had unambiguously thrown its lot behind some elements of the Northern Alliance and did not seem too concerned that such a complete reversal of fortune might alienate many Afghans: "Afghans change their turbans," Putin said. But he was wary of Afghans from the diaspora. He contrasted "those who fight and die, and those who sip coffee." The peace conference was not going to be a conference of reconciliation; it would be a conference of victors. Washington was much more interested in removing the Taliban than in shaping the future of Afghanistan.

Countries closer to Afghanistan could not afford to be indifferent to its future, and the protracted discussions on where an Afghan conference should take place soon showed that they had very different ideas on what Afghanistan should become. The Russians and the Iranians wanted the rapid convening of a conference in Kabul, which would confer international legitimacy to their protégés in the Northern Alliance and consolidate their grip on central power. This was the nightmare scenario for the Pakistanis, who warned that accommodating one side would not provide a sustainable solution. They were interested in convening a conference in the Persian Gulf, where they would have more influence, and they hurriedly arranged a mostly Pashtun conference in Peshawar, trying to ensure that they would have a dominant role. In the end, a compromise was reached. The conference was convened on December 5, 2001, in Germany, in a secluded chateau located on a mountaintop near Bonn. That made posturing in front of press cameras more difficult, and it complicated the efforts of the various outside players who wanted to influence the outcome.

The Bonn Agreement

The composition of the Afghan delegation to the conference was the work of Lakhdar Brahimi, who consulted closely with the United States, knowing that nothing could be sustained without strong U.S. support. Rabbani did not get the dominant role that the Russians had wanted for him and was not a signatory of the final document. The Panshiri group within the Northern Alliance, the Shura I Nizar, which had early on shown that it was aware of the dangers of abusing victory, was in the end the great victor, getting control of the key ministries of defense, interior, and foreign affairs—a result that displeased powerful warlords belonging to other components of the Northern Alliance, like Abdul Rashid Dostum and Ismaïl Khan. Of critical importance was the fact that while a clan of the northerners had won, the historic place of the Pashtun in Afghanistan was not ignored. A Pashtun, Hamid Karzai, whose name Brahimi had mentioned just a few days before the opening of the conference, was appointed chairman of the interim authority. He had the great advantage of not being a warlord, which was a good signal for the new Afghanistan, but Pashtun warlords like Abdul Rab al Rasul Saiaf and Haji Abdul Qadir felt cheated.

At the last minute, the effort almost collapsed: the United Nations and the human rights community had wanted to insert in the final agreement a clause that explicitly excluded war crimes and crimes against humanity from an amnesty. In a country that had experienced close to a quarter-century of extreme violence, many felt long-term peace could only be established on foundations of justice and accountability, but several of the Afghans sitting at the table were not prepared for that. In the end, there was no clause on war crimes, but the final Bonn Agreement stated that the "United Nations had the right to investigate human rights violations and, where necessary, recommend corrective action." The language on the presence of foreign troops was purposefully vague. It called for the deployment of an international security force to "assist in the maintenance of security for Kabul and its surrounding areas" and mentioned that "such a force could, as appropriate, be progressively expanded to other urban centers and other areas." In addition, "the participants in the UN talks on Afghanistan pledged to withdraw all military units from Kabul and other urban centers or other areas in which the UN mandated force is deployed." This vague wording reflected very different views on the size of the force to be deployed: some British diplomats had mentioned a figure of 50,000, which at the time seemed impossibly high. Meanwhile, Rabbani was thinking of about 200 advisers.

Lakhdar Brahimi would later be criticized for having conceded too much to the warlords of Afghanistan, and in 2007 I heard one Afghan complaining that all the difficulties that Afghanistan now confronted had their origin in the Bonn Agreement and the flawed loya jirgas, or grand councils of Afghan leaders, that followed. But Brahimi remembered the disastrous loya jirga of 1992, which unraveled into violence and civil war, and in his opening speech in Bonn, he reminded the participants of that terrible precedent. His task was further complicated by the fact that he not only had to negotiate with the Afghans, he also had to get the backing of the United States, which was looking for a quick exit and had at the time limited war aims. He knew that the international community had little appetite for transforming political declarations into actual commitments on the ground, especially military commitments.

In hindsight, I believe that what was achieved in Bonn was almost miraculous, considering the odds against success when the conference took place. There were deep suspicions between Iran and Pakistan, and profound divisions among the Afghans; the international community had no common vision, no willingness to commit significant military forces, and no understanding of their possible use. The UN "witness," to employ the word that Brahimi used when he signed the Bonn Agreement, had in effect very little leverage. Even so, he transformed a problem into an opportunity: the lack of a clear strategic vision at the highest level of the U.S. government allowed him to play a masterful tactical game with the help of an astute Afghan American close to the Bush administration, who later became a successful U.S. ambassador to the UN, Zalmay Khalilzad.

The greatest achievement of Bonn was to keep the door open, to establish a process that could have allowed for a gradual evolution of Afghanistan. It is when a war ends that guns have the greatest sway, and it is always dangerous to try to settle all issues at that particular moment. Peace agreements that make such an attempt inevitably consolidate the power of those who have waged war, as was the case at Dayton after the Bosnian wars. The Bonn Agreement did not ignore the power of the warlords—otherwise there would have been no agreement—but by taking a step-by-step approach it kept open the possibility that a legitimacy other than the legitimacy of the gun would eventually prevail. It provided for an interim authority, to be chaired by Karzai. A special independent commission of twenty-one members would then determine the composition and procedures of an emergency loya jirga of 1,500 delegates, which would convene six months later to elect a head of state and establish a transitional administration. A constitutional loya jirga, convened within the next eighteen months, would draft a constitution, followed by elections. It was not an unreasonable hope that in the meantime militias would have been disarmed, the tense political context of a war would have changed, and the atmosphere in which the constitution would be drafted would foster a more sustainable compromise than the one that would have emerged if that elaborate and complicated sequence had been compressed. But obviously Bonn was only the beginning, and a good outcome would depend on the Afghans and the international community being able to agree on a strategic vision for Afghanistan and stay the course.

In Bonn, and later in Kabul as the head of the UN mission, Lakhdar Brahimi allowed the United Nations to play a much bigger role than would normally have been the case, and he did more than one could hope to put Afghanistan on the right track. In spite of their differences, many Afghans are still grateful for the role he played and consider him a kind of friendly "uncle" of the nation. When I reflect on the qualities required of a special representative of the secretary general (SRSG)— as the position of head of a UN mission is described in the jargon of the organization—I immediately think of Brahimi. This is one of the most difficult, and most unrecognized, jobs on earth. All at once, you become a key political figure in a country that is not your own. The foundation of your role is the trust you are able to build with the people of the country: they expect you to be their advocate and protector; but your influence on national leaders is directly linked to the perception they have of your influence with key international stakeholders, who themselves want you to be the implementer of their often conflicting agendas. The position, because it is so operational, summarizes all the tensions and possible contradictions of the United Nations, an organization whose raison d'être is to serve the people, but whose influence depends on the capacity to generate and manage the support of powerful member states.

Members of the Security Council have often characterized Brahimi as "shrewd" and "wily," and ambassadors believe they pay him the ultimate compliment by calling him a great diplomat. He undoubtedly was, as he maneuvered the shoals of conflicting agendas of powerful member states and avoided head-on clashes with the United States while protecting his credibility with the Afghans and many countries that were anything but friends of the Bush administration. But in Afghanistan, as in Haiti and South Africa, where he had also held this same position of SRSG, he proved to be much more than a diplomat. The most difficult challenge for a foreigner who becomes involved in the aftermath of a civil war is to find the right balance between the humility to listen and the courage to press hard. You are in a country that is not yours, and it is not your future that is at stake, which means that you will not have to bear the consequences of the choices that are being made, but also that you may have a more balanced, and less impassioned, understanding of the issues at stake. You must be impartial: you should not be indifferent, but you do not have to add your own passions. Societies that have gone through a civil war are indeed full of passions, and they are in no need of more of them, although I have observed how often foreigners take satisfaction in vicariously joining sides, and being part of the emotional battle, once the physical one has ended. It takes wisdom and humility to resist that impulse, and Brahimi always did. He built trust not by flattering his interlocutors and encouraging their passions, but by showing that his differences with particular viewpoints were borne out of a sense of care for the people. Such empathy won him the respect and friendship of many Afghans.

Commitments Made, But With Reluctance

The following months were to confirm that Brahimi had been right not to overplay a weak hand, as the international community struggled to follow up on its ambiguous commitments. The Bonn Agreement had been signed on December 5 and provided for the interim authority to start working in Kabul on December 22, barely two weeks later. I went to London to discuss with British officials a possible military deployment, since the United Kingdom was, with Turkey, the country most often mentioned as a possible leading nation of a multinational force. It immediately became clear that on December 22 the best scenario one could hope for was a symbolic international security presence in Kabul. With the exception of France, the United Kingdom is the only European military with a solid tradition of expeditionary deployments. However, aside from the United States, even the most efficient military has great difficulty deploying and sustaining a full battalion in less than three weeks. Beyond the practical difficulties of a rapid deployment, I discussed underlying political issues that could create more lasting difficulties. The British were rightly concerned about being left to negotiate the status of the force with various Afghan factions. The Bonn Agreement was vague, and they knew that only the United States had enough clout with all their Afghan interlocutors, not just with Mohammad Qasim Fahim, the Tadjik minister of defense. They wanted to make sure that the United States would be part of the negotiation, and they also were keen to have a reliable connection with the U.S. chain of command for close air support and for intelligence. Their concern was operational but also political: they wanted the United States to be part of the picture so that the policies on the ground would be aligned. After all, the memories of Bosnia, when the Europeans were on the ground, with the United States providing support from the air, were not so distant. And the operational environment was not appealing. As a British general put it to me, this is a situation of low consent, and low capabilities. Under such circumstances, the British confirmed that they were ready to lead the operation provided it was for a limited period of time, and limited to Kabul; only the United States or NATO, in their view, had the command capacity to lead an operation for the whole Afghan theater.

There was during that period a lot of talk about a multinational force that would be composed largely of Muslims. From the outset, I had strong reservations about such a concept: religion should not be a selection criterion when it comes to supporting peace. The Indians, with the experience of a country that has to accommodate several religions, were also publicly opposed. But in reality, there was never much of a chance that such a force would ever be deployed. As an ambassador from a possible troop-contributing Muslim country told me: "We do not want to be left behind in Afghanistan to fix the country, while the Western forces, having evicted al Qaeda and the Taliban, decide they have accomplished their mission and pack up and leave!"

Units from the developing world eventually would be deployed, but the international security force would remain an essentially Western force. Setting it up was proving harder than some had anticipated. The views of Rabbani had been overcome, as the influence of Defense Minister Fahim, a young and dynamic Panshiri, grew. It was now agreed that the international security force would not be just a symbolic deployment of advisers, and Fahim had actually accepted that the force deploy beyond Kabul. The new minister of defense wanted a national army, but he understood that it would take time. He was willing to accept in the interim a credible international security force, to avoid a vacuum that would be filled by local militias. The problem was therefore less with the demand than with the supply. The British, who had accepted to take the lead just before the Security Council resolution authorizing an International Security Assistance Force (ISAF) was adopted on December 20, were keen to hand over the lead role quickly to another nation.

The resolution reflected the lack of enthusiasm of the international community for a major engagement in Afghanistan. It used the exact terms of the Bonn Agreement ("to assist") and defined the area of operation as "Kabul and its surroundings." The Bonn Agreement had mentioned the possibility of an expansion beyond Kabul, but as it was becoming apparent that offers of troops would not be forthcoming, ambitions were scaled down. When the members of the Security Council had their first monthly luncheon of 2002, at the beginning of January, the French, the British, and the Russian ambassadors all stressed that the force should limit its deployment to Kabul, and that it was for the Afghans to take responsibility for the security of the provinces. Kofi Annan had doubts about this minimalist approach. A few days later, he shared them with several American experts from foundations and universities he had invited to reflect with him and the UN senior staff on the priorities of his second term as secretary general. He noted that the "Western engagement in Afghanistan was limited, in its geographic scope as well as in its duration," and asked, "What would happen six months from now?"

He then took advantage of the Davos meeting at the end of the month to press the Turks, since Britain did not want to continue as the "lead nation."

Turkish foreign minister Ismail Cem was noncommittal, although not negative. He played down Turkey's links with Dostum, the Mazar warlord, and asked why the Germans had had second thoughts about leading the force. While Kofi Annan had mentioned the prospect of the June emergency loya jirga, whose preparation would require nationwide security, Cem made clear that an expansion of the operation beyond Kabul would be full of dangers.

No progress was made at a Security Council luncheon in February. Kofi Annan decided to have more restricted meetings in his private conference room. Two took place in the following days. The five permanent members were there, but also the international security force members sitting on the council (Bulgaria and Norway), along with Germany and Turkey. He asked critical but difficult questions: How big should the force be? Who would determine the right figure? Who would lead the force, and under which conditions? If the force was not expanded beyond Kabul, how would security be provided? Was it realistic to rely on warlords? Would there be alternative arrangements? He raised the issue of reforming the army and the police, asking for more specific information from the United States and the United Kingdom about the army, and from Germany about the police. The answers he got were vague. The Europeans, who had joined to show solidarity with the United States but had no strategic interest, were already looking for the exit, and the United States itself did not have a very clear message. Ambassador Richard Williamson, the deputy permanent representative of the United States to the UN, was satisfied with what had happened in Kabul and wondered how it could be replicated elsewhere, and how a UN civilian presence could be considered in other cities. The assumption was that the Taliban were no longer an issue, and the U.S. priority was now the fight against al Qaeda.

The secretary general had been in Washington shortly after the first February meeting on Afghanistan, and he was well aware of the limits of U.S. political engagement. He had met Senator Joe Biden, then the senior Democrat on the Foreign Relations Committee and later U.S. vice president, who had expressed his support for an expansion of the security force, but the views in the Bush administration were quite different from those of the senator. Annan had a testy exchange at a dinner with Secretary of Defense Donald Rumsfeld. He asked Rumsfeld, "Are you not creating new warlords?" to which the secretary had quipped, "No, we are not creating new ones, we are giving guns to old ones!" suggesting that this was the "Afghan Solution" that the United States had in mind. The Bush administration was keen to keep the war against al Qaeda and the Taliban as a distinct U.S.-controlled effort, separate from a broader Afghan strategy, for which there was little appetite in Washington. At the end of February, Ari Fleisher, White House spokesman, had reiterated the official position:

"The President continues to believe the purpose of the military is to be used to fight and win wars, and not to engage in peacekeeping of that nature."

In several meetings, Brahimi had tried to puncture the prevailing mood of complacency, noting that "the Taliban might have been routed, but they were all over the place." And in the report that was to serve as the basis for adopting the resolution establishing the UN civilian mission (the United Nations Assistance Mission in Afghanistan or UNAMA) at the end of March, the secretary general appealed to the Security Council to expand ISAF:

> The Force remains limited to Kabul, while the main threats to the Interim Administration emanate from the provinces. There is a continuing danger that existing security structures, both Afghan and international, will not adequately address the security threats that are currently discernible and that are likely to increase as the convening of the emergency Loya Jirga approaches. I hope that the Security Council will consider these factors and support the wish of the Afghan people for the expansion of the Force.[2]

Kofi Annan was even more explicit when he spoke, telling the members of the council: "We are struggling." He had good reason to be increasingly worried. Even in Kabul, the situation was far from satisfactory. In February, on the same day where there had been such reluctance to increase the international security commitment to Afghanistan in a meeting in New York, and just as the International Security Assistance Force was reaching its full complement of 4,800 troops, an Afghan minister had been murdered at Kabul airport. Contrary to assurances, there were still some 10,000 Afghan soldiers in the capital, confined in barracks, but their disarmament had not yet started. And powerful Afghan leaders, like Gulbuddin Hekmatyar, Abdul Rasul Sayiaf, and Rabbani were actively opposing the emergency loya jirga planned for June. There had also been violent incidents between Tadjiks and Uzbeks in Mazar-e Sharif, a large city in north-central Afghanistan. The reality was that the agreement reached in Bonn was extremely fragile. The "victors" were deeply divided among themselves, and the vanquished were just biding their time. Moreover, the swift victory of late 2001 had made the United States and its allies very complacent. The downsizing of U.S. forces, which had no interest in peacekeeping, was taken as a given at the time, and other countries deployed in Afghanistan were only concerned about managing its consequences.

2. "The situation in Afghanistan and its implications for international peace and security," Report of the Secretary-General, March 18, 2002, United Nations (http://unama.unmissions.org/Portals/UNAMA/SG%20Reports/18%20March%202002.pdf).

International Confusion and a Lack of Strategy

By the spring of 2002, it was clear that a stronger military commitment in Afghanistan was not a realistic option. If the international community did not really agree on an overarching strategic goal in Afghanistan, how would it agree on a comprehensive military strategy?

The Security Council was becoming more divided on other issues, including increasing violence between Israelis and Palestinians, and when Afghanistan was on the agenda, ideology on the U.S. side and lack of political will on the European side prevented a serious discussion. The International Crisis Group had called for a stronger international force, boldly recommending 25,000 to 30,000 troops, rather than the simple doubling of the existing force of under 5,000. Brahimi also advocated for a stronger force, which might have given the international community the leverage it needed to promote a more balanced dispensation of power in Afghanistan. But the Americans were only interested in defeating al Qaeda, and the Europeans had little appetite for a grand strategy if it required a more serious military engagement on their part. Clever ambassadors found clever ways to pretend that an expansion of ISAF was not needed. The usually wise representative of one of the major European powers, which would later become very engaged in Afghanistan, spoke of the "ISAF effect" beyond Kabul and bluntly concluded: "We have to put aside the dream of a wider ISAF." Another one suggested to think "outside the box" and "be creative." He emphasized the power of money: "Karzai can have leverage with cash. . . . We should channel money only in those places where human rights are respected." As for the idea of a mobile force, "it was not needed, since there was U.S. air power. The stick was in the air, it might still be needed in the coming weeks, but hopefully it would be unnecessary afterwards." The question was no longer whether there would be an expansion but how big the downsizing should be. Britain generously announced that it would keep 700 troops, while France stated that the reduction of its presence would be gradual. On May 23 ISAF was extended for another six months without any expansion of its area of operations. It would actually take another eighteen months and the takeover of the command of the multinational force by NATO for an expansion to be agreed. Even then, the expansion would be extremely gradual and cautious, focusing on those parts of the country that were the safest. No effort was then made to integrate in one single vision the U.S.-led war that continued in the south and the NATO-led "peacekeeping force" that started to deploy in the north in 2004.

Washington, which from the outset had a limited anti-terrorist agenda, quickly lost interest in Afghanistan, focusing instead on Iraq, where it launched a war in March 2003. The Europeans, with limited capacities to project force, were not prepared to fill the vacuum; their posture also was determined by their bilateral relationships with the United States, not by the needs of Afghanistan. Entrusting the security of Afghanistan to largely ethnic Tadjik and Uzbek forces was therefore the default option, even if it alienated the Pashtun South and laid the ground for a Pashtun insurgency that would identify itself with the Taliban. The international forces were weak, and they could effectively limit neither the political dominance of the Northern Alliance victors of 2001 in the north nor the resurgence of the vanquished Taliban in the south. When President Barack Obama decided on the surge of U.S. forces in 2009, it was much too late: the Taliban had regained the initiative and the window for an effective politico-military strategy had closed.

In the end, a confused international community, which had become embroiled in a faraway country, of which it knew little, out of solidarity for the United States rather than a genuine concern, could only rally around a strategy that would be largely nonpolitical. Initially, the humanitarian impact of the military campaign was the main concern. Much time was spent discussing logistical support and coordination of humanitarian aid, in the belief that there was an impending humanitarian crisis. The European Union, as well as NATO, was keen to show its relevance, and the rumor even went around that the UN had asked NATO to support its humanitarian operations. In reality, the only major humanitarian emergency was the issue of the refugees in Pakistan and in Iran. If the war intensified, the risk of more Afghans crossing the border into Pakistan was a serious concern for the Pakistani leadership; conversely, if the situation improved, the return of some 3.5 million Afghans who had taken refuge in Pakistan and Iran would raise major humanitarian as well as political issues. Would they be forced to return? What would be the political impact of their return on their home communities? How could the international community help manage their voluntary return? Curiously, I have no recollection of those issues being discussed in any depth at a high level. But the office of the United Nations High Commissioner for Refugees (UNHCR), which was headed in Afghanistan by an extremely competent and self-effacing Italian, Filippo Grandi—who would later become the head of the UN agency that provides basic services to Palestinians, UNRWA—quietly helped manage the return of millions of refugees to Afghanistan; perhaps this suggests that while strategic issues do need to be discussed at the strategic level, many practical issues are best left to responsible operators in the field, provided they are given adequate resources.

Once the moment of immediate humanitarian concerns had passed, the reconstruction of Afghanistan became the focus of world attention. Indeed, there was much to be done in a country ravaged by two decades of war, and this was an extraordinary opportunity to mobilize much-needed resources. The year 2001 had not even ended when a donor conference was already being planned for January 2002 in Tokyo. Brahimi noted that it might be a bit early, and that we could possibly give the Afghans time to settle down in Kabul. When the conference effectively took place on January 21–22, $4.5 billion was pledged, but Kofi Annan noted that $10 billion would be needed over a period of ten years. The United States had already lost interest and committed a minimal amount of money for the reconstruction effort.[3] But the machinery of international aid was starting to move, with its usual emphasis on eye-catching numbers and headline goals that have little connection with the realities on the ground. Brahimi had experienced firsthand the natural tendency of bureaucracies—national as well as international—to develop agendas that have more to do with their own expansion than with the interests of the people they are supposed to serve. As a result, he was determined to impose as much discipline as possible at least on the UN system so that its actions in Afghanistan would all be harnessed in support of one single overarching goal: help Afghanistan become a functioning state in charge of its own destiny. He knew how desperately poor Afghanistan was and how much it needed help, but he was concerned that the massive engagement that the international community was beginning to trumpet—with huge dollar figures—would raise high expectations among the Afghan people. He had learned from experience that the capacity of the international community to actually deliver on its commitments is very limited. He wanted the UN mission in Afghanistan to be "integrated," not because he had any ambition of becoming the new governor of Afghanistan, but to have some control over the various UN agencies operating in Afghanistan, which themselves would only be a small part (10 percent to 15 percent) of the whole international contribution. But this was no easy task: some agencies that had no capacity and zero experience of Afghanistan were in a hurry to send their "experts" to Kabul even if what they were planning to do was already better done by another agency with experience of Afghanistan. A high risk remained that the efforts of the international community would be driven by supply—or more accurately, the illusion of supply—rather than by the needs and demands of the Afghans.

3. Donors pledged $1.8 billion for 2002 and $4.5 billion over a five-year period. The U.S. contribution ($296 million in 2002) was dwarfed by the European Union commitment of $500 million in 2002. Japan also pledged $500 million over a thirty-month period.

The following years confirmed Brahimi's fears. Because of the vast amounts that were eventually committed to Afghanistan in high-profile international conferences, the confusion reached an order of magnitude that is less visible when less money is at stake. International NGOs, keen to deliver services so as to show results to their donors, often short-circuited the state they wanted to build, thus perpetuating its weakness, and donor nations were wary of entrusting funds to Afghan institutions that they deemed corrupt and unresponsive to the needs of the people. A valiant effort was made to prepare an Afghan National Development Strategy. However, the need to adhere to an international timetable, and the weakness of Afghan structures, meant that the development strategy often ignored local needs. Moreover, the administrative organization of Afghanistan, which gave limited budgetary powers to provincial governors, made it very difficult to connect national plans to local needs, and the provincial councils were confined to an advisory role. The program that came closest to empowering Afghans in a way that would reconcile the need for a national vision of Afghanistan with local accountability was the National Solidarity Program of the World Bank. The World Bank allocated funds to ministries in Kabul, but those funds were then disbursed on the basis of proposals made by self-defined communities that had a responsibility for monitoring the implementation of the proposals they made. A link was established between the local and the national level of government. Overall, however, the gap between Afghan expectations and actual delivery remained wide.

Meanwhile, as the security situation deteriorated, the military gradually became more involved in development tasks, and more money was made available, but at a time when it was becoming more difficult to spend it because of renewed violence in much of the country. NATO understood that a purely military effort would not produce results. The Provincial Reconstruction Teams (PRTs) were the response. They appeared first in the north, when ISAF began to expand beyond Kabul in 2004. Each contributing country would deploy civilians as well as nonfighting military units that would rebuild roads, train police, support irrigation projects, and refurbish schools. These PRT units were located in a military camp next to a fighting component known as the "maneuver force." The intent was laudable, and it expanded on the practice of all forces deployed in a stabilization operation to conduct so-called heart and minds campaigns, which are a well-developed feature of many UN operations. The United States and NATO countries had much more money to throw at the effort, leading to much criticism from the humanitarian and development communities, which are often unhappy even with the incomparably more modest efforts of traditional UN military programs. The PRTs were an attempt to bring together two strands of the international effort:

military and development. However, the leading role that NATO gave to the military commander meant that development became an adjunct of the military strategy rather than a component of a broader political vision. And the Afghans had no control over the budget of the PRTs, which further marginalized already weak Afghan institutions. ISAF thus acquired a civilian component, with command-and-control arrangements that varied from one contingent to the other. In some PRTs, the civilian component could make its own plans; in others, the military commander had simply acquired a civilian adviser, who played some role in the "coordination" of the civilian effort, but to advise is not to command.

Development efforts, which had been a substitute for a political strategy, were now being harnessed to support the tactical efforts of a failing military force. In the south of the country, where security steadily deteriorated, vast amounts of money were made available by the U.S. government, which allowed some remote border provinces to build vocational training schools, repair bridges, and embark on a multitude of useful projects; it was certainly a most welcome windfall for the beneficiary communities. In the quieter north, where most of the non-U.S. PRTs were initially deployed, there was much less money. A relatively rich small province of the south could suddenly acquire hundreds of kilometers of asphalted roads, courtesy of the United States, while the provinces of the Central Highlands, reputedly one of the poorest parts of the country, still had only three kilometers of asphalted roads in 2008. The governor of a still-peaceful province asked me: Do we need to plant bombs to get some real development money?

With all the PRTs, I felt the same embarrassment that I experienced in many UN operations: the contrast between local people living in absolute misery and an international camp with all the amenities of the modern world—amplified in Afghanistan by the wealth of the troop contributors, and in the north of the country by the relative calm in which they were operating. There was no doubt that these impressive fortified camps, fully lit at night next to cities without electricity and regularly supplied by heavy transport planes and helicopters, were the most expensive way to deliver a limited amount of aid to very poor people.

By the end of 2007, the disarray of the international community was more and more apparent. The international community had supported the Northern Alliance because it was the cheapest way to defeat the Taliban. It had then backed Karzai, often hiding behind a process that enabled it to avoid having to make decisions of substance. There had been some remarkable achievements: Brahimi and Khalilzad, the American ambassador, had gradually brought significant Pashtun influence into the debate, and the Afghanistan that emerged at the end of the 2002–05 constitutional process was very different, and more inclusive, than the Afghanistan that had been represented at Bonn. But that reconciliation was extremely fragile. For instance, when the constitution was being discussed before the loya jirga, the idea had been broached of having a prime minister as well as a president, to allow for a broader distribution of power. But it became clear that in the circumstances of the time, this might easily lead to a fractured leadership and possibly resumption of civil war, if the Northern Alliance controlled one position and the Pashtun the other. The idea was, probably wisely at the time, abandoned (although it was revived in 2014 to settle a disputed presidential election). Because of the same fear that factions could easily return to war, and the lack of support for a strong parliament, the electoral system had been designed to discourage the formation of political parties. The international community was now frustrated that political life in Afghanistan was all about personal deals and patronage, and that Afghanistan was not the dream country it had claimed to build. It was easier, in Western capitals, to blame the Afghan government than an inadequate international engagement, although the same capitals expected the United Nations to deliver the criticism to President Karzai, while they would cover him with praise in public events. I saw this at the NATO summit in Bucharest in 2008, when the speech of the secretary general sounded tougher than most of the national speeches. As often when things are going substantively wrong, the temptation grows to find some magic institutional fix, rather than to address the substance.

Indeed, the structure of the international engagement in Afghanistan was excessively complicated, with the juxtaposition of NATO, the UN, and the United States. But the UN found itself in an even more difficult position after the Afghan parliamentary elections of 2005, which essentially completed the Bonn process. The elections meant that the UN mission no longer had a road map to frame its relationship with the Afghans. Meanwhile, the deteriorating situation put it in an increasingly difficult situation as more civilian casualties resulted from an intensifying war. As a protector and friend of the Afghans, the UN would lose its moral authority if it did not condemn the "collateral" damage to civilians, but it was also more and more dependent on the protection of NATO, with which it was essential to maintain good relations. After 2005 Afghanistan took a turn for the worse: the Taliban insurgency, once confined to the south, spread throughout the country in spite of the buildup of American troops decided by President Obama in 2009. Even now, as I write years later, the fragile institutions put in place by the Bonn process are under siege, and in need of reform, as the international community is packing up.

A Very Long Detour to Reach Peace

What went wrong? Among my many visits to Afghanistan, one particular moment stands out because it captures all the ambiguities of the international effort, the hopes, the cynical calculations, the insurmountable distance between the story the international community wanted to hear and the realities of Afghanistan. It is December 19, 2005, and I am in the main chamber of the parliament, where refurbishing work was still being completed the day before. President Karzai has been sitting for a while in the chair reserved for him, and the room is filled with excitement that is gradually turning into annoyance. During the past twenty minutes, everybody has been waiting for the most important guest to arrive: Vice President Dick Cheney, who is representing President Bush at the inauguration of the parliament, the first one elected in decades. And Dick Cheney is very late. A ceremony that means so much to the Afghans is delayed because a foreigner, a powerful foreigner, is late. But the delay has one great advantage: the new parliamentarians are milling around, and it is an extraordinary opportunity to observe the diversity of Afghanistan. There are, of course, many Pashtuns, and most conform to the cliché that they should have eagle features, piercing eyes, and splendid turbans. There are round faces out of a Persian miniature: many come from Herat in the west, but they may also be Shia Hazaras from the central highlands of Afghanistan. The Asian looks and the pointed hats of some other members of parliament reveal that they come from Badakshan, the mountainous valley that connects Afghanistan with China. Maybe it is the isolation that has protected their traditional costume, but it is reminiscent of the Sassanid Empire that extended to Afghanistan and Pakistan 1,500 years ago, before the caliphate and Islam took over. I am told the blue eyes are a legacy of the soldiers of Alexander who walked across the many mountains of Afghanistan, because they wanted to see what was behind the next mountain range. They did not settle until they found the fertile plains of the Indus. It may just be a nice story, but the Hellenistic coins representing Bactrian kings that one finds in remote villages of Afghanistan, and the ruins of the Greek city of Taxila in the suburbs of Islamabad, show that indeed the Greeks marched all the way through Afghanistan. While most members of parliament have flowing robes, there are also many wearing business suits, which reflect the long engagement of Afghanistan with the industrial world, whether it be the Soviet Union of Brezhnev or an American university.

The U.S. vice president has eventually arrived, and Karzai begins his speech. He speaks alternatively in Dari and Pashtun, and I am listening to the English translation. The first part of his speech is too technocratic. He begins by saying everything the international community wants to hear and draws a long catalogue of all that needs to be done in Afghanistan: security, good governance, justice, basic infrastructure, education, health, and so forth. The list is daunting. And then, toward the end, as he looks at all the people assembled in the hall, he has tears in his eyes, and so do many in the audience. He talks about what it means for Afghanistan to come together, what it means to have been through so much violence and suffering. He makes everybody in the hall aware of their responsibilities, of the immense hopes that have been vested in them and in the legislative institution they embody.

The word *democracy* has many meanings, and has often been misused. Each time Kofi Annan met George W. Bush, even after the situation had begun to seriously deteriorate, the president of the United States would always stress how good things were in Afghanistan, how "democracy" was winning. There was something forced and mechanical in the way he said it, and I could not resist an internal smile. But on that morning of December 2005, as I look at the people around me—more than a quarter women, which is truly revolutionary for the country—I have to recognize the formidable strength of the idea. A human community is coming together, and for once, it is united in a common hope.

That community is very different from the American ideal of democracy. The hope for the future is balanced, and complicated, by the memories of a long past. The people in the hall are all victims of that past, but many of them also have been perpetrators, and they know it, and they know who did what to whom. And the hard battles of power have not disappeared. Until the last minute there has been a bitter fight for the election of the speaker. Some of the commanders wanted Sayiaf, a Pashtun who took an active part in the violence and abuse that opened the way to the Taliban, but his election was resisted by all those who wanted their country to move past the era of commanders, past the age of the gun as the ultimate source of legitimacy. Eventually, Yunus Qanooni, a well-educated Tadjik, will be chosen. It is already a remarkable victory that the give-and-take of parliamentary discussion has been accepted. But that victory is fragile.

Nine years after that ceremony, there is much complaint and frustration among Western powers about the corruption of the Afghan government, and many Afghans seem to have lost confidence in their own young institutions. Two more presidential elections have taken place, but there is a sense that the window of opportunity that opened after the first parliamentary election, in December 2005—I remember Ashraf Ghani, then the minister of finance mentioning eighteen months—was lost, because the billions that were thrown at

Afghanistan were often wasted; actually, much of that money never reached the Afghan budget. While the lives of ordinary Afghans improved, nothing irreversible was achieved. Some big investments were made. For instance, a ringroad, of great importance to end the isolation and fragmentation of that mountainous country, was partially built at great expense, with Japanese funding, but no effective provision was made for its maintenance, and the unforgiving Afghan winter is already taking a toll on that investment. Millions of children, including girls, were brought back to school with the help of UNICEF, but millions more remain without any education, and many teachers themselves have a minimal level of education. The hopes of December 2005 have not been fulfilled, and corruption is rife. Indeed, the sudden influx of billions of dollars in one of the poorest countries in the world whetted appetites, and the boom of international aid, combined with the boom induced by the drug trade, created a new class of Afghan millionaires, feeding resentment in a population that did not want abusive armed commanders being replaced by, or transforming themselves into, exploitative businessmen and political entrepreneurs.

The world of wealth and power has little self-awareness, and it is as ignorant of its impact as the terrorists who struck on September 11 were of the society they were attacking. Whether it is the power of money or the use of force, the rich and powerful tend to be somewhat casual about the impact of their actions. In 2001 the United States sent an unequivocal message to the world that any state that deliberately provided a safe haven to enemies of the United States would be held responsible and would have to face the consequences. The swift overthrow of the Taliban regime made that point. But once that was done, policymakers in Washington gave little thought to what force was really meant to accomplish. During my visits to Afghanistan, I was generally struck by the quality of U.S. commanders at the battalion level: they worked hard to understand the difficult situation they had been thrown into and gained detailed knowledge of their theater of operations, but the rapid rotation of personnel meant that they were at their greatest level of efficiency when they were about to leave. I remember a candid conversation with a bright American colonel who was on his second tour of duty in Afghanistan. He said bluntly that during his first tour, they had it all wrong: "It was all about the kill rate," which he discovered was not a relevant yardstick. He now understood the complexities of tribal relationships and was aware of the risk that in some situations tribal solidarity would outweigh resentment against the cruelty of Taliban chiefs, and that it was all about tradeoffs: Afghans wanted better governance, more honesty, but they also were generally loyal to their traditional leaders who would sometimes be honest, sometimes not. The revised U.S. doctrine of counterinsurgency, which put the emphasis on protecting the civilian population, rather than killing enemies, was an admission of the limits of force, but it begged the question of the trust that the Afghans had in their own government. What did it mean to protect civilians from Taliban attacks if they were not prepared to rally around their government?

I went back to Kabul in the summer of 2010, and I saw how Afghanistan had changed since my first visit. Kabul now looked like a city under siege, with high cement blast walls and checkpoints everywhere. At the checkpoints, Afghans had better uniforms, but the most conspicuous change was the ubiquitous presence of employees from private military companies, wearing dark glasses and toting high-powered guns to protect foreigners. Today, the Afghans resent military actions that still kill civilians and that support a government that many do not trust; they see the deterioration of their security, and they do not see the concrete impact on their lives of the huge amounts of aid that were promised. A growing number of Afghans now say: "If the foreigners don't give us security, if they violate our customs, and if they do not provide riches, they should leave!" Over the last twelve years, the Afghans have had firsthand experience of the fickleness of the international community. The current war in their country started as a revenge of a wounded country that had to reestablish its preeminence, and those who promoted it, like Donald Rumsfeld when he met the secretary general and made his quip about old warlords, had no reform agenda; they just wanted to topple a group that had helped terrorists. But that was not enough for democratic public opinion in the Western world, and the engagement in Afghanistan evolved into a bold experiment in societal transformation of an extremely poor country.

Brahimi was well aware of the risk that the international community would not stick to a consistent strategy, and in 2001 he had made sure that the United Nations was not given the expansive executive role in Afghanistan it had been given in East Timor or Kosovo, two much smaller territories where it had effectively taken over and acted as the government. He had strong doubts about the wisdom of such ambitious undertakings, for which the international community does not have the resources and which quickly antagonize those who are supposed to "benefit" from international help. Brahimi had been a militant anti-colonialist in the fight of Algeria to free itself from France. He knew what many proponents of "trusteeships" for "failed states" seem to ignore: we do not live in a colonial age, and no neocolonial endeavor, as well-intentioned as it might be, can succeed, even if it is wrapped in the blue flag of the United Nations. Freedom, for millions of people around the world, is not just individual freedom; it is also the collective freedom for a human community to determine its own future without foreign interference. Afghanistan belonged to the Afghans, and the sooner a legitimate Afghan authority took charge, the better.

Brahimi's vision then had the full support of a remarkable Afghan who combined a rare expertise on Afghanistan with experience of development economics and also, most important, development bureaucracies. Ashraf Ghani is now well known for his work as the minister of finance of Afghanistan from July 2002 to December 2004, which laid the ground for his candidacy to become president of Afghanistan. But in late 2001 he was only known to development experts for a sharp tongue and an independent and creative mind: he could intimidate, and sometimes alienate, more traditional bureaucrats. From the outset, in a meeting that took place in November 2001, he had stressed that the reconstruction of a country broken by conflict was an essentially political affair. He noted that contrary to clichés often heard about Afghanistan, that country has had a functioning state, of one kind or another, for more than two centuries. There was a long period of the twentieth century during which the state found the right balance with the many tribes of Afghanistan that live in valleys often isolated for several months in winter: it was a reassuring but not-too-interfering presence. During the devastating civil war that destroyed so much human as well as physical capital in Afghanistan, any sense of trust was lost. Rebuilding that trust was the priority in 2001, and remains the priority today. All the discussions about military or development strategies are a distraction if that foundation is missing. Today, the election of Ashraf Ghani as president and the agreement reached with his competitor, Abdullah Abdullah, give some hope: a political vision of what is required to build a functioning state may at last be implemented.

The Gap between Goals and the Effort to Achieve Them

What will be the political cost of that long and painful detour? Will the international community, now so eager to hand off its commitments to the Afghans, give the needed support? As NATO countries are ending the greatly expanded ISAF mission, one can ask what it means to enter a country with such expansive but ambiguous goals. The Western intervention in Afghanistan began with the strategic objective of uprooting the terrorists. It became easy to conflate this goal with a broader objective of making the world a safer and better place and improving the lives of the Afghan people. Indeed, improving the lives of the Afghan people was an important tool for gaining domestic support for such a costly international intervention. But the two are not the same, and the gap between our stated goals in Afghanistan and the seriousness, or

to respect the distance, while celebrating our common humanity. I will never forget a cold winter night in the eastern city of Gardez, where I visited the UN mission's regional office, which at the time was led by an intelligent and resourceful Australian named Tom Gregg. The Afghan staff of the United Nations gave me a mysterious package, and I was wondering why they were so excited, laughing while waiting for me to open their present: it was a pressure cooker, a most common kitchen utensil in Afghanistan, and maybe an appropriate symbol of the state of the country. We had a good laugh together. I was no more the foreign official in a position of power, and they were the ones who had made a good practical joke, sharing their lives and making me another villager of Afghanistan.

two

IRAQ

Lingering Damage to the Idea of Collective Action

President George W. Bush fired the opening shots of what was to become the most damaging confrontation between the United States and the United Nations on September 12, 2002. Although the resistance of Saddam Hussein to inspections of Iraq's weapons programs had already raised the possibility of an attack on Iraq—and we now know that U.S. preparations for a war against Iraq were started soon after 9/11—until that point there was not yet much public debate about a possible U.S. attack. President Bush was in New York to deliver, as president of the host nation, his annual speech to the General Assembly. Before delivering his speech in the great hall of the UN, he had the traditional meeting with the secretary general, in a room located next to the hall. He was in a fiery mood, speaking in short sentences. His first words set the tone of the meeting and of the debates to come: "I do not want the United Nations to be the League of Nations." The message was clear: the relevance of the UN was at stake, and if the UN did not support U.S. policies of confronting a "new Hitler," the UN would become as irrelevant as was the League of Nations in the run-up to World War II. And when the secretary general, trying to show support, replied that the Iraqis "will have to comply," Bush was quick to retort: "Comply with what? There have been sixteen resolutions!"

In hindsight, that remark said it all. The time for diplomacy was gone, and the die was already cast. There was no expectation, at the highest level of the U.S. government, that Iraq would ever comply. Bush then added, becoming more emotional: "I love my country. . . . Democracy sounds like American democracy. . . . But freedom is created by God!" The born-again Christian was, consciously or not, challenging the institutional dimension of the American experience, and its roots in the age of enlightenment. It was fascinating to observe how a not-particularly-intellectual president was expressing profound tensions that go back to the founding fathers and that, to this day, are a big part of the ambiguous attraction of the American dream, which rests on the enduring power of institutions but also on the central role of the individual who can shape his or her destiny. The UN note-taker at that meeting was an outstanding young American, one of the best experts on the Middle East, Rick Hooper. He would die eleven months later, in the bombing of the UN building in Baghdad.

We then rushed to the great hall of the United Nations to listen to the speeches of Bush and Kofi Annan. Their logic was profoundly different. Bush focused on Iraq, using the now infamous description that it posed a "grave and gathering danger" and making clear that what was at stake was the credibility of the international community. He mentioned in the same sentence Afghanistan, Iraq, and Palestine, as three countries that held the promise of democracy and could become examples for the Middle East and the Islamic world.

Kofi Annan used his own speech to make the case for multilateralism. "I stand before you today as a multilateralist—by precedent, by principle, by Charter and by duty," he said at the outset. His speech was very focused. After reminding his audience that the meeting of the General Assembly was taking place just one day after the first anniversary of the terrorist attacks of September 11, he deliberately chose to concentrate on four critical issues, rather than going through the usual rambling catalogue of world problems: the Israel-Palestine conflict, Iraq, Afghanistan, and the nuclear dimension of the India-Pakistan conflict. This was a courageous choice on many counts: putting at the top of the list the Israel-Palestine conflict ran directly against the logic of U.S. policy at the time, while even a careful allusion to the India-Pakistan conflict was bound to irritate powerful members of the Security Council who do not want that particular issue to be discussed at the United Nations.

Another UN tradition is the "P5 luncheon." Each year, during the ministerial week that opens the General Assembly, the secretary general invites to his dining room on the thirty-eighth floor of the UN tower the foreign ministers of the five permanent members of the Security Council. They sit at the table with their ambassadors, and the secretary general is accompanied by five or six of his key advisers. This makes for a very cramped dining room, in which the note-takers sitting behind have barely enough room to spread their papers. In 2002 the luncheon took place the next day, on September 13, and it provided a first opportunity to begin the discussion on the next steps that the Security Council should take with respect to Iraq. The signals were ambiguous: On the one hand, there was a real difference of approach between Secretary of State Colin Powell, who wanted a resolution with a clear timeline for action, and Foreign Minister Dominique de Villepin of France, who stressed the need for a two-phase approach. From the outset, the French believed that it was necessary first to send a clear signal, with precise demands to Iraq; only after evaluating Iraq's response should the Security Council decide to take further action. On the other hand, the careful choice of words by Russian foreign minister Igor Ivanov—he did not exclude the use of force but said it would be "difficult"—gave the impression that a negotiation was possible and that finding common ground was within reach. A few days later, when the Security Council had its usual monthly luncheon, France implied that it would be ready for the use of force after the vote of a second Security Council resolution. In these early days of discussion, there was no perception that the fracture within the council would become irreparable. However, in hindsight, when on September 16 the council, in response to its demands, received a conciliatory letter from Iraq, the obvious U.S. disappointment was another indication that the United States might not really be looking for a diplomatic solution.

From the outset, Kofi Annan was very much aware that the Iraq crisis would be a defining moment for the relations between the United Nations and the United States. I had no direct responsibility during the Iraq crisis, since peacekeeping was rightly not considered a realistic possibility, but I was nevertheless deeply involved in advising the secretary general who felt, at that difficult juncture, that a collegial style of management was particularly needed. Throughout the crisis, he relied on a small but diverse group of advisors, and our internal debates would reflect the broader discussion that was going to seize the whole world. As early as February 2002, in an internal seminar that the secretary general had convened to reflect on the objectives of his second term, Louise Fréchette, the Canadian deputy secretary general, had stressed how fragile the improvement of relations between the United States and the UN was. Several participants had noted the emphasis of the U.S. administration on the use of force, the huge growth of military spending, and the lack of consultations with traditional allies. The situation in the world could become much worse, one participant had said. The impending crisis with Iraq called for a continuation of the earlier discussion, and Kofi Annan convened another internal meeting at Glen Cove in the last days of September. He was afraid that the UN could easily become a forum that countries usually very deferential to U.S. policies might use to show some token independence. "The UN must not become a place to let off steam against the U.S.," he said. "We must keep the U.S. in the fold."

The discussion oscillated between those who wanted to reach out to the natural allies of the UN and those who felt nothing would work without U.S.

support. Jeffrey Sachs, then a special advisor to the secretary general, noted how new centers of power had emerged, each with an interest in the UN. Other members of the Annan team, mainly from the developing world, reminded the group that many countries were now deeply suspicious of multilateralism, which they saw as a way for the rich and powerful to impose their own rules. We had to convince them of the utility of the United Nations for their countries. Others—including Mark Malloch-Brown, then head of the United Nations Development Program, and Sergio Vieira de Mello, who at the time was the UN's high commissioner for human rights—insisted on the need to engage the United States, to convince Washington that multilateralism was in the U.S. national interest. Kofi Annan tried to bridge the divide in his concluding remarks: "We have to engage the U.S.," he said, "but the resolution [on Iraq] should not be seen as a setup, as an excuse for military action, and there should not be any whiff of regime change in it." Jeffrey Sachs made a powerful case, which stands the test of time very well, against the prospect of a war in Iraq. He argued that the only good scenario would be a very short war, followed by the quick installation of a stable regime, with immediate control of oil and increased oil supplies. But that scenario, he noted, was unlikely, and the alternative scenarios would lead to huge fiscal imbalance and financial fragility of the United States. I nevertheless think that at this early stage, the secretary general probably was already convinced that the conduct of Iraq and the U.S. position would make a war inevitable, but he was thinking of what would come afterward. He stressed what would become a leitmotif of all his interventions, the importance of a united Security Council: "The crisis has to be handled in a way that makes it possible to turn to the international community and the UN later. Hence the difficulty for the U.S. to go it alone." He added, "The strongest argument against unilateral action is the fear of unintended consequences."

Meanwhile, Hans Blix, a former Swedish foreign minister who also had served as the head of the International Atomic Energy Agency and had a reputation for remarkable perseverance and integrity, was working hard to put together a credible program of weapons inspections in Iraq. His challenge, as U.S. defense secretary Donald Rumsfeld would say, was to prove a negative. It is much harder to prove that a country does not have weapons of mass destruction, if it does not have them, than to prove it has them, if it actually has them. Where there is no fire, there is no smoke, and no smoking gun, but that will never be enough for those who have suspicions. I remember an evening in early October, when I had stayed late in the office and was one of the last to leave a deserted UN building; Blix was also leaving late and he looked weary. He had informed the Security Council in the morning of his discussions with the Iraqis on the modalities of inspections and shared his views on a few critical issues: How to guarantee the safety of inspectors' planes in the no-fly zone over part of Iraq? How to organize inspections in so-called presidential sites? He felt that even on those sensitive points, an agreement with Baghdad might be possible, but he was worried that the joint U.S.-U.K. position, according to which troops and representatives of the P5 should accompany inspectors, was a step too far. The concept of inspection was based on cooperation, and coercion would change the whole nature of the effort.

The month of November gave hope to all those who wanted to avoid a destructive clash in the Security Council. For once, it seemed that the unrelenting pressure of the United States and the United Kingdom, and the more cautious approach of the other members of the council, would produce a result that would be better than either the U.S. or French positions: the tough stance of Washington and the threat of war would lead to a hardened inspection regime, while the French emphasis on diplomacy would open the opportunity for Iraq to comply. This might be multilateralism at its best. By early November, the United States and France were apparently agreed on a draft resolution. There would be no need for a second resolution once the first one had been adopted, which is what Washington wanted, but there would be a second debate, which is what Paris wanted. Russia eventually joined the agreement, and on November 8 the council unanimously adopted Resolution 1441. Even Syria joined the consensus. This was a considerable success for Colin Powell, who could now tell those who had questioned his efforts in the UN Security Council that diplomacy had paid off. There was a fleeting moment when everybody could hope against hope that the Iraq debate would not end in disaster.

But U.S. claims that incidents concerning the no-fly zone in northern Iraq were violations of the resolution—which they were not—quickly brought back a more sober assessment of reality and sparked one of the first real clashes between Kofi Annan and the United States over Iraq. As he was visiting Kosovo, the secretary general was asked in a tiny Serb village about the issue, and his clear answer was that indeed the no-fly zone incidents were not violations of Resolution 1441. His statement was picked up by wire services and stopped an incipient U.S. campaign to ratchet up the pressure. The hawks in Washington did not like it. It was clear that Washington was still determined to go to war, but the diplomatic success in the council meant that the risk of a unilateral U.S. move had become less likely. President Jacques Chirac captured the mood of the moment when he told Kofi Annan, in a meeting in Paris on November 25, that he was a "little less pessimistic." Chirac had spoken in Prague to Bush, who had confided that National Security Adviser Condoleezza Rice had to manage Vice President Dick Cheney, Rumsfeld, Deputy Defense

Secretary Paul Wolfowitz, and other hard-liners in the administration. The business community, according to Chirac, was in favor of the war, but public opinion was beginning to have doubts. And British prime minister Tony Blair himself was concerned. It would be difficult politically for the United States to go it alone without the United Kingdom. But Chirac concluded on a more bellicose note: "If Saddam makes a mistake, we go . . . and Saddam is a specialist of mistakes!" France seemed to be genuinely open to a range of possible outcomes.

A lot hinged on the detailed information that the Security Council had demanded from the Iraqis. The dossier prepared by Iraq was brought to the president of the council, Ambassador Alfonso Valdivieso of Colombia, on the weekend of December 8. The file had 12,000 pages, and Valdivieso immediately shared it with the five permanent members of the council, which irritated the elected members. There were issues of confidentiality because some of the documents, including lists of suppliers, might not only open a window on illicit activities of Iraq but could also serve as a guide for other would-be nuclear proliferators. It was eventually agreed that Blix would be the custodian of those sensitive documents, and that he would have the authority to censor sensitive information. The United States was quick to point out the gaps in the file, which further irritated those who had not had the time to sift through the mountains of documents provided by Iraq.

As 2002 drew to an end, I headed for Kuwait to check the state of preparedness of the UN mission monitoring the border between Iraq and Kuwait, which had been in place since 1991 to watch the demilitarized zone between those countries. I arrived in the evening of January 2, 2003. Flying alongside the border in a UN helicopter brought a clearer message than a careful reading of the discussions and resolutions of the council. One could see thousands of troops and tanks taking position on the Kuwaiti side of the border and getting ready to destroy the sand berm that had been erected to stop Iraqi incursions. When I crossed into Iraq in a UN convoy to visit our base in Um Qasr, the tired Iraqi soldiers who waived us in looked as if they had lost the war before it had even started. It suddenly felt as if the eleven years between the first Gulf war and the oncoming conflict had just been a temporary truce, and the unfinished business of 1991 was now going to be completed. The sunken ships, still rusting in the muddy waters of the Shatt al Arab, were a visible sign that normalcy had not returned to Iraq after the first defeat of Saddam. At the beginning of 2003, there was a sense of inevitability: war had to happen. The only real question, as in Greek tragedies, was how?

The road that eventually led to the launch of hostilities on March 20, 2003, was not straight. The military timetable played a more and more dominant role, even though Kofi Annan stressed that it should not influence the political timetable. But it obviously did: tens of thousands of troops had already been deployed, and everybody knew that a military campaign needed to take place before the scorching heat of spring and summer. This was especially true if one believed that the risk of Iraq using chemical weapons was real: wearing an anti-chemical weapons suit on top of combat gear is uncomfortable enough; doing so would be almost unbearable once the summer heat had set in.

The secretary general, in spite of the growing inevitability of the war, was trying to cling to a compromise position and thus salvage the unity of the Security Council: acknowledging that the show of force was useful to extract concessions from the Iraqis, but reminding France's Villepin that if inspections were to be considered a success, it would be important to manage a possible de-escalation in a way that would save face for Washington. I wonder whether he really believed at this late stage that war could be avoided, but until the very end he genuinely tried to keep all options open.

The general sentiment was that Iraq was not helping its case much. Chirac's observation that "Saddam is a specialist of mistakes" seemed to be confirmed. The file produced by the Iraqis in December, voluminous as it was, had proved to be remarkably empty of significant content; the Iraqi cooperation with inspectors remained minimal; and Western intelligence services were reinforcing each other's certainties about Iraq's weapons arsenals: I was thus told by a French nonproliferation specialist, who was a great supporter of going to war and was very critical of the French position, that indeed she knew for a fact through intelligence reports that aluminum tubes bought by Iraq were used for uranium enrichment. Blix himself, when he briefed the council at the end of January, made it clear that Iraq was not playing a straight game, though he later qualified his declaration, which had been seized upon by the hawks, in an interview with the *New York Times*.

The UN Caught between Rival Powers

The discussion came to a head on February 5, 2003, when the Security Council again met at the ministerial level and Colin Powell famously presented the case of the United States against Saddam Hussein. Powell had nothing more than circumstantial evidence, but I suspect that most of those who watched him deliver his message believed that Iraq had indeed some clandestine weapons programs. This was the most logical—but in hindsight wrong—way to explain the continued lack of genuine cooperation of Iraq. But positions had hardened, and nobody was ready to claim the benefit of the doubt, neither the hawks who wanted their war, nor the opponents of the war who were afraid that any acceptance of the possibility of Iraq's possessing weapons of mass destruction would lead them to eventually accept war. The debate was not framed in a way that allowed for admission of uncertainty and compromise, in spite of the heroic efforts of Hans Blix, who was gradually accumulating enough information to make an objective decision based on facts possible. But he needed some more time, and the United States was not willing to wait. At the monthly luncheon of the Security Council, on February 6, the French ambassador presented ideas for reinforced inspections, which were quickly rejected by the U.S. and U.K. ambassadors. It was becoming more and more apparent that there was no interest, among the permanent members of the council, in bridging the deep divide that had opened between them, and that they were all now engaged in a tactical game of blame-shifting, which profoundly dismayed the elected members and brought the council to a standstill.

Kofi Annan had a different, and broader, perspective. A multilateralist by principle and by duty, as he had said in his speech at the General Assembly, he knew that the conditions under which war would happen could have major consequences for international law, for international institutions, and for nonproliferation. Would preventive war formally become the official new U.S. doctrine, setting an example that could undermine one of the most important articles of the UN charter, article 51, which authorizes the unilateral use of force only in self-defense? Would the Security Council be ignored, against the will of a clear majority of nations, and risk marginalization? Would nonproliferation be managed through treaties in multilateral frameworks, or through unilateral actions, thus creating a powerful incentive for proliferators to acquire weapons of mass destruction?

The secretary general, now convinced that war had become inevitable, used the opportunity of a speech at the College of William and Mary to outline his position. He stressed the importance of using multilateral approaches to enforcing nonproliferation regimes, noting that "when states decide to use force, not in self-defense but to deal with broader threats to international peace and security, there is no substitute for the unique legitimacy provided by the United Nations Security Council." He then pointedly observed that the authors of the UN Charter were not pacifists and that the Security Council might have "to face up to its responsibilities: sometimes force has to be met by force." He called on U.S. leadership: "When there is strong U.S. leadership, exercised through patient diplomatic persuasion and coalition-building, the United Nations is successful and the United States is successful." His implicit message was that the United States should go the extra mile to gain support in the council, as Washington had done to get the first resolution. At the time, I felt he was being too accepting of war and should not create the impression that he was giving up. I would have liked him to take a stronger stance. In hindsight I probably was wrong, and not consistent with my own position, which was also that war had become inevitable.

But the United States was less and less interested in diplomacy, and France, convinced that any effort to stop the war was pointless, drew the opposite conclusion of Kofi Annan: the tactical goal of France was no longer to preserve the unity of the council but, on the contrary, to make sure that a war would not have the council's support. The French believed that since the majority of the world seemed opposed to the war, it was important, for the future credibility of the council, not to be associated with the war. I disagreed with my compatriots on that issue: from a national standpoint, I thought that France, as an ally of the United States, should avoid a frontal collision with Washington. I thought that it was more important to protect the capacity of France to influence the postconflict phase than to fight a rearguard battle against a war that would happen anyway. In the postconflict phase, legal issues such as the control of oil revenues would acquire a vital importance, and the United States would need the authority of the Security Council, since the U.S. Army could create facts on the ground but would not be in a position to create legal facts. It was better to keep one's political capital for that crucial phase. And as a matter of principle, although I could not accept a war of choice, because all wars create immense suffering and have unintended consequences, I did not approve of the smug self-righteousness of the opponents of war. I accepted the possibility that Saddam Hussein might have weapons of mass destruction, and I had no doubt about the awful nature of his regime. More fundamentally, I feared that a collision between the United States and the United Nations would do enormous damage to the Security Council and to international law. I wrote a letter to Dominique de Villepin's chief of staff to suggest that a more moderate posture of France was advisable. France should tell the Bush administration that it did not agree with the war but that, for the sake of U.S.-French relations, it would not actively oppose it, but abstain. But the mood in France was exactly the opposite, and my views were very much in the minority. One of the most respected strategic experts of France, who had been the director of the International Institute for Strategic Studies in London and is now its chairman, François Heisbourg, reflected the prevailing consensus well when he wrote in the *Financial Times* that the United States was going to face a new Vietnam, and that it was good not to be associated with a policy that would eventually fail.

under the guise of nonproliferation, this was a red flag and put even more distance between the opposing camps in the council. Time was running out, and compromise seemed less and less likely. As Kofi Annan put it, "The permanent members of the council were talking past each other." The Canadians had launched a trial balloon, suggesting that a clear deadline be set for Iraqi actions to take place: the idea could have helped the antiwar camp to climb down from its position and allow for a consensual decision to go to war, but that is precisely what the French and others did not want. They considered the Canadian idea a dangerous ultimatum. British diplomats, who saw a looming diplomatic disaster, were making desperate efforts, with their usual ingenuity, to square the circle: Would it be possible to draw a list of disarmament tasks to be performed by the Iraqis that would be sufficiently significant to be a good test of Iraqi compliance, and sufficiently limited to be achievable in a very short timeframe? In the end, this attempt also failed: the antiwar camp was wary of the automaticity implied in the British efforts, the undecided members were suspicious of British intentions, and the United States remained noncommittal. The "undecided six," as the six elected members of the council who were the swing votes were called, wanted to hear from Hans Blix and Mohamed El Baradei, who succeeded Blix as the head of the International Atomic Energy Agency, rather than the United Kingdom, on the "remaining tasks of disarmament." Blix had used the image of a "down payment" to characterize the demands made on Saddam Hussein, noting that, in view of Iraq's past record, the down payment should be significant. The undecided six, who genuinely wanted to disarm Iraq but also wanted to avoid a war, trusted the integrity of Blix and El Baradei and hoped against hope that the council could rally around an objective and balanced answer provided by two respected international civil servants. They deeply resented the fact that France and like-minded countries had actually given up on trying to stop the march toward war.

The protracted drama came to an end on a weekend in mid-March 2003, when a hastily convened summit took place in the Azores. The abundance of flags at the press conference compensated for the small number of countries attending. President Bush thanked his host, Prime Minister José Manuel Barroso of Portugal, for arranging the meeting "at such short notice." Prime Minister Blair and Prime Minister José Maria Aznar of Spain also attended. The declaration that was issued referred to the unanimously adopted Resolution 1441 and previous UN resolutions. It recalled "the serious consequences" foreseen in case of noncompliance by Iraq, signaling that the effort to adopt a second resolution had now ended. It outlined the "war aims" of the emerging coalition, which undertook a solemn obligation to help the Iraqi people build a new Iraq at peace with itself and its neighbors. The Iraqi people deserve to be lifted from insecurity and tyranny, and freed to determine for themselves the future of their country. We envisage a unified Iraq with its territorial integrity respected. All the Iraqi people—its rich mix of Sunni and Shiite Arabs, Kurds, Turkmen, Assyrians, Chaldeans, and all others—should enjoy freedom, prosperity, and equality in a united country. We will support the Iraqi people's aspirations for a representative government that upholds human rights and the rule of law as cornerstones of democracy.

The declaration did not close the door on future cooperation with the United Nations. On the contrary, the conclusion was an appeal for solidarity.

In the Security Council, the mood was certainly not inclined to cooperation, and when the council reconvened on Monday, March 17, there was a lot of petulance and bitterness. The cosponsors of the new draft resolution told the press that they had decided not to put the resolution to a vote because of the announced French veto. They said they wanted to protect the United Nations. This triggered angry comments from the French ambassador, who observed that it was unusual for cosponsors of a resolution to inform the press before they inform the council and pointedly noted that the reference to a French veto was incorrect, since there was no majority in the first place. Ambassador Jean-Marc de la Sablière was right, but my compatriots had made it easier for the coalition to blame France by so frequently brandishing the prospect of a French veto in the previous weeks. U.S. ambassador John Negroponte also told the press that the secretary general of the United Nations had been notified that military operations would be launched (Kofi Annan had received a call from Negroponte on Sunday evening) and that no further notification would be issued.

The antiwar camp in the council was nevertheless determined not to make life easy for the United States and other members of what was beginning to be called the "coalition." Several ambassadors requested that inspections continue and asked to be briefed on the future "program of work" of inspectors. The Chinese ambassador soberly observed that if the withdrawal of the draft resolution signaled an effort to reach consensus, it was welcome; if it signaled war, it was "very regrettable." Blix, as unflappable as ever, announced that he had prepared a working document on twelve key remaining tasks that could be made available to the council in the afternoon. If Iraq was "pro-active"— and Blix noted that Iraq was making great efforts to prove that it had destroyed unauthorized weapons—completing disarmament tasks would be "a matter of months, not weeks, not years." This was a timetable that was not compatible with the military realities that were beginning to unfold.

As the head of peacekeeping with a mission deployed on the frontline between Kuwait and Iraq, I had a problem that needed to be solved in a matter of hours, not days or weeks. When Iqbal Riza, Kofi Annan's chief of staff, had called me on Sunday night to inform me of Negroponte's phone call, we had agreed to start immediately the evacuation of the peacekeepers deployed on the Iraqi side of the border, in the base that I had visited at Um Qasr. A handful of UN troops were not going to make any difference and stop a massive military operation, but they would be in serious danger if they remained in a place that was to be at the center of the first battle. At the same time, it was important for the United Nations not to give the impression that peacekeepers were rushing to get out of the way to make war easier. The antiwar members of the council were watching us, as they were watching what would be decided for the weapons inspectors and for the personnel managing the UN's oil-for-food program in Iraq. They understood the operational necessities on the ground, but they wanted a bit of theater in the chamber of the council. In the Secretariat, we did not want theatrics to lead to loss of life. So we adjusted our plans a bit in the early hours of Monday: the column of peacekeepers leaving Um Qasr was temporarily stopped, so that the secretary general could inform the Security Council that he was ordering UN personnel to pull out for their own safety. Sergei Lavrov, the Russian ambassador, "took note," the authority of the council was safeguarded, and I ordered the troops to complete their withdrawal before nightfall. Two days later, in what was the middle of the night in Baghdad, military operations started, as big explosions, apparently aimed at the Iraqi leadership, shook the capital of Iraq.

Looking to the UN's Post-War Role

As soon as the secretary general had reached the conclusion that war was inevitable, he had started to explore the role that the UN could play in the postconflict phase. He was probably influenced by the Kosovo experience in 1999. The Security Council had then been badly divided, and the war had been launched without a council resolution, but the members of the council found agreement on the management of the postconflict phase through Resolution 1244, which was unanimously adopted and entrusted the management of Kosovo to the UN. Now, nearly four years later, at the beginning of March, Jay Garner, a retired U.S. general who had been appointed by the Pentagon to run the Office of Reconstruction and Humanitarian Assistance in Iraq, came to the United Nations. Garner's office was tasked with overseeing planning and assistance to Iraq and would be in charge of administering the country after the war. His visit apparently signaled that the United States did not exclude a role for the UN, underscoring the conclusion of the Azores declaration. Privately, Powell had mentioned to the Security Council that the United States might turn to the UN after the conflict, and Condoleezza Rice had mentioned to Sergio de Mello, who had just been appointed high commissioner for human rights and had had the rare honor of a meeting at the White House, that "the administration was looking hard at how the UN might play a legitimizing role."

It was clear that no decision had been made in Washington, and Kofi Annan wanted to take advantage of that vacuum to offer some ideas and re-insert the UN in the process. He was concerned that Washington had not thought through a number of important issues (among them the management of the oil-for-food program, which had become a central piece of the Iraqi economy) and felt he had a duty to call them to the attention of the Americans. He did not waste any time. Even before military operations had started, on the same day as the meeting of the Security Council where he had announced that he was pulling UN personnel out of Iraq, he convened a meeting to discuss the role of the UN in the postconflict phase. Tony Blair, who had worked so hard, but failed, to convince the United States to seek a second resolution, was now deploying the same energy to have UN involvement in the postconflict phase. The Azores declaration was a first indication of that policy. The secretary general referred to a call he had received from Blair, who had asked him for help. The model was Afghanistan, with a strong special representative of the secretary general who would do what Lakhdar Brahimi was doing in Kabul: facilitate a political process and the emergence of new legitimate authorities.

We were all agreed that the comparative advantage of the UN was its capacity to build trust and produce legitimacy, but legitimacy requires independence, and there was no clarity on how the UN would fit into a process driven by the American administration. Kofi Annan asked Rafeeuddin Ahmed, a Pakistani who had played a critical role in the UN engagement in Cambodia thirteen years earlier, to prepare a report on the issue. He would be helped in this delicate task by Salman Ahmed (no connection to Rafeeuddin), who had already shown his exceptional talent helping Brahimi write the landmark report in 2000 on peacekeeping reform that bears his name and had then played a decisive role in helping me implement it. But the most immediate issue was the oil-for-food program: the supply of humanitarian goods to the Iraqis should not be interrupted, but the atmosphere in the council was so poisoned that there was a serious risk that whatever proposal was put forward by one of the permanent members would be rejected by one of the other P5. To avoid that outcome, Kofi Annan took the unusual step of sending a letter to the president of the council outlining in great detail—including language that could be put in a resolution—the adaptations he thought were required for the oil-for-food program not to come to a sudden stop that would hurt the Iraqi people. The United States could not resist making its own proposals, which were not well received, but the proposals made by the secretary general eventually paved the way for the winding down of the oil-for-food program.

The more political issue of the role of the UN in a post-Saddam Iraq was a different matter. Villepin was very pessimistic about the future course of American policies, telling the secretary general that he expected Washington's imperial ambitions would not stop with Iraq. It was very important, in such circumstances, for the UN not to be associated with the U.S. adventure in Iraq, and Villepin explicitly excluded a resolution along the lines of Resolution 1244 on Kosovo. On the opposite side of the argument, Clare Short, who was the U.K. minister for development and cooperation and would later resign from the U.K. government, insisted with Kofi Annan that the UN had to take a leading political role, which would be, according to her, a condition of legitimacy. Her attitude was representative of the left wing of the Labor party. She rebuffed Jeremy Greenstock when the British ambassador mentioned that some measure of "fudging" might be necessary, considering the views in the U.S. administration and Condoleezza Rice's lack of support for a political role for the UN. The British government had made a commitment to the parliament, Short said. And when the deputy secretary general, Louise Fréchette, trying to be pragmatic, mentioned that there were many ways for the UN to be involved, she was also rebuffed: the political role of the UN was the key. Kofi Annan, mindful of what he had heard from Villepin, was delivering messages to Clare Short that he probably hoped might reach Washington through her or through Blair: "There was going to be a lot of resistance in the council, and a U.S.-U.K. plan would not succeed if it appeared to be non-negotiable. Several members of the council feared that Iraq was just a first step, and it was important to reassure them." A brief discussion followed on a possible UN envoy to Iraq. Bernard Kouchner, who had served in a similar post in Kosovo, had called me to express his interest, and I was glad that Kofi mentioned his name. Short mentioned Sergio de Mello, but the secretary general immediately replied that he would not be available.

The war had now started, and everybody was trying to make sense of the news coming from Iraq. The initial night, when several precision-guided missiles and bombs hit command centers, had not produced the checkmate that some may have hoped for. As often happens in wars, absurd mood swings followed, and the difficulties encountered by advancing U.S. forces in Nazarieh and Najaf were quickly interpreted as signs of difficulties to come: self-proclaimed military experts were pontificating on the challenges of the "war of cities." Coalition prisoners had been—contrary to Geneva conventions—paraded on Al Jazeera, and U.S. Army general John Abuzaid admitted on March 23 that "it had been the toughest day." There was a visible, and sad, schadenfreude in many parts of the world, and it was palpable in the corridors of the United Nations. Few wanted the United States to lose, and any sensible person knew that it was not a possibility, but many were not unhappy that things were not going too well for the coalition. That meant that no negotiations on postconflict arrangements could seriously start before the war had ended.

Three more weeks would pass before triumphant U.S. troops entered Baghdad cheered by Iraqis celebrating the end of Saddam's rule. During that period, intense private discussions had taken place in the UN and also, obviously, in the U.S. government. The divisions in the UN Secretariat were almost as deep as in the Security Council. Kofi Annan was receiving contradictory advice from his closest aides. When, on March 27, he called me into his office for a long tête-à-tête on Iraq, I argued that the UN should not rush and should avoid being in a position of demandeur. If the UN role in Iraq was perceived as a response to U.S. and U.K. requests, it would be compromised from the outset and of little use. What the UN could bring was the facilitation of a political process within Iraq, and a regional role to prevent Iraq from becoming a battleground between rival powers in the Middle East: the two were linked and connected to the future of Shia-Sunni relations and Persian-Arab relations. I argued that the best criterion for a significant political role of the UN should be the end of occupation. So long as there was occupation, the responsibilities of the occupying powers should not be diluted, and the UN, on the ground, but not necessarily in the region, should confine itself to a humanitarian role, as UNRWA does with the Palestinians.

In the United Nations, many were arguing for a greater role of the organization, and Kofi Annan, who was more realist than I, had been cautious but more open when he met with Tony Blair. His "red lines" were that the UN should not be "subordinated" to the coalition and that the coalition should not expect an ex-post legitimization of the war. The United States changed the nature of the discussion when, a few days later, Colin Powell made clear to the secretary general that the coalition would take full responsibility for the political process. What Washington was apparently considering was a conference that the United States would organize, but where the UN would be in attendance: this was the exact opposite of the Bonn process for Afghanistan, which had been organized by the UN, with a U.S. presence, and it would obviously have major consequences for the credibility and legitimacy of the whole process. This was a far cry from what Clare Short had anticipated, and closer to the "fudge" that pragmatic British ambassador Greenstock had predicted. As Kofi Annan had said early on, this was not going to be a "neat process." Ironically, the more it became clear that the political role of the UN would be minimal, the more Washington and London pressed the secretary general to appoint an "envoy." Kieran Prendergast sadly, and disapprovingly, commented that the UN role was now "to add tone." This was humiliating and dangerous, but could the UN say no? That was my preference, but one could argue that, over time, the U.S.-led coalition would see the benefits of using the UN, and the possibility therefore existed to gradually insert a dose of multilateralism and international legitimacy into a unilateral process. As Greenstock told the secretary general, do not rule yourself out of the game.

The UN fought a rearguard battle, which in hindsight probably made little sense. The secretary general decided to appoint Rafeehudin Ahmed as his personal adviser for Iraq, not as an envoy, to make the point that the UN was keeping its distance from the coalition, and not—at least not yet—taking any new role in Iraq. When the secretary general formally introduced his "adviser" to the members of the council—which is what the United States and United Kingdom wanted, to make the insignificant role of the UN as visible as possible—Jeremy Greenstock asked if the adviser would be allowed to travel. The Russian ambassador, Sergei Lavrov, immediately retorted that any contact while Iraq was still occupied would be inappropriate. At a press conference in Belfast, Bush brushed aside all these diplomatic niceties, welcoming the "vital role" of the United Nations and the appointment by the secretary general of a "personal representative."

Putting the UN's Imprimatur on the Occupation

The UN had already lost the spin battle and was now embarked on a course that it would not be able to control. On the one hand, there was unrelenting pressure from the United States and the United Kingdom to have some light UN wrapping on the occupation of Iraq. On the other hand, the countries that had opposed the war did not have clear policy goals: they were exhausted by the bruising political battle they had waged before the war, and they were not prepared for more battles with a now-triumphant United States. Moreover, like the secretary general himself, they were not sure of what was good for the UN. The "vital role of the UN" became the cliché that reconciled those who were actually running the show in Washington with those who would have liked to pry away Iraq from U.S. control but had no idea how it could be done. And the UN was caught in the middle. The discussion had shifted from substance to perception, and Tony Blair, expert as he was in the management of perceptions, captured the situation well when he told the secretary general: "We will navigate our way between, on the one hand, the idea that the UN takes over, and on the other hand, that it is a rubber stamp." The secretary general had to transform that rhetorical fudge into a political line, which was not easy. In a conversation with Colin Powell, he seemed to accept that "it would be difficult for the U.S. to hand over Iraq after having won the war," but he added that "it was important to recognize that the UN membership was anxious not to be seen as rubber-stamping." The buzz word, which cleverly fudged who was in charge, was found, unsurprisingly, by Blair: "partnership."

By the second half of April, the fudge had become policy, and the mood in the Security Council and in the world had radically shifted. The British foreign minister, Jack Straw, had told his European colleagues: "The train is leaving the station, and you are asking where the train is going?" The most vocal opponents of the war, France and Russia, were now prepared to consider the appointment of a special representative of the secretary general, stepping up the UN's role. When Mexico, which was holding the presidency of the council for May, organized a debate on the role of the UN in postconflict situations, the expected differences emerged as the United States attributed success in East Timor to Australia, while France celebrated the role of the UN, but the fireworks of the previous period were conspicuously absent. Diplomacy was back, and the council wanted to make a deal.

On May 1 Kofi Annan once again convened a private meeting with all the council members in his conference room to start a process of reconciliation among them. He outlined a menu of activities that could be undertaken by the UN, from humanitarian assistance to reconstruction and political facilitation. He made clear that Iraq was not a place for blue helmets and that security would have to be the responsibility of coalition forces. Greenstock spoke first and brought some clarity to the discussion. He confirmed the obvious, that the United States and United Kingdom were occupying powers, and that any country joining the coalition would also be an occupying power. This was an intelligent way to remind the Americans that all forces deployed in Iraq were not all-powerful, but were bound by the Geneva Conventions, while at the same time clarifying that the coalition did not need a mandate of the council. Instead, the mandate was provided by international law and the Fourth Geneva Convention, which defines the responsibilities and obligations of an occupying power. He then went on to describe four possible "phases": coalition, interim authority, transitional government, and finally a sovereign Iraqi government with full authority. He envisaged a role for the UN in the areas described by the secretary general in all the phases and noted that the process of transfer of responsibility from the coalition to the final sovereign Iraqi government would be gradual. He used, like his prime minister, the conveniently ambiguous word "partnership." And he elegantly glossed over the fact that the occupying powers were going to organize a process that would, in effect, fundamentally change the political and administrative order in Iraq: according to international law, an occupying power cannot do that.

But the members of the council were not in a very combative mood, and Gunter Pleuger, the German ambassador who spoke immediately after Greenstock, agreed with the need to go one step at a time and to be pragmatic. What was important was to have a process that would be accepted by the Iraqis, by the region, and by the world, he said. Lavrov was not duped by the sophisticated description of phases and bluntly said that what mattered was the overall design. He pressed on a point that Pleuger had alluded to and could not be dealt with through a diplomatic fudge: who would sell the oil? He, perhaps mischievously, wondered whether the secretary general could be put in charge. Referring to the partnership mentioned by Greenstock, he said there could be no senior and junior partners, only equal partners. La Sablière for France and Wang Guangya for China wanted answers from the coalition before expressing a national position.

John Negroponte, the American ambassador, spoke last. He was not in a comfortable position, because he obviously was waiting for decisions that had not yet been made in Washington. He could only confirm that already approved contracts of the oil-for-food program would be executed. But he was vague on the role of the interim authority in Iraq, stating that he believed that the position expressed by Condoleezza Rice—the authority would not be the government—was still "probably" the position of the U.S. government. At the end of the meeting, the frustrated Mexican president of the council asked when the United States would be in a position to present concrete proposals, and Negroponte bluntly replied: "When we call a meeting!" The United States clearly was unhappy with the initiative of the secretary general, but I thought it had nevertheless served a very useful purpose. Members of the council had been given the opportunity to share concerns and raise questions before positions were finalized in Washington. I observed that Kofi Annan would often use such tactics with an administration that was not naturally inclined to consultations. This was an intelligent way to prepare the ground for consensus and encourage genuine interaction between members of the council who would otherwise easily revert to a confrontational mode.

Expediency Defeats Coherence

On May 8 the British and American ambassadors sent a letter to the president of the council outlining their responsibilities as occupying powers, and the next day they presented the draft resolution for which everybody had been waiting. This was a very clever sequence, which seemed close to what Greenstock had said a week before: the council did not have to enter into a divisive debate on the authority of the coalition, which was derived from its responsibilities as an occupying force. On that basis, the interim authority acquired full control over the resources of Iraq and of the oil-for-food program for an unlimited period. The only constraint was an advisory board including the United Nations and the Bretton Woods institutions—the World Bank and International Monetary Fund (IMF)—which had a limited and vague supervisory role. The role of the UN was described in a paragraph that was as long as it was vague: the secretary general was requested "to appoint a Special Representative for Iraq whose independent responsibilities shall involve reporting regularly to the Council on his activities under this resolution, coordinating activities of the United Nations in post-conflict processes in Iraq, coordinating among United Nations and international agencies engaged in humanitarian assistance and reconstruction activities in Iraq" in addition to coordinating with the coalition to assist the people of Iraq perform a dizzying list of tasks from safely returning refugees to rebuilding infrastructure to supporting economic reconstruction and protecting human rights.[1]

The man chosen by Kofi Annan to play that impossible role, in which he would have to meet maximum expectations with minimum powers, was Sergio

---

1. The full list is: "(a) coordinating humanitarian and reconstruction assistance by United Nations agencies and between United Nations agencies and non-governmental organizations; (b) promoting the safe, orderly, and voluntary return of refugees and displaced persons; (c) working intensively with the Authority, the people of Iraq, and others concerned to advance efforts to restore and establish national and local institutions for representative governance, including by working together to facilitate a process leading to an internationally recognized, representative government of Iraq; (d) facilitating the reconstruction of key infrastructure, in cooperation with other international organizations; (e) promoting economic reconstruction and the conditions for sustainable development, including through coordination with national and regional organizations, as appropriate, civil society, donors, and the international financial institutions; (f) encouraging international efforts to contribute to basic civilian administration functions; (g) promoting the protection of human rights; (h) encouraging international efforts to rebuild the capacity of the Iraqi civilian police force; and (i) encouraging international efforts to promote legal and judicial reform."

de Mello. The Americans had lobbied hard to have him appointed, and they eventually overcame the initial reluctance of the secretary general.

The contrast between the bitter battle that had led to a disastrous impasse before the war and the quick adoption of Resolution 1483 on May 22 was extraordinary. I think even the Bush administration must have been surprised to have such a complete victory after the debacle of the failed war resolution. When I heard the result of the vote, while on UN business in Kinshasa, I felt relieved that the council was able to come together, because I knew that this was absolutely necessary for the Congolese effort in which I was engaged to succeed. But I was also somewhat despondent that there was so little coherence and strategic thinking among the powers in the Security Council that have the responsibility for peace and security. As I had anticipated, the countries opposed to the war, exhausted by the fight in which they had spent substantial political capital, were now ready to concede everything. Considering the political dynamics of late April and May, there was probably no other possible course of action, but it was astonishing to see how easily expediency had won over coherence.

The United Nations, caught in the middle, was to pay a heavy price, in political and in human terms, for that fudge. In Iraq, the situation was not good. Three weeks after his arrival, Garner had been replaced by U.S. diplomat Paul Bremer, and after the looting of the Baghdad museum and the spreading violence, it was already evident that General Eric Shinseki, then U.S. Army chief of staff, had been right when he had recommended a much bigger force than the troops that were actually deployed. But it was also becoming clear that Washington's diplomatic success in the Security Council would not translate into significant troop deployments from other countries beyond a small core of supporters. In particular, the hope that Muslim countries like Jordan or Pakistan would provide contingents quickly evaporated. Among other major traditional peacekeepers, India, which would gradually become a strategic ally of the United States during the Bush administration, was also reluctant to be drawn into Iraq and be associated with what could turn into a sectarian war. Other former colonized countries were not keen to become occupying powers. Meanwhile, on the economic and financial front as well as the political front, it also became clear that the United Nations was not going to play a substantive role any time soon.

On the financial front, the issue was the amount of power given to the "international advisory and monitoring board" overseeing the "development fund" created by Resolution 1483 in May 2003. Since the resolution had explicitly put the development fund of Iraq—which was going to collect all the oil revenues of Iraq—under the authority of the occupying powers, the only international oversight of this huge financial resource would rest with the

International Advisory and Monitoring Board, authorized by Resolution 1483. The World Bank and the IMF were not able to take a strong position on the issue, and Bremer was keen not to have his power limited. Sergio de Mello, who could see from his position in Baghdad that this was one of the few leverage points that the UN might still have, insisted in a videoconference we had with him in June that the UN fight over the terms of reference of the board. The UN was isolated in its position, however, and that battle was quickly lost.

The last possible tool of influence for the UN was the political expertise that it could deploy in Baghdad, which might influence U.S. policies. Sergio de Mello had moved quickly to Baghdad. His reputation in the UN and the active support of Kofi Annan had allowed him to deploy an A-team, combining people who had a deep knowledge of the Middle East and Iraq with experts on peacekeeping, some of whom had worked with him in East Timor and Kosovo. I knew many of them. His key political adviser was Ghassan Salame. He is one of the best specialists of the Middle East, a rare man who is at the same time a sophisticated political analyst and professor as well as a very effective political operator. Salame, although he has spent much time as a professor at the Institut d'Etudes Politiques in Paris, keeps an extensive network of contacts not only in his native country, Lebanon, where he has been a minister and an influential political figure, but throughout the Middle East. And indeed, in June and early July 2003 Salame and a few other Middle East experts played a very useful role in helping Sergio de Mello make contacts with a large spectrum of Iraqi personalities from Sunni secular personalities like diplomat Adnan Pachachi to key Shia leaders like Ayatollah Sistani. For a few weeks, the UN could at a minimum provide sound political advice to Bremer. Bremer understood that the UN could help him, and probably listened to some of its advice as he was putting together the Iraqi Governing Council. But as soon as the composition of the Iraqi Governing Council had been announced, Bremer had little use for the UN. In a humiliating meeting a few days before the bombing that killed him, Sergio de Mello reminded Bremer that the UN could bring a unique legitimacy to the reconstruction of Iraq, but Bremer replied bluntly that it was not the case in Iraq, now that the Governing Council had been installed. And in any case, he added, what was the international authority of the United Nations, with a divided Security Council that the United States had ignored to wage war?

A Tragic Day in Baghdad

The news of the Baghdad bombing reached me in Europe, on the afternoon of August 19. Kofi Annan later said that on that fateful day, we lost our innocence. And it is true that none of us had really thought that the UN as such could be targeted. Of course, we knew what had happened on 9/11, and that the UN building had been a possible target of al Qaeda. But I think many of us unconsciously differentiated between the UN headquarters, where international politics, and all its moral dilemmas, are debated, and the UN in the field, where people risk their lives to save other people's lives. This was certainly what the UN people who had gone to Iraq thought they were doing. Many of them had deep misgivings about the war, but they sincerely hoped that the UN could now help build a new Iraq, and that the success of postwar engagement would help overcome the disastrous diplomacy—or absence thereof—that had led to the war.

On August 19 I did not feel I had lost my innocence. I felt immense anger. The UN staffers who died on that day—like the peacekeepers who are killed in action every year around the world—are but a fraction of the tens of thousands of civilians who are the victims of conflict every year, but they are the embodiment of that still unfulfilled dream: a real international community that cares. What had been until then a political discussion on the appropriate role of the UN in an occupied country had become a very personal wound.

I knew five of the twenty-two victims personally: Sergio de Mello, Jean-Selim Kanaan, Fiona Watson, Rick Hooper, and Nadia Younes. Jean-Selim was the husband of Laura Dolci, one of the young and committed staff of the Department of Peacekeeping Operations (DPKO) who give energy and a moral dimension to peacekeeping. I had seen both of them a month before, in Geneva, where they were together for the birth of their first child: Mattia-Selim, as he was named, was born less than three weeks before his father died. On August 20 I rushed to Geneva, presented my condolences to Annie Vieira de Mello on behalf of the secretary general and went to visit Laura and her baby. I later represented the UN in Cairo at the funeral of Jean-Selim, who combined French Protestant roots through his mother and Egyptian Christian roots through his father. His Egyptian family greeted me with exuberance and generosity. Each of us is the product of so many strands, but during the oriental Christian rites, as I was listening in a cloud of frankincense to the litany of prayers, I felt that the unique mix that had been Jean-Selim—and would be further enriched in his son Mattia-Selim—represented exactly the diversity and richness that a genuine encounter between East and West, between the Orient and Europe, can produce. This is the best response to all the bigots.

In Cairo I also visited the family of Nadia Younes, who came from a very different part of Egyptian society, the rich Sunni entrepreneurial class, at ease in Cairo but also in London, Paris, or New York: that dynamism had made the success of Nadia, who had been the spokesperson of Kofi Annan and a chief of protocol before joining Sergio de Mello in Baghdad, and whom we all admired for her natural empathy and warmth. My deputy Hedi Annabi went to Edinburgh for the funeral of Fiona Watson, the quiet, smart young Scottish girl who had, like Laura Dolci, worked in the peacekeeping department and would have lived had she not rushed back to her Baghdad assignment one day earlier than scheduled. Later, we were all in New York to attend a service for Rick Hooper, the trusted adviser of Kieran Prendergast, who was in Baghdad on the day of the bombing because he was filling in for a friend and fellow staff member.

Sergio, Jean-Selim, Nadia, Fiona, and Rick came from four different continents and represented everything that is right about the UN. Their brutal deaths were unbearable to all of us, but what was particularly painful for me was that it was not clear what they had died for. Prendergast, cruelly, but with some truth, had said that the UN had been in Iraq "to add tone," and that was certainly not a reason to die. In my tenure at the helm of DPKO, I inevitably witnessed many deaths of those on UN assignments: some the result of tragic accidents, like the helicopter crash that killed twenty-four Pakistanis in Sierra Leone, some the consequence of hostile action, like the nine Bangladeshi soldiers who were ambushed in Ituri. Each time, I had a sense of personal loss, but I always felt that these personal tragedies, which left families grieving, had not been in vain: they were part of a risky but useful enterprise that helped change the lives of millions of people. In this abominable summer of 2003, I was not sure that our friends who had died in Baghdad were making a real difference, except through the example of commitment they were setting. And for that, they should all be remembered.

New Questions about the Occupation and the UN's Role

After the bombing, the international presence of the UN was dramatically curtailed in Iraq, and the Iraqi UN staff, which had already paid a very high toll to terrorism—seven of the twenty-two killed on August 19 were Iraqis—was for a while the only significant UN presence in the country. In New York, a protracted discussion on the security conditions for the return of international staff to Iraq had started, which was in fact a discussion on the role of the UN in Iraq. What role would warrant a UN presence, given the inevitable risks of that presence? That was the real question, but it was almost impossible to raise it in such blunt terms. Many of us reiterated that the UN presence could become significant only once the occupation ended.

At the traditional meeting between the secretary general and the U.S. president in September, for the opening of the General Assembly, the tone of President Bush had somewhat changed, and there was some shrillness in the way he reiterated that the United States would prevail in Iraq. But the sequence anticipated by his administration for the emergence of a sovereign Iraq had not changed. Bremer was still adamant that sovereignty would be transferred to the Iraqis at the end of the process, and that a constitutional agreement would be quickly drafted before the transfer. Bremer wanted to keep tight control as long as possible. He understood that the underrepresentation of Sunnis was a major issue, but he wanted, through carefully controlled caucuses, to oversee the "outreach" to new political players. Kofi Annan clearly expressed the reservations of the UN about the U.S. approach at the monthly luncheon of the Security Council in October. In essence, the UN was recommending the opposite of the U.S.-planned sequence: a quick transfer of sovereignty, followed by a long process of constitutional drafting. The result was another fudge, Resolution 1511, which was adopted in mid-October.

In Washington, there was a growing awareness that the timetable for a transfer of sovereignty had to be compressed. One month after the adoption of the resolution, a new agreement offered some of the answers requested by the resolution. There would be a transitional constitution, and an interim government emanating from a transitional national assembly elected through caucuses would be formed, to which sovereignty would be transferred in mid-2004. Key religious Shia leaders like Ayatollah Sistani had always made clear, including in a meeting with Sergio de Mello, that elections had to take place before any constitutional process could start, and they were unhappy with the caucus process. The United Nations was drawn into the controversy when a Shia leader formally asked the secretary general whether elections were possible before mid-2004. Brahimi, in response to a request of the secretary general, concluded that elections would not be possible before mid-2004, but that the caucus system was also unsatisfactory. He then helped put together the Iraqi government that replaced the U.S.-appointed Iraqi Governing Council on June 1, 2004. This formally ended the occupation on July 1, when the Coalition Provisional Authority, which succeeded the Office of Reconstruction and Humanitarian Assistance, was officially dissolved and Bremer left Iraq. The UN went on to help organize elections, and Sergio de Mello eventually had a successor when a former ambassador of Pakistan to the United States, Ashraf Qazi, was appointed special representative of the secretary general and settled in Baghdad.

Discussions in the United Nations continued on the appropriate size of the UN presence and on the security arrangements that had to be put in place to protect UN staff. Artificially complicated schemes were imagined to try to find troops that would protect the UN without being part of the coalition forces. Military logic, as I had hoped, prevailed. It was eventually concluded that the security of the UN was the responsibility of the coalition, but that a dedicated unit would be assigned to the static protection of the UN. The close protection of UN staff was the responsibility of the new UN Department for Safety and Security that had been created after the Baghdad bombing. I was glad that blue helmets were not involved. In hindsight, however, I underestimated the consequences for peacekeeping, worldwide, of the new situation created by international terrorism: the fact that the UN had to build a significant internal security component to protect itself against new threats signaled a major evolution, which changed the nature of the relationship between the UN and the host populations and, by implication, the posture of the peacekeepers themselves. The blast walls that were erected around UN compounds in Iraq and Afghanistan were the physical expression of the divide that had opened between the UN and possibly millions of people who did not actively engage in terrorism but who were no longer prepared to stop it when it threatened the UN. The United Nations had begun to lose its single most important asset: the trust of the people.

As I look back at the intense debates we went through in the UN over the role of the organization in Iraq, it seems that we all exaggerated the importance of the posture of the UN Secretariat. In the end, the organization is obviously in the hands of its member states, and in particular the most powerful ones. They will not hesitate to ditch the UN if it stands in the way of their immediate political goals and will come back to it with equanimity if political circumstances change and doing so suits them. The "political credibility" of the UN is a relative concept. I think that Kofi Annan was concerned that if the UN stayed on the sidelines in Iraq, it would be perceived as irrelevant by the United States and thus might be mortally wounded. In the end, I believe such concerns, and the hope that an active role of the UN would address them, were probably both exaggerated. If the United States had had a fully triumphant path in Iraq, all the efforts of the UN to demonstrate its relevance to Washington would not have changed U.S. views. Conversely, the difficulties encountered by the United States in Iraq led the Bush administration to make limited use of the UN. But those difficulties did not alter Washington's fundamental views of the organization, and the UN role remained very limited, in spite of all the emphatic declarations on the UN's "vital" role.

I was probably also wrong to be so concerned that the UN would lose its credibility if it did not stick to a principled position that would have excluded any political role in an occupied country. While I still believe that it would have been tactically better not to be in a position of *demandeur*, I was exaggerating the level of expectations that people with no power have with respect to what the UN can do to challenge power. I still believe that the United

Nations has nothing to stand on if it does not stand for principles, and the UN must not disappoint that hope. But there is greater tolerance than I thought for compromise and adjustment, and the Iraq crisis is just an episode in the never-ending battle between the dream of a genuine international community governed by principles and rules and the reality of a world of states that have only limited trust in the utility of principles. Given such a reality, those of us who believe that a world governed by rules and principles would be a better and safer place should probably not entertain the illusion that they are going to beat the practitioners of realpolitik at their own game, and a lot of the efforts of the UN to position itself were, in hindsight, futile. The only criterion should be the difference that the UN will or will not be able to make in the lives of people who have no other friends than the UN. In the case of Iraq, the UN did not have much political space and therefore could not make much of a difference. The trade-off between the risks it took, in terms of its reputation and tragically with the lives of some of its best people, and the contribution it could realistically make was not acceptable. Even so, the trade-off was the result of a particular political configuration that the UN could probably not resist, rather than the consequence of a deliberate choice.

For the UN, the most painful lesson of Iraq is actually how little care, political as well as human, key member states showed for the organization they had created in 1945. This was particularly in evidence in the diplomatic debacle that preceded the war, which will probably remain a textbook illustration of what not to do in diplomacy. The United States had wrong assumptions, but in a way the most coherent position. The Bush administration was convinced that a new era had started, and authors like Elliot Cohen pontificated that the rest of the world was begging for the assertion of U.S. power. If the United States wanted to exercise its power unfettered, the UN was an unnecessary complication, to be ignored or circumvented. If it had not been for the insistence of Tony Blair, the United States probably would not have made the long and damaging detour of trying to get a second resolution before eventually going to war on the basis of the first resolution. Avoiding a return to the Security Council undoubtedly would have triggered negative reactions, but it would have been a much less bruising battle than the failed attempt to get a second resolution. The combination of U.S. neocon hostility to the UN and shallow Blairite support for multilateralism was deadly. It meant Colin Powell had to fight on the home front, not traveling very much in the crucial first months of 2003, instead of seriously fighting internationally for the U.S. position, which was necessary if the multilateralist approach was to have a chance of success. The British lost everything: they fought hard for a second resolution, with the half-hearted support of Washington, but when it became apparent that they would not get it, they abandoned their principled position, sacrificing their political credibility in Europe without gaining much credibility or leverage in the United States. Washington had wasted time and political capital following bad advice from London and now had confirmation that its British ally would always fall in line anyway.

The French thought they had won the glory of being right and of representing the majority of the world in the Security Council. In a way, they had a point: Foreign Minister Villepin got genuine applause in the Security Council, and I heard many diplomats privately complimenting the French on their "courageous" position. They were happy that the French were saying in a flamboyant way what they did not dare express, even quietly. But France was taking a Gaullist stance in a world that was profoundly different from the world of Charles De Gaulle. The cold war was over, and the disagreement of France with the United States could not be compensated by a French expression of solidarity with Washington on the most strategic issues, as De Gaulle had done at critical moments like the Cuban crisis. Even if wrongly, Iraq was now the strategic issue for Washington, and French disagreement was seen in the United States as radical disloyalty. Internationally, there was no other pole at the time than the United States: China and Russia, while they were close to the French position, were happy to leave it to France to carry the banner of the opposition to war. But France could not pretend to be a pole by itself. This was a very different situation from the one De Gaulle had dealt with: De Gaulle could claim at once to reject the division of the world in two camps, while affirming the solidarity of France with the United States. The situation differed from the period of de Gaulle also with respect to the UN. De Gaulle did not have much consideration for the UN, which he disparagingly characterized as "le machin," or "the thing." The Chirac administration was much more supportive of the UN and genuinely thought that it was helping the UN and the legitimacy of the Security Council by not associating it with a war that would eventually be seen as a failure. But in hindsight, the bitter battle in the Security Council probably did more harm to the institution than a less dramatic confrontation would have done. It certainly emphatically made the point that the authority of the council could be ignored, which was bad for the council as well as for nonproliferation policy.

I came out of the Iraq crisis convinced that it is dangerous for the Security Council to pretend to address a crisis in which a major power believes it has a strategic interest, and when that power's interests conflict with the views and interests of other powers. The international community is not enough of a community, and the Security Council still is not a robust enough an institution, to withstand the tensions that such crises will inevitably provoke. The

UN did not solve the cold war, nor did it make any pretense it could. That is how the UN survived and could play a very useful role in crises of a lesser order, which could have escalated if they had not been addressed. As the head of peacekeeping, I became more and more convinced that the best may be the enemy of the good, and that the pretense of ambitious goals can actually kill more limited but important endeavors. But the clarity of the cold war is lost, which means that the range of crises that the UN can address is less well-defined. The experience in Iraq demonstrates the costs when the Security Council is careless, both in terms of human lives and institutions whose currency is trust. The United Nations suffered a considerable blow to its credibility through the Iraq crisis, and all the Security Council members came out burned by the experience, though some worse than others. What happened in Iraq undermined the ability of member states to speak for a common good and damaged the idea of collective efforts embodied in the United Nations. We continue to see the scars of the Iraq crisis on the United Nations as an institution.

The threat of weapons proliferation is real, and remains of the first order, but it requires collective action. Here lies the challenge: the exaggeration of the threat by the Bush administration in the case of Iraq raised questions about the effectiveness of multilateral instruments to address that threat, while the unilateral use of force by the United States created a powerful incentive for would-be proliferators to do the opposite of Saddam Hussein. Countries that perceive themselves to be under threat have good reasons to try to discreetly acquire a nuclear breakout capacity, and countries that want to uphold the nonproliferation regime will find it more difficult to win the trust of those countries. The protracted negotiation with Iran shows how difficult it now is to build mutual trust and to agree on an effective international regime after the Iraq experience.

three

GEORGIA
The War That Could Have Been Avoided

Some peacekeeping operations have been in existence for decades, a fact that is often held against peacekeeping in general. Some critics have charged that peacekeeping operations perversely contribute to prolonging conflicts, since the parties lose the incentive to settle their differences. I never accepted the argument, because the cost of each of those peacekeeping operations that have stretched over decades has been much smaller than the cost of even a small war, in both human and financial terms. A "frozen" conflict is still better than a hot conflict. But these critics are nevertheless right to point out the complacency not just of the parties, but also of the international community when it comes to long-standing missions. Preventing war has undeniable value, but that does not mean that the international community should lower its ambitions so much that the absence of war comes to be equated with genuine peace.

Early in my tenure at the United Nations, I decided that I should review these long-standing peacekeeping operations to see what could be done to bring them to closure. I went through a process of elimination but found there was nothing I could do about the two longest-standing missions. The oldest was the observer mission in the Middle East (UNTSO, in UN terminology), created to monitor the cease-fire between Israel and its Arab neighbors after the war when Israel was born in 1948. Almost as old was the observer mission in Kashmir (UNMOGIP), created in 1949 to monitor the cease-fire line after the first conflict between newly independent India and Pakistan. The observers of UNTSO are now seconded to the mission in Lebanon (UNIFIL) and the mission on the Golan Heights (UNDOF). While from a management standpoint closing UNTSO certainly would make sense, maintaining the mission makes the political point that the conflict between Israel and its Arab neighbors remains a single big issue. Most Arab countries would be opposed to closing UNTSO so long as there is not a comprehensive peace. The political battle therefore to terminate UNTSO was not worth the benefit, considering the small additional cost of keeping a mission that is distinct from UNIFIL and UNDOF. The South Asia mission, UNMOGIP, presents a similar story. From an operational viewpoint, the forty-five observers deployed along a frontline of 700 kilometers cannot make much of a difference, and India, which has never really accepted that Kashmir be put on the agenda of the United Nations, does not want UNMOGIP to play a significant role. For the opposite reason, Pakistan is keen to keep UNMOGIP alive, to ensure that Kashmir is—in principle if not in reality—on the agenda of the Security Council. There again, the political cost of closing the mission is not worth paying, considering the limited financial burden it puts on member states.

Two other missions have lasted for too long: MINURSO, which deployed in April 1991 to monitor the cease-fire that ended the conflict between Morocco and the Polisario Front, and UNFICYP, which has been monitoring the cease-fire between Turkey and Cyprus since 1964. But in both missions, there was nothing useful I could contribute. In Western Sahara, a violent conflict had pitted the Polisario Front, the liberation movement that also had fought Spain in the region, against Morocco. The protracted conflict ended in 1991 with a cease-fire, and the two sides agreed that a referendum would resolve their dispute. However, the conditions under which the referendum would take place are still being debated more than two decades later, despite a strong effort in 1997 by James Baker, the former U.S. secretary of state, to find a compromise. Without genuine reconciliation between Algeria and Morocco, no resolution of the conflict is possible. I was not going to try where Baker had failed.

In the case of Cyprus, I did not get involved because Kofi Annan had asked one of the UN's best negotiators, Alvaro de Soto, a Peruvian diplomat who had joined the United Nations when Javier Perez de Cuellar was elected secretary general, to help find a solution that would end the division of the island. Cyprus is a full member of the United Nations. It has joined the European Union, with the strong support of Greece, while the Turkish Republic of Northern Cyprus, on the northern part of the island, survives in diplomatic isolation, recognized only by Turkey, which has maintained troops there since 1974. The capital, Nicosia, is the last divided city in the world. De Soto worked hard for five years to find a way to resolve the practical issues as well as questions of principle in the conflict. The failure of his efforts was in large part a consequence of the disconnect between a traditional diplomatic process and the politics of Cyprus. The time when diplomats could, through astute negotiations, resolve the destinies of people without their involvement was gone, for good and for bad. In the age of television and mass media, no diplomatic subtlety will work unless it is rooted in a public discussion that connects the inevitable complexities of a diplomatic compromise to the popular mood—but, of course, popular mood does not make it easy to devise subtle compromise. The island remains divided after forty years, and it is now quite possible that the Cyprus partition has become permanent.

The one frozen conflict where I felt I might be able to make a difference was between Georgia and Abkhazia. I was worried that the indifference of the international community to the situation in the Caucasus could one day lead to a resumption of war. The conflict between Georgia and Russia that exploded in the summer of 2008 proved me right, but it also showed the limits of what the UN can achieve in a divided international community. As the divisions of the Security Council deepened, there was little the Secretariat of the UN could do to stop the slide toward war. This was too big a game, and the Secretariat, without a powerful ally ready to support a principled position, was eventually powerless.

The conflict in Abkhazia had its origins in the breakup of the Soviet Union. Georgia had become part of the Russian empire in the early nineteenth century and had been briefly independent after the Bolshevik revolution, before being integrated into the new Soviet Union. Its western part, Abkhazia, became part of the Russian empire in the middle of the nineteenth century. Until then, it had a significant Muslim population, which subsequently emigrated to territories controlled by the Ottoman Empire. The vacuum created was then filled by a variety of Georgian and Russian immigrants. These varied histories led to different legal status once the entire region was incorporated into the Soviet Union. Georgia became a Socialist Soviet Republic, and Abkhazia was eventually made an Autonomous Socialist Soviet Republic within Georgia. Even more important, the "imagined communities"—to borrow a concept coined by Benedict Anderson—produced by those divergent histories were profoundly different. The Georgians were proud of a history that went back to the ancient kingdom of Colchis and included the territory of Abkhazia, while the Abkhaz were wary of Georgian intentions and were grateful to Moscow for protecting their limited autonomy. It now matters little that the privileged status Moscow awarded to the Abkhaz may have been motivated more by a cynical policy of divide-and-rule than by a genuine concern for the Abkhaz identity. When the breakup of the Soviet Union forced a choice, the overwhelming majority of non-Georgian Abkhaz wanted to remain a part of a reconfigured Russia, while the overwhelming majority of ethnic Georgians in Abkhazia would have none of it and wanted to be part of a restored independent Georgia.

Georgia became independent in 1991 and a year later abolished its Soviet-era constitution. Non-Georgian Abkhaz, concerned that their autonomy was going to disappear, reacted by declaring their independence and violently expelling Georgian officials. In 1992 Georgian troops entered the secessionist republic. A nasty war followed, which eventually ended in 1994 with a cease-fire agreement brokered by Russia; a cease-fire line with exclusion zones was drawn. Peacekeeping troops theoretically provided by the Commonwealth of Independent States (CIS)—actually by Russia—were deployed, and a UN observer mission started monitoring the cease-fire. The agreement was a compromise in which the Abkhaz, who had received support from Russia during their conflict with Georgia, gained the reassurance of a Russian military presence under the guise of the CIS, while Georgia obtained a UN observer presence (called UNOMIG, for United Nations Observer Mission in Georgia), which would constrain Russian actions and put the Georgia-Abkhaz conflict on the agenda of the Security Council. Most of Abkhazia (except for the Kodori valley, a mountainous region, inaccessible in winter, which provides a corridor to the capital of Abkhazia, Sukhumi) was under the control of a secessionist Abkhaz government with close links to Russia. An estimated 250,000 ethnic Georgians had fled and were now living in refugee camps on the Georgian-controlled side of the cease-fire line. And there was no peace process to move away from that rather desperate situation. The stage was set for another frozen conflict.

My first trip to Georgia, which I combined with a trip to Moscow, took place in November 2002 at the very moment when the Iraq controversy was heating up. I was observing in New York the steady deterioration of relations between the United States and other key members of the Security Council and the militarization of foreign policy as the "global war on terror" was eroding principles of law and pushing countries to take the law into their own hands. Nationalism is a contagious disease, and it was striking to see how American nationalism and Russian nationalism could reinforce each other. I have no doubt that even if the Bush administration had pursued wiser policies, the sense of humiliation in Russia after the breakup of the Soviet Union would have fueled Russian nationalism, but the negative dynamics of the Iraq crisis probably amplified the trend. The world was again in a zero-sum-game pattern, and we were entering a kind of "mini–cold war." Georgia could not get closer to the United States without getting farther from Russia. When the United States, concerned that Chechen terrorists might enter Georgia through the Pankisi valley, sent a few Special Forces there to encourage the Georgians to take the fight against terrorism seriously, the Russians naturally were suspicious. A vicious circle had set in, in which every action was interpreted negatively by the other side.

Georgia is a beautiful country, and Abkhazia, at its western end, is particularly beautiful; the snow-capped mountains of the Caucasus are the backdrop of hills covered with Mediterranean vegetation overlooking the Black Sea. After Abkhazia had become part of the Russian empire, it was the favorite destination of Russians who wanted sun and beautiful beaches. It was in effect an extension of the Russian Riviera and bears striking resemblance to pictures of the French Riviera in the early 1900s. Except for the odd and hideous sanatoria built in the 1960s, and the bulbs of a few monasteries, which are a reminder that this is a place where Orthodox Christianity chased away Islam, the only buildings emerging from forests of eucalyptus and gardens of cypress are charming art nouveau villas reflecting the economic boom that preceded World War I. I slept in one of them near Sukhumi, the villa of Stalin himself, the most famous Georgian of the twentieth century. The plumbing was vintage Soviet era, with tepid water trickling into an old bath tub, and the towel did not dry. These were the sediments of history: a solid bourgeois villa built by some Russian entrepreneur in the early 1900s; decrepit remains of Soviet luxury from the 1950s. And then, left to the imagination, were the ghosts of the tragic twentieth century: Joseph Stalin, but also his terrifying chief of secret police, Lavrenti Beria, whose villa was within walking distance, and Leon Trotsky, who, following Stalin's treacherous advice, fatefully stayed in Sukhumi instead of rushing back to Moscow to safeguard his own position after the death of Lenin.

As I was leaning on the balustrade of the terrace watching the moon rising over the Black Sea, framed by palm trees, I wondered about the thoughts of my hosts, former officials of the Communist Party of the Soviet Union, who were now running Abkhazia. The next day, I met in Tbilisi with their former colleague, now the president of Georgia, Eduard Shevardnadze. In many ways their experiences were shared. They could all say, like the French who survived the turmoil of the Revolution and the Napoleonic wars, *"j'ai vécu"*—"I lived," or more accurately, "I survived." They had been part of the tragedies of the twentieth century, and none of them could have gone through the experience unscathed. None of them was known for having committed crimes, but none could have prospered without accepting that crimes were being committed. And now they were on opposite sides. Shevardnadze had helped manage the disintegration of the Soviet empire and then had become the president of an independent Georgia. There was a certain irony in the fact that a Georgian had played such a decisive role in building the Soviet empire on the ruins of World War II and that another Georgian had helped manage its unraveling.

Local Conflict, Global Dimensions

When I saw Shevardnadze in Tbilisi, he had aged and looked, probably misleadingly, more like a benevolent grandfather than a formidable political operator who had earned the nickname of White Fox. He gave the impression of a man whose time was running out—he even reminded me that he had only two years left as president—and who understood history but had given up on shaping it. "If the war of Abkhazia had been described accurately, as ethnic cleansing and genocide, there would already be a solution," he said, without elaborating on the fact that the war had started at the initiative of Georgia and that he had not done much at the time to stop it, although he certainly showed bravery, staying in Sukhumi until the last moment as the city was being retaken by Abkhaz forces. He was now worried that the Georgian exiles from Abkhazia were getting more and more impatient and would threaten his own position in Tbilisi.

Here was a man whose whole life could be read in two opposite ways. On the one hand, he had seen his father arrested by Stalin's secret police, but he had himself joined the Communist Party at the height of Stalinism in 1948 and had a long career at the heart of the police system that ruled the Soviet Union. He was a master survivor. On the other hand, as the foreign minister for Mikhail Gorbachev, he had agreed, at a critical moment in the late 1980s, that maintaining an imperial power was not worth using force and shedding more blood. For that, he had won the gratitude of millions of people, and the lasting resentment of other millions. He was thus probably still Marxist enough to be convinced that it is sometimes pointless to stand in the way of historical forces, ideological or nationalist, that are stronger than the will of any individual, and at the same time, he was no longer a Bolshevik, being acutely aware of the limits of the use of force and of its possible unintended consequences. He appeared wary of the new course of American policies, which superficially brought Washington and Moscow closer in a common fight against terrorism but actually encouraged unilateral action and a militarization of foreign policy that was bound to pull the two countries apart. He made it clear to me that no solution to the Abkhaz conflict could be reached without the Russians and stressed that his discussions with Vladimir Putin had led to more conciliatory positions in the Kremlin, but not all Russians would follow Putin's instructions, and Putin himself could evolve. Shevardnadze favored transitory arrangements, for a period of approximately ten years, that would give enough time to digest the legacy of the Soviet system. For peace to settle in, he seemed to believe that a new generation was needed, which would not bear the scars of a tragic history. The war of 2008 did eventually prove him wrong: Putin and Shevardnadze's successor, Mikheil Saakashvili, both belonged to the new generation, but they did not bring peace. On the contrary, the caution of the older generation seems to have been lost.

After my meeting with Shevardnadze, I flew to Moscow to meet with Russian officials. A meeting of the "friends of the Secretary General for Georgia" was also planned; the group had been formed at the time of the Georgia-Abkhazia conflict to build a united front of the international community, which would encourage the two "sides" to compromise and negotiate. It was composed of the three Western permanent members of the Security Council, plus Germany and Russia. While it symbolically tried to bridge the gap between Russia and the West, Western countries had a clear majority and the group was perceived to be tilting toward the Georgian position. When I arrived in Moscow, a Russian diplomat told me that Abkhaz prime minister Anri Djergenia would attend the meeting of the group of friends. This was a surprise, as was the unexpected presence in Moscow of Sergei Lavrov, who was at the time the Russian ambassador at the UN. The "Western" friends, who did not want Djergenia to attend a meeting involving members of the Security Council because they feared it would give too much legitimacy to the Abkhaz authorities, became highly suspicious. In the end, the meeting did not take place because the Russians wanted the Western friends to present their position separately from Russia, which would have visibly broken the precarious unity of the group and also defeated the goal of applying joint pressure on the parties. Only a few days later, the ailing president of Abkhazia, Vladislav Ardzinba, fired Djergenia.

That first visit to Georgia, the Russian surprise in Moscow, and the sudden firing of Djergenia only weeks after the Russians had tried to build up his international legitimacy gave me a hint of the complexities of the conflict. To borrow from U.S. secretary of defense Donald Rumsfeld's quip about Iraq, the Georgia file has many known unknowns, and some unknown unknowns too. There are quite a few players involved in the management of the Abkhaz file in Moscow, and a lot of intrigue among the Abkhaz themselves. Many Abkhaz leaders had careers in the former Soviet Union, often in the security organs. Some of them were born in Russia, and most have apartments in Moscow and feel at home in the Russian capital. Their personal rivalries and ambitions play an important part in determining their political choices. Russian policies had just as many complexities. There was the army, which had bases in Georgia and wanted to keep them, at least partially because army leaders liked being deployed in a pleasant country. There were the various security agencies, which have offered patronage and support to their clients and correspondents in Georgia. There were the business people, sometimes linked to criminal interests, who see Abkhazia as a good place to make money. They are busy restoring old hotels in Sukhumi, investing in a booming tourist industry, and hoping to benefit from the growth of a new Russian middle class. There was the Ministry of Foreign Affairs, which does not want Abkhazia to become an irritant in the relations between Russia and the West but is wary of U.S. intentions in the Caucasus. At the time of my visit in 2002 the diplomats did not seem to exclude a solution that would keep Abkhazia within Georgia in some kind of loose confederation, but they were not prepared to push for that solution to the point where Russian-Abkhaz relations would suffer. These various strategies sometimes conflicted and sometimes complemented each other, but an additional complicating factor was Russian domestic politics. Supporting a tough posture in Abkhazia gave politicians patriotic credentials in Moscow and provided an easy way to make a name for oneself in Russian politics.

On the Western side, my visit had confirmed what I feared: there actually was not much interest in the issue. Britain and France were members of the group of friends, and Britain had even appointed a former British ambassador to Russia, Sir Brian Fall, as its representative. But the permanent members of the Security Council had other, more important, priorities, and it was hard to put Georgia on the agenda at top-level meetings. I can remember only one lunch at the Elysée Palace in Paris where Georgia was briefly discussed between Kofi Annan and Jacques Chirac. Sergei Ordjonikhidze, a senior UN official of Russian nationality with a famous Georgian origin, was present, and he commented that there was no real problem between Russia and Georgia, and that difficulties would go away when Shevardnadze left power. This exchange was typical of the prevailing complacency, and of a tendency to interpret the conflict in personal terms that ignored the more strategic issues. The United States and Germany had, for different reasons, a more strategic approach. Germany continues to have a huge stake in the stabilization of central and eastern Europe and seems to have been guided, ever since the fall of the Berlin Wall, by three complementary, and sometimes competing, considerations: first, a solid alliance with the United States; second, a European commitment; and finally, a cooperative relationship with Russia. The same three considerations would apply a decade later to the Ukraine crisis, where they would be even more difficult to reconcile. German diplomats saw how a festering Georgian conflict might make it difficult to reconcile those three competing goals, but Berlin had little leverage to influence events in Georgia.

The key players were Moscow and Washington, but in both there seemed to be several competing policies. Rumsfeld's Pentagon was obviously keen to strengthen military ties with Georgia and was engaged in a program of military cooperation that would eventually lead to a small Georgian role in the occupation of Iraq (the protection of the UN compound in Baghdad). Georgia is in a strategic location, close to the Middle East, notably Iran, and this is of some value to the U.S. military. The State Department looked at Georgia in a broader context and did not want to precipitate a crisis with Russia. It nevertheless was clearly in favor of eventually bringing Georgia into NATO. The ideologues of the Bush administration were initially suspicious of the Georgian leadership and felt that there was unfinished business in Tbilisi. One year later, in November 2003, the so-called Rose Revolution would take care of their concerns, as it toppled Shevardnadze and brought to power a new Georgian leadership squarely allied with Washington. The common thread that bound together policies that could differ on tactics was a clear vision that Georgia could be brought unambiguously into the Western camp, and that the correlation of forces with Russia had changed in such radical ways that Russia would not be in a position to resist such an evolution. President Bush's envoy, Ambassador Rudolf Perina, an experienced diplomat who knew the Caucasus very well, hinted that Georgia indeed was a place where Washington and Moscow had a real difference, but in the end Moscow would have to accept a new state of affairs. Furthermore, he believed this evolution to be legitimate because it reflected what the people of Georgia wanted. The time was past when powerful states could carve out spheres of influence in their neighborhoods or even halfway around the world. I was initially sympathetic to that view. The memory of the displaced Georgians living in camps was fresh in my mind, as was the harassment of Georgians who had stayed in the Abkhaz-controlled Gali district. I had visited the miserable schools where they sent their children and where nearly everything was missing, including textbooks written in Georgian. Shevardnadze was right that this was ethnic cleansing, and nothing could justify such abuse of force.

Diplomatic Approaches to the Conflict

What could be done? The question was not on the agenda of heads of state, but diplomats who followed the issue understood that it was time to try to restart some kind of process. For several years, the head of the UN mission, German diplomat Dietrich Boden, had tried to develop a position that would reconcile the Western and the Russian views. The result had been the "Boden paper," which referred to the "territorial integrity" of Georgia. Having Russia accept a document that included those two words was considered a diplomatic victory by Western powers. But that "victory" had been short-lived. The Abkhaz, from the outset, made clear that they would not accept the Boden paper because it challenged their fundamental position, and the Russians were of the view that nothing should be forced on the Abkhaz. That opposition had destroyed whatever limited unity of the friends Boden thought he had achieved: the Western powers expected Russia to "deliver" the Abkhaz, and Russia was not prepared to act. The discussion on the Boden paper and the conditions under which the Abkhaz might receive it had become a distraction. It was unrealistic to take as the starting point of a negotiation what would at best be the optimal end state. Boden's approach, focused on the fundamental underlying issue of the status of Abkhazia, had failed. Prior to his effort, other special representatives had taken another approach, focusing on practical issues and confidence-building measures. They had also failed. It was necessary to try a different approach. That new approach came to be known as the Geneva process.

It was now clear that there would be no solution to the conflict without addressing three distinct but related sets of issues. The first, most visible and most pressing, was the relationship between the Abkhaz and the Georgians. I had been told that, historically, Abkhaz and Georgian people got along well, and that the Abkhaz culture was as threatened by the expanding Russian influence as it was by Georgian dominance. But the violence of the war, in which a quarter million Georgians had been displaced, had destroyed that relationship, and there was now poverty, fear, corruption, and banditry in a lawless area where the only source of wealth was the yearly harvest of blueberries. Unless that was fixed—and fixing it required an effective state, accountable police and administration, as well as authorities whose legitimacy would be accepted by all—no real peace was possible. I had many diplomatic sessions devoted to Georgia in which words seemed very removed from reality, but I never forgot that in the end, the justification for the whole effort was to bring a modest improvement to the lives of people who had been caught in events over which they had no control and who were now the pawns of political plays in which they did not matter much.

The second set of issues that needed to be addressed was the relationship between Georgia and Russia. Historically, Georgians and Russians have also had a good relationship; and the kind of ethnic and religious divisions that destroyed Yugoslavia were largely absent in Georgia. On the contrary, many Georgians rose to prominent positions in Moscow, and there were many mixed marriages and a shared antipathy for the Ottoman Empire. Economically, the connections between Georgia and Russia also were tight; while the high east-west mountain range of the greater Caucasus creates a natural barrier between North and South Caucasus, the coastal corridor through which the train used to run provides an easy entry into Armenia and Azerbaijan and connects Georgia with the Russian part of the coast along the Black Sea. Physical geography in the Caucasus creates a natural east-west axis of communications, and Georgia is right at the center of it, provided its western border with Russia is opened. But the cease-fire line separating the Abkhaz-controlled part of Georgia from the rest of the country had severed that link, interrupting the train service that used to run between Sochi and Tbilisi. What would define the relationship in the future: the old links of history and geography, or a new dynamic shaped by the asymmetry between Russia and Georgia? This asymmetry at a structural level obviously favored Russia, with its enormous landmass and its still considerable army, which would dwarf any Georgian effort but played in favor of Georgia at a psychological level: it was Russia that was shrinking and felt defeated, while Georgia, now a friend and ally of the only remaining superpower and an aspiring member of NATO and the European Union, had a new horizon opening.

The third, and most fundamental, issue was the relationship between Russia and the United States: Was Georgia going to be the last symbolic battlefield of the cold war, or a bridge between a reborn Russia and a reborn "West?" In the years that followed the fall of the Berlin Wall, joining NATO and the EU became the strategic goal not only of central European countries that had been under the domination of the Soviet Union but also of former parts of the Soviet Union itself. The aspiration reflected a desire to join a democratic family that provided freedom and prosperity at last; it was also an insurance policy against any resurgence of Russian imperialism. The combination of Western euphoria and Russian weakness that characterized the period led to a series of NATO and EU enlargements, including the three Baltic states. For the acceding countries, the EU and NATO were two facets of the same dream: the first brought the prospect of European prosperity; the second brought a U.S. security guarantee. There was, however, an unfortunate institutional competition between the two organizations that did not allow for a strategic discussion of the longer-term implications of their parallel enlargement. The expansion of the EU had immediate practical implications, as borders were open to movements of goods and people, and the acceding countries had to meet EU standards. The EU was therefore wary of expanding too quickly, but it did not want to lag behind NATO. And NATO did not want European links to be ahead of transatlantic links. The expansion of NATO would have less visible, if not less fundamental, implications than the EU expansion: the perimeter of the security guarantee provided by article V of NATO's Treaty of Washington would in principle require major adjustments for U.S. and European military planning. But at the same time, it was assumed that Russia was no longer a military threat, which made an extension of the U.S. security guarantee a less weighty decision. This would eventually prove to be the basic flaw of the whole process. The fundamental reason why new NATO members wanted to join was their perception of a virtual Russian threat, but their request was accepted because the NATO leadership believed Russia was not a threat any more. The contradiction was not ignored by Western policymakers, who wanted to respond positively to the new applicants without antagonizing Russia. Their response was to try to change the relationship between NATO and Russia, first through the inclusion of Russia in the North Atlantic Cooperation Council (1991), then in the Partnership for Peace (1994), and finally through the establishment of a Permanent Joint Council (1997), which became the NATO-Russia Council in 2002. Would those various attempts to bring Russia partially into the NATO camp be enough to blur the dividing line between a Western alliance and Russia? The Georgia conflict and the relationship of Georgia with the United States and NATO were going to test the limits of that policy.

At the end of 2002, as I was discussing those ideas with representatives of the group of friends, I was under no illusion that there could be any quick fix. But I saw the benefits of having a process that would bring together envoys appointed by their respective capitals. They would have a better chance to convey the strategic implications at the highest level, and they would not be caught up in the passions of the diplomatic community in Tbilisi. I also foresaw a much more dynamic role for the UN than in previous "groups of friends." Considering the deep divisions among the friends, I felt that a leading UN role could be helpful and reassuring to the parties because it would not ignore the framework laid down by Security Council resolutions but would nonetheless try to insert some flexibility, and it would not be bound by national positions. If managed well, it would help the parties engage directly. It was agreed that I would chair the meetings, but that the special representative of the secretary general in Georgia would also attend. On the substance, the compromise that would make it possible to go beyond the sterile discussion of the Boden paper was to address confidence-building measures as well as humanitarian, political, and security issues. At first, it seemed to work. In February 2003 I chaired the first meeting of the new Geneva process. We agreed to discuss three baskets of issues: the economy, dominated by the question of the railway coming from Russia; the return of displaced persons; and political and security issues. This was a good balance. The Abkhaz and the Russians were happy to discuss confidence-building measures and the Georgians to push on issues related to returns, security, and status. It was agreed that the group would again meet at high level in June. A process had been started.

But again came a Russian—and Georgian—surprise, when Russian president Putin invited President Shevardnadze for a meeting in Sochi in March with the prime minister of Abkhazia. The communiqué mentioned cooperation on the railway, on electricity, and on return of displaced persons, but superbly ignored the UN. Some of the friends were very unhappy, all the more so when it transpired that President Shevardnadze had not pushed for a UN role. The Russians—at least some of them (interestingly, Valery Loschinin, the Russian envoy and deputy minister of foreign affairs, was not present at the Sochi meeting)—were still uncomfortable with a UN format in which the Western friends could easily put them on the spot. As for the Georgians, they also were probably of two minds on how to deal with Russia. As Shevardnadze had told me, the key to the Abkhaz issue was in Moscow. Bringing the UN and the Western friends in might help put some pressure on Russia, but it could also lead to a hardening of positions. Was it better to try to disconnect the Georgia-Russia relationship from the broader East-West strategic relationship, or on the contrary, to make it a part of some grand bargain? In the tense atmosphere that characterized the run-up to the Iraq war, the "White Fox" Shevardnadze could see some merit in the first option. We agreed with the Western friends that it was better to put a brave face on this new Russian initiative, and the head of the UN mission in Georgia, Ambassador Heidi Tagliavini, with great tenacity worked hard to bring the two processes together.

A Peaceful Revolution in Georgia

The meeting of the friends that had been planned for June did take place, and it was the first of its kind where both Abkhaz and Georgians joined the proceedings. Loschinin, who represented Russia, was suave, and the discussions were smooth. The Georgian side wanted concrete progress on the return of displaced persons and security in the district of Gali, on the Abkhaz side of the cease-fire line. There had been a clear Georgian majority there before the war. Most Georgians had now fled, but a few would return to look after their abandoned houses and collect blueberries in the summer. However, the lack of security impeded permanent returns. The Georgians, backed by the United States, suggested a special interim administration of the district. That was obviously unacceptable to the Abkhaz, who saw it as a challenge to their sovereignty, but the discussion evolved when Loschinin quietly noted that ideas that can scare at first may eventually become acceptable once one looks at the details. He mentioned the police as a part of government where a new approach could be tested. The concluding statement referred to the proposal, and at the end of July, the

Security Council authorized the deployment of twenty additional police officers in the UN mission. This was a long way from the interim administration that the United States and the Georgians had suggested for the Gali district, but it was a promising if modest beginning. The Geneva process had stimulated some policy initiatives and time would tell whether real evolutions would eventually be possible. In the meantime, there was, as I put it cautiously, "the impression of movement." This was certainly not enough, but without it, the pressure to use force would increase and would certainly make things worse.

By accident rather than design, I was in Georgia when the Rose Revolution brought down Eduard Shevardnadze, and a new strategic configuration began to emerge gradually. I arrived in Tbilisi on the evening of November 20, 2003, as the results of the chaotic legislative elections of November 2 were being announced and were immediately questioned. The official figures gave 21 percent of the vote to a coalition of parties supporting Shevardnadze; 12 percent to the Labor Party of Georgia; 18 percent to the opposition National Movement headed by Saakashvili; and 18 percent to the party of Aslan Abashidze, the leader of Ajaria, another secessionist province in Georgia.[1] Abashidze had sent his militants to Tbilisi to support Shevardnadze during the campaign, and the Labor Party also supported Shevardnadze. Officially Shevardnadze had won, since his coalition had enough support to maintain a majority in parliament, but there was a widespread suspicion of foul play and a view that he now was really in the minority. This was a dangerous situation. The risk was high that a protest demonstration planned by the opposition on November 22 would turn into a bloody confrontation. Even so, the foreign minister, with whom I spoke on the eve of the planned demonstration, was reassuring; the president, he said, would not declare a state of emergency. But events were accelerating. By the afternoon of November 22, demonstrators occupied the parliament building while Shevardnadze was speaking. He barely had time to leave. Saakashvili and Nino Bujardnadze, the speaker of the outgoing parliament who had broken with Shevardnadze, addressed a cheering crowd from the balcony of the parliament building. Bujardnadze announced that she was assuming the presidency of Georgia temporarily until presidential elections could be organized. In Tbilisi, more and more police units were siding with

---

1. Ajaria has no common border with Russia, being in the western corner of Georgia, adjacent to Turkey. The main resource of Ajaria is the harbor of Batumi, and the secession movement seemed to be more about control of wealth than about politics. The electoral results in Ajaria were particularly dubious, as Abashidze's party captured some 97 percent of registered voters, whose number had increased by 22 percent since the previous election.

the demonstrators, although Shevardnadze had announced that he would not resign. I was in Sukhumi for the day, and the Abkhaz leaders were not hiding their concerns. They disliked Shevardnadze, but in a strange way he was still a colleague from the old time. The new Georgian leadership was untested, and the Abkhaz did not know what to expect. For decades, decisions in the Caucasus had been produced not by ideology, not by democratic aspirations, but by apparatchiks groomed in the art of accommodating various bureaucratic pressures while not completely ignoring popular demand, if only for the sake of tranquility. What was new was the possibility of untidy democracy and outside interference. And both prospects were deeply upsetting.

I was back in Tbilisi on the evening of November 23. There was no particular agitation at the airport, and the police car that opened the way from the airport to the city had no difficulty ordering vehicles to pull aside. The president had lost his authority, but the police still could handle traffic. This was the second or third time I was a witness to a revolution, depending on how one defines a revolution. I had been in Portugal in 1974, working as an intern at the French embassy in Lisbon: from week to week I had seen power shifting, as communists and socialists vied for power after the fall of the dictatorship. Before that I had taken part as a student in the events of May 1968 in Paris: this was more the theater of revolution than a real revolution, and I remember how we were discussing the occupation of the parliament as if it was going to be as easy as the occupation of the Sorbonne, but there was a fleeting moment when indeed it seemed possible. One speech by President Charles De Gaulle after twenty-four hours of uncertainty turned that situation around.

In all three cases, I felt I was observing an experiment in political science. There is nothing quite like a revolution to show the abstract nature of political power. Authority is a concept, all in the mind: the minds of those who usually defer to it but under some circumstances suddenly lose their deference, and also, crucially, the minds of those who are in power. In most revolutions, the sitting government loses its control over power not because it no longer has the means to defend itself, although there are examples of that. In August 1792, for example, the Swiss guards who were protecting Louis XVI in his palace did not surrender; they fought, but were overwhelmed. But in most recent revolutions, from those in Europe in 1989 to the "awakening" in Egypt in 2011, the sitting authority loses power not because it is overwhelmed but because it loses confidence in itself and is no longer prepared to use force. That is, thankfully, what happened in Tbilisi in those fateful days of November 2003. But as events were unfolding, there was no assurance that the revolution would be peaceful.

I could not go back to the government guesthouse where I was staying because of roadblocks and demonstrators. Shevardnadze was rumored to have found a temporary refuge in that particular building, which was now surrounded by a big crowd. I went to the UN compound and waited for things to get quieter. The Russian foreign minister, Igor Ivanov, had arrived, and he first paid a visit to the opposition, a gesture that was seen by supporters of Shevardnadze as a mortal blow. He told the demonstrators that Russia would not intervene. He then had a meeting with Shevardnadze, and again with the opposition. He eventually brought Saakashvili to the residence of Shevardnadze, after which Shevardnadze announced his resignation. The revolution was over. In the streets, honking cars drove at high speed with flags flying through open windows, like soccer fans after a victorious match. What a contrast with the tragic faces of the refugees I had visited in the morning, in the town of Zugdidi, on the Georgian side of the cease-fire line with Abkhazia. The cheering crowds in Tbilisi believed they were making history, while the refugees of Zugdidi knew they had been the victims of history: expelled by the Abkhaz, ignored by the Russian troops, and used by the Georgian authorities in their propaganda war. The news they had heard of Shevardnadze's imminent demise had brought some smiles, but they did not have too much hope in the future; they had had too many disappointments in the past.

Tbilisi was full of rumors, and I had a particularly good source in the new French ambassador, Salome Zourabichvili. She is probably the only French diplomat of Georgian origin and the only French citizen to become the foreign minister of another country. I had first met her when she had just joined the Quai d'Orsay and was a junior officer in the policy planning staff, working on the Soviet Union. She had won the respect of her colleagues because she was never afraid of speaking her mind, even if it did not exactly reflect the official line. In the late 1970s and early 1980s, she was a definite skeptic about détente policies. She was tough and articulate. Maybe because she had beautiful dark blue eyes, she made a point of being always extremely professional and matter-of-fact, in a world dominated by men who were not indifferent to her charms. I worked with her again when I was ambassador to the Western European Union and she was my deputy. It was a strong partnership, because she knew how to hold the line in difficult negotiations, and I was in the comfortable role of being the one who would make the minor concession that she had prepared for me. In Tbilisi, she immediately made her mark. I had dinner with her and Heidi Tagliavini, the head of the UN mission, in a deserted restaurant, once the demonstrations had subsided. She was extremely happy that the possibility now existed for Georgia to free itself from its past of secret deals and corruption and become a truly democratic country. I did not imagine at the time that her deep love for Georgia would lead her to abandon the comfort of the French civil service and to become the foreign minister of

Georgia when Saakashvili, a few months later, made a surprise request to Chirac during an official visit to France. She would eventually not last very long in that position for the same reason that she had accepted it. Her commitment was to her idea of Georgia, and she was not prepared to compromise, even if she made many enemies that way.

In the discussions I had before leaving Tbilisi, it was striking to observe two opposite visions on how history is made. On one side were all those who had played a part in the revolution and wanted to believe in "people's power." I saw one of them the next morning, when I went to the parliament to congratulate the new president ad interim, Nino Bujardnadze. She had spent the night in her office in the parliament building; she was exhausted, but it did not show. She exuded calm and confidence and was focused on the economic situation of Georgia. She had little to say about the politics of the next few weeks and projected herself in the future, as if the immediate future were already a done deal. She did not sound like a politician, and there was a great contrast between her and Saakashvili, who was on all the television screens and spoke in an exalted manner—but both seemed to believe that this peaceful revolution had forced a new way of playing politics.

On the other side was the old guard of Georgian politicians, all the orphans of Shevardnadze, who still clung to the view that everything happens through secret deals in which everyone gets a little piece of the cake. They were a bit lost because the rules of the game they knew—raw force and the naked play of interests—did not seem to apply in this case. They were trying to reassure themselves; one of them told me that Georgians, going back to Stalin, like strongmen, and that among those who were emerging from the revolution, the populist Saakashvili was the one with the right profile. And they were confident that at some point they would reassert themselves. Ajaria was a case in point. Abashidze, the strongman of Ajaria, had real leverage, they said. If Ajaria were to secede, the new Georgian authorities would rule over a rump Georgia. Abashidze would have to be accommodated, and the best way was probably to make him the speaker of the new parliament. He would be less present in Ajaria, and such a step would send a signal to secessionist regions that they can have a place in Tbilisi. But as they were speculating on the next deal, they were baffled by Russian policies. What was Moscow up to? They had been used to a world of shadow puppets in which the puppeteer controls the play. They had noted every move of Ivanov. In a country that had not controlled its destinies for such a long time, it was difficult to imagine that Russia had just been watching. Had Russia accompanied a movement it could not control, or was there some more complicated plot? At a minimum, Ivanov, by shuttling at the most critical hour between the main protagonists, had given an implicit blessing to the opponents of the president, which was disappointing for those who had thrown their lot with Shevardnadze, but also was reassuring because it meant that this was still a world of deals made by power brokers. And they looked at what Russia would do with Ajaria. Before flying back to Moscow, Ivanov had gone to Batumi, the capital of Ajaria, where he had met with Abashidze. What had he told Abashidze? Had Ivanov encouraged moderation and restraint, or the opposite?

These questions did not receive immediate answers, and no decisive conclusion could be drawn on the basis of the events that took place in 2004, the first year after the Rose Revolution. The first important episode was the Ajaria crisis in the spring of 2004. Saakashvili, who had won a rushed presidential election in January, sent an ultimatum to Abashidze to fall in line, and Russia did nothing to prevent the fall of Abashidze. At the time, the moderate course taken by Russia was probably misread by Saakashvili, who later drew the wrong conclusion that he could play the same tough game with Abkhazia; this would prove to be a disastrously mistaken assessment. There were hints as early as 2004 that both Georgia and Russia might be tempted to create "facts on the ground" concerning Abkhazia. Russia was already generously conferring Russian citizenship to any Abkhaz who requested it. On the one hand, this could be seen as a humanitarian gesture to facilitate travel for Abkhaz who refused to use a Georgian passport. On the other hand, it was an ominous sign, especially if it was combined with a declared Russian policy of unilateral protection of Russian nationals. For the Baltic states and Ukraine, all of which have significant Russian minorities, Abkhazia was thus seen as a laboratory of a neo-imperial Russian policy that could one day threaten their own independence. Meanwhile, the bloody denouement of the Beslan terrorist attack of September 1, 2004—in which at least 330 people, almost 200 of them children, died after more than 1,100 people were held hostage in a school in southern Russia—had shown the risk of extreme violence in the Caucasus region, and was likely to lead to a greater role for security organs and a tougher Russian policy in the region. On the Georgian side, during the summer of 2004 the warning shots fired by the Georgian navy toward a boat that was sailing to Sukhumi seemed to indicate that Tbilisi did not rule out the use of force. There were also clashes between Georgia and South Ossetia, a secessionist region in northern Georgia, which stopped only when Georgian forces had to pull back. A significant increase of the Georgian military budget added concern.

Nevertheless, several encouraging evolutions were occurring in Georgia. The appointment of Salome Zourabichvili as foreign minister, for example, was a sign that Georgian foreign policy would not be dominated by ultranationalists. I sensed that the Georgian military's lack of success in South Ossetia had strengthened the camp of those who warned against the use of force and who wanted to use diplomatic means to restore the unity of Georgia. Among them, a key figure would be Irakli Alasania, who was put in charge of the Abkhaz file. I would eventually know him well and admire his wise patriotism.

These conflicting signals were reflected in the meeting of the friends group I chaired in Geneva in December 2004, which was inconclusive. Everything was on hold. I had convened it at the instigation of the friends, who were concerned that the deterioration of relations between Russia and Western countries might spill over to Georgia and Abkhazia. There had indeed been serious tensions between Russia and Western countries in 2004 related to elections in Ukraine, a meeting in Sofia of the Organization for Security and Cooperation in Europe had been a miserable failure, presidential elections in Abkhazia—obviously not recognized by Georgia—had developed into a crisis because the Russian-backed candidate was not winning, and the situation in Sukhumi had become unsettled. The crisis of the presidential elections in Abkhazia was not yet resolved, and the Geneva meeting of December was therefore about damage limitation: avoiding a final rift between Russia and the Western friends by keeping the process going, with a practical focus on the very real issue of the return of displaced persons. The UN high commissioner for refugees joined the meeting to show that the UN system was ready to help in a very concrete manner if the political will was there. The meeting was a success insofar as it had maintained a modicum of common ground between the friends. Loschinin, suave as ever, even referred to the Boden paper, the kind of harmless little diplomatic gesture that diplomats love and that politicians despise, but no concrete progress had been achieved. I clearly saw the risk that the Geneva process could become a kind of smokescreen conveniently giving cover for an utterly deadlocked situation.

A Brief Window for a Settlement

In early January 2005, what had been a very ambiguous situation suddenly became a fairly hopeful one. A rerun of the Abkhaz presidential election took place, and it was won by Sergei Bagapsh, a former leader in the Communist Party turned businessman, who also had been a prime minister in the late 1990s. This was seen as a sign that not everything in Abkhazia was controlled by Moscow, and the fact that Russia did not prevent the election of a man who was apparently not its preferred candidate was encouraging. It was time to check whether a window was opening for diplomacy.

I decided to go again to Georgia in February 2005. This was certainly the most encouraging of all the visits I made to the country, and I actually believe that a window for a negotiated solution of the Georgia-Abkhazia conflict—and most likely also the South Ossetia conflict—did open and close in the first half of 2005. For the first time I had a feeling that I was meeting with interlocutors on both sides who might, with some international reassurance, talk to each other. The Abkhaz wanted security guarantees, and the Georgians wanted the return of displaced persons to Abkhazia. On both sides, the willingness to engage in a practical manner was palpable. The most encouraging sign was a sense of mutual respect, which was a precondition to establishing any measure of trust. We were all agreed that it was essential to try to build on that momentum, and a meeting of the friends was convened in June 2005. Georgia and Abkhazia joined for the first time since the meeting in 2003, and there was some genuine dialogue. The atmosphere was very different from June 2003. On the Abkhaz side, Minister for Foreign Affairs Sergei Shamba was more than an apparatchik; he obviously had his own constraints, and the rhetorical fireworks in the first part of the meeting made me concerned that the meeting would be another fiasco. It was a reminder of the mixed messages I had heard in Sukhumi when I was there in February. The new Abkhaz president, Bagapsh, seemed genuinely open and focused on practical ways to foster economic development and an evolution of relations between Abkhazia and Georgia, but he was an isolated man who did not have much of a team. He was surrounded by apparatchiks who limited his margin for maneuver. When I visited him, part of the conversation had to take place in his garden; at least we knew the flowers were not bugged. The harsh words of Shamba on the first day of the meeting in June might well reflect those constraints. But when we reconvened the next day, Shamba showed a real willingness to engage on practical issues related to the situation of the district of Gali, where the majority of Georgian Abkhaz is concentrated and where the majority of returns would take place if a measure of confidence was to be restored.

On the Georgian side, Georgi Khaindrava, the state minister for conflict resolution issues, and Irakli Alasania, aide to the Georgian president, were willing to engage. Alasania in particular was carefully avoiding provocative statements and trying to make progress on practical issues without abandoning the principled position of Georgia. I could see that the Abkhaz, who had always felt that their basic position was not even acknowledged by the Georgians, for the first time did not have a sense of humiliation that made them defensive and intractable. While the Georgians were obviously not going to concede on the independence of Abkhazia, they seemed prepared to consider actions that mattered to the Abkhaz.

I had noted during my visits to Tbilisi that there were really two camps in Georgia when it came to the issue of sanctions against Abkhazia. One group of people stuck to the traditional Georgian view. They saw any lifting of the sanctions that had been imposed against Abkhazia as a prize that would reward the Abkhaz for abandoning their position on the independence of Georgia. Any step in that direction and, a fortiori, any enhanced cooperation between Georgia and Abkhazia, should come at the end of the process, and certainly not at the beginning. Alasania had, in my view, rightly concluded that the development of more open economic relations should not be seen as a reward but as an incentive, which therefore should not wait for the end of the negotiation. Judging from the example of Cyprus, this was probably the right path to take. The only positive change in Cyprus came when the two human communities of Cyprus began to interact with each other. In Georgia, the greater the separation between Abkhazia and Georgia proper, the greater the risk that the distance—human and political—between Abkhazia and Georgia would grow, as Abkhaz-Russian economic and human relations intensified and Georgia proper got closer to the European space. The smart policy was not to punish the Abkhaz, but rather to entice them by making Georgia attractive to Abkhazia, while acknowledging the reality of Russian economic interests in Georgia.

The contours of a process that would not result in a big bang but would set the stage for a gradual evolution were emerging in side discussions as the meeting was progressing. From the Georgian standpoint, the test would be a significantly improved security and human rights situation in the Gali district of Abkhazia. Such improvement would be the result of UN engagement, but more important, of the goodwill of the Abkhaz, who would show in a concrete way that they were now ready to encourage rather than discourage returns and were thus willing to begin to reverse the ethnic cleansing of the 1990s. From the Abkhaz standpoint, a straightforward declaration by Georgia that it would not use force, along with more effective cease-fire arrangements in the upper Kodori valley, would be the test that Tbilisi was not going to try to bully Abkhazia into submission. Meanwhile, increased economic relations would benefit both sides and would bring the two parts of Georgia closer, without prejudging the final deal. Such a process would have fallen short of a clear reintegration of Abkhazia into Georgia, which was rejected by the overwhelming majority of Abkhaz, but it did not close the door to it and left an ambiguity that might, if circumstances changed sufficiently on the ground and if the appeal of a tolerant and prosperous Georgia grew, eventually lead to some kind of confederation, or some special status for Abkhazia—à la

Monaco, as one Georgian told me—that Abkhazia might call independence, but that also would satisfy Georgia.

The Window Closes

After the war of 2008, the recognition by Russia of South Ossetia and Abkhazia, and the following hard partition of Georgia this rosy scenario sounds naive and out of reach. The small window that had opened in early 2005 was gradually shut in the following period. It is hard to point to a particular event as the crossroads where history took a turn for the worse. Rather, it was a series of actions that destroyed the possibility of a negotiated settlement. The fragile trust that had begun to develop between Shamba, the Abkhaz official in charge of the process, and Saakashvili's aide Alasania did not survive the dismissal of the latter, who was appointed ambassador of Georgia to the UN in New York and lost the capacity to be a central player in the negotiation. Salome Zourabichvili's resignation as foreign minister in October 2005, and her subsequent joining with the opposition to Saakashvili, was another sign that a subtle differentiated approach to the relations of Georgia with the European Union and with NATO had been replaced by an all-out push for a quick integration in NATO. On the frontline, the installation of a Georgian youth camp very close to the cease-fire line, in an area where the Inguri River did not clearly mark the separation, was a legal but risky move that heightened the risks of incidents. And incidents were occurring in other areas of the zone of conflict. Their origins were impossible to identify, but collectively they were a clear sign that the cease-fire arrangements were unraveling. Just as worrying, no side had much interest in making a real effort to address their weaknesses. More meetings of the group of friends were held, but they had no substance. The Germans were making efforts to salvage the process, and they insisted one of the meetings take place in Bonn. Heidi Tagliavini, whose integrity and persistence had won the respect of the parties, had now been replaced by Jean Arnault. He was one of the most experienced negotiators in the UN. He had managed political processes in places as diverse as Guatemala, Burundi, and Afghanistan, where he had been the deputy of Lakhdar Brahimi before replacing him as the head of the UN mission. The UN Secretariat was taking Georgia seriously, but to no avail.

From 2005 on, the signs of instability became more and more worrying. The Russians were busy creating new legal facts on the ground, as a growing number of Abkhaz citizens were acquiring Russian passports. At all levels, a deterioration was visible. At the strategic level, the continuing crisis over the status of Kosovo was beginning to have an impact on Georgia, as Russia regularly drew a parallel between the two situations, implicitly suggesting that coherence was needed in resolving the two conflicts, which would imply independence for Abkhazia. President Bush had a triumphal visit in Georgia in May 2005, which was reciprocated in July 2006 by a visit of Saakashvili to Washington, during which President Bush called him "my friend." Meanwhile, the Georgian parliament was demanding the withdrawal of Russian peacekeepers. Moscow was pointedly withdrawing its troops from bases outside Abkhazia and South Ossetia, but certainly not from the two breakaway republics. This was clearly a zero-sum game, and the rapprochement with the West and the United States in particular was happening at the expense of Georgia-Russia relations.

A number of incidents contributed to the deterioration on the ground. Unexplained explosions, which Georgia attributed to Russian covert actions, curtailed gas and electricity imports from Russia in January of 2006, in the middle of a harsh winter. Georgian military operations in the Kodori valley, the only part of Abkhazia not under the control of the Abkhaz authorities, led to violent clashes in the summer. Then a Georgian military helicopter carrying the Georgian minister of defense was shot at while flying over South Ossetia. Russian officers were arrested as spies in the fall of 2006, which led to more Russian sanctions against Georgia. By 2007 the cease-fire arrangements looked increasingly precarious, and the political process seemed to have reached a dead end. In the fall, Saakashvili announced that in the face of a continued stalemate he wanted a review of the situation. From the Georgian perspective, this was a way to signal unhappiness with the UN—which was deemed to be too much under the influence of Russia—and it would put political pressure on the Western friends to deliver. Jean Arnault, head of the UN observer mission, and I were under no illusions that the review could find some new unexplored way to resolve the conflict. If that was the purpose, it was a dangerous move, because it would raise expectations without providing the means to respond to them. But it could be used to draw the attention of the two strategic players, the United States and Russia, to the dangers of benign neglect.

Much is made of conflict prevention and of the importance of early action by the Security Council to stop a situation from deteriorating. Experts have often stressed the need for stronger analytical capacities—including in the UN—and one of the recommendations of the 2000 Brahimi report on peacekeeping reforms was precisely to beef up the early-warning capacities of the UN. While the secretary general of the United Nations would be in a stronger position to call the attention of member states to their responsibilities when confronted with the risk of future conflict if he could rely on solid and dedicated professional advice, I am convinced that the lack of knowledge or analysis is not the main problem. The main problem is the lack of political will among member states, and the months that preceded the Georgian conflict of the summer of 2008 are a sad confirmation of that. I myself underestimated at the time the risk of a hot confrontation, as I was more focused on Sudan, the Democratic Republic of the Congo, and Afghanistan. But Jean Arnault was raising the alarm, as it became more and more evident to him that there was not even the semblance of a political process, and that the immediate priority should be to strengthen the cease-fire arrangements to minimize the risk of resumption of conflict. In the spring of 2008, he presciently suggested in an internal note, which I still have in my files, that the secretary general could "express bluntly his concerns about the present danger of escalation in the Georgian-Abkhaz conflict [and] point to the major powers' responsibility to address this danger, remind them of their shared commitment before the United Nations to preventing war and call upon them urgently *to work together.*" But the major powers were not interested. In all so-called frozen conflicts, consolidating cease-fire arrangements in the absence of a credible political process is often criticized as a cowardly acceptance of the status quo, which in fact it is, although the alternative course is to challenge the status quo by all means, including the use of force. Georgia is a good example of the unwillingness of the international community to consider honestly such hard choices, something that, of course, also would require a greater commitment to addressing the underlying issues.

The Western friends of Georgia nevertheless were all publicly calling for moderation, and apparently in the weeks preceding the conflict, U.S. secretary of state Condoleezza Rice made it clear to the Georgian leadership that the United States was opposed to the use of force and that Georgia would be on its own if it used force. But except for a courageous German diplomatic initiative to defuse tensions and re-energize a dying political process, the UN's calls for a greater focus on cease-fire arrangements did not get much traction. In the spring of 2008, there was no need for specific intelligence to predict that the risk of an armed conflict in Abkhazia or South Ossetia was steadily increasing, and that we would all be lucky if the summer of 2008 passed without one.

The detailed circumstances of the conflict have been described in a report commissioned by the European Union, led by Heidi Tagliavini. I was a member of the advisory board that she consulted as she was drafting it. From the evidence that was presented to the board, there is little doubt that Georgia initiated hostilities against South Ossetia. This led to a powerful counterattack by Russian forces, which quickly entered the theater of operations through a tunnel that connects South Ossetia with Russia. A lot of attention has been given to who started the war, and indeed, this is a relevant question if international law is to be upheld and if article 51 of the UN Charter, which allows for the use of force only in self-defense, is to remain relevant. But what I found most striking in the analysis of the conflict is the attitude of the United States and Russia. Both countries have at all times detailed knowledge of what happens in Georgia, Russia because of the many connections created by more than a century of common history, the United States because it is engaged in extensive military cooperation with Georgia—with 1,000 military advisers deployed there. The conflict that started during the night on August 7 was not a minor skirmish. It was preceded by significant military preparations, and it is hard to believe that both countries were equally blind to what was brewing and were caught by surprise. And yet, at least judging by the actions that were made public, they did nothing to stop it: on August 3 the Russian Foreign Ministry said that the risk of large-scale military operations was increasing, but there was no serious effort to get the attention of the Security Council. This lack of serious effort suggests that maybe both countries thought a fait accompli might well suit them. They just did not expect the same fait accompli. Did some in Washington believe that a quick and bold Georgian action would settle once and for all the Ossetia file, as the Ajaria file had been settled? Were some in Moscow waiting for the Georgian leadership to make a major blunder, so that Abkhazia and South Ossetia would decisively consolidate their position, and Tbilisi and the West would finally learn a lesson on how not to deal with Russia?

By then I had left the United Nations, and I am not in a position to answer those questions. The actual conclusion of my engagement with Georgia had taken place a few months before, in May 2008, when I accompanied the secretary general to Bucharest to attend a NATO summit. It was my first visit to Romania since the early 1990s, when I had gone to Bucharest shortly after the fall of Nicolae Ceausescu as the head of the French policy planning staff. The contrast could not be greater, and it was a lesson in what was done right and what was done wrong in the two decades since the end of the cold war. Bucharest had changed radically, for the better; the city was clearly benefiting from the integration of Romania into the European Union, and there was an atmosphere of prosperity that contrasted with the eerie devastation of the Ceausescu period, when gigantic palaces sat amid empty spaces and half-demolished apartment blocks, like stranded whales. The palace of Ceausescu was still there, now hosting, of all things, a NATO summit, and we were all trying to find our way in its oversized corridors. Romania was legitimately proud to host a summit of the most powerful security organization in the western world, but underneath the surface of pan-European reconciliation, there were some deep currents of resentment.

At the official dinner that concluded the summit, the presence of Bush and Putin at the same table could not hide the divides and the bitterness. Bush had pushed hard to bring Georgia and Ukraine into NATO. France and Germany had successfully resisted the push, and Angela Merkel had drafted compromise language that allowed the process to start but with no certainty that it would be finished. This was probably the worst of all worlds. Saakashvili, by coincidence almost alone at his dinner table, was sulking, probably more than ever convinced that he had to push harder, to create the kind of fait accompli that his weak European partners would have no other option but to swallow. Russia was under no illusion that the United States would continue to push. As for the members of the European Union, two foreign ministers from central Europe sitting at my table were complaining about "old Europe," confirmed in their belief, as one of them put it, that "at the hour of danger, there is only the United States one can count on." Only the foreign minister of Slovenia, Dimitrij Rupel, wisely noted that narrow national interests were more than ever driving policy, and there was little common strategic vision in Europe.

The end of the cold war had destroyed a physical separation and brought prosperity. But it had not destroyed mental walls, the result of different memories built on different histories. And that was, and still is, the tragedy of Georgia. There is no genuine common understanding on what Europe should look like, and even a compromise like the one that was reached in 1955 on Austria, when the Soviet Union pulled out its troops in exchange for Austrian neutrality, is today impossible. Paradoxically, in 1955 the admission of the reality of the divide made it easier to reach a compromise. Today, we pretend to be less divided, but competing ambitions and fears make it almost impossible to build a common strategic vision. Considering their past, it is unthinkable for countries like Georgia or Ukraine to surrender their sovereign right to join NATO. Indeed, for all the countries that were once under Soviet domination, the fear of Russian imperialism remains the most powerful factor shaping their foreign policies. For them, the aspiration of other European countries to build a cooperative relationship with Russia is seen at best as naive, at worst as cynical and cowardly. Depending on where you sit in Europe, and what your relative power is, the definition of realism differs radically. If you are in the east and weak, you see no alternative to a strong military alliance with the United States. If you are further west in Europe, and more powerful, you begin to question the wisdom and feasibility of a military balance of power as the foundation of peace, and you look for some agreed understanding of what a European status quo should look like, one that would not be threatening to Russia but also would not limit the sovereignty of its neighbors.

From that standpoint, the last two decades are, in hindsight, lost decades, as the present Ukraine crisis shows. Every actor shares a responsibility in that failure. The European Union has been politically too weak to project a sense of nonaggressive self-confidence that would reassure its new members without threatening Russia. NATO is still perceived by Russia, as well as by its new members, as an essentially anti-Russian alliance. Russia for its part has been unable to define a constructive relationship with the countries it used to dominate and seems to believe that its own security is better assured by the weakness of its neighbors than by their success. And the United States has been unable to forge a steady long-term strategy with Russia. But the result is that Europe cannot entirely leave the prison of its tragic past. In Georgia and now Ukraine, that means the divides of yesterday cut across countries, and so the whole region that borders Russia, which could have been a bridge anchoring Russia to Europe and projecting Europe into a new space, has not yet found a modern balance. The Achilles' heel of the European Union enlargement policy is the absence of a genuine European policy toward Russia. Maybe that outcome was inevitable, considering the different pasts of different parts of Europe, and it raises questions about the possibility of a real common European foreign policy. I could not help thinking that there was some irony that at the 2008 Bucharest summit, the other important item on the agenda was Afghanistan: Here was a distant land with which Europe, except for the British Empire, had never had much interaction. But it was on the agenda because it mattered to the United States, which had made it a test of NATO solidarity. And the United States mattered to Europe.

As for the people of Afghanistan or the people of Georgia, they were caught in strategic plays that went far beyond them. In the case of Georgia, the United Nations tried to create some political space that would help the Abkhaz and Georgian people find a modus vivendi, so that Georgians would not live in internally displaced person camps and Abkhazia would not be a rump pariah state. We failed. The steady deterioration after 2005 culminated in the hot war of the summer of 2008 and the hard partition of Georgia. In the end, the frozen conflict UN observer mission that I worked to bring to closure ironically was closed, in 2009, only after the situation heated to war, as consensus on its deployment eroded in the Security Council. I have a strong belief that, like most conflicts, the 2008 war was eminently avoidable. One cannot point to a single cause, but rather a series of policy failures that took place in Tbilisi, Moscow, Washington, and European capitals. Those who had a responsibility in shaping the strategic posture in Washington and Moscow showed little concern for the impact of their policies on the people directly affected by those policies. Europeans were weak and reacted too late. Meanwhile, those who were making decisions on the ground seemed to have had little understanding of what the bigger strategic picture was. Because of that, people died, Georgia is durably divided, and the broader European strategic picture remains unsettled.

four

CÔTE D'IVOIRE

Elections Are Rarely the Shortest Route to Peace

The news media look at the various crises that the Security Council has to address as if they are independent problems that are dealt with in isolation. Nothing is further from the truth, and I learned in 2003—a year during which the Security Council had to deal with several crises at once—how difficult it is to actually address each crisis on its own merits, and not make it a bargaining chip in a broader game. The year 2003 was, of course, dominated by Iraq, which reverberated on every aspect of the council's work. The Iraq debacle in the council actually helped in the case for action in the Democratic Republic of the Congo because the council was eager to show that it could again work in a cohesive manner, and there was a genuine possibility of convergence. Stopping the violence in the Ituri region of Congo would not be an American, British, or French victory: it would be a victory of the council.

Côte d'Ivoire was a different matter: it had traditionally been very close to its former colonial master, France. Forty years after independence, there was still a very big French community in Abidjan, and French troops were stationed in the country on the basis of a bilateral agreement. For most members of the council, France "owned" Côte d'Ivoire, and if there was trouble, it was for France to fix. At a time when France had been the flag-bearer of the opponents to the Iraq war, that historic relationship was not going to help in Washington, in case some UN involvement was needed.

As the crisis in Côte d'Ivoire began to unfold in 2002, I knew it would be serious and could not be ignored. In several West African countries, there is a divide between the coastal south and the northern hinterland, which reflects tribal differences exacerbated by the history of colonization. The slave trade was, of course, first a coastal trade, and the colonization that followed also started from the coast. The consequence has been a generally Christian south

93

and a Muslim north, with often more differences in the same country between the tribes of the south and the tribes of the north than between tribes separated by a border in the north. This is all the more so in the case of Côte d'Ivoire, because during the colonial period, there was just one Afrique Occidentale Française, which was broken up into several countries at the time of independence.

When a civil war pitching the northern part of the country against Abidjan and the south erupted in the fall of 2002, the concern was immediate in all the countries that are members of the Economic Community of West African States (ECOWAS), a regional organization with a focus beyond economic issues extending to matters of regional security and stability. The north-south divide had been an important factor in the conflicts that devastated Sierra Leone and Liberia; it is latent in Ghana and a major risk in Nigeria. Meanwhile, for landlocked countries like Mali and Burkina Faso, a war in Côte d'Ivoire was an economic as well as a human tragedy. West African states were also very aware of the risks of conflict spillover in a region with very porous borders. Côte d'Ivoire, which had for decades been the economic engine of Francophone West Africa, was the natural outlet for their international trade, and host to many of their citizens, who represented some 25 percent of the population. This very high figure—in what other country do immigrants represent a quarter of the population?—reflected in part the labor-intensive nature of the cocoa culture, which plays a central role in the Ivoirian economy (Cote d'Ivoire is the source of almost half of the world production of cocoa). It was also a consequence of the great uncertainty on the definition of Ivoirian nationality.

That uncertainty was at the heart of the crisis. It had been brewing for several years, ever since Konan Bedie, from the dominant ethnic group of the south, the Baoule, had become president, following the death in 1993 of Félix Houphouët-Boigny, who had led Côte d'Ivoire since independence. Bedie, to prevent his rival from the northern part of the country, Alassane Ouattara, from running, put the emphasis on *ivoirité*, casting doubt on the nationality of his competitor and fanning the flames of xenophobia. Bedie eventually was overthrown in a military coup led by a disgruntled general, General Robert Guei, but ten months later, in October 2000, the only candidate allowed to run against Guei, Laurent Gbagbo, won a surprise victory. Opposition leaders like Ouattara, who had been excluded from running, called for fresh elections, while General Guei claimed polling fraud but fled in the wake of a popular uprising. Gbagbo was now president of Côte d'Ivoire.

Whatever misgivings one could have about the way the election had been conducted, this was a watershed for Côte d'Ivoire. For decades, a narrow elite had run the country, courting the favor of Houphouët-Boigny, who had managed the independence from France so smoothly that it had barely registered. Côte d'Ivoire had enjoyed a relative prosperity, compared to its neighbors, that dampened possible tensions. There had been some waste, like the bizarre construction in Yamoussoukro of a basilica modeled on Saint Peter's in Rome, but in West Africa Côte d'Ivoire had been widely perceived, until the military coup, as a haven of prosperity and stability. Coming after the coup of Guei, the election of Laurent Gbagbo confirmed that the era of traditional Ivoirian politics had come to an end, even if superficially one could have an impression of continuity.

Laurent Gbagbo, like all the Ivoirian politicians of his generation, had been educated in France, had many friends in the French Socialist Party, and ultimately picked France when he had to go into exile. And he was, like Houphouët-Boigny and Bedie, from the south, but unlike them, he did not belong to the dominant Baoule group. He was from the smaller Bete tribe. More important, unlike them and also Ouattara, he had never been part of what some called the "Houphouët-Boigny system." On the contrary, as the leader of the leftist Front Populaire Ivoirien, he had actually been an opponent to Houphouët-Boigny, spending some time in jail (when Ouattara was Houphouët-Boigny's prime minister), some time in exile, and even running against Houphouët-Boigny in the presidential election of 1990 and winning a seat in the first open parliamentary election of the same year. Gbagbo was not a full member of the old club of Ivoirian politics: the unprecedented military coup had been the first signal that the veneer of peace and civility that had hidden underlying tensions was coming off. The surprise election of the populist Gbagbo was the confirmation that new dynamics were at play; the same dynamics would soon lead to a civil war and years of crisis.

The depth of the divide was not immediately clear. On the contrary, there initially was some encouraging news: municipal elections were organized, in which for the first time all parties could participate, and the return of Ouattara from exile in late 2001 seemed to signal that the national reconciliation forum that Gbagbo was promoting was gaining some traction. Those efforts culminated when Gbagbo, Ouattara, and Bedie met in Yamoussoukro in late August 2002 and a broad-based government was formed. But shortly after, as garrisons mutinied in the north of the country, the civil war erupted. The rebels quickly took control of the northern half of the country, and they would have taken control of Abidjan if pre-stationed French forces had not stopped them. That is when I heard for the first time a mention of Côte d'Ivoire in the context of my UN job: President Jacques Chirac, who was receiving Kofi Annan at the Elysée Palace in late November 2002, expressed extreme concern, noting that the *ivoirité* promoted by Bedie had created a very dangerous dynamic, that Gbagbo was under the wrong influence, and that the country was now full of weapons. Chirac, who had a genuine interest in Africa, appeared well informed, and he expected the worse. "Côte d'Ivoire," he said, "is a real disaster." It was now urgent to get Ouattara out of the country for his own safety and to try to limit the damage.

French diplomacy, led by Dominique de Villepin, was immediately engaged. At Chirac's invitation, a peace conference was convened in January 2003 near Paris, in Linas-Marcoussis, chaired by a respected member of the constitutional court of France, Pierre Mazeaud. All the belligerents were in attendance, and after much prodding an agreement was reached. It contained a list of ambitious undertakings: a government of national reconciliation was to be appointed, led by a "consensus prime minister" who would stay in office until the presidential election could be held. It was agreed that the prime minister would not be a candidate in the presidential election. The agreement did not shy away from the contentious issues that had triggered the conflict: nationality, the eligibility of Ouattara as a candidate, reform of the armed forces, disarmament, and the media. A monitoring committee, which included ECOWAS, as well as the African Union, the European Union, the Organization de la Francophonie, the Group of 8, and the United Nations, was set up. The French wanted to make sure that the agreement the Ivoirians had reached behind closed doors would be supported and overseen by the whole international community. Two days after the signature of the agreement, a conference was convened in Paris, co-chaired by Chirac, Kofi Annan, and President Tabo Mbeki of South Africa, who at the time was also president of the African Union. Eleven African heads of state were in attendance. This was a remarkable diplomatic success and an example of enlightened diplomacy, even if holding the conference in the former colonial power sent a wrong signal. The French had managed not only to produce a substantive agreement among reluctant Ivoirian parties, but they had also garnered the support of all the international organizations that mattered. This was no small achievement.

At the beginning of 2003, I had one clear priority concerning Côte d'Ivoire: I needed to prepare a possible UN peacekeeping operation. French and ECOWAS forces monitored the precarious cease-fire that cut the country in half along an east-west axis, but the French were eager to play a less central role, and the African forces needed logistical and financial support if their presence was to be sustained. Even before the Linas-Marcoussis meeting, Villepin had broached the idea of a UN peacekeeping operation. The French military had observed the success of the British operation in Sierra Leone in 2000, and had very bad memories of their experience with UN peacekeeping forces in Yugoslavia; they did not want their forces to be put under UN command. My concern was that the French presence in Côte d'Ivoire was much bigger than the force deployed by the British in Sierra Leone, so that the comparison did not really apply. What we feared was a repeat of Somalia, when an uncoordinated U.S. operation against Mohamed Farrah Aideed, a Somali warlord, had ended in disaster, leading to the precipitous withdrawal of the UN mission. I made clear to General Henri Bentegeat, the chief of the French defense staff, that the UN wanted to avoid the risks inherent in having two parallel chains of command in the same theater of operations. Always a practical man who wanted to find solutions, as I would experience again in Congo soon after, he offered to send military planners to New York to work with our own planners.

In Côte d'Ivoire, however, events were not waiting for our planners to develop their plans. I began to have a nasty feeling that the orderly process that had been concocted in Linas-Marcoussis might easily go off-track. As head of state, Gbagbo had left the signing of the agreement to the representative of his party, establishing a distance between his constitutional authority and a deal signed at a lower level on the territory of the former colonial power. And the atmosphere in Côte d'Ivoire was very different from Linas-Marcoussis. On February 2 some 100,000 people demonstrated in Abidjan against the power-sharing agreement that had just been signed in France. Radio stations and television propagated xenophobic messages. And the French were in a weaker position than I had thought. Indeed, their presence had stopped the rebels and protected Gbagbo, but the threat of withdrawal from Abidjan was not very credible: there were some 20,000 French citizens (many dual nationals) in the city, and Paris could not abandon them. The French were as much the hostages of the mobs in Abidjan as Gbagbo was dependent on the French presence.

Divergent Interests in the Security Council

Meanwhile, the Security Council was consumed by Iraq, as Secretary of State Colin Powell was presenting to the Security Council "evidence" on Iraqi weapons of mass destruction, and U.S.-French relations would soon reach their nadir. It was becoming increasingly unlikely that the United States would agree to authorize a peacekeeping mission in Côte d'Ivoire to satisfy the French, especially with an unsettled situation: there was no government of national unity, no "consensus prime minister," no effective cease-fire. But the West Africans were very concerned by the backsliding that was happening, and they had asked the UN to continue to prepare for a peacekeeping mission, while they would make a push on the politics. The president of Ghana, John Kufuor, convened a meeting in Accra in March, which produced tangible results: the Ivoirian parties finally agreed to let consensus prime minister Seydou Diarra form the cabinet. This was the first of many attempts by the countries of West Africa, which had the greatest stake in the resolution of the crisis, to move the process forward. What became known as the Accra II Agreement had the great merit of being an agreement signed in Africa and sponsored by an African country. The Côte d'Ivoire peace process was no longer only a French issue, and that was important in Washington as well as in Abidjan.

In Washington, it would be harder to resist calls for a peacekeeping operation if they were coming from the region. But there was still a lot of resistance, which was more ideological than practical. The United States was prepared to give $9 million to ECOWAS to support the deployment of forces from the region but was negotiating hard to avoid a UN peacekeeping operation. To facilitate the transition, we had proposed to first deploy "military liaison officers" instead of military observers, which would have sounded more like the advance party of a UN peacekeeping operation. The United States agreed to liaison officers, but it was now trying to bring their number down, although the budgetary cost was negligible. I was always amused to see how important these little games with words became. They tricked no one, and most of the time common sense would eventually prevail, but they mattered, even for the most powerful member states. If they were the price to get things done, it was a small price to pay.

The Security Council, however, was not yet ready to authorize a UN peacekeeping operation large enough to replace the ECOWAS and French forces that had been deployed to consolidate the cease-fire. After much haggling, the council only authorized for one year a mission with no blue helmets. During a visit to West Africa in June, the council congratulated ECOWAS and French forces on their good cooperation and called for more voluntary contributions to support African troops, but did not mention the deployment of a UN operation. The local rhetoric was encouraging that benign attitude. In a well-publicized meeting at the presidential palace, military leaders and rebels solemnly declared that the "war is over." This was only the first of many declarations and judging by what was actually happening, this was a somewhat premature statement. There still was no agreement on the appointments of the ministers of defense and national security, and in September 2003 the ministers of the major rebel armed group, the "Forces Nouvelles," walked out of the government of national unity. The progress achieved by President Kufuor and ECOWAS at Accra in March was now unraveling. A month later a French journalist had an altercation with a policeman and was shot dead. There were several instances of sporadic violence, which in December would escalate to attempted crossings by armed groups of the fragile "confidence zone" that served as a cease-fire line. The combination of an insufficiently resourced West African force with a French force that was strong but conjured, among the Ivoirian population, memories of the colonial past was not going to stabilize the situation.

The West African leaders had known it for a while, but their call to the Security Council during its visit for a UN peacekeeping operation had been watered down in the official report of the council's visit, which just mentioned "serious needs for additional resources from the International Community." In November, as the situation continued to deteriorate, regional demands became more pressing, and the very able foreign minister of Ghana, Nana Akufo-Addo, led an ECOWAS delegation to the council. He had strong arguments, and he was, as usual, most articulate in presenting them. To help him put pressure on the council, I agreed with Kofi Annan to send an assessment mission to Côte d'Ivoire, which would develop initial plans for a UN peacekeeping operation.

Ever since President Chirac had raised Côte d'Ivoire with Annan, I had been thinking about what my role should be in a crisis where France was so much involved. I knew that the closeness of France with Côte d'Ivoire, which had been so much in evidence when France was able to convene the Linas-Marcoussis conference, would sometimes help—orphan conflicts do not usually generate much international interest—but would also be a complication. Côte d'Ivoire would be the first test of my ability to convey France's perspective to the secretary general: why appoint a Frenchman to run peacekeeping if it did not facilitate relations between the Secretariat and a permanent member of the Council? But I needed to remain a loyal international civil servant with a clear moral compass, to serve the best interests of the desperate people who had been dragged into a conflict by bad politics. A further complication, which I observed time and again, is that most interlocutors in conflict countries don't take very seriously the explicit prescription of the UN Charter that as a UN civil servant you are to take instructions from the UN, not your home capital. In the passionate climate of Côte d'Ivoire, there was little doubt that the first reaction would be to see me as a French agent. I therefore decided that I would initially avoid taking a too visible role, and I asked my experienced deputy Hedi Annabi to lead the assessment mission. A Tunisian who had been in the Department of Peacekeeping Operations since its creation, he had more experience of peacekeeping than most and was known as a shrewd and cautious political operator who usually knew before everybody else where a fractious discussion in the Security Council would end. Crucially, everybody respected his impeccable integrity. After the assessment mission returned, the secretary general weighed in further and explicitly called for the deployment of a UN peacekeeping operation.

The impact on the ground of those diplomatic initiatives was almost immediate, an indication of the importance of politics and international engagement in managing fragile peace processes. The Forces Nouvelles announced that they were ending their boycott of the government. The time had come for the final push, and the secretary general, reporting on the good news that was coming from Côte d'Ivoire, reiterated his call for the deployment of a UN peacekeeping operation. On February 27, 2004, the Security Council finally authorized the mission; it would integrate some of the ECOWAS troops and complement them with troops from other parts of the world. A whole paragraph of the resolution detailed the tasks that the French forces would perform in support of the UN mission. Integration of the French forces into the UN mission had never been an option in Côte d'Ivoire, but the resolution was sufficiently specific that it mitigated the danger of having two separate chains of command for the same theater. The benefit and risk of having an independent expeditionary force from a powerful nation was that it provided a capacity to escalate that no UN force ever has. Years later, in 2011, that French presence would prove to be decisive. I saw the advantage and the insurance policy that such a presence provided; I would find out about the risks a few months later.

The UN had now been put at the center of the engagement of the international community in Côte d'Ivoire, and a bigger peacekeeping operation was starting to deploy. But I knew that in Côte d'Ivoire, as in all post-conflict situations, while military force could sometimes contain the violence and block spoilers, it would not by itself bring peace. Peace would be the result of a political process, of an agreement between the key players, and in the past twelve months, that agreement had proven elusive, with many false starts. It was time to try to capitalize on the momentum that a new mission might create. Encouraged by various members of the Security Council and with the full support of ECOWAS, I accepted to lead a delegation of senior officials to Côte d'Ivoire. Its unusual composition reflected the newfound unity of the international community: three permanent members of the Security Council, France, the United Kingdom, and the United States, were represented at a senior level, but what was most significant was the presence of Ibn Chambas, the Ghanaian top official of ECOWAS. This was a powerful message to President Gbagbo and the Forces Nouvelles that they would not be able to play West Africa against the Security Council.

When I arrived in early May 2004, the climate was very tense. Shortly after the adoption of the Security Council resolution, the situation had again taken a turn for the worse: a demonstration by the opposition had been violently repressed, shattering the hope that some opposition leaders may have had that street power combined with the engagement of the international community would push out Gbagbo in the same way President Jean-Bertrand Aristide had been ousted in Haiti a month earlier. A UN team was now investigating the violence that had caused more than 100 deaths. The media were full of incendiary rhetoric, and a troubling parallel could be drawn with the role played by radio stations in the Rwandan genocide in 1994. And yet, driving along the beautiful avenues of Abidjan, it was hard to believe that the country could tip into extreme violence. In spite of the division of the country and one-and-a-half years of political paralysis, the capital city did not seem too affected. It still deserved, with its skyscrapers illuminated at night, its nickname of the Manhattan of Africa. I was told it was a different story in some of the sprawling suburbs, in the countryside, and in the north of the country, where economic activities had been brought to a standstill.

What was striking, and worried me the most, was the series of meetings I conducted with the parties to the conflict. The message of our delegation was simple and straightforward, but their response was not. We told them that the deployment of a peacekeeping operation in one of the richest countries of West Africa was not a favor that the Ivoirian people were making to the international community, but a favor of the international community to Côte d'Ivoire. There were many other places in the world that needed support. So it was essential that they all stop playing games and drop the preconditions that prevented any progress. The roadmap that had been outlined at Linas-Marcoussis and confirmed at Accra was clear: there would be a presidential election and the armed forces of the country would be reunited.

The rebels from the north wanted a genuinely open presidential election, and that required credible electoral lists and eligibility criteria that would not exclude a potential candidate like Ouattara. This in turn required some legislative measures as well as determined administrative actions. The rebels did not trust a state apparatus controlled by the president for a credible implementation; that concern had led to the compromise of an empowered "consensus prime minister" who would lead a coalition government with a careful distribution of key ministries among the main actors. On the presidential side, Gbagbo and his party also had clear demands: they wanted the rebels to disarm and stated that no credible election could be held so long as a secessionist group was allowed to keep its weapons and challenge the constitutional order. The compromise would be their integration into the national army. Most of our interlocutors had great talent in making their case, and it often sounded like a Sorbonne seminar, in which the debaters enjoyed exchanging clever arguments, except this time human lives were at stake. However, it quickly became clear that their respective positions were entrenched and incompatible.

Elections: Essential but Not Sufficient

I was beginning to understand that the basic flaw of the process was the reliance on an election to resolve fundamental differences. In a country at peace, an election is always a divisive moment, but losers accept their defeat because they trust the winners will not abuse their victory. How, in a country that had been bitterly divided by war, would leaders suddenly become so confident and generous that they would entrust to the uncertainties of an election their future and maybe their lives? I would find in the following years that the innumerable technical battles over the preparation of an election and the difficulties that would keep popping up as soon as one issue had been resolved were a sideshow. Presidential elections did not take place in Côte d'Ivoire for almost eight years not because there were some unique technical issues to be resolved, but because none of the key actors was willing to let the election go ahead unless he was assured of winning it. Obviously, that was not achievable unless one of the candidates miscalculated (which is what eventually happened). In the meantime, even if it was flawed, there was no game in town other than the process that had been painfully agreed at Linas-Marcoussis and Accra, and I felt it was vital to keep it alive. Gaining time is a tactic that sometimes can become a strategy. The perspective of an election was certainly a factor that could be used to make violence less attractive, and the more time passed, the more time there would be for possible negotiations between key leaders on what should happen after the presidential election. Actually, a postelection deal was the only hope to ever have a peaceful election; the absence of such a deal in the election that finally took place in 2010 would actually precipitate Côte d'Ivoire into its worse crisis since 2002.

In 2004 the risk of violence was high, and keeping on board the various signatories of the agreement was hard. At first glance, it did not seem so difficult: they all knew each other, they had studied at the same French universities, and they sometimes came from the same villages. And most of them seemed to share a great appetite for power and wealth. One was thus reminded of the Houphouët-Boigny period, in which loyalties were maintained through clientelism. But at the same time, it was clear that this new period was different, not just because Gbagbo had challenged the old club, but also because on both sides of the divide, there was a new generation, often less educated, who had discovered the power of the street, and the older politicians were only too happy to have found this new tool that they could now use to further their goals. They could turn on the violence when it suited them. They had henchmen who knew how to run militias and commandeer assassinations. I met a few of them, in both camps, and was not reassured. Did we have any leverage to stop them and make sure that the competition for riches would not turn into a vicious ethnic war? During this first visit to Côte d'Ivoire, many observers told me that sanctions, personal sanctions, were the most effective tool in the box to address that threat. There were some real thugs backstage, who were probably more concerned about their wallets than their tribes. However, they were ready to trigger a spiral of ethnic violence to fatten their wallets, and the best way to stop them was to scare them: they had to be afraid of losing their bank accounts and nice apartments in Europe or America.

Leverage required a unified international community. The delegation I had led to Abidjan had been a first very modest attempt of the UN. Building on this effort, in June President Gbagbo met Kofi Annan, President Kufuor, and Nigerian president Olusegun Obasanjo, all of whom pressed him to soften his stance, but demonstrations by "jeunes patriotes," the militia that supported Gbagbo, during a visit of the Security Council to Abidjan had shown that the street could still be "turned on" and that nothing was really settled. What was needed was a much more vigorous international engagement, at the highest level. The closest we got to a concerted effort to engage Gbagbo was in the margins of an African Union meeting in Addis Ababa in July and a follow-up meeting in Accra the same month. Kofi Annan was willing to push hard during the meeting of the African Union in Addis. But how can one put pressure on a head of state when he is smart, expecting to be pressured, and reasonably confident that he is in a strong position? I was to witness different techniques with different partners, but the encounters with President Gbagbo were my first lesson. Kofi Annan, who was well aware of the immense talent for procrastination of his interlocutor, started his first meeting with an optimistic rhetorical question: "So, now that you have met with your opponents, everything is settled, isn't it?" Gbagbo replied: "Well, we had a good meeting, and we decided to meet again." He added, "I have transmitted all the draft laws," suggesting that the ball was no longer in his camp, but in the National Assembly (where it would easily remain stuck). And then he added, with a sigh, elegantly moving the conversation toward generalities, while creating a kind of complicity with the secretary general: "It is so complicated to run an African State!" Annan would have none of it and brought the conversation back to specifics: "We need to set a date for a summit of heads of state in

Accra," he replied. As the meeting came to an end, and Gbagbo was smoothly preparing to take leave, he said: "La Côte d'Ivoire, it's a crisis that can be resolved. The war is over, and what keeps things going is politics! I am embarrassed, Mr. Secretary General, to take up your time."

The president of Côte d'Ivoire had to go through one more painful experience before flying back to Abidjan: the mini-summit of July 6, where he was confronted by many of his African peers behind closed doors. Obasanjo spoke first, and he set the tone, saying at the outset: "After the Abuja summit, Gbagbo kept his word for the first time! We have to help him." Ghana's Kufuor added: "This is a crisis of confidence." President Omar Bongo of Gabon, who was considered the "wise man" of the meeting because of his long tenure in office, concluded this opening volley: "The one who is accountable for Côte d'Ivoire is Gbagbo!" Gbagbo may have been a bit shaken by this broadside, but he remained very smooth, and his answer was a variation of his reply to the secretary general the day before: "The problems of Côte d'Ivoire, they are really tiring, we are going in circle. . . . Côte d'Ivoire, it is like the Bastille days of colonial times, when we were climbing on greasy poles for the village fair!"

What was at stake was indeed very serious: would there be a meeting at Accra, three weeks later, where the roadmap leading to elections would eventually be finalized, on the basis of a substantive agreement between Gbagbo and his opponents? The cajoling and the jokes kept the tension under control, but the political reality was that the whole of West Africa was telling President Gbagbo and his opponents that they had to come to terms. Gbagbo felt the pressure and accepted the creation of mixed commissions to prepare for the meeting in Accra. The meeting took place at the end of the month, and at the time it was considered a success. The parliament would adopt the necessary laws, the president would resolve the issue of eligibility to the presidency—though how he would do it was still unclear. The prime minister would be empowered, and the rebels would start disarming by October 15 at the latest.

On October 15 the legislative package still had not been adopted, no disarmament had started, and there were rumors that the rebels and opposition leaders might actually be quite comfortable with a situation in which the president's mandate would have lapsed, and the legal vacuum thus created would lead to some exceptional arrangement supported by the international community. This was called the "Haiti scenario," after the way Aristide had left the country and been replaced by an interim president supported by the international community. Gbagbo had no intention of becoming an African Aristide and surrendering his position. Three days before the mid-October deadline, he had delivered an eloquent speech that many in the international community had received positively. The rebels were clearly not interested in disarming at this stage, and many in the international community, including in France, appeared to be ready to throw their weight in support of Gbagbo. Many anticipated the possibility that the army would launch operations across the buffer zone that separated the south from the rebel-controlled north and were prepared to look the other way.

When I was in Abidjan, I had met a European ambassador who had no patience for a UN operation that would support a process rather than a person. He had told me: "In Africa, you need victors and vanquished." It was becoming clear that the diplomatic efforts of the United Nations and West Africa had stalled and key actors in the international community were ready for a Gbagbo victory, provided appearances were saved and the Linas-Marcoussis deal was not too blatantly sidestepped. So I was not too surprised when the Ivoirian army launched operations in the north on November 4. The secretary general immediately characterized the offensive of the army, or "FANCI" by its French acronym, as a "major violation of the ceasefire," but he did not have much support in the Security Council to take any action. A draft statement circulated among members of the council actually paid tribute to the speech of President Gbagbo on October 12; only at the very end did it condemn the military operations, and it was careful not to implicate the president.

Everything changed in twenty-four hours. In the morning of November 5, 2004, a French military camp was attacked by fighter planes of the Ivoirian government, and several French soldiers were killed. One would never know how deliberate the action was, although it was hard to believe it was a mistake, considering the circumstances of the attack. I learned of it in the very early hours of the morning, when I received a call from Michele Alliot-Marie, the French minister of defense; she had a very strong message to deliver. She officially informed me that the French were retaliating in self-defense against the Ivoirian forces and had destroyed the two Sukhoi jetfighters responsible for the attack. Actually, the French, who could not take the risk of another attack, had destroyed the whole Ivoirian air force, four jet fighters and five attack helicopters. The Ivoirian crisis had entered a new phase.

In Abidjan, the destruction of the air force by the former colonial power created a deep sense of humiliation, and the party of the president had no difficulty stirring the passions of nationalism. Television and radio broadcast heinous messages, and tens of thousands of "jeunes patriotes," the pro-Gbagbo militia, took to the streets of the capital. The four French lycées were reportedly burned down, and thousands of French nationals were evacuated. The French troops were in a very difficult situation, as they were confronted by angry crowds, some armed, that they could barely control. There was gunfire, and people were killed.

The French were, as one would have expected, very concerned for the safety of their troops and worried that the Ivoirian forces might again become a threat if they were quickly reequipped. On November 16 the Security Council unanimously adopted a resolution that imposed an arms embargo on Côte d'Ivoire. This was the first of a series of steps the Security Council would take to try to take charge of the peace process in Côte d'Ivoire and force a solution. The initial unanimity would not last, and the prolonged crisis in Côte d'Ivoire would expose strains within the international community as well the limits of what a peacekeeping operation can achieve when it is confronted by unwilling partners.

Immediately after the attack, there had been reactions in Africa that revealed cracks in the apparent unity. Obasanjo had convened a summit in Abuja, which called for an arms embargo, but President Mbeki had not been in attendance. Mbeki had been mandated by the African Union to be a mediator, and he went to Abidjan, when the tension was at its highest, and met with President Gbagbo. Mbeki was keen to play a role in the Ivoirian crisis, and Gbagbo played to his strong anticolonial convictions. I had the impression that, for Mbeki, the Ivoirian crisis was essentially a delayed decolonization crisis. Which it partially was, as Côte d'Ivoire had never emotionally broken up with its former colonial master, and the outpouring of anti-French emotions in the streets of Abidjan was the result of too many years of pent-up resentment.

In the following months, Mbeki would usually take positions favorable to President Gbagbo and blame Prime Minister Diarra, the rebels, or the UN for delays and setbacks. Mbeki would remain the African Union mediator until October 2006, and he was very active in that role, particularly in 2005; in April, he called all the parties to a meeting in Pretoria and managed to have them all sign the "Pretoria Agreement." Once again, all the Ivoirian parties "solemnly declared the end of the war." More significant, they agreed to hold a presidential election in October, to strengthen the authority of the prime minister, to take practical actions for the reunification of the army, to make the necessary amendments to laws, and to rely on the mediator for the resolution of the issue of the eligibility of presidential candidates. The composition of the independent electoral commission was further refined, and the UN was expected to participate in the organization of general elections. When violent incidents took place a few weeks later, President Mbeki reconvened the parties at the end of June to review progress and to renew their commitment to presidential elections in October 2005. By the fall of 2005, Mbeki felt he had done his part, using his good relations with Gbagbo to get the legislative package through and resolve the question of the eligibility of presidential candidates. In his view, the ball was now clearly in the court of the rebels, who were stalling on disarmament.

Obasanjo and other West African leaders had a very different reading of the crisis. They blamed Gbagbo as much as the rebels for the stalemate and were very concerned that Gbagbo was playing with fire and could enflame the whole subregion. They felt it was necessary to be much tougher with the president. Some probably thought Mbeki did not have a real understanding of the crisis, and the competition between Nigeria and South Africa for a permanent seat in the Security Council further complicated the relationship. This led to a bad pattern: the African Union Peace and Security Council, where South Africa had influence, would usually take positions that helped Gbagbo, while ECOWAS would take a harder line. Ivoirian parties skillfully played one institution against the other.

Meanwhile, the French were eager to see the UN mission take a more forceful role. I had a first taste of the high expectations put on the UN at a meeting in the margins of a summit of francophone countries in Ouagadougou. The adviser of President Chirac for African affairs asked me how the UN mission could enforce the embargo. I was at pains to explain that peacekeepers, unless they were prepared to go to war with the country in which they were deployed, which nobody suggested, had to work with the government for practical reasons, and that invoking Chapter VII of the UN Charter made little difference in that respect. At best, if so mandated, troops could go to a harbor in Cote d'Ivoire and ask to inspect a ship. If access was denied, then they could report to the Security Council, the same way that inspectors did in Iraq when they were refused access to a particular facility. The fact that the peacekeepers had guns would not change the situation, because they would not force their way if stopped by Ivoirian troops.

Unrealistic Expectations of the UN

I found time and again, from Côte d'Ivoire to Sudan or Lebanon, that powerful member states, which usually have a keen sense of what force can achieve, and which certainly would never accept bullying by the United Nations, often had unrealistic expectations of what a peacekeeping operation can deliver. They exaggerated the authority of the Security Council and were unwilling to accept that peacekeeping troops, when confronted by a reluctant government, have only a symbolic authority that can easily be brushed aside, especially if the Security Council is not prepared for any political escalation or to back them with force, as the French finally did in 2011. A month later, the French minister of defense called again to insist that "Accra had to be imposed," referring to the peace agreement, and that it was "necessary to show one's force." I wish it had been possible, and I certainly agreed that too often the United Nations adopted a weak posture that made the peacekeeping operation irrelevant. Internally, I was always pushing the troops and the heads of mission to be strong and avoid meekness. My compatriots were doing their job in pressing a structurally weak UN to show some toughness, and I was doing mine in lowering their expectations, because I knew the limitations under which we were working.

The discussion moved to the Security Council. The French wanted a resolution that would give the UN force additional tasks in the implementation of the embargo, while the United States did not want to put any additional resources into Côte d'Ivoire. The all-too-typical compromise was easy to reach, at the expense of the UN: more tasks and no resources to perform them. The inconsistency of the council was worrying, but its consequences were limited. While a better-resourced and proactive force might have made a difference in the game of chicken of an uncertain peace process—and I was doing my best, with limited resources, to stiffen the spine of the force—I was under no illusion that the critical element remained political: How united would the international community be? How effective could external pressure be on actors who were fighting for their political survival?

After the Pretoria Agreement, the secretary general had appointed, at the request of Mbeki, a high representative for elections who, in principle, had quite extensive powers, giving the United Nations an unprecedented role in elections. Antonio Monteiro was a shrewd Portuguese diplomat, and he was working intensively, but the progress was very slow. By July it was clear that the October presidential election was not going to happen, a situation that would need to be managed. The institutional vacuum that would be created was dangerous.

There were widely diverging assessments of the situation; in mid-2005 Mbeki was reasonably optimistic, while the leaders of Nigeria and Ghana were extremely concerned. The efforts of West Africa on the one hand, and of South Africa on the other, instead of adding up, were subtracting from each other. In September the secretary general organized a meeting where he brought together Mbeki and Obasanjo, to try to change that dynamic and develop a consistent African position. But the maneuvering continued. While a meeting of ECOWAS in the Nigerian capital was seen as a defeat for Gbagbo, a meeting of the Peace and Security Council of the African Union two weeks before the deadline of the end of October agreed on a twelve-month extension of his mandate. The oversight mechanism that was put in place reflected the delicate balance of competing ambitions between South Africa and Nigeria: South Africa would have responsibility for day-to-day monitoring in

Abidjan, while Olu Adeniji, the foreign minister of Nigeria who had successfully led the UN Sierra Leone mission, would chair a monthly meeting of an "international working group." It was also decided that a new prime minister would be appointed, but that took some time. The first consensus prime minister, Seydou Diarra, had shown subtlety and finesse, but he had gradually lost support in Côte d'Ivoire as well as in the international community. Reaching an agreement on his successor was difficult, however. Thankfully, Nigeria and South Africa made a joint effort, and in early December 2005, all the parties agreed on the appointment of Konan Banny, a respected technocrat who was the governor of the central bank of West African states. His authority was immediately tested when he had a conflict with President Gbagbo on the appointment of the minister of finance. He wanted to control that key ministry, and Gbagbo eventually relented.

Was 2006 going to achieve the breakthrough that had eluded the international community in the past three years? The appearance of a greater coherence of international efforts, which had led to the appointment of a new prime minister, was a source of hope. The UN high representative for elections—who was now a tough Swiss diplomat, Gérard Stoudmann—was continuing to push hard. But in July 2006 it was again becoming apparent that preparations for elections were slipping and the deadline of October was again going to be missed.

Kofi Annan, who had invested so much in trying to solve the crisis of Côte d'Ivoire, and whose term as secretary general was coming to an end in December, made a last-ditch effort. At the African summit in Banjul, Gambia, in early July 2006, he convinced Gbagbo to have a summit immediately after, in Yamoussoukro, which was attended by all the key protagonists of the Ivoirian crisis, as well as Mbeki and Obasanjo. Before the summit, the secretary general had separate meetings with Gbagbo and Prime Minister Banny. We had hoped that there also would be a joint meeting, to demonstrate that the president and the prime minister were willing to work together, but that was too ambitious. Banny hosted the secretary general at the Fondation Houphouët-Boigny, while Gbagbo held the meeting in a huge room of the presidential palace. The setting and the atmosphere of the latter meeting were a vignette of all the ambiguities of Côte d'Ivoire: a splendid late Renaissance Beauvais tapestry provided the backdrop of the meeting with the president and made a strange contrast with the unappealing late 1960s–early 1970s architecture of the building. Drinks were brought. The secretary general soberly drank coconut milk; President Gbagbo, who never missed an occasion, when we met, of mentioning the memory of my leftist father, encouraged me to have a glass of rosé champagne.

That was, unfortunately, the high point of the summit. The subsequent discussion was disappointing, and although we managed to get agreement on a list of specific action points that were supposed to be reviewed in September, it was obvious that the momentum was not there. Stoudmann had told me there was no way to hold elections before the spring of 2007, even in a best-case scenario. The divisions of the international community were as wide as ever. While the French, the West Africans, and the secretary general wanted to take a strong position by giving a central role to the Security Council, President Mbeki continued to harbor doubts about that forceful approach, and his doubts were undermining it. But he had genuine reasons to harbor them, and I wonder whether what he saw happening in the fall confirmed his views.

Gbagbo did not attend the September review meeting on the action points. The protracted battle between the international community and President Gbagbo had now come to a head, as the October deadline loomed closer and the patient efforts to overcome, through technical means, the roadblocks that had been put in the way of elections, disarmament, and peace obviously had failed. What could now be done? The most ambitious scenario was that Gbagbo would be forced to surrender the presidency. That was unrealistic, for practical as well as political reasons. The president was not going to be legally deposed in Côte d'Ivoire, and he still had enough international support to exclude such a possibility. But the West African countries and France wanted to make his authority more dependent on decisions by the Security Council and to alter, through a resolution of the Security Council, the distribution of power in Côte d'Ivoire. The constitutional mandate of President Gbagbo had lapsed in October 2005, and that provided for an opening; the same month, Resolution 1633 had endorsed the decisions of the Peace and Security Council of the African Union and extended Gbagbo's mandate for one year, making the legitimacy of the president partly dependent on Security Council resolutions. But its language was careful, and it essentially called for the implementation of the Linas-Marcoussis agreement. The anti-Gbagbo camp now wanted to go further.

The Limits to Security Council Authority

Resolution 1721, adopted in November 2006, was the culmination of those efforts. The negotiations before its adoption, as well as its eventual failure to produce a breakthrough, provide a sobering lesson on the limits of the authority of the Security Council. What was at stake was the capacity of the Security Council to alter the internal constitutional order of a member state of the United Nations. Gbagbo immediately understood that if the debate was framed as a choice between national sovereignty and international law, many countries would balk, and he would win, as the guardian of Ivoirian national sovereignty. The negotiation leading up to the resolution was therefore quite difficult, as countries like China, Russia, but also the United States needed to be convinced that it was now necessary to go beyond the cautious language of 2005. Eventually the resolution affirmed that the "provisions [of the resolution] are intended to be applicable during the transition period until a newly elected President takes up his duties and a new National Assembly is elected." This bold language had been agreed only as an interim arrangement to fill a vacuum, but the wording gave a constitutional flavor to the resolution. However, the subsequent "provisions" described intentions and obligations rather than practical arrangements. And the apparent victory of those who supported the authority of the Security Council over national constitutional law was quickly undermined when a few days later the American ambassador in Côte d'Ivoire, after a meeting with President Gbagbo, clarified that indeed the Ivoirian constitution had a superior authority. The resolution, which was at the outer limit of what a Security Council mindful of state sovereignty could accept, did not achieve what its promoters had hoped for, and at the end of 2006 President Gbagbo seemed to be in a stronger position than a year earlier. Kofi Annan, who had shown a particular interest in trying to resolve the crisis, was leaving his position as secretary general, and it was not in Côte d'Ivoire but in France that a presidential election was going to take place. The symbolism of President Chirac leaving the Elysée before Gbagbo left his own presidential place was not lost on those who had toiled for four years to get closer to a political resolution of the crisis.

When President Gbagbo first met the new secretary general, Ban Ki-moon, in January 2007, he told him wearily: "Everybody is tired." Everybody was indeed tired, and that created an opportunity that Burkina Faso, a neighbor of Côte d'Ivoire, seized. On March 4, 2007, under the aegis of President Blaise Compaore, a new power-sharing agreement was signed between President Gbagbo and the rebels. Guillaume Soro, the leader of the Forces Nouvelles, the group that represented the core of the armed rebellion, was appointed prime minister. At thirty-five, he was from a much younger generation than Konan Bedie, Ouattara, or Banny, and he represented those who had guns. The heads of traditional parties might not be very happy with the arrangement, but there was little they could actually do to oppose it. It was hard for them to resist the push of Compaore, who was rumored to have given military support to the rebels in the past (many rebels were of Burkinabe origin, and the questioning of their *ivoirité* was a key element of the crisis). Many rumors then began to spread, suggesting that some secret deal had allegedly been made on the distribution of key positions after an election.

After the March agreement in Ouagadougou, the political dynamics shifted. Progress was expected—not from pressures of the Security Council, the African Union or ECOWAS, but from the direct engagement of the parties, prodded by the president of Burkina Faso. Nothing could be taken for granted, and an attempt against Soro's life in June 2007 was a stark reminder that there were still forces in Côte d'Ivoire that were not ready for a political deal. But the UN was not in a position to broker a better deal than the one on which Compaore was apparently working. Everybody in the Security Council and the Secretariat agreed that at this stage, the best option was to let the president of Burkina Faso lead. For the first time, thanks to him, instead of short and inconclusive summits, there was quiet but sustained engagement between the two sides. The role of the United Nations had changed. As Alpha Oumar Konare, who as a former president of Mali also had a keen interest in the resolution of the Ivoirian crisis, put it to the secretary general, the UN now had to "accompany the process." The UN was expected to continue to work on the technical arrangements needed for an effective disarmament and a credible election.

In April 2008 South Africa, which at the time was an elected member of the Security Council, organized a public debate on the conflicts of Africa. President Gbagbo spoke, and he drew conclusions that certainly pleased President Mbeki, but also Muammar Qaddafi of Libya (I heard him make exactly the same point to the secretary general). He said that the United Nations should focus on the resolution of interstate conflicts and should leave it to regional and subregional organizations to address intrastate conflicts. It was a self-serving point, but it also reflected the fact that the best hope to resolve the crisis had been brought by the neighbor who had the greatest stake in resolving it—a neighbor who also was close to one of the parties to the conflict. I was, however, not convinced. I had seen how decisive the role of the United Nations had been in ending the civil wars in Sierra Leone and Liberia, and I had little doubt that if the Democratic Republic of the Congo was to stabilize, it would need strong international engagement. I had seen time and again how the parties to many African conflicts were often suspicious of the intentions of their neighbors and actually called for an engagement of non-African countries. And in Côte d'Ivoire I had seen how actors managed to play the efforts of the AU and ECOWAS against each other. But it was also true that from the beginning of the crisis the attempts of the Security Council to force a solution through sanctions and increasingly tougher wording of resolutions had failed. Until 2011 there was no sense that Côte d'Ivoire was such a critical issue for the Security Council that it would be prepared to up the ante. Except for the West African countries of ECOWAS, no country, including South Africa and

France—which had first supported Gbagbo and then had consistently tried to weaken him—had a vital interest in the solution of the crisis. Burkina Faso did have such an interest. At the same time, looking back at the strenuous efforts that we made to maintain a flawed process on track, I think they were not in vain; they certainly did not produce a solution, and the unity of purposes more often than not was missing. There was no common vision between West Africa and South Africa, and France had its own agenda. But without those relentless pressures, without the threat of sanctions against individuals who were ready to use the dynamics of violence and hatred to advance their cause, it is very likely that Côte d'Ivoire would have again slipped into violence. International pressures were never going to produce peace, but they may well have prevented another war, and that is a worthwhile result. Frozen conflicts are better than hot war.

In 2010 the long-awaited presidential election finally happened. I was no longer working at the United Nations, and I had no inside knowledge of the efforts that had made such an outcome possible. I imagined that there had been some deal between the key protagonists—Gbagbo, Ouattara, and Bedie—because I never believed that Gbagbo would abandon power willingly. And I was astonished when I discovered that there was no such deal: the election had gone ahead because Gbagbo was convinced he would be the winner. He lost because Bedie—who had introduced the concept of *ivoirité!*—allied himself with Ouattara, thus dividing the southern part of the country while Ouattara could count on a united north. Unsurprisingly, Gbagbo did not accept the result, and the most serious crisis since the civil war of 2002 began. The international community showed surprising unity. Gbagbo had exhausted its patience, and the secretary general, the Security Council, the African Union, and ECOWAS, all called for his resignation. Predictably, he did not resign, but he was crushed by a combination of French and UN forces, and the elected president, Alassane Ouattara, took office.

For the first time in Africa, the result of an election was upheld through the intervention of foreign forces. In 1999 the American analyst Edward Luttwak wrote a provocative article in *Foreign Affairs* titled "Give War a Chance!" It was a kind of epitaph to the inconclusive posture of the international community during most of the Yugoslav conflict. In 2011 war was indeed given a chance, and this was an extraordinary outcome. I want to believe that this "happy" ending will mark the end of a long civil war and a victory for democracy. But I am still afraid that it may be only a temporary lull in the confrontation that pits the north of the country against the south. So long as Ouattara remains president, one may hope that he will be able to rein in the militias that supported him, and to reach out to the supporters of his former opponent; the rapid economic development of Côte d'Ivoire is another hopeful sign. But Ouattara has lost an important ally with the fall of Compaore in neighboring Burkina Faso in late 2014, and it is far from assured that the younger, more militant generation of Ivoirians is ready for reconciliation. The north-south issues that divide West African countries are still not resolved, and what happens in Côte d'Ivoire can become a life-or-death issue not only for Ivoirians but also for the citizens of neighboring countries working in Côte d'Ivoire, and by implication for the whole region.

Making elections the centerpiece of the solution raises the stakes in a dramatic way. If differences of opinion have been so fundamental that they have led to a war, it is very risky to expect those who were ready to die for their cause to accept the results of an election as if it was the judgment of God, in some modern form of a medieval tournament. For one side to win everything and for the other to lose everything is unlikely to work for very long. This all-or-nothing approach is a precarious foundation for peace, if it is not complemented by a much broader effort.

I am again reminded of what the European ambassador had told me at the height of the crisis: "In Africa, you need victors and vanquished." At the time, I had replied that the United Nations cannot and should not pick a winner; it can only support a process. I still believe it, and I think the UN loses its most valuable asset, the trust of the people, if it becomes a cover for a strategy designed by outsiders to empower a handpicked leader. But supporting an electoral process is not enough. A lot of time and effort could have been saved, in Côte d'Ivoire and other countries, if the focus of the international community was from the outset to help broker solutions in the success of which all actors would have a stake. Hiding behind an electoral process is more comfortable, but it is not necessarily more democratic, and certainly not more ethical. If the winners are not prepared to respect the losers, if the losers are not prepared to concede—in other words if the foundations of democracy have not been built and have not been widely accepted—an election may well become the trigger of a new cycle of violence. I hope it will not be the case in Côte d'Ivoire.

five
DEMOCRATIC REPUBLIC OF THE CONGO
The Limits of the Use of Force

The idea of humanitarian intervention has an appealing moral clarity. It was not seriously considered in 1994, when the Rwandan genocide happened, however. It was tested in 1999—at the price of deep divisions in the Security Council, which did not authorize the operation—when NATO intervened in Kosovo to stop ethnic cleansing. Four years later, in 2003, the Security Council was again confronted, repeatedly, with the question of intervention. The Iraq war was not a case of humanitarian intervention, and no agreement was reached on the use of force. But while most of the world was focused on Iraq, three African crises developed, all of which had the potential to become immense tragedies and raised the question of humanitarian intervention. I was involved in all three: What I did and did not do at the time illustrates the ethical dilemmas facing an international civil servant. Did I tell the Security Council what it "needed to know" rather than what it "wanted to hear," to quote the 2000 Brahimi report on peacekeeping? Was I forceful enough? The three crises unfolded in very different ways, and they illustrate the difficulty of answering those questions even years later.

As described in chapter 4, the first crisis was in Côte d'Ivoire, where the extremely violent tone of the media had ominous similarities with the hate messages of *Radio Mille Collines* of Rwanda at the time of the genocide. The Ivoirian crisis would actually last several years, and although it never exploded into a full-blown civil war, there were several dangerous spasms. The United Nations played a patient and thankless role, managing a delaying game that may have contributed to avoiding the worst, but there was never—until 2011—a decisive moment, just a long series of aborted dramas. The second crisis was in the Darfur region of Sudan, which was largely ignored in 2003 and early 2004, when violence was at its worst, but became a global cause in the middle of 2004. That is when I myself became deeply involved. The third crisis took place in the Democratic Republic of the Congo (DRC). For 4.5 million Congolese living in Ituri, the north-eastern corner of Congo, 2003 was the year when they came terribly close to a total breakdown, as violence spiked and the prospect of massive killings—if not genocide—became more and more real. For me, those fateful weeks of May 2003 were to be the longest in my life, as I realized that I was facing in Congo the possibility of a replica of Srebrenica, Bosnia—where 7,000 people were murdered on the UN's watch—or even Rwanda, where 800,000 people were murdered in 100 days, while the international community stood by.

More than a decade after that decisive period in 2003, both the Democratic Republic of the Congo and Sudan are still in crisis, and the risk of major violence is still there. And yet, they are the two countries where the United Nations has invested the most. For the millions who mobilized to "save Darfur," and for me, who spent more personal efforts on those two countries than on any other, it is time to ask harsh questions: Did we do the right thing? Or was it all futile agitation? I will examine both cases in detail. In the case of Darfur, I have doubts. In the case of Congo, I continue to believe that we made a difference, but I now better understand how important luck and sometimes sheer coincidence can be, and how the moral and operational clarity of the public debate on humanitarian intervention does not really help us find our way in the fog of imperfect peace. In the confusion of events, we have to move one step at a time, exploiting momentum when we can, but sometimes even backsliding. In that protracted chess game with the devil—I should say devils, there are many of them, large and small—there is never a checkmate moment. The story I want to tell is the story of that uncertain march, in which you know that abstention would be wrong, but you can never be sure that you are doing right.

From the outset, the international community had no grand design for Congo, and the members of the Security Council who at the end of 1999 authorized the UN mission known as MONUC in the newly renamed Democratic Republic of the Congo had no idea of what they were going into. The world stumbled into Congo.

The Democratic Republic of the Congo is a huge country, the size of western Europe, with the second-largest rainforest of the world and with few interconnecting features beyond the River Congo itself. Its transportation infrastructure is nonexistent or dilapidated and fails to bind the country together. It is a kind of inland archipelago, with islands of urban and mining centers in an ocean of forest. The longtime dictator Mobutu Sésé Seko controlled the country, then known as Zaire, by dominating urban centers, as he was able to quash any resistance one city at a time. But with the end of the cold war, Zaire had lost its strategic importance for his Western patrons, and Mobutu was on his own. He opened up to opposition leaders in 1991, but kept control of the security forces. It was the facade of a state rather than a real state, as public administration was weak, the considerable resources accruing from the mines were largely diverted into private pockets, and most of the security forces were rarely paid, except for those dedicated to the security of the president. It should therefore not have been a surprise that in the immediate aftermath of the genocide in neighboring Rwanda, the Hutu *genocidaires* who had been defeated by opposition leader and future Rwandan president Paul Kagame crossed the borders into the DRC, accompanied by hundreds of thousands of Hutus who were fleeing the revenge of Kagame's Tutsi forces. A controversial French-led European operation temporarily alleviated the suffering of many of the refugees who were caught in the turmoil, but in the midst of them were many killers who had taken active part in the genocide. The contrast could not be greater between densely populated Rwanda, with few natural resources, and the loosely controlled vastness of Congo, full of riches and now a haven for some of the leaders of the genocide, as well as for those who felt threatened by the new regime in Rwanda. This was a situation that Kagame, now in control of Rwanda, did not accept, and together with an anti-Mobutu rebel, Laurent-Désiré Kabila, he swiftly captured much of eastern Zaire by late 1996. Revenge killings took place, and in the process many Congolese people were killed, becoming collateral victims of the Rwandan genocide. Kabila then went all the way to the capital Kinshasa in May 1997, where he was installed as president. But the alliance between the two leaders quickly broke down, and in the summer of 1998 war resumed. Two rebel movements opposed to Kabila, the Movement for the Liberation of Congo (MLC) and the Congolese Rally for Democracy (RDC), supported respectively by Uganda and Rwanda, tried to march to Kinshasa. Meanwhile, Namibia and Zimbabwe joined the fight on Kabila's side and would later be followed by Angola. A second full-fledged civil war then started, involving six African countries. Congo was now cut in two, and it took more than a year for the six countries and three rebel movements assembled in Lusaka to reach a cease-fire agreement that detailed the modalities for the eventual withdrawal of occupying armies and the reunification of the country. The July 1999 agreement, which had been negotiated by African leaders and not by the UN, nevertheless called on the United Nations for its implementation.

When it established the MONUC mission in November 1999, the Security Council limited its tasks to monitoring the cease-fire and subsequent withdrawal of the armies that had fought during the first Congo War to overthrow

Mobutu. However, the resemblance to a traditional peacekeeping mission in which UN observers monitor a cease-fire and report violations was superficial at best. This was not Cyprus. First, some of the national armies that were parties to the agreement had weak chains of command, and once in Congo, the attraction of its considerable resources was to prove irresistible. The rebel movements were even less accountable, however, and their strong ties with neighboring countries raised the questions of possible ulterior motives for their actions: They were rebels; they could also be proxies. And a fundamental ambiguity remained on the status of the parties: while the Lusaka agreement specified that all parties would "enjoy equal status," it also affirmed the sovereignty of Congo, of which the government in Kinshasa considered itself the depository.

Further complicating the UN's efforts, several armed groups were not signatories of the cease-fire agreement. The main group was the Forces Democratiques de Liberation du Rwanda (FDLR), the core of which were the former genocidaires of Rwanda, who had now settled in the forests and mining areas of the Kivu in the eastern DRC. The Lusaka agreement provided that such armed groups should be "tracked down" by the forces that were party to the agreement. Who would "track down" genocidaires in the vast Congolese jungle was unclear, however, and this task would be further complicated by the fact that those fighting under the FDLR label also included a range of Hutu opponents to the regime of Paul Kagame; these opponents had not committed crimes during the genocide but had challenged his leadership, including some of them by military means. Meanwhile, from the perspective of some officials in Kinshasa, the FDLR was a proxy force and an ally on which they relied to fight the Rwandan enemy.

The Security Council, when it adopted Resolution 1291 creating MONUC, referred to the Lusaka agreement but refrained from tasking MONUC with "tracking down" the FDLR in the forests of Congo. Where should MONUC's priorities then be? There were deeply conflicting expectations. The Congolese leadership in Kinshasa wanted the UN to kick out foreign troops and help re-establish the sovereignty of the country. The Rwandan leadership expected MONUC to "track down" the genocidaires; the view of Kigali was that because the international community had done nothing to stop the genocide, it now had a duty to pursue the genocidaires. As President Kagame once told me, the issue of the genocidaires was not a Rwandan issue, it was an issue for the world. As for the Western permanent members of the Security Council, they were divided by their own historical infighting over the DRC: Rwanda had represented a fault line between francophone and anglophone Africa, and the victory of Paul Kagame, who had spent years of exile in English-speaking

Uganda, clearly tilted Rwanda toward anglophone Africa. In that context many Congolese saw France as a natural ally of francophone Congo while they suspected Britain and the United States of supporting Rwanda. While divided by history, all the members of the Security Council were united by a shared sense of guilt. But guilt did not lead to a clear strategic direction. On the one hand, the nations represented on the council understood the difficulty of military action and did not want to have any part in it. France, for example, was initially wary of an emphasis on military means that would legitimize Rwandan actions in the DRC and further tilt the strategic and economic balance in favor of Rwanda and Anglophone Africa. On the other hand, all the members of the council were uncomfortable at the prospect of being accused of not doing everything to suppress the genocidaires.

This lack of strategic clarity led to a long proxy war between Rwanda and the DRC, and an extension into DRC territory of Rwandan domestic politics. Over the years, the FDLR mingled with the Congolese population, as Hutu combatants and noncombatants took Congolese wives. After years in the bush and effective Rwandan operations in the early 2000s, the FDLR have been considerably weakened; there are probably no more than a few thousand FDLR combatants today, a far cry from the tens of thousands when MONUC was first deployed, and they no longer present a significant military threat to Rwanda. But within the DRC they have remained a dangerous armed group that greatly contributes to the suffering of the Congolese population, as they exploit natural resources and take revenge on the population when challenged. They also are a lingering political threat to Rwanda. The continued refusal of the majority of FDLR to disarm reflects both the control of the FDLR leadership over its rank and file—exercised through the most brutal means—and also the lack of trust that many Rwandan Hutus who took refuge in the DRC have in the possibility of a genuine reconciliation in Rwanda.

I became aware only gradually of these strategic and moral ambiguities as my knowledge of Congo developed. I visited the Democratic Republic of the Congo nine times during my tenure—more than any other country with a peacekeeping operation. When the crisis of 2003 started, I had already been in Congo three times, including one visit with Kofi Annan in September 2001.

In the early days of 2001 the UN troops deployed essentially were guard units that were protecting the small UN bases that had been established along the cease-fire line, each positioned so that the circle defined by the range of an MI-8 helicopter would overlap with the circle of the next base. Because the DRC is such a big country, the total number of peacekeepers—some 5,000— appeared large on paper, creating the false impression that MONUC had greater capacity to intervene and protect civilians than it actually had, given its sprinkling of small detachments scattered around the country. At the time, I even considered the possibility of reducing the number of UN troops, as foreign armies began to withdraw, to remind the world that MONUC essentially was an observer mission whose mandate was to monitor the withdrawal of foreign forces, not to establish peace in the DRC. There was a narrow technical logic to that position, but while hiding behind a flawed mandate might superficially protect the UN, it would not help the people, as I would find out in my first visit to the DRC in the spring of 2001. In the east, MONUC was seen as the force that would free the country from its occupiers, and when a Moroccan battalion started deploying in Kisangani in April 2001, the welcoming crowd was so big—to the great displeasure of the rebel movement allied with Rwanda that controlled the city, the Congolese Rally for Democracy-Goma (RCD-Goma)—that it took hours for the troops to get from the airport to their camp. MONUC did not have much capacity, but it raised expectations; this could be very dangerous. The Moroccans in Kisangani would soon enough find out how difficult it was to be caught between the RCD-Goma, the Rwandans, and the Congolese population. One year later, on May 14, 2002, in what was later called the May Rebellion, more than 150 Congolese would be brutally killed in Kisangani, as the RCD-Goma and the troops of Laurent Nkunda—a Tutsi officer backed by Rwanda who would play a central role in several crises—asserted their domination of a restive population. MONUC troops, vastly outnumbered in this large city, watched and did not halt the violence. In 2002 the killings in Kisangani played an important role in delegitimizing the presence of foreign troops in Congo: the incident was the first of several in which MONUC failed to meet the expectations of the people it had come to help. In the spring of 2001, however, what was most apparent was the dynamic of reunification that the deployment of MONUC was encouraging.

Laurent-Désiré Kabila had been assassinated in January 2001, in circumstances that remain unclear to this day. While he had appeared to support military options to end the occupation of the DRC by Rwanda and Uganda, his son Joseph, who succeeded him, seemed more inclined to favor political solutions. A "prayer breakfast" in Washington in February 2001 provided the occasion for the first meeting between Paul Kagame and Joseph Kabila. But the mistrust between the two leaders ran deep, and when I arrived in Kinshasa in April 2001, its "Grand Hotel" was still full of officers from the countries allied with Kabila. The country was cut in two, and Kinshasa was the capital of a country at war. The Grand Hotel was a bizarre mix, part military headquarters, with officers in military fatigues who would have found it insulting to pay for their rooms, and part brothel, judging by the number of prostitutes in the corridors.

The job of MONUC was extremely difficult: monitoring the cease-fire rigorously would have meant reporting every instance in which one of the parties used some proxy force to enlarge the area it controlled. Both sides did it, and MONUC, whose headquarters was based in the capital of one of the parties, often turned a blind eye on violations committed by the Kinshasa side. That had not protected it from the hostility of Laurent-Désiré Kabila, who expected the mission to shore up his authority against rebels. The special representative of the secretary general, Kamel Morjane, was a Tunisian who had made a priority of helping the reunification of the country under Kinshasa's terms and did not want to damage his relations with the president. In the absence of a clear political process, it was unclear on whose terms unity would be achieved, but there was a sense of hope, and all the talk was about withdrawal of the foreign forces and reunification. Morjane was focusing on practical measures, working hard to reopen the River Congo, the main artery of the country, to civilian traffic. But we knew that more fundamental issues would need to be addressed: the reconciliation of the DRC with its neighbors, the reconciliation of the Congolese with themselves, and the creation of an effective state.

In the early 2000s Congo was an occupied country, and the most pressing questions were how to trigger the departure of foreign troops and then manage the consequences of their departure. There were two main levers to encourage the departure of foreign troops. One was to embarrass the states whose troops were present in the DRC by raising questions about the motives behind their presence. The second was to deprive them of any legitimate rationale for their presence in the DRC.

The embarrassment was provided by the report of a UN Panel of Experts on the Illegal Exploitation of Natural Resources and Other Forms of Wealth of the Democratic Republic of the Congo. The panel had been created by the secretary general at the insistence of the president of the Security Council in June 2000.[1] The report issued in April 2001 was damning for all the armies present in the DRC and the respective states they came from.[2] They were each accused of exploiting the natural resources of the country. The report did not single out one side; Zimbabwe, an ally of Kabila, was accused as well as Uganda and Rwanda. The Ugandans reacted furiously, and their ally in the DRC, Jean-Pierre Bemba, the leader of the newly formed union between RCD-ML and

1. Presidential statement of the Security Council, June 2, 2000 (S/PRST/2000/20).
2. Report of the Panel of Experts on the Illegal Exploitation of Natural Resources and Other Forms of Wealth of the Democratic Republic of the Congo, April 12, 2001 (S/2001/375) (www.un.org/news/dh/latest/drcongo.htm).

the MLC, the Congolese Liberation Front (CLF), violently rejected its con-clusions. I first met Bemba in his provisional capital of Gbadolite, a dilapi-dated city that nevertheless boasted one of Mobutu's palaces and an airport with a runway long enough for Mobutu to land his chartered Concorde when he flew back from Europe. Bemba said the report was part of a plot against him and Congo, a "Plan Malachite," cooked up by France and Belgium, and he insisted he had documents to prove it; they were in his safe and would be released if anything happened to him. The leader of the RCD-Goma, Adolphe Onusumba, was also very vocal about the report, but it was not even men-tioned by my Rwandan interlocutors when I went to Kigali.

Depriving Rwanda and Uganda of any legitimate rationale to be in Congo required the elimination of the threat posed by former genocidaires. This would be more difficult. In Kigali, my Rwandan interlocutors were stressing the need to forcefully disarm the genocidaires and were accusing Kinshasa of giving support to them. In September 2001, the idea of a joint force combin-ing the RCD-Goma and the MLC—the two movements allied respectively to Uganda and Rwanda—that would disarm armed groups was mentioned. Rwanda was of course right to have doubts about the realism of voluntary dis-armament for hardened genocidaires. But the 40,000 members of the Hutu militia known as the *interhamwe* that Rwanda claimed to be in eastern Congo were not all hardened genocidaires, and the international community (and MONUC) was right to advocate voluntary disarmament for the majority of them. The reason was that the more coercive disarmament was mentioned and military operations were launched by Rwandan or RCD-Goma troops against FDLR and *interhamwe*, the less likely it was that members of the armed groups would risk crossing "enemy lines" to surrender their weapons in a process of voluntary disarmament. The long saga of a group of some 3,000 Rwandan Hutus who were cantoned in a military base at Kamina provided a good illustration of the problem. They did not want to go back to Rwanda, and Rwanda did not want them back; this led to endless negotiations. Even-tually, in April 2002, South Africa organized the forced repatriation of a few of them. Instead of unblocking the situation, this hardened the position of those Hutus left behind. Suspicions between the two capitals ran deep, as Kigali knew that Hutu fighters in Congo were getting support from Kinshasa. Peace in eastern Congo requires an understanding between Kigali and Kin-shasa, which did not exist in 2002, but also needed is a profound evolution in the internal politics of Rwanda: a new attitude toward the Hutus, who repre-sent 80 percent of the population. That still has not happened.

The ambassadors of the United Kingdom and France to the United Nations, Jeremy Greenstock and Jean-David Lévitte, understood that the positions of their respective countries could have a great influence on the relations between Kigali and Kinshasa. So long as Rwanda felt supported by London and the DRC by Paris, there was little hope for compromise and progress. The two ambassadors convinced their respective foreign ministers, Jack Straw and Hubert Védrine, to undertake a joint visit to the Democratic Republic of the Congo and to Rwanda in January 2002. The trip was carefully prepared, and the two ministers spent enough time in the two countries to ensure that their visit would be more than a photo opportunity. It was a great success on several counts. For Rwandan as well as Congolese leaders, the mere fact of a Franco-British joint effort was deeply disturbing, in a very positive way: it challenged the basic assumptions underpinning the hard-line positions that Congo and Rwanda took on their bilateral relations. For the two European ministers, it was a reality check that helped both countries recognize that their respective "protégés" needed to be more strongly encouraged to soften their positions. I was told that the conversation in Kigali had not been easy.

I would have a flavor of the tone of the meeting a few weeks later, when I had my own first personal encounter with Rwandan president Kagame in Kigali. I had met him with Kofi Annan before, but I had seen only his aides in another visit to Kigali without the secretary general. The president of Rwanda obviously managed his time very carefully, and probably initially thought that a French head of UN peacekeeping was just a puppet of France. But in February 2002 he decided that it was now time to meet me, and I was asked to come to the presidential mansion in the evening. I was ushered into a meeting room a couple of minutes before the scheduled time, his aides showed up just before the president, and the president himself appeared exactly on time. I would observe the same ritual in all my subsequent visits. The message of control and organized power was not lost on me. The conversation lasted an hour and a half, and I understood why Kagame is one of the most respected, but also most feared, leaders of Africa. There was no small talk, nothing gratuitous in what he said, every sentence had a message, and all his points were woven together in an impeccable logic. He reminded me that getting rid of the genocidaires was an international responsibility and that Rwanda was doing what the international community should do, what the DRC was apparently unable to do. One could sense the distance between him, who was running his country like a little Prussia, and his weak neighbor to the west. When I told him that the extended presence of Rwanda in the DRC was not making friends for his country there and was undermining the Congolese ally of Rwanda, the RCD-Goma, he cut me off sharply: "We are not in Congo to be liked!"

It was a lesson in realpolitik, and realpolitik did lay the groundwork for the eventual withdrawal of foreign troops. In addition to the Franco-British rapprochement on Congo, several factors played a role. The May Rebellion in Kisangani in 2002 against Rwandan-supported RCD-Goma forces showed that the occupation and division of Congo was unsustainable, and it was an embarrassment for the Security Council, which had been discussing the "responsibility to protect" at headquarters almost at the same time. The position of the United States also was evolving toward a more balanced approach to the DRC and Rwanda. A few days after the event in Kisangani, Steve Hadley, President George W. Bush's national security advisor, informed me that while Clare Short, the strongly pro-Rwanda development minister of the United Kingdom, had tried to block IMF support to the DRC, her move was not only defeated by France but also by the United States, which had hardened its position on Rwanda and now wanted Rwandan troops to withdraw from the DRC. Meanwhile, on the Kabila side, quiet efforts had been made to accelerate the disengagement of the "allies" as Namibian, Zimbabwean, and Angolan troops were called. Angola very astutely convinced Zimbabwe to leave. The "allies" were now leaving, and they would all be gone by the end of 2002.

A Turning Point

The political turning point was reached in July 2002, at the summit in Durban that transformed the Organization of African Unity into the African Union. The creation of the African Union was a major diplomatic achievement for South African president Thabo Mbeki, who also was gradually increasing South Africa's role in the DRC peace effort. South Africa was now host, in Sun City, to the Inter-Congolese Dialogue, which brought together all Congolese factions, and President Mbeki used the momentum of the summit to organize a meeting between President Kagame and President Kabila in Durban. Three weeks later, in Pretoria on July 30, the two presidents, in the presence of President Mbeki, signed a far-reaching agreement: Rwanda pledged to withdraw its troops from the DRC, while the DRC pledged to "track down" the Hutu fighters, known as ex-FAR *interhamwe*, who had been members of the armed forces of Rwanda during the 1994 genocide. Rwanda, however, did not commit to absorb any of the ex-FAR. A "third party verification mechanism," comprising South Africa in its dual capacity of chair of the AU and facilitator of the Congolese peace process and the United Nations, was instituted to monitor the implementation of the agreement. The United Nations had not been involved in the negotiation, which was managed entirely by South Africa, and I was initially quite skeptical that it would be a strategic turning point. I was wrong. The government of the DRC took action against FDLR leaders, declaring twenty-five of them persona non grata and arresting and transferring to an international court a well-known genocidaire. Although a meeting between President Kabila and President Kagame scheduled for the end of August in Kinshasa was eventually canceled (Kagame visited Kabila in Kinshasa for the first time in 2010), on September 13 the two presidents met in New York, in the presence of Kofi Annan, George W. Bush, Thabo Mbeki, and Uganda's Yoweri Museveni. On September 17 President Kagame made the spectacular announcement that Rwanda was starting to pull out its troops from the DRC. Two weeks later, on October 5, the withdrawal of 23,000 Rwandan troops was completed. This was an extraordinary logistical and political achievement, which demonstrated the remarkable capacity of Rwanda to take and implement bold decisions. It fit a pattern that I would observe time and again. President Kagame was capable of swift action, realistically taking into account the international configuration of forces, but never appearing to bend to pressure, as the rapidity of his actions went beyond what was expected and conveyed a message of decisiveness and strategic vision.

The withdrawal of Ugandan troops would prove to be a more complicated and dangerous affair. In Luanda on September 6, 2002, Museveni and Kabila had signed, in the presence of Angolan president José Eduardo Dos Santos, who was the facilitator of that particular process, an agreement that provided for the withdrawal of Ugandan forces. It was important that parallel progress be made by Congo in its bilateral relations with Uganda and with Rwanda: the two eastern neighbors of the DRC have a complicated relationship. Kagame was for many years of exile hosted by Museveni, but the relationship between the two countries has fluctuated considerably over the years. They are competing for influence and economic rewards in eastern Congo, to the point that Congo has sometimes been a kind of battleground for an indirect war fought through proxy militias. Neither of the two countries can afford to let the other have a dominant influence over their common neighbor, and each therefore watches carefully what the other is doing.

After the swift withdrawal of Rwandan troops, the conditions under which the Ugandans would effectively withdraw, and which authority would fill the void created by the departure of foreign troops, had to be addressed. In areas previously controlled by Rwandan troops, there were some attempts to tip the military balance against Rwanda's Congolese ally, RCD-Goma, which wanted to maintain control. The town of Uvira in South Kivu, for example, was temporarily occupied by Mai Mai forces (the Mai Mai, present throughout the east, are a Congolese group usually aligned with Kinshasa) who were allied with the ex–armed forces of Rwanda (ex-FAR) *interhamwe*. But after a strong protest by Kigali, they withdrew from the town, which was then reoccupied by RCD-Goma forces.

The situation was much more complex in Ituri, which was occupied by Ugandan troops. This remote district of rolling hills in the northeastern corner of the DRC has easy connections to both Uganda and Rwanda, and it has its own political dynamics, distinct from North and South Kivu. It traditionally feels neglected by Kinshasa, but it is the richest district of Orientale Province. Ituri boasts the biggest gold field in the world, Kilomoto, and it also produces coltan, a mineral used in microchips for cell phones. Ethnically, this district of roughly three million people is much more complex than the Kivus. While much has been made of the opposition between the Hemas, who are of Nilotic ethnicity and are often compared to the Tutsi, and the Lendus, who are Bantus and often compared to the Hutus, the existence of many other ethnic groups has historically been a stabilizing factor preventing the dangerous ethnic polarization between Tutsi and Hutus that tore apart Rwanda and Burundi. But in 2002–03 the appetite for the vast resources of Ituri and the manipulation of traditional ethnic tensions were a deadly combination. I had had a first hint of the possibility of murderous ethnic violence during my first trip to the DRC, in April 2001, when a young Togolese, Gilbert Bawara, who would later become a minister in his own country but at the time was working for MONUC, had shared with me his fear that the eastern DRC—the Kivus and Ituri—might be torn apart by ethnic violence. He recommended that we address that threat through local political mechanisms that would bring the various communities together. Nothing had been done, however, and the security situation was deteriorating. A few people were trying to call the attention of the international community to the violence that was steadily killing people in the Kivus, but there was little interest in MONUC for a strong engagement, all the more so as it would have meant challenging the government's policies, which preferred integrating Mai Mai fighters into the Congolese army, rather than supporting mediation efforts between the Mai Mai and the RCD-Goma, a strategy that would have opened a political space in the Kivus. It was in any case difficult to have an ambitious political strategy in an occupied country where MONUC played a marginal role. Ituri was a different case because it involved not only the proxy war between Kinshasa and its eastern neighbors of Uganda and Rwanda but also the rivalry between Uganda and Rwanda. As early as 2001 violence had flared against international actors when six employees of the Red Cross were murdered near Bunia, the capital of the district, and questions were raised whether that brutal act was a warning of what was in store if the international community persisted in demanding the departure of all foreign troops. By the end of 2002, the situation was deteriorating in the northeastern DRC. Just before the new year, I received a worried call from Lena Sundh, the Swedish deputy special representative of the secretary general, who was afraid that the situation in Beni, a key town on the road that connects Ituri to the Kivus, might get out of hand. The situation was further complicated by the prospect of an Inter-Congolese Dialogue: each group wanted to create facts on the ground and control as much territory as possible to strengthen its position at the negotiating table, which led to an intensification of fighting. In early spring 2003, massacres started in Ituri, and on March 10 I informed the Security Council, which certainly had other priorities since we were just ten days away from the start of the Iraq war.

The head of the peacekeeping mission in Congo since the fall of 2001 was a dedicated Cameroonian with a strong humanitarian background, Namanga Ngongi. He had spent most of his career with the World Food Program, where he had become the second-in-command, and he brought to Congo a profound empathy for the people of the country. He was less interested in politics than in saving lives. He did not believe in guns and worried both his bodyguards and me by insisting they be unarmed. But in the critical months of 2003, his dedication would make an enormous difference; without him, many more people would have died in Ituri. He made strenuous efforts in March 2003 to negotiate a cease-fire in Ituri as tens of thousands of people were being displaced by increasing violence. He finally succeeded on March 18, and part of the deal was that the Ugandan troops would leave by April 24. This was important to Rwanda, which was threatening to come back to Congo if the Ugandans did not leave. Bunia, the capital of Ituri, had changed hands a couple of times, and the situation there was dire. Militarily, the inadequacy of the UN mandate and of the UN force was becoming more obvious every day. The plan that we had proposed to the Security Council envisaged a two-phased voluntary disarmament process focused on the ex-FAR *interhamwe* of the Kivus. There was little appetite in Kinshasa for its implementation, and it did not correspond to the reality in Ituri, which involved several ethnic militias loosely connected to Rwanda and Uganda. The news that reached New York was horrific. Acts of cannibalism were perpetrated by the same militias whose leaders were negotiating the future of Congo, and their position in that future, in the luxurious South African resort of Sun City. Special Representative Ngongi was pleading to deploy troops in Ituri. But the disarmament task forces, composed of South African and Bangladeshi soldiers, had been planned for the Kivus, not Ituri. The South Africans were complaining that the UN was slow in organizing their deployment, but they were not themselves ready.

The Crisis in Ituri

I made the most important decision of my tenure as head of peacekeeping at the beginning of April, when I decided to deploy a Uruguayan battalion already stationed in Congo to Bunia. Miraculously, the government of Uruguay agreed to the transfer. Ngongi had pushed hard for the move. I saw all the risks of the decision. From a narrowly legal standpoint, my hands were not tied: so long as we had no troops deployed in Ituri, we had no formal obligation to protect the population there, since the resolution empowering MONUC carefully specified that MONUC was to protect civilians in imminent danger only "in the areas of deployment of its infantry battalions and as it deems within its capabilities." If we deployed, the legal situation would change, since we would have created a legal obligation for ourselves. I was never convinced by such technicalities. In the face of a human tragedy, I knew I would find little solace in the knowledge that I had not been legally obliged to intervene. Having deployed, the real question was: could action be taken that would be effective and stop the violence? And the answer to the question was morally and operationally difficult to formulate. Morally, any deployment would immediately raise expectations, and the desperate people of Bunia would see it as a promise of the United Nations to ensure their safety. But would we be able to keep our promise, or would we have another of the UN's darkest moments, another Srebrenica?

The crisis of Ituri confronted me for the first time with a dilemma that is at the heart of peacekeeping: it is the choice between the risk of a failed intervention—which can damage the credibility of peacekeeping so much that peacekeeping is no longer available for those situations where it could make a real difference—and the risk of abstention in a situation where intervention could have prevented mass atrocities. What is worse? To lose the capacity to help in the future for the pretense of helping in a hopeless situation, or to live with the thought that horrors happened that you might have stopped if you had acted. You know the answer only in hindsight. In Ituri, I decided for intervention. It was a huge gamble. The Uruguayan troops were a guard unit not really prepared for the immensely difficult situation of Bunia, and I was more doubtful than SRSG Ngongi of their capacity to make a critical operational difference on the ground. Actually, what we had feared almost immediately happened. As soon as the Uruguayans began to deploy, thousands of desperate displaced persons made their way to the airstrip where they were landing and to the UN compound in the center of the city. Two large spontaneous camps appeared in a matter of days. The people believed we had made them a promise, and I knew how uncertain and fragile that promise was.

My hope in making the decision for deployment was to have a political impact as much as an operational one. In the best-case scenario, the bold gesture of deploying UN blue helmets in the middle of a crisis could change the political dynamics on the ground, as various troublemakers would understand that the commitment of the international community was stronger than they had anticipated. The Ugandan troops were reluctant to withdraw, and there were rumors that chaos might be organized to prove how necessary it was that they stay in Ituri. A UN deployment would reinforce the message that they had to leave, and it would make it more complicated to escalate the violence. In the more likely worst-case scenario, UN troops would not stop the violence, but their presence would draw the attention of the whole world to an unfolding tragedy that otherwise might go unnoticed, and that focus might make it possible to build enough political momentum to deploy an emergency bridging force, and then transform MONUC into a stronger and more proactive force.

From the moment the decision was made, implementation was a race against time. The Uruguayan battalion had no capacity to support itself, the only way to bring troops to Bunia was by air, and the airstrip was in poor condition. This was an enormous logistical challenge for the understaffed and under-resourced UN, and our logisticians and staff officers had to show a lot of ingenuity to make a rapid deployment possible. The armored personnel carriers (APCs in military parlance) of the Uruguayan unit were airlifted using the MI 26, our most powerful helicopter. C-130 and small Antonov transport planes moved troops, rations, ammunition, and all that was necessary to build a military camp, from prefabs to generators and concertina wire. Every day, at the morning meeting in New York, I would be told how many Uruguayans and how many APCs had arrived in Bunia, and how many were operational. The first days were particularly tense, when the numbers deployed were so small that they could not have defended themselves at all if attacked.

By April 26 there were 225 troops in Bunia. On that same day, however, we learned that a military observer had been killed sixty-five kilometers north of Bunia when his vehicle hit a freshly laid mine. This was an ominous sign. Even as we gained small standing in Bunia, the situation was continuing to deteriorate throughout the district of Ituri. It looked more and more like the second scenario I had envisaged. The situation in Bunia was awful: our troops provided limited protection to thousands of terrified Congolese who were huddling near our camps, people were getting killed by mortar shells, the sanitary situation was appalling, and women and children with horrific wounds caused by machetes found limited relief in an emergency room that had been improvised in a decrepit building.

By the end of April, I knew that the UN alone would not be able to stop the horror. The only hope was the deployment of a strong multinational force that would send a clear message to all actors that this time, the international community was not going to run away, as it had done nine years before in Rwanda. But the difficulty would be to find a "lead nation." A multinational force cannot be launched if it is not anchored by a strong army around which armies of other nations can rally. And there are very few countries in the world that have the capacity to deploy an expeditionary force at short notice. On the African continent, South Africa was the most likely candidate, but I knew it was already stretched and had difficulties accelerating its deployment in MONUC. In America, the United States obviously was focusing on Iraq, and Canada, traumatized by the experience of Rwanda, where a brave Canadian general, Roméo Dallaire, had been abandoned by the international community, was not going to come back to Africa in any significant way. In Europe, the United Kingdom was engaged in Iraq. France was the only option: it had strong experience of deployments in Africa and had already been in the eastern DRC when it led the deployment of "Operation Turquoise" in Goma after the Rwandan genocide. The French experience was a double-edged sword, however, as "Turquoise" was considered by the Rwandan leadership to have helped the génocidaires flee to Congo.

I raised the alarm in the Security Council on Monday, May 5. I now needed the support of the United States and the engagement of France. I soon learned that my briefing had had an impact on the United States. This was of critical importance. The Security Council was still reeling from its battles over the Iraq war, and without strong American support, there was no realistic prospect that the council would authorize the deployment of a multinational force. But the French mission to the UN was less than enthusiastic. How could I turn the crisis of Iraq into an opportunity for Congo? How would I line up the right set of personalities to make the right decisions?

The Security Council was in disarray. All its members were still in a state of shock that the council had been sidelined when the United States and United Kingdom decided to go ahead with the war in Iraq. Both enemies and friends of the UN were questioning the relevance of the institution. If it was seen to be incapable of stopping what could become another genocide, its future might well be in danger. This consideration should be particularly relevant for France, whose clout, as a permanent member, was linked to the clout of the council itself. France had taken the lead of the anti-Iraq war camp, rightly convinced that its position echoed the views of many countries around the world. But it also was witnessing how the world responds to power, and that many countries, even if they had misgivings about the U.S. decision to go to war, did not want to cause any lasting damage to their relations with Washington. The crisis in Ituri could provide an opportunity for the Security Council, and especially for France and the United States, to come together and move on after the painful battles over Iraq. These political considerations were important, but who would be the flag-bearers who would turn them into operational decisions? In May 2003 we were all incredibly lucky to have the right mix of people in a few critical places of the machinery of governments.

In the U.S. mission to the United Nations, the deputy ambassador following African affairs was a political appointee who, as an attorney, had been active in Republican politics in Illinois. "Rick" Williamson, who would later become special envoy of the Bush administration for Darfur, cared about people in Africa, and he was not hampered by diplomatic conventions. In those critical weeks, he became a strong ally, pleading the case of Congo in Washington because he believed it was the right thing to do.

On the French side, it was more complicated. I knew I would be better off going directly to the decisionmakers in Paris, rather than through the French mission at the UN, which was all too well aware of the potential difficulties of a Congo operation. I felt I could have an ally in the chief of staff of the French army, General Henri Bentegeat; he had been involved in several operations in Africa, he knew how to evaluate risk, and he was not afraid of speaking his mind to politicians. I spoke to him to prepare the ground for a conversation between Kofi Annan and Jacques Chirac. He was cautious, but I felt he would not advise against a French military involvement. He understood how tragic the situation was, and he would make every effort to find practical solutions if his political masters so decided. Bentegeat is a man with a profound sense of ethics, and I knew he would not refuse to help if he could, even if that entailed some risks. And he did help. Once the groundwork had been laid with him, a phone call between Kofi Annan and Jacques Chirac was arranged. It took place on a Saturday morning, when I was with Annan and the Security Council at a retreat at the Rockefeller Estate at Pocantico Hills, near New York. The retreat discussion was on the role of the Security Council, and the Angolan ambassador, Gaspar Martins, had mentioned the situation in Congo and the lack of action by the council. He did not know that, as he was speaking, the UN Secretariat was quietly working to convince a key member of the council to lead a multinational force and radically change that situation. Annan left the room to place the call and asked me to join him immediately afterward: from his jubilant smile, I immediately knew the conversation had gone well. We were both extremely excited. Chirac had promised to help. He liked Kofi Annan, and he had a genuine interest in Africa. I suspect Bentegeat had already spoken to the French president, who understood that even a limited deployment could make a big difference; it would change the dynamics on the ground, and it would also begin to change the dynamics in the Security Council. The timing could not have been better. The first phase of our little plot had succeeded and I was relieved: we now had a green light from the top. I admired the way Kofi Annan had weighed in at the right moment, with the right words. Of course, Chirac had responded well for more fundamental reasons than his friendship with the secretary general, but that friendship certainly had helped. While Kofi Annan knew how to use the authority of his office, he also knew that the real power was not with him but with the heads of state, who need to be cajoled and persuaded rather than bullied. And he did it very well. But one positive phone conversation was not enough to turn the multinational force into an operational reality. It was just the first step in a battle that would have many twists and turns.

I waged that battle on several fronts. In Bunia, the Uruguayans, confronted with a situation they could not control, were more and more nervous, and there was a risk they might decide to withdraw, which would have made any future deployment of a multinational force impossible. I polished my rusty Spanish to speak to the president of Uruguay and convince him to keep his troops in Bunia. To this day, I am immensely grateful that this small nation, which had no national interest in Congo, eventually decided to stay the course and support the UN.

Locally, the political and military balances were shifting. On May 12 one of the tribal groups, the Hemas, retook Bunia from its rival, the Lendus. This was to have tragic consequences for the UN mission: A few days later, 60 kilometers away, two of our military observers, who had desperately radioed to be evacuated, were barbarically assassinated by a Lendu militia, which wanted to punish MONUC for not having prevented the capture of Bunia by the Hemas. A MONUC helicopter had come to pick them up, but did not see them and left the area without landing, and the two were left to their tragic fate. This was a somber day; MONUC was overwhelmed, and I wondered whether we would be able to stop the tragedy from escalating. I was at the top of the chain of command, giving strategic direction, but well aware that peacekeeping, like war, is all in the art of implementation. Thousands of men and women, uniformed personnel as well as civilians, were engaged in a huge effort, with dozens of different specialties: staff officers monitoring radio communications, movement control personnel approving helicopter movements, political analysts reviewing the security situation on the ground, military observers reviewing the deployment of their colleagues. Many of our staff demonstrated extraordinary commitment and a sense of duty, but the quality was uneven. Our command-and-control procedures were weak, and there was no redundancy built in our systems, so that a lot—too much, in fact—depended on the quality of the individuals in charge. The loss of our two observers played a large part in my subsequent efforts to professionalize peacekeeping and build more robust structures. This was not just about efficiency; it was about saving lives.

Meanwhile, President Kabila was threatening to break the Lusaka cease-fire agreement and deploy his own troops to Bunia. They were perceived as allied with the Lendus, which in all likelihood would lead to an escalation of the violence, not stabilization.

After the positive conversation between French president Jacques Chirac and Kofi Annan, the French diplomatic staff had very professionally established a list of conditions for the engagement of France. My compatriots were doing their job, and I would have done the same had I been working at the Quai d'Orsay, making sure that French interests were protected and that the French army would not walk into a disaster. But my job as an international civil servant was now to mobilize the resources of a powerful nation for a broader interest and reconcile legitimate national concerns with the higher goal of saving lives in Congo. I felt that in most situations, national interests are not incompatible with the goals of the UN charter, but harnessing them for that purpose is hard work and sometimes requires a bit of clever diplomacy. In the case of the Ituri operation, each of the French conditions was certainly a daunting challenge:

—An area of operation limited to Bunia and its airport.

—A strict time limit on the deployment; it should end in September.

—Involvement of a coalition to make clear that the operation was not a French operation.

—A written agreement of Uganda and Rwanda.

The first condition—a deployment limited to Bunia—was very worrying, and some on my staff thought we should reject the French offer. Their concern was that a French deployment limited to Bunia might well displace rather than stop the violence; the situation would stabilize in Bunia, but violence would spiral out of control in the rest of the district, and several thousand more Congolese would then converge toward Bunia, creating chaos and more tragedy. I was concerned about that scenario as well, but I believed that if it happened, the French force would be compelled politically and operationally to go beyond Bunia. France would not be able to hide behind a self-imposed technical limitation of the area of operation in the face of an unfolding humanitarian disaster, and the military would not want to deal with a growing flow of panicked refugees. I felt that the less the issue was discussed, the better. Ambiguity on the exact area of operation was our best chance to create a political dynamic in which stabilization would start with Bunia, but gradually spill over to the whole of Ituri.

The second condition was much more problematic for me. We could not afford a security vacuum when the multinational force left, and it was important to have some overlap with a follow-on force. But how could we possibly deploy the follow-on troops by late September? This would require a new resolution authorizing a bigger MONUC, enormous goodwill from the troop contributors who would replace the multinational force, and a massive logistical effort, far superior to what we had just done to deploy the Uruguayans.

The third condition was another challenge: the situation in Ituri was scary, and many countries were quite happy to let the French do the job. Some were also nervous about being associated with the French, because of the ambiguous legacy of "Turquoise" in Rwanda. I agreed with Paris that it was very important that this not be a "French operation." There was a risk otherwise that the force would not be seen as impartial and would be dragged into a posture where it would unwittingly have to align itself with one of the militias. In the ten days following the successful conversation between Chirac and Annan, I spoke to officials in more than twenty countries, extracting a valuable special forces company from Sweden, transport planes from Portugal and Belgium, and a small unit from the United Kingdom. I was particularly keen to have Britain on board. The symbolism of Britain's Union Jack and the French tricolor floating together would establish the impartiality of the force vis-à-vis Rwanda and Uganda, and it would also show that the relationship between London and Paris was no longer defined by their differences over the Iraq war. As a committed European, I also thought that a European force—willing to work with African countries such as South Africa and to deploy to Ituri— would send a badly needed signal that the European Union was beginning to repair the wounds caused by the bitter debate that had preceded the Iraq war. An EU operation could provide a great opportunity for the Europeans to move on. Javier Solana, the EU's high representative for foreign and security policy, immediately agreed, and the Ituri deployment, later known as "Operation Artemis," became the first test of UN-EU cooperation in Africa.

A meeting was hastily arranged in Brussels on May 19, and for the first time in ten days, I began to be more optimistic. The frantic work of the past week had not been in vain, and that most elusive element, political momentum, had been created. In forty-eight hours, we received several pieces of good news. The meeting in Brussels had gone well, the British representative had given Her Majesty's government's support to what had now become "the French initiative," and Prime Minister Tony Blair, when called by Kofi Annan, confirmed that there would be British participation. In Bunia, a truce had been agreed, and the Congolese Red Cross could accomplish its grim task of recovering abandoned corpses that littered the town. Uganda, which had been accused of having contributed to the chaos so it would be called back into Ituri to stop it, was now publicly supporting the deployment of the European force. British and American diplomacy also was very helpful. President Bush's national security adviser Condoleezza Rice had called President Kagame, and Rick Williamson was lobbying in Washington to get the State Department's approval for the reinforced MONUC that would replace the French-led multi-national force in September. He told me he was "out on a limb," which I could easily believe, considering the state of Franco-U.S. relations and what the last few months had been like in the Security Council.

The multinational force and its UN replacement were becoming a reality, and for me it was now time to go to Congo, Rwanda, and Uganda. The situation there could still easily unravel, and one key French condition in particular was not yet met, as the French ambassador drily reminded me on the phone, to dampen my optimism and to put pressure on me, as I was driving to Kennedy airport: Rwanda had not yet given its written consent, and without that consent, there would not be an operation.

My first meeting in Kinshasa was with President Kabila, on May 23. I pleaded with him not to deploy Congolese troops in Bunia. I was not too reassured by his answers. There would be battles, he said, and his army would have to fight. I also informed him of the replacement of UN special representative Namanga Ngongi, who had been pushing so hard for the international deployment, but was now ready to leave, by William Swing, an old Africa hand at the State Department who had been until two years earlier the U.S. ambassador to the Democratic Republic of the Congo. He had been introduced to me at the time by Kamel Morjane, and I immediately thought he could serve the UN. After he retired from the U.S. diplomatic service, Kofi Annan had appointed him his special representative in one of our most static missions, Western Sahara. He had done well there, but his arrival in Congo would have bigger strategic implications: This was a mission in crisis, and the arrival of an experienced American diplomat, who already knew Congo very well, could achieve many goals at once. It signaled U.S. interest, making it more difficult for the Congolese to ignore the UN and also more difficult for the United States to walk away from Congo. Actually, during his tenure as special representative of the secretary general in the DRC, Swing proved to be an extremely effective advocate in the U.S. Congress of UN involvement in the DRC. Discussing with President Kabila such an unusual appointment in the middle of the Ituri tragedy was a good way to demonstrate the commitment of the UN to the DRC, but it also made it very difficult, for those advisers of the president who were uneasy with the appointment, to block it. In the middle of a major crisis, the resolution of which so much depended on the UN, it would have been hard to question the intentions of the secretary general.

In Kinshasa, there was no sense of the tragedy that was unfolding a thousand miles away to the east. The food and wine at diplomatic dinners were as good as ever, and the conversation of some diplomats as bad as ever. It was painful to listen to a retiring European ambassador pontificating on Congolese corruption. His theory, that he was so obviously pleased to share with his dinner partners, was that it would be much cheaper to buy one thousand Congolese to have peace in Congo than to deploy troops. He seemed oblivious to the many decades during which his country and others had condoned the corruption of Congo, and he did not care too much about the impact of such practices on the miserable people who did not have much of a say on the way their country had been governed since independence. In Kinshasa, the future of Congo was still largely seen as a diplomatic game.

A Tense Situation in Bunia

Bunia stood in stark contrast to the capital. A few days earlier, the plane of a Congolese minister had been hit by a surface-to-air rocket and had to make an emergency landing in Kampala, Uganda. The Hema militia of the Union of Congolese Patriots (UPC) controlled the road between the airport and the city, and the grip of our Uruguayan troops was tenuous at best. A unit of Congolese policemen sent from Kinshasa had collapsed soon after its deployment, and they were now idle, representing a potential additional cause of unrest, as well as more mouths to feed. The perimeter of the airport was not really secured, and thousands of displaced people were sleeping in tents along the runway. In Bunia itself, the market, usually bustling with activity, was deserted. The only human presence was of young men with guns; a boy, barely twelve years old, was trying to carry a machine gun and a round of ammunition obviously too heavy for him. One was parading a bin Laden T-shirt, and another one a Coca Cola T-shirt. The political messages were not self-evident. But the consequences of violence were for everybody to see in the "hospital" about which I had read so many depressing reports. The "hospital" was a big room in which the "operating room" was just a corner isolated by a curtain. Women lying on cots with their children, a little cupboard with some medication, men with an arm or a leg missing, reminders of what I had seen in Sierra Leone, and extraordinarily committed nurses and doctors, making do with very little and probably wondering why they had to waste time with a bureaucrat from New York.

I then met with one of the leaders of the Union of Congolese Patriots, the big Rwandan-supported Hema militia that was momentarily in control of the town. He was in his twenties, surrounded by even younger bodyguards, many of whom seemed to be on drugs. The "boss" very much wanted to show he was the boss, continuously interrupting himself to make calls on his cell phone; "I have to discuss with my chief of staff!" he replied when I mentioned that stealing medical supplies was not advancing any particular cause. The meeting was both frightening and somewhat bizarrely reassuring: I could feel that things could go terribly wrong very quickly, and that for some of the militia leaders, human life had no more value here than in a video game. At the same time, this was obviously not a professional force, and a lot would depend on psychological factors, and on the capacity of the international community to project a sense of strength and determination—to intimidate and deter. But nothing was assured. While I was discussing with the humanitarian community what could be done to alleviate the suffering in Ituri, the meeting had to be interrupted because gunfire was getting a bit too close. Through the wide-open windows of the room where we were meeting, we could hear and see a band of militias taking potshots at the two armed personnel carriers that were protecting us. We had to beat a prudent retreat to a safer place behind concertina wire and sandbags.

The gunfire died down, and I was able to start my meeting with Pétronille Waweka, an unassuming lady who had played a decisive role with Special Representative Ngongi in bringing about a precarious cease-fire to Ituri. She belonged to the Alur tribe, a smaller tribe than the two dominant tribes of the Hema and the Lendu, which allowed her to more effectively mediate disputes. I would much later read a wonderful—apocryphal?—story about her grandmother, who was said to have stared down a lion, on her way home, until the lion walked away. She may have inherited from her grandmother that capacity of staring down much more dangerous threats than lions: militia leaders. In the cramped bunker where we were meeting, she was giving a face and a voice to the simple needs of the people of Ituri.

In many African conflicts, reports of horrific deeds create a distance that protects smug Westerners from unwelcome emotions. They see the conflicts of the Great Lakes region as barely human, remnants of a primitive world they left behind long ago and about which they can do little. What they should see is actually the opposite. Human beings may have very different ways of managing social links, and when they rupture, the worst is always possible, everywhere. But people have universal aspirations, and the aspirations of Pétronille Waweka were those of every mother in a similar situation: "Save our children from being killed or becoming killers, save our girls from being raped! Deploy a strong force to once and for all take the power away from the guns. And deploy it now! We have suffered too much! We cannot wait any longer!" I did not have any good answers, because I was not yet in a position to promise anything. Nothing was confirmed. I could not make a false promise, but I could not add to the despair. I tried to explain honestly what we were doing, and what obstacles still had to be overcome: agreement of Rwanda to the deployment of the multinational force, good cooperation by Uganda, no further deterioration in Bunia, and effective logistics to repair a decaying runway and allow for a fast deployment of the multinational force. They were definitely many ifs.

I went to Uganda the next day to visit President Museveni at his farm. France had reinstated its bilateral aid with Uganda, and the Ugandan leader was in an ebullient and jocular mood, half old tribal chief, half school teacher. I think he was intrigued and possibly amused by this tall Frenchman who wouldn't let go. When asked which tribe I came from, I said I was a "Breton" and explained to him some of the alleged characteristics of Bretons: we are independent-minded, and we are persistent, some might even say stubborn. His answer was to enunciate and carefully write on a page of yellow-pad legal paper the ten commandments of peacekeeping, and then give them to me as a *vade mecum*. I left Kampala confident that Uganda would not stand in the way. The president had made the strategic decision to go along with the force and not to play havoc with Ituri, provided his Rwandan neighbors did the same.

The most important meeting was still to come, on May 28, with President Kagame in his office in Kigali. In the plane that was taking me to Rwanda, I immersed myself in the works of Machiavelli, thinking I would find some rest in the company of one of the best minds of the Italian Renaissance. His writings, like Shakespeare's plays, are as good an introduction to the politics of the Great Lakes as any learned book on the tribal makeup of Congo. They are all about power, how it is kept, and what combination of symbolic deeds and brutal actions ensures control over people.

In Ituri, the militias of Jean-Pierre Bemba, which had once been in alliance with the RCD when Uganda and Rwanda were allies, were now seen as enemies by Rwanda. Rwanda was adjusting its posture, and the Rwandan-supported UPC militia had just strengthened its grip on Bunia. There even were rumors that the forces of the RCD-Goma in North Kivu might move further north, toward Butembo and Beni, connecting the Kivu and Ituri theaters of operation; that would be bad news, as it would create a continuum between the RCD-Goma–dominated North Kivu and the UPC in Bunia. Uganda would most likely be very unhappy with such a configuration, which would give too much influence to Rwanda.

I knew that the clock was ticking for the deployment. The French had not waited for adoption of a resolution by the Security Council to start their preparations, but they needed the resolution to move ahead, and there would be no resolution without a letter from President Kagame. The council was going to have a meeting on Congo a few hours later on the very same day I was meeting with President Kagame thanks to the time difference. Would the letter reach the council in time? I was very nervous, and I asked the president, as politely as I could, to send the letter . . . immediately! In hindsight, considering the way in which I have seen President Kagame always operate in a strategic manner, I should have been totally relaxed. Kagame would not have received me if he was ready to precipitate a crisis, and the international alignment of forces was such that it should have been clear to me that he had made a strategic decision. The choice of timing was to underline its strategic importance, not to create uncertainty. He had shifted gears to a political strategy— which was not incompatible with the pursuit of some territorial gains by the RCD-Goma to strengthen its political hand in power-sharing arrangements.

President Kagame's letter was brought to the council chamber in the afternoon, and two weeks later, on June 10, the first elements of the multinational force landed in Bunia. It was quickly tested by the UPC, and successfully passed the test. Not only did the situation in Bunia rapidly improve, but the situation in the rest of Ituri also improved. The momentum we had hoped for had been created, and nobody wanted to pick a fight with the European force; for any potential troublemaker who might have had second thoughts, the Mirage jetfighters, which flew over Bunia from time to time, inspired the fear of God.

We had bought ourselves a window of calm, but another race against time had now started: What force would we be able to deploy after the multinational force left, and when? I had tried to convince the European Union to agree to keep an "over the horizon" force, in case things went wrong. The troops would have been stationed in Europe, but would have been sent to Congo if warranted. At a European Union Council meeting with Solana on July 18, the EU rejected the idea. I also tried to convince Sweden to transfer to MONUC its Special Forces Company when the multinational force left. As a precedent, in East Timor, Australia, after having been the lead nation of the multinational force that stabilized the situation when the violence exploded in 1999, had, with New Zealand and other multinational force contributors, stayed behind when the multinational force left, and that continuity had been a decisive factor in ensuring the operational and political credibility of the successor UN force. I was concerned that in Congo, spoilers would challenge the UN force as soon as the multinational force had left. These requests were rejected, however, and it became all the more important to have as strong a force as possible to replace the multinational force. Throughout July, there were discussions involving key members of the Security Council to strengthen MONUC. On July 28 the council agreed to bring the numbers of MONUC up to 10,800 and expand its mandate. But we now had only a few weeks to deploy before the multinational force would begin to pull out. Miraculously, by late September, thanks to enormous efforts of troop contributors, the first additional troops of what was now called the Ituri brigade began to deploy, and the vacuum I had feared was avoided. I later learned that the French military, who were used to the slow pace of UN deployments, had never expected that we would meet the deadline, and were very surprised when we did.

This reinforcement of MONUC was highly significant. MONUC from now on would be a completely different mission, although I was well aware that the brigade in Ituri, with less than 5,000 troops, would have a hard time dealing with the whole of Ituri. That number was not much higher than what the French-led multinational force had deployed—and that deployment had been limited to Bunia—but as usual, the UN was expected to do more with less. We would need to have good troops, good command, and a very strategic use of force if we wanted to maintain the credibility that the international community had just acquired, and which it was now bestowing on the UN.

Some Progress but No Genuine Reconciliation

The following years were to show how difficult such a strategic use of force would be, and how essential it was that it be a part of a political strategy. Military force had its own limitations, and without an effective political process, it was bound to disappoint.

By March 2004 the situation in eastern Congo was again deteriorating. After the creation in 2003 of a government of national unity that was supposed to bring together the former enemy factions, an agreement on the senior posts in the army had eventually been reached, but there was still no genuine integration, and no serious effort was made to begin building a national Congolese army. A meeting that I had convened in February in New York to get support from international donors and develop a more coherent and ambitious approach reforming the security sector had not produced any results. The fundamental ambiguities of the Congolese transition government were playing out at all levels of the army, where the former enemies were jockeying for influence and control.

The simmering conflict came to a head in Bukavu, the capital of South Kivu—a city of critical importance in eastern Congo. The precarious balance between the Kabila camp and the RCD-Goma in Bukavu was broken when disagreement between a newly appointed military commander belonging to the Kabila camp and South Kivu's governor, Xavier Chiribanya Chirimwami, who belonged to the RCD-Goma, gradually got out of control. The governor was suspended in February 2004, and the commander of the military region was eventually relieved of his duties. The conflict escalated when the new commander appointed by the government, General Félix Mabe, was challenged by his deputy, Colonel Jules Mutebutsi, a Tutsi close to Rwanda, who had also been relieved of his duties but stayed in Bukavu with troops loyal to him. Fighting broke out in Bukavu. General Laurent Nkunda, the same Tutsi officer close to Rwanda who had been responsible for the Kisangani massacres in 2002 and who would again wreak havoc in eastern Congo in the fall of 2008, announced that he was moving from his base in North Kivu to help Mutebutsi in South Kivu. MONUC, which favored a political solution and had also declared its opposition to General Mabe, on the government side, when he had entered the town, issued an ultimatum announcing that it would use force if Nkunda persisted in his intentions. But when Nkunda ignored the warning, an order from Kinshasa was given to the UN troops not to take a blocking position, even though the commanding officer was prepared to stand his ground. I was on the other side of the Atlantic and learned only after the fact about that disastrous reversal. The consequences were catastrophic: from June 2 to 9, Bukavu was under the control of forces that had openly challenged the government of national unity. Several hundred people were killed, and MONUC had shown its impotence. Eventually, under intense political pressure, Mutebutsi fled to Rwanda and Nkunda pulled back to North Kivu.

But the damage had been done: MONUC had lost whatever credibility and momentum Operation Artemis had created. The Europeans who had given a helping hand to MONUC a year before were quick to express their disappointment. At a retreat of the Security Council, the French ambassador said that MONUC "had made a fool of itself." For me, the crisis was a confirmation of my concerns about the real capacity of MONUC; 10,000 not-very-mobile troops in a country the size of Europe were not much of a deterrent, especially if command and control was hesitant. I was determined to use this crisis to deepen the engagement of the international community. I knew that no reinforcement of MONUC would ever be sufficient to bring peace in a country as big as Congo, but military capacity was one of the foundations of political leverage, and it could be used strategically to achieve political goals, and to help bring about more stability. One needed to combine a stronger MONUC with a more politically engaged international community.

When in September 2004, in the margins of the General Assembly, Kofi Annan had his customary meeting with the president of the United States, he raised the issue of Congo. We had decided not to self-censor ourselves, and the Secretariat was asking for 13,100 additional troops; this was unprecedented and would have represented more than a doubling of MONUC. At the time of the meeting, the United States had agreed only to 3,000 more troops. We had a long way to go. So Kofi Annan mentioned to President Bush that the United Kingdom was now ready to support an increase of 6,000. The president had not been briefed, and he understood that 6,000 British troops were going to deploy to Congo—if only! In spite of the magnitude of the Congolese tragedy, the DRC issue was not yet, and actually would never become, an issue of the first order for the world's great powers, followed with sufficient attention by top leaders. But the intensive lobbying of the secretary general paid off, and eventually the Security Council agreed on an overall ceiling of 17,000, which was less than what we had requested but still a significant reinforcement. Meanwhile, the United States was getting politically more and more engaged; in September 2004 Washington brokered an agreement under which Rwanda, Uganda, and the Democratic Republic of the Congo created a tripartite commission to work together on normalizing the situation in eastern Congo and completing the tasks listed in the Lusaka, Pretoria, and Luanda agreements. The agreement was extended to Burundi in 2005.

The last months of 2004 were, however, a dangerous period. MONUC had not yet been strengthened, and contrary to the hopes raised by the tripartite agreement, the relations between Rwanda and Uganda had deteriorated again; there were rumors that some Rwandan troops were actually in eastern Congo, which were neither confirmed nor denied by Rwanda. President Kagame was blowing hot and cold on Congo. At one point Kigali threatened to conduct a surgical operation if Kinshasa did not take action against the Hutu FDLR. Later, Rwanda offered—and Kabila refused—to put Rwandan troops under Congolese command, an offer similar to the one that Rwanda, with remarkable strategic continuity, would make again in 2009, and which would then be accepted, to have joint Rwandan-Congolese operations in eastern Congo.

I went to Congo in October to reorganize the military command and try to restore the credibility of the mission. Traditionally the force had been commanded from Kinshasa, but the "main effort" was clearly in the east, and the disastrous episode of Bukavu showed the importance of empowering the local commanders and being close to the theater. I felt it was now essential to have a general who would push the troops to take a more dynamic posture. And I had the right person for the job: the Dutch marine general Patrick Cammaert, who had led the UN deployment in Eritrea and had been the military adviser of the Department of Peacekeeping Operations for the past two years. He was familiar with Congolese military challenges and was respected by our major troop contributors. He had always been more at ease commanding in tough operational situations—he had first worked for the UN as battalion commander in a Khmer-Rouge area of Cambodia—than in the corridors of headquarters. A division headquarters was created in Kisangani, reporting to the overall force headquarters in Kinshasa, and Cammaert was appointed division commander. The 6,000 additional troops were now deploying. The bulk of them was from South Asia, and the eastern division looked a bit like a restoration of the British Raj; we had Bangladeshi, Indian, Nepalese, and Pakistani troops. On the occasion when the new secretary general, Ban Ki-moon, made his first visit to Congo, the four South Asian contingents showcased their respective military bands, and it was a competition on who played the bagpipe best. A more sensitive issue was how to organize the interaction between India and Pakistan, two countries that have been at war several times. I had Indian and Pakistani officers working together in New York, but I was worried when I learned that India was the only country to offer attack helicopters, which were essential for close air support. How would Indian close air support work with Pakistani ground troops? I was told this would not be an issue, and it actually was not.

The operational tempo changed quickly as the new division commander pushed his troops. The troops were no longer confined to static camps; they deployed in mobile operating bases, patrolled at night, and regularly launched "cordon and search" operations. The civilian support capacities of the mission were stretched, as commercially contracted helicopters were tasked to transport troops according to operational needs. The procedures of the UN had not been designed for such operations, and there was a lot of bureaucratic resistance to operations that were redefining peacekeeping. The mission now had the initiative and could shape perceptions and build political momentum. This new posture carried risks. In March 2005 the force was tragically tested; north of Bunia, a patrol was ambushed and nine Bangladeshi soldiers were killed. Bangladesh took the loss with great courage, and General Cammaert reacted swiftly. Several dozen militia fighters were killed in a counter-operation. At the beginning of April, the force issued an ultimatum to the militias of Ituri to disarm, and it acted on its ultimatum: the military credibility of MONUC was restored. Eventually, 15,000 militia members would disarm, and the military actions of the UN transformed the situation in Ituri. And this remarkable success happened with a force that was not even one-tenth of the force that experts would recommend for effective protection of the civilian population. In their most recent manual on counterinsurgency, the

U.S. Army and Marine Corps assert that counterinsurgency is about protecting people rather than killing insurgents, an approach that makes the discussion of force ratios for counterinsurgency pertinent for robust peacekeeping. The recommended ratio is 20 soldiers for a population of 1,000 to protect. If such a ratio had been applied to Ituri, some 90,000 troops would have been required.

The Ituri campaign of 2005 was undoubtedly the most successful operation of MONUC, and it showed the decisive impact of good command. As the year was coming to an end, however, the UN was confronted with a military challenge of a different order of magnitude: it was no longer about providing security in a district of 4.5 million people, but ensuring the security of elections in a country of 60 million—a country that had been deprived of multiparty elections for forty years. I was aware that ensuring a safe environment throughout the country was way beyond the capacity of MONUC, even if it had regained some credibility. We would have to count on creating the right political dynamic, so that major actors would be under pressure not to disrupt the process. Could we turn again to the European Union? The Europeans had kept a good memory of their operation in Bunia, which had been an extraordinary success, operationally and politically. It had helped MONUC recover from a desperate situation, it had sent a salutary message of European commitment and watchfulness to the Congolese and their neighbors, and it had begun to familiarize the European Union, as an institution, with Africa. Congo had gained, the UN had gained, and the EU had gained. My deputy Hedi Annabi and I thought we could build on that first success of EU-UN cooperation in Africa and repeat the experience. This time, it would not be an emergency deployment, but a well-prepared reinforcement during the election period. Javier Solana saw the benefits for the nascent European common foreign and security policy of the European Union, and we started working quietly with the secretariat of the Council of the European Union in December 2005. In the last days of the year, a formal letter requesting the military support of the EU for the elections was sent to the British presidency of the EU, which liked the idea. A few days later, Germany was taking over the presidency of the European Union. It was not thrilled when it discovered the request, and it was my mistake not to have prepared the ground with Berlin. The engagement of Germany outside Europe is a gradual and sensitive process, and German public opinion shows great reluctance to any engagement on the African continent. Berlin felt that the two secretariats had plotted behind its back. I believe that for international institutions to work, and especially for the European Union, which has the ambition of being more than a regional organization, it is essential to allow international secretariats to develop concepts without letting member states kill them quietly before they are hatched. For an international civil servant, there is a fine balance to strike between pushing states to act in a way that goes beyond their narrow national perspective and embarrassing them by ignoring their domestic political constraints. I may have been a little too pushy on that occasion, but it eventually worked.

The European Union agreed to deploy troops during the Congolese elections, and it turned out to be an extraordinarily successful psychological operation. The deployment was limited to Kinshasa, and the number of fighting forces actually deployed during the elections was minuscule with no more than two companies, but the existence of an over-the-horizon force—essentially French troops already stationed in Gabon—and the public information campaign that accompanied the deployment massively amplified the perceived capacities of the force. In the end, potential spoilers felt that all the military power of Europe would fall on them if they made trouble, the elections were peaceful, and the European Union could proudly convince itself that it had ensured their success.

Operation Artemis in 2003, the Ituri campaign of General Cammaert in 2005, the EU deployment in support of the elections in 2006: these were the three moments before the creation of the "intervention brigade" in 2013 (see below) when military force made a difference in Congo during the last fifteen years. It is important not to draw the wrong conclusions from these examples of success. No decisive battle was won; no militia was crushed. A force was deployed, and in some instances used, essentially to create momentum, to shape perceptions, by astutely picking fights that it was sure to win, by putting up a show that was sufficiently intimidating to transform the political dynamics. It was largely political theater, and that "show," more than the immediate impact of a specific operation, made the difference between success and failure. And indeed, good command and the right mindset also made a big difference. But the political context in which the force was operating was the most critical factor. In Ituri, the militias that MONUC confronted were a tactical rather than a strategic challenge. They were poorly trained groups of criminals, often on drugs, and the military actions of MONUC were backed by constant political support of key powers and had the support of the Kinshasa government. This has never been the case in the Kivus, where there is a superficial consensus of the major powers to address the threat posed by the FDLR genocidaires, but there is no international consensus on the underlying unresolved political issues, in particular the conditions for a genuine Rwanda-DRC reconciliation.

This was sadly demonstrated a few months after my departure from the UN, when the Security Council, eager to address the FDLR threat, but with no clear vision of what an accountable national Congolese army should look like, mandated MONUC to provide logistical support to Congolese troops. I had always resisted such calls for joint operations because I doubted their operational effectiveness, unless they were decided on a case-by-case basis. No serious progress had been made in the reform of the army, and many units had little or no discipline. This lack of progress was a symptom of a more fundamental issue: there was no agreement between the international community and the Kinshasa leadership on what a national Congolese army should look like. In the absence of any genuine reform of the army, the UN would find itself allied with factions, rather than with a truly national army, and that alliance had the potential to trigger even more violence. When in 2009 parts of Nkunda's Rwandophone militia, the National Congress for the Defense of the People (CNDP), were integrated in the Congolese army, the international community was relieved that a dangerous group had been neutralized and that the Congolese army would be stronger in its fight against the genocidaires. It overlooked the fact that integrating units and commanders who had themselves committed atrocities was sending a terrible signal to other militias. Some of the Mai Mai groups, which had not been included in the Lusaka agreement and were allied to the genocidaires, unsurprisingly drew the conclusion that committing atrocities indeed might be the best way to attract attention and eventually reap rewards. The mass rapes of Congolese women that occurred in the summer of 2010 were committed by the FDLR but also by some of their Mai Mai allies who resented the fact that parts of the CNDP militia had been integrated in the Congolese army and were now taking over lucrative mines not for the benefit of the Congolese people but for their own personal benefit. The desperate people of the Kivus were not gaining the protection of an army that they could trust; they were just getting new masters because the politics of creating an accountable army had not been addressed.

Force matters, and I spent much time focusing on the peacekeepers, trying to salvage desperate situations and to turn crises into opportunities. Indeed, had we had a better conduct of military operations, had we had more campaigns like the Ituri campaign of 2005, the United Nations would today be in a stronger position to contribute to the political stabilization of the country, although any foreign intervention, whether it is under the flag of the United Nations or not, eventually will generate hostility, and the political leverage provided by a military presence produces diminishing returns. But in hindsight, I believe the main mistake was of a political nature: military operations became a convenient distraction, which allowed the Security Council to neglect the politics of Congo.

The recent creation by the UN of the intervention brigade and its contribution to the defeat of the M23, the last incarnation of a Rwandan-supported militia in the eastern DRC, show at once the importance and the limits of military force. The most hopeful sign in the defeat of the M23 in 2013 is actually the role of the Congolese armed forces; their courage and professionalism made all Congolese proud and demonstrated a patriotism that may be more important for the future of the country than the military victory itself. But force alone will not bring peace to eastern Congo, and one should not draw the wrong conclusions from that success of robust peacekeeping in support of the Congolese army. There is a tendency to exaggerate what force can achieve in the stabilization of a country, as if it were only a question of cleaning up some bad neighborhoods with an international SWAT team.

In the end, robust peacekeeping is an empty concept if it is not supported by a robust political posture. The United Nations does not have the capacity to enforce peace. And actually no nation, even the United States, has that capacity, as is clear from the recent experiences in Afghanistan and Iraq. What the United Nations has, that no nation has, is the capacity to create trust in its fairness and impartiality. That requires a very rigorous and disciplined use of force. If civilians are killed under the UN's watch, and the peacekeepers are seen to be passive, not only has the UN failed in its mission to save lives, but its political credibility is destroyed, which will prevent it from playing an effective role in promoting a political process. But if the UN becomes the auxiliary of a government whose legitimacy and representativeness is still questioned, it may lose not only its military credibility but its political legitimacy, putting at risk what is potentially its most valuable contribution: the capacity to foster compromise among various groups as the indispensible base of lasting peace. In Congo, although the leaders are now elected, that contribution is still much needed. Stability requires much more than crushing the former genocidaires, and lasting peace depends on how the government of the DRC will assert its authority throughout the country. Recruiting criminals to defeat other criminals, as it did in the past, will not end the cycle of violence. Building a professional and accountable army will. The most difficult challenge in Congo has never been a military challenge: it is to build trusted institutions.

six
DEMOCRATIC REPUBLIC OF THE CONGO
Was It Worth It?

There never has been clarity on the political goals of international involvement in the Democratic Republic of the Congo, and the immensity of the humanitarian crisis in the country has only contributed to the neglect of politics. The horrors of sexual abuse have drawn international attention, including from Hillary Clinton when she was secretary of state. The plight of Congolese women is only the worst symptom of a deeper political problem: the collapse of state institutions, itself the result of a failed political process. The first peace agreement, the Lusaka Accord of 1999, did not ignore the need for a political process, as it provided for an Inter-Congolese Dialogue that would bring together the Congolese government in Kinshasa, the rebel movements, and all the major organizations and groups of the recognized representative political opposition as well as representatives of the main components of Congolese society, what the French call the *forces vives*.

The accord also acknowledged the connections between the internal peace process of Congo and the regional dynamics: Congo had become a battlefield for its neighbors and a haven for the genocidaires because of its own weakness. But the accord could not address the fundamental unresolved issue that has now plagued the country for more than a decade: how could the country recover if the region was not willing to accept a stronger Congo? An agreement among the Congolese is an indispensable foundation for regained strength, but it is not enough. The domestic peace process and the regional peace process have to be closely coordinated. This would be fully recognized by the United Nations only in 2012, when Mary Robinson, former president of Ireland and UN high commissioner for human rights, was given a very broad peacemaking mandate, which included internal as well as regional reconciliation. This role is now fulfilled by Said Djinnit, an Algerian who very effectively draws on his previous experience as commissioner for peace and security of the African Union.

As a follow-up to the Lusaka agreement, the Organization of African Unity in December 1999 had appointed Sir Ketumile Masire, an elderly former president of Botswana, as facilitator for the domestic process, and he was supposed to complete the process in only three months. The Kinshasa side, which was deeply suspicious of a process that gave legitimacy to the rebel movements it was fighting, very grudgingly accepted his appointment. The fact that Masire belonged to the "anglophone" sphere and had several British advisers did not help with his Kinshasa interlocutors, who saw him as too close to their anglophone enemies in Uganda and Rwanda. And many Congolese leaders do not speak a word of English. After the assassination of Laurent-Désiré Kabila and the February 2001 meeting between his son and successor Joseph Kabila and Rwanda's Paul Kagame, things began to move. During Kofi Annan's visit to the DRC in September 2001, Kisangani was mentioned as a possible venue for the dialogue. It would be a great symbol that the Congolese were claiming back their country and taking charge of their future if the conference took place in a city located right in the center of their country, one that had itself witnessed terrible devastation. This choice of venue, which would have required the demilitarization of Kisangani, proved to be too ambitious. The Rwandan-backed rebel group Congolese Rally for Democracy-Goma (RCD-Goma) and Rwanda, which controlled the city, were not ready in 2001 for the demilitarization of Kisangani, despite the loud demands from the city's people I witnessed during my visit there in early 2002. It would take the international outrage that followed another round of violence during the May Rebellion of 2002 in Kisangani to raise the pressure to the point where Rwanda decided that holding on to Kisangani and the east was becoming politically untenable. The decision was eventually made to hold the Inter-Congolese Dialogue outside the country. There was a false start in Addis Ababa in October 2001. Only 70 delegates out of 320 invited showed up, and the talks collapsed barely a week into the meeting when the delegation of Kinshasa pulled out; the government of South Africa rescued the dialogue by inviting the parties to a luxurious South African resort, Sun City.

I went to Sun City two days after the formal opening of the dialogue, on February 25, 2002. In any negotiation to end a conflict, the venue matters a lot. Too comfortable, and you create an incentive to drag on the negotiation forever; too austere, and you may not attract some of the players, who need to be bribed into making peace. Sun City is an amusement park, and it was certainly not too austere. I could not help feeling a bit uneasy. Two days earlier, I had been in Goma, where I had heard horror stories about what happened when the nearby Niyragongo volcano had erupted, cutting the city in two with lava and forcing thousands of people to run for their lives. Some leaders of the RCD-Goma, who controlled the city, had then shown more greed than human compassion, seizing the opportunity to steal cars and plunder abandoned houses. The contrast was stark, as we were sipping nice drinks in bougainvillea gardens with some of the very people who had committed atrocities.

Of course, ignoring the guns that controlled the country would have been unwise, and it was absolutely necessary to bring on board those who controlled the most guns in Congo. Without their participation, any agreement would be meaningless. The same moral dilemma comes up in every peace negotiation, and the challenge is to create some balance, so that those who have no guns, and who actually are the victims of the guns, also have a voice. In the Inter-Congolese Dialogue, that was supposed to be the role of the *forces vives* and the *opposition politique*. But when I arrived, the discussion on the *opposition politique* was actually dominated by a negotiation among those who had guns. Would the *opposition politique* be on the Kinshasa side or on the side of the Movement for the Liberation of Congo (MLC), which was backed by Uganda, or the RDC-Goma, backed by Rwanda? In a country that had not had free elections for decades, and where political parties proliferate but most do not have many more members than their leader, it was technically and politically very difficult to make the distinction between self-appointed civil society or political party leaders who are often the proxies of those who have the guns, and genuine voices who should be empowered. In Sun City, the space given to such voices was limited, and the agreement was essentially shaped by the major military actors.

For several months, progress was very slow, and in June 2002 Kofi Annan appointed Moustapha Niasse, a former prime minister of Senegal, to help move the negotiation forward. I was initially concerned that there would be too many cooks in the kitchen. But Moustapha Niasse was very shrewd, very patient, and very persistent. Soft-spoken and discrete, he was not inclined to boast about his successes, but he quietly and efficiently pushed his agenda. He also had an excellent team, including Haile Menkerios, a former Eritrean ambassador to the United Nations whom Kofi Annan had recruited to the UN staff when he could not work anymore with the president of Eritrea. Menkerios would help build relations with Paul Kagame and many of the other key players whom he knew personally. Haile Menkerios had a misleadingly unassuming appearance, but his years spent as a guerilla fighter in the Eritrean war of independence had made him a tough realist who understood the difficulty of transitioning from war to state-building. Later on, when the issue of the army and the distribution of senior military posts became a major stumbling

strong international backing. Azarias Ruberwa, the leader of the RCD-Goma, had wanted Etienne Tchisekedi, a politician from Kasai who had symbolized the democratic aspirations of Congo in the last years of the Mobutu regime, to be chosen. If he had been, that would have meant that three of the four vice presidents were not in the president's camp. There was a fear, among key international actors, that this could dangerously weaken the president and could lead to a resumption of war, since there was too much uncertainty about the military situation and the true intentions of the rebel movements and their alleged backers. The choice of Z'Ahidi Ngoma was a compromise that consolidated a precarious political balance: two vice presidents would be on the president's side, and two on the rebel movements' side. In the early summer of 2003, the priority was to establish a balance of power between the Kabila camp and the rebel movements backed by Rwanda and Uganda, and to prevent any centrifugal tendencies. But the exclusion of Etienne Tshisekedi—a major Congolese political figure and a symbol of the opposition to Mobutu—was indeed problematic.

My hope was that an inclusive government could help repair relations between Congo and Rwanda. When I met Paul Kagame in May 2003, he told me that all the problems of the DRC would disappear once there was an inclusive Congolese government. This was an acceptable statement if it meant that Rwanda wanted to have friends in Kinshasa as a guarantee that Congo would be a friendly neighbor. But Kagame's position also put the Congolese "friends" of Rwanda in a dangerous situation where they would always be suspected of looking after the interests of Rwanda before those of Congo. When the agreement on the four vice presidents was reached, I encouraged the leader of the RCD-Goma, Azarias Ruberwa, to go to Kinshasa, take his position as vice president, and begin to repair his fractured country. A lawyer by training, Ruberwa is a Congolese Tutsi for whom the support of Rwanda was critical. As one of the most thoughtful and articulate Congolese leaders, he always seemed to be torn between his alliance with Rwanda, which he saw as a life insurance for him and the tiny minority of Tutsi in Congo, and his understanding that any real reconciliation between the Congolese themselves would require that nobody be suspected of being a proxy of foreign interests. But would foreign powers such as Rwanda allow their friends in Congo not to be proxies?

In the end, raw power, rather than any internal arrangement within Congo, has shaped the relations between Kinshasa and Kigali. Rwanda pulled out of Congo in 2002 because of the combined pressures of South Africa and the United States. Nearly six years later, in the fall of 2008, it was a combination of weaknesses that led Congo and Rwanda to reach a new understanding. The military offensive of the Congolese armed forces against a Rwandan-backed militia, the National Congress for the Defense of the People (CNDP), had failed completely, and the European Union was no longer willing to come to the rescue as it had done in 2003. Meanwhile, the Netherlands and Sweden had suspended their budgetary aid to Rwanda. The two leaders, Kabila and Kagame, then quickly reached an agreement, without any mediator and outside any established institution. The Congolese government integrated into the Congolese army the Rwandan-backed militia it had fought for years and launched operations against the former genocidaires, with whom some of its forces had sometimes been allied in the past. In 2013 the defeat of the Rwandan-supported M23 was also the result of raw calculations of power: the forceful posture of the United Nations, the determination and courage of Congolese forces, and the direct pressure on Rwanda through suspension of budgetary aid by important donors. Fleeting moments when both countries were in a position of weakness have done more to change their relations than years of diplomacy, but such improvements remain as fragile and superficial as the stabilization of Congo itself. The present stability of Rwanda reflects genuine economic progress, but also tight political control; below the surface, unresolved political tensions simmer, which could one day boil over. Neither country has enough self-confidence to develop a mutually beneficial relationship with the other.

The Limits of Foreign Intervention

No UN peacekeeping mission has been more costly than the Congo mission, and no country hosting a full-fledged peacekeeping operation has seen more human suffering than the Democratic Republic of the Congo. To many, the failure of the United Nations in Congo is an indictment of the whole enterprise of peacekeeping, if not of the very concept of intervention. I have often asked myself if the whole effort was worth it, and what could and should have been done differently.

A frequent criticism is that the international community's engagement in Congo was always half-hearted, both militarily and politically, and that the Congolese people were never given a voice. I have explained in the previous chapter the limits of forceful military engagement. Forceful political engagement is no less difficult. The United Nations is that organization whose charter starts with the bold assertion: "We the people of the United Nations." In Congo, the United Nations tried to build a bridge between the interests of states and the aspirations of people. Mechanisms were designed to put pressure on states, like the political committee created by the Lusaka agreement, which was meant to monitor the implementation of the accord, or the Comité

International d'Appui à la Transition, through which ambassadors of major powers based in Kinshasa accompanied the process agreed in the Inter-Congolese Dialogue. The Congolese leaders never liked such structures, and they could easily mobilize Congolese nationalism against them, so that the leverage of the international community on state leaders was always weak. When the international community claimed to speak on behalf of the Congolese people, it could easily be suspected of neocolonialism.

The answer of the international community, in Congo as in other countries emerging from conflict, has been to give priority to the organization of elections. In 2005 and 2006 a constitutional referendum, as well as presidential and parliamentary elections, took place. For the United Nations, it was the biggest electoral operation ever. The logistics were daunting, the final bill would reach close to half a billion dollars, and thousands of people, Congolese and international, would join the effort. In the United Nations, the election owes a lot to two men. One was a New Zealander, Ross Mountain, deputy special representative of the secretary general and resident coordinator of the United Nations Development Program, who led the effort in the same way he had dealt with humanitarian emergencies in previous phases of his life: with a practical mind, an unlimited energy, and a great capacity never to take an administrative "no" for an answer. Helicopters were deployed, bulletins were printed, and electrical generators were sent to remote voting centers. For the presidential elections, some 50,000 polling stations were opened. Another person essential to the election process was a quiet university professor from Togo, Tadjoudine Ali-Diabacte. The two of them, with critical support provided by South Africa, made a huge difference. But the most important actor was the Congolese people themselves. Visiting the independent electoral commission a few months before the first election was a moving experience for me. In Kinshasa, the digital foundation of a new democracy was being built and the excitement of electoral workers was palpable. Their leader was a clergyman and university professor, Abbé Malu-Malu, who was the chairman of the independent electoral commission. He gained the respect of everybody by effectively registering millions of voters and establishing the credibility of the electoral process. His impartiality would later be questioned, as he increasingly would be seen as close to the president.

Did we succeed, did the people of Congo, for decades deprived a voice, speak up? At one level, they did: throughout the country, people who sometimes could not read had walked for miles to register, for the first time in their lives, at remote registration centers. They had become citizens, and these new citizens—25 million of them—were becoming "the people," a polity, as their names were entered in electronic databases. But in hindsight, there is little doubt that the sequence of elections made little sense. As one of the more thoughtful Congolese leaders told me in October 2004, it did not make much sense to have as the first free and fair Congolese election in half a century a referendum on a constitution drafted by a parliament of unelected members. A constitution is always a complicated document that voters can hardly relate to, and as the European discussion on the ratifications of the Maastricht and Lisbon treaties has shown, voters do not necessarily decide on the merits of the document, and a popular referendum may not be the best option. The massive victory of the yes vote (84 percent) in Congo was a costly foregone conclusion. It would certainly have been more honest to admit that a constitutional referendum was an expensive and unnecessary formality. Ideally, it would have been preferable to elect the assembly charged with drafting a constitution, rather than have a referendum on the constitution itself. Meanwhile, the priority given to national elections (of the president and parliament) meant that the consolidation of local institutions was delayed. The direct election of the president, which was pushed by the international community in Congo as in Afghanistan, was a strategic choice fraught with risks. It certainly strengthened the office of the president, who became the symbol of the restored unity of the country. But ominously, the Mobutu tradition of a Kinshasa-centric regime was not broken: the distribution of power in the capital remained the central focus, dangerously raising the stakes, and almost derailing the electoral process. The question of the participation of long-time opposition politician Etienne Tchisekedi in the presidential election thus became a major issue at the beginning of 2006. Would the historic leader of the Union for Democracy and Social Progress (UDPS), who had not been chosen as the representative of the political opposition when the four vice presidents of the transition were appointed, re-enter political life through the presidential election? He seems to have been hesitant. He initially asked his supporters not to register for voting. When the registration phase was over, however, he made the reopening of registration a condition for his own candidacy, although his earlier call for a boycott of registration did not seem to have had much of an impact, and a reopening of the registration would have further delayed the election. When I went to Congo in 2006, I pleaded with him to participate, but I do not think there was much appetite in the international community for his participation. While many in his entourage probably would have liked him to run, Tchisekedi himself, who was then seventy-four years old, did not seem ready for this new phase of Congolese politics. Maybe he preferred keeping his legendary image as the man who had reintroduced the idea of democracy in Congo than actually be confronted with the risk of failure in the first democratic election of a president.

The non-participation of Tchisekedi opened the possibility for Jean-Pierre Bemba to be the challenger of Joseph Kabila. Bemba, the son of a very rich businessman who made his fortune during the Mobutu years, attracted part of the Tchisekedi vote, especially in Kinshasa, which did not give a majority to Kabila. A petulant populist who enjoys the rough and tumble of politics, he is in many ways the opposite of Joseph Kabila; he talks a lot and tends to overwhelm his interlocutors with colorful stories that may or may not be true. His campaign was strong enough to force a second round, which made some in Kabila's entourage very nervous but actually confirmed that the election was not a fraud. And when Kabila eventually won the second round with 58 percent of the vote at the end of October 2006, the initial claims by Bemba that the election had been fraudulent sounded hollow.

Despite its success, the presidential election confirmed my fear that politics in Congo remained dangerously polarized along geographic fault lines. Bemba received 42 percent of the vote, but he won a plurality of votes in all the western provinces of the DRC, including Kinshasa, with more than 90 percent of the vote in his home province of Equateur. Kabila won the election with 58 percent of the vote nationally because he had a plurality in all the eastern provinces, with more than 90 percent of the vote in the two provinces of Kivu and in Katanga. Bemba eventually conceded, and when I came for the inauguration of President Kabila in December 2006, I encouraged Bemba, unsuccessfully, to attend the ceremony. The relationship between the two Congolese leaders actually degenerated into a grave crisis in April 2007 when fighting broke out in Kinshasa between government forces and the militia that was protecting Bemba. Under heavy bombing by government forces, Bemba had to take refuge in the South African embassy and was eventually allowed to leave the country. A year later, he was arrested in Brussels on the basis of a warrant issued by the International Criminal Court because of his command responsibility for war crimes committed in the Central African Republic by militias allegedly under his authority. Congo had, at least temporarily, lost a controversial but central figure in its politics.

At enormous and unsustainable cost, the international community consolidated the presidency through elections and largely ignored the other institutions of the state: The parliament was gradually weakened; justice remained elusive; the reform of the army and police stalled for many years; and provincial institutions remained weak, perpetuating the risk that provincial politics would be manipulated from Kinshasa and that neighbors would abuse institutional weakness. There was no international reaction when Bemba left Congo, nor when elections of provincial governors were manipulated or even bought. A strategic choice was made, by default more than design: peace would not be anchored in institutions but in fragile—and reversible—deals between leaders, in Congo and in the region. When five years later, in 2011, national elections were again organized, the international community had essentially given up on free and fair elections as a key foundation of legitimacy. This time Etienne Tchisekedi did run against Joseph Kabila, and Congolese civil society was mobilized. The electoral law, which provided for a second round if no candidate had reached 50 percent of the vote, was changed without any protest from the international community, which looked the other way when very credible allegations of significant fraud were proffered. Such indifference did not serve Congo well, and I do not think it served President Kabila, who needs a strong mandate and uncontested legitimacy to transform his country. It did not help the very low credibility of the international community and could only breed despair and cynicism among the many Congolese who want their country to change.

The strengthening of institutions was my main concern during my last two meetings with President Kabila. They were two long tête à tête: one in his suite in the Waldorf Astoria in New York, in September 2007 when I was still the head of peacekeeping; the next in his office in Kinshasa, where I went in the fall of 2009 to help the Open Society Institute support a more vibrant dialogue among the Congolese people. I discussed with the president the long and difficult road that still lay ahead. He and his country had gone a long way since our first meeting in April 2001, a few months after the assassination of his father. But there was still much unfinished business. There was still no effective justice in Congo, even if the arrest and transfer to the International Criminal Court in the Hague of one of the worst militia leaders of Ituri, Thomas Lubanga, had sent a signal that the reign of impunity might come to an end. Another indictee of the International Criminal Court, Bosco Ntaganda, was still free, in spite of an arrest warrant, and that situation would get worse when in 2009 the deal with Rwanda to integrate Rwandan-backed militias allowed him to join the Congolese armed forces. The capacity of the country to handle through institutions political differences also remained very weak. I stressed to the president that Congo was still too fragile to afford to exclude any significant component of the political spectrum. In both meetings, I insisted that the parliament had an important role to play, and that strong institutions were actually power multipliers. Congo would be in a better position to have stable relations with its neighbors in the east if its provinces became stronger and the state was more visible and accountable.

As the 2011 elections attest, I did not convince the president, nor the big powers that could have made a difference. Since the high point of the 2006 elections, the fragile unity of purpose of the international community has been replaced by competition for lucrative mining contracts. That competition was exacerbated when China invited itself to the table, to the great satisfaction of the Congolese and dismay of Western countries that felt they were losing leverage and market share.

The Congolese people and their leaders have gradually lost confidence in foreigners, and the international community, tired of its own efforts, has lost any ambition. Fifty years after independence, Congolese leaders are suspicious of the Western agenda, and they are proud that the Democratic Republic of the Congo is at last on its own. Today, Congolese nationalism perfectly suits international exhaustion. The creation of the intervention brigade and the appointment of Mary Robinson and then Said Djinnit as special envoys appear as ultimate efforts to help Congo take the right path. But I wonder at this stage what leverage and influence the international community can still muster. In any intervention, the political credibility of foreigners is a wasting asset, and the window when people in desperate need of help are open to foreign advice and influence is a very short one, which needs to be exploited momentarily, before it closes.

My greatest regret is that the breathing space that the peacekeepers created was not used early enough to build institutions, when there was still some trust between the Congolese and the United Nations. Today, both the Congolese leadership and the international community are gambling the future of this vast country on deals, often cut from a position of extreme weakness, and there is neither the commitment required on the part of the international community nor the trust needed on the part of the Congolese. It is in the early days and months of an intervention that the course is set. That is when we should put the most resources, political and military. In Congo, as in Afghanistan, we did the opposite: starting small and only gradually strengthening our military and political posture, when maybe it was too late.

And yet, I do not think the whole effort was wasted. The desperate people whose lives were saved by the United Nations in Ituri, the heated discussions with Congolese debating the future of their country are facts that cannot easily be dismissed, and for me they make the effort of all those years worthwhile. But it may have been a mistake not to radically alter the role of the UN after the 2006 elections. The United Nations kept a central military role, becoming almost an auxiliary of the government in the east, although the international community had lost its political oversight mechanism when the Comité International d'Appui à la Transition was disbanded after the 2006 presidential election. The United Nations found itself in the worse of all worlds: it still had responsibility, but it had lost most of its authority and legitimacy. A cleaner cut would have been preferable, as in Sierra Leone, where the United Nations started downsizing its force before it was asked to do so. But a clean cut—if it was not to be reckless—would have required a much earlier and much more strategic engagement in the politics of Congo, so that viable institutions and not just a fragile presidency were in place when the United Nations started leaving. I repeatedly pushed for such engagement, but was often distracted by the more immediate pressures of military operations.

There was never any clarity on the degree of support that the international community would be willing to provide to the United Nations for a more ambitious and more focused political strategy. One should not have expected from the Security Council, which includes democracies as well as authoritarian regimes, a unified and coherent strategy on how to consolidate state institutions. This is true even though all countries, democratic and nondemocratic, are wary of the unpredictability of a democratic process in a country emerging from civil war. What is stability, after all? The capacity for a government to control dissent, or the capacity of institutions to manage differences? An exhausted and skeptical international community clearly prefers the first option, even if democracies rhetorically support the second.

In the end, only the Congolese people can transform Congo. My own commitment to Congo found its inspiration in them, in the many brave people who after several decades of dictatorship and two decades of war want to build their country. Some, like Floribert Chibeya, the president of the NGO The Voice of Those Who Have No Voice, who was assassinated in 2010, have paid for their commitment with their lives. Many others are patiently beginning to transform Congo. The engagement of the United Nations has certainly not met their expectations, but it helped end the division of Congo and a full-fledged civil war. Today, the Congolese economy is growing at a fast clip, and the lives of many Congolese have improved, but state institutions remain weak and almost irrelevant.

We have to accept that in a country that is not theirs, peacekeepers can play only a limited role: they help contain the most extreme violence, and they open a fragile, and constantly threatened, path toward a more open society. Ultimately, they cannot go much further than the leaders of the country in which they are deployed want them to go, and their impact is a reflection of the commitment of the international community. But on those occasions where they succeed against all odds, their success can make all the difference between life and death for millions of people, and that slim hope is worth risking many failures.

seven

SUDAN

Dangers of a Fragmented Strategy
for a Fragmented Country

The year 2003 was when the killing began in Darfur. In the UN, only two people had raised the alarm in internal meetings of the Secretariat of the United Nations: Mukesh Kapila, the senior development official of the United Nations in Sudan, and Jan Egeland, the head of humanitarian affairs in New York. But it was only in June 2004 that the crisis in Darfur became a big issue at the United Nations and in the global international debate. Iraq had been the dominant international issue in 2003, and my main focus that year was on the crisis in eastern Congo. A year later, we were again moving backward in Congo, with the failure of the UN mission in Bukavu, and I also was concerned about the hardening of President Laurent Gbagbo's position in Côte d'Ivoire. I did not have my eyes trained on Sudan.

I can still recall the silence in the room when a courageous woman from Pakistan, Asma Jahangir, who was then the UN special rapporteur on extrajudicial, arbitrary, and summary executions, spoke up in a meeting of the Executive Committee on Peace and Security, an internal UN structure that Kofi Annan had created precisely to ensure that nobody would be in a position to claim not to know about crisis situations. At the same time, Andrew Natsios, who was the head of the U.S. Agency for International Development, made a special trip to New York to see the secretary general. His interest in Sudan was not recent, and he would prove to be the senior official of the George W. Bush administration most knowledgeable about Sudanese issues. When he met with Kofi Annan, he brought maps of Darfur, which showed with great precision the extent of the destruction: hundreds of villages had been burned down, and the survivors had moved to huge camps of displaced persons, where they survived only with international aid. I do not recall the word genocide being used in those meetings, but it was clear that a great tragedy was happening in Darfur.

At the same time, there were signs that the long war that had devastated the south of Sudan might come to an end. Building on the framework agreement they had signed in Machakos, Kenya, in 2002, the government of Sudan and the main rebel movement in the south, the Sudan Peoples Liberation Movement (SPLM), were able to sign a wealth-sharing agreement in January and a power-sharing agreement in March. In early June, the Security Council made the decision to establish a precursor mission that would pave the way for a full-fledged peacekeeping operation once a peace agreement was signed. Kofi Annan decided to appoint as his representative Jan Pronk, a strong personality who did not fit the traditional diplomatic mold. Pronk had been a leftist development minister in the Netherlands who did not hesitate to challenge governments with patchy human rights records. He had resigned from the cabinet when the UN issued in 1999 its harsh report on the failure of peacekeepers to protect Muslims in Srebrenica, Bosnia; with that resignation, Pronk took political responsibility for the conduct of Dutch troops in Srebrenica. He would bring to Sudan the same personal commitment that he had shown throughout his political career, winning the respect of many—including unlikely interlocutors like the president of Eritrea—for his integrity, but eventually breaking his relationship with the Sudanese authorities.

The year 2004 also was when the Peace and Security Council of the African Union became operational. The institutional transformation, from the Organization of African Unity to the African Union, had an enormous symbolic meaning for many Africans, and for nobody more than Alpha Oumar Konare, the volcanic former president of Mali, who had considerable ambitions for Africa and was the first chairman of the newly created Commission of the African Union. The vision of an Africa that could take charge of its own affairs was now to be tested, as African observers were being deployed to Darfur. Would the prospect of peace between North and South Sudan and the hope that Africa was going to have a new dawn with the creation of the African Union be confirmed or shattered by its response to the tragedy of Darfur? From the outset, there were competing agendas concerning Darfur. There were the grassroots movements of Western countries, particularly active in the United States, which had put Darfur on the Western political map; their goal was to prevent the international community from once again looking the other way, as it had done before when confronted by mass atrocities. For many of them, the Darfur situation called for a humanitarian intervention. There was the U.S. government, reacting to the public pressure of grassroots movements, with no intention to intervene, as it was busy trying to stabilize Iraq, but with no sympathy for the regime of President Omar al-Bashir. Some African countries were actually suspicious of the intentions of Washington and concerned that the Bush administration wanted to achieve regime change in Sudan through support of rebel movements. And there were the new leaders of the African Union, keen to demonstrate that they could effectively resolve conflicts in Africa.

The United Nations was at the epicenter of those conflicting expectations, and Kofi Annan decided to visit Darfur with U.S. secretary of state Colin Powell before attending the African Union summit in Addis Ababa. At the end of the visit, the United Nations and the government of Sudan were able to agree on a joint communiqué, which could have paved the way to a cooperative relationship between Sudan and the United Nations if it had ever been implemented. The UN and the government recognized the "need to stop the continuing attacks on the targeted civilian population in Darfur, particularly by the Janjaweed and other outlaw armed groups, and to ensure security in the region consistent with the humanitarian cease-fire agreement signed by the government of Sudan and the rebel groups (SLM and JEM [the Sudan Liberation Movement and the Justice and Equality Movement]) in May." The United Nations committed to more humanitarian aid and help to the African Union in deploying monitors, while the government pledged to step up its efforts to disarm the Janjaweed, which were informal pro-government militias, and to facilitate humanitarian access.

In Addis, Konare was already planning the deployment of a force of 300 soldiers who would protect monitors supervising the "humanitarian ceasefire" that had been agreed in April. The implicit hope was that the government of Sudan, which had initially used Arab militias to quell a rebellion that was challenging its army, was now ready to put the genie back in its bottle, and might welcome some international help. But were the rebels ready for an agreement? Konare privately expressed his concern that rebels were being encouraged by Eritrea not to attend the talks. And from the outset, there was an ambiguity on the role of military deployments. Obviously, in an area with more than 6 million people, spread among hundreds of small villages, a "force" of 300 soldiers was not an adequate force, and the credibility of monitors depended entirely on the strength of the agreement that they would oversee. But the hardware of troops and military observers was easier to support than the more elusive concept of a political process. The focus on peacekeeping and deployment of a force, African or international, was a diversion, but for heads of state, as well as for grassroots movements, it would become the main issue.

Back in New York, Kofi Annan warned the Security Council, at its monthly informal lunch, on the limits of military threats. The new American ambassador was a former senator from Missouri, John Danforth, a principled man ordained as an Episcopalian priest, who had a personal commitment to bringing peace to Sudan. In one of the first meetings he attended, he observed with some melancholy that the United States did not prefer unilateral action, but that no country was willing to engage, and he took Darfur as an example. On July 22 I was with Kofi Annan for a meeting in his conference room with Colin Powell, Andrew Natsios, and John Danforth. Powell, who a few weeks later would characterize the situation in Darfur as "genocide," agreed that the solution would not come from troops but from an agreement among the Sudanese themselves. There was deep and justified skepticism about what could be achieved by additional deployments of Sudanese police, or soldiers from South Sudan, as John Garang, the leader of the SPLM, had offered. Jan Egeland, who was a very effective advocate for the humanitarian community, noted that the situation had temporarily improved with the massive deployment of humanitarian aid, but he was pushing for more "intervention." There was no obvious way forward on the political front, as the rebels were more and more divided. It was agreed that increased political pressure would be applied through monthly reports that the Secretariat of the United Nations would submit to the Security Council. But I doubt anybody seriously believed that anyone would make a difference.

In effect, the option of military deployments gained ground by default rather than by choice. General Patrick Cammaert, the military adviser of the Department of Peacekeeping Operations, was tasked to develop plans for an African Union mission in Darfur. He went to Darfur and came back with a plan for the deployment of a force of 3,200 troops and 1,200 police. The plan suited everybody: the United Nations, which did not have to deploy a mission that did not look promising; the African Union, which was keen to flex its new political muscles; and the leading Western countries, which wanted "to do" something, but certainly were not prepared to deploy their own troops and did not want to pay too much. A price tag of $228 million to fund an African mission looked like a reasonable bargain to escape an uncomfortable situation.

The situation took a significant turn in September when in testimony before the Foreign Relations Committee of the U.S. Senate, Colin Powell famously declared: "Genocide has been committed in Darfur and the government of Sudan and the Janjaweed bear responsibility—and genocide may still be occurring." This short sentence immediately made headlines, as it should have. For most people around the world, the word genocide conjures memories of the Holocaust, of Cambodia, of Rwanda. It is a stark reminder of the lack of will of the international community to prevent those immense crimes. It was therefore not surprising that when the secretary of state of the most powerful nation on earth made such a categorical statement, many would expect the United States to take decisive action to prevent a repetition of the past. But a careful reading of the full statement of the secretary showed that Colin Powell had good lawyers but poor political advisors and spin-doctors. The statement was based on a long legal analysis referring to the terms of the UN's Genocide Convention. The convention defines genocide broadly as "acts committed with intent to destroy, in whole or in part, a national, ethnical, racial, or religious group."

And indeed, Janjaweed or Jingaweit militias, as they are alternatively known, had committed large-scale acts of violence against non-Arab tribes in Darfur. It was not hard to argue that the widespread burning of non-Arab villages, accompanied by rape and looting, was indeed genocide as defined by the 1948 convention, which is much broader than the usual understanding of the word. However, because the convention captures a wide range of acts that can be characterized as genocidal, it is also more cautious in the answer that it prescribes. On the basis of the convention, Colin Powell recommended a formal UN investigation into all violations of human rights that had occurred in Darfur; in other words, a report but no specific action to be taken. After the use of the word genocide, this was a somewhat lame response. The secretary of state noted that the United States saw the situation in Darfur as genocide, but the international community needed more evidence. And he was clear that the investigation provided an opportunity for the government of Sudan to redeem itself "before it is taken to the bar of international justice" by taking action and "holding to account those who are responsible for past atrocities." Invoking genocide was a diplomatic tool to gain time, rather than a moral determination that something needed to be done.

The stage was now set for a long series of equivocations and obfuscations that have prolonged, rather than shortened, the tragedy of Darfur. This became clear at the next monthly lunch of the Security Council, where several states from the developing world asked that incendiary words that divide not be used and called for "incentives." But the U.S. diplomatic strategy, which would come to be supported by all Western countries, was more about punishment than incentives. It assumed that if the government of Sudan did not take action to prevent acts of genocide, it was itself an accomplice to genocide. Was it acceptable and realistic to conduct a genuine negotiation with such extreme accusations looming in the background? If you were on the side of angels, negotiating with the devil was unseemly, and if you were accused of being the devil, the road to heaven looked like a long and arduous path.

As for the United Nations, it was caught in the middle of those contradictions. Ambassador Danforth, to win support for the resolution initiating the investigation called for by the United States, had softened the language of the secretary of state, saying that genocide was likely to have happened, and the resolution that came out of the deliberations of the Security Council on September 18 (Resolution 1564) was ambiguous: The real political goal was not to establish facts, but to build pressure and buy time. The resolution mixed threats of "additional measures," meaning sanctions, with expectations of cooperation with the government of Sudan. Meanwhile, the situation in Darfur had not improved much, and Kofi Annan could not accept that while the diplomats were buying time, people continued to die. Although Colin Powell had told U.S. senators that the African Union was willing "to provide a significant number of troops" and had commented that this was "the fastest way to bring security to the countryside," we had no illusions, and Kofi Annan reminded the Security Council of its responsibilities. The deployment of African troops was the fastest way only because there was no other way.

Kofi Annan asked me to call the European Union and NATO to check whether they might make troops available. I doubt he believed there was any possibility that it would happen, but I think it was a way for him to put on notice the rich countries that had played the critical role in raising international awareness of the Darfur tragedy. I doubted that any military deployment could make a difference in the absence of a political agreement, and I was concerned that all this saber rattling was a political show with little meaning; it intended to put pressure on the government of Sudan, but it was a bluff that would most likely harden Sudanese resistance. Though I was not convinced, I made the calls. A few days later, when President Jacques Chirac came to New York for the General Assembly, he chided me for having called on NATO: "It would be utter folly to have NATO in Darfur!" he solemnly said. I agreed with him, but the prospect of a serious NATO presence in Darfur was always remote. Meanwhile, African countries were making extraordinary efforts to deploy quickly, and by October some 2,000 African troops were present in Darfur. This was all the more remarkable as the rivalry between South Africa and Nigeria for a permanent seat at the Security Council made it impossible to organize the AU mission around a "framework nation" that could direct and structure the expeditionary force.

The Western world was satisfied that something had been done about Darfur so it could move on to other challenges, or at least wait for the results of the UN inquiry, which would not be ready before 2005. Later in the fall, an opportunity presented itself to the Security Council to take a truly strategic approach and consider not just Darfur, but the whole of Sudan. The peace talks between the SPLM and the government of Sudan were making steady progress, but the Security Council was not much involved. The UN Secretariat sent a supporting team to the talks, in preparation for the deployment of a peacekeeping operation to implement the future peace accord between Khartoum and South Sudan. The UN had a lot to catch up with. The negotiation until then had been tightly controlled by a small group of "observer" countries: Italy, Norway, the United Kingdom, and the United States. They now saw the need to enlist broader support, and John Danforth, keen to move the peace process forward, convinced the Security Council to hold a special meeting in Africa, with a focus on Sudan and Somalia. This was an intelligent and courageous decision, which would allow the other members of the Security Council, who were little informed about Sudan, to take ownership of one of the most strategic issues for the future of Africa. The council met on November 18 in Nairobi to discuss Sudan. This was only the second meeting of the Security Council in Africa—the first had happened thirty years earlier in Addis Ababa and had focused on decolonization—and it was only the third or fourth outside New York.

Sudan, prior to its ultimate partition in 2011, was the largest country in Africa. Its size, which put its northern border with Egypt 2,000 kilometers away from its southern border with Uganda, and its position, east of the Sahara desert, created a unique situation. The divide between Arab and black Africa cut right across the country, but the Nile—whose two branches, coming from the depths of black Africa, merge in the capital Khartoum—provides a physical link between two very different worlds: the green world of swamps and lush forests in the south and the world of the desert in the north. For many centuries, going back to ancient Egypt, the people of the north have preyed on the south, bringing from the depths of the continent slaves, gold, and ivory. In modern times, the Arab tribes of the Nile around Khartoum have been the dominant actors in Sudan, building their wealth on north-south and east-west trade, as Muslim pilgrims from West Africa crossed through Sudan on their way to Mecca. A century of British colonial rule did little to change the pattern. The colonizers dealt primarily with the Arab elite, and their presence in the south, except for some garrison towns, remained minimal. When Sudan became independent in 1956, there were only six trained doctors for the whole south. The only real legacy of the colonial period in the south was Christianity, promoted by Protestant missionaries, which added another layer on some of the greatest and most complex civilizations in Africa, among which the Nuer kingdoms are the most famous. When independence came, there was little to unite the Arab tribes of the north with the people of the south, as the colonial period had exacerbated the differences, and Sudan has been engulfed in a succession of internal conflicts almost continuously since 1956. And yet, the Arab leaders, after centuries of trade, have more African blood than they would like to admit, and the divide today is often more in the minds than in the color of the skin. Many "Arabs," including in Darfur, which geographically belongs to the north, have dark skin, and I remember Hassan Tourabi, the Islamist leader, reminding me that the word Sudan means "the country of the blacks." There was a hint of bitterness in the reminder, and the relations between the Arabs and the Africans of Sudan would probably be less difficult if the Arabs of Sudan were more assured of their own Arab identity. The militant Islamism of Tourabi or President Omar al-Bashir may be a way to compensate for the hybridization of the country.

The Security Council meeting in Nairobi took place in a big hall quite representative of the bland buildings of the 1960s or early 1970s, a rather good illustration of the pseudo-homogenization of the modern world at its most mediocre. This was a historic occasion, but not a historic building. I had never met John Garang, the leader of the SPLM, before. He was a towering figure, and one could see, beyond the romanticized legend of the freedom fighter, the tough strategic mind of a man who probably was not a democrat, but who had a vision for his country. He was a popular leader not just in the south, but also in the north, where many black Africans live, especially in the slums of Khartoum. When he spoke about the "earthquake of peace" that an agreement would bring, it was more than rhetoric on the part of a man who had fought for decades. And when he called on the Security Council to be the guardian of the agreement, it was more than a diplomatic nicety. They were the words of a rebel leader entrusting the future of his people to the international community. The representative of the government in Khartoum, Vice President Ali Osman Taha, was more polished, but he too was not a mediocre figure. It was significant that he spoke unequivocally of federalism and decentralization. One had a sense that the two men who had been instrumental in moving the negotiation forward might agree on a vision of a "new Sudan." As for the African leaders, they had their usual ambivalence about the role of the United Nations. Yoweri Museveni, the president of Uganda, spoke in favor of African solutions and African troops, remarking that in Africa, there are people of all colors, including blue, like John Garang!

The most immediate issue was the army of the future state. The proportion between north and south was not easy to agree to, because it required an agreement on the baseline, on the balance of forces as it was, which is a sensitive issue when you are fighting a war. Garang was apparently prepared to make concessions and to agree to a 70/30 ratio between north and south, but he wanted the army to be paid by the central government, so that the funds allocated to the south would fund development rather than armed forces. He spent a lot of his speech addressing pending technical issues in the negotiations, rather than explaining how the "earthquake of peace" that he was hoping for could be consolidated in a strategic way.

A Lost Opportunity

In hindsight, the meeting in Nairobi was a lost opportunity. It had not been well prepared, many members of the Security Council were not well informed, and those who knew the real issues were not sure that broadening the circle of engaged countries would bring more results. The secretary general nevertheless stressed the need to make sure that the peace process between north and south and the Darfur peace process were made compatible and that peace in Sudan was considered as a whole. "Only a comprehensive political solution for the Sudan as a whole offers any longer-term hope of stability in the country," he said. He called for a national conference involving all Sudanese stakeholders to discuss the future governance of the country. Vice President Taha, while he took exception to the secretary general for singling out the government of Sudan for violations of the Darfur humanitarian cease-fire, nevertheless responded positively, stating that "the peace agreement opens the door to conducting a national dialogue to form a popular, broad-based government." John Garang was less explicit in his speech, and the Western countries that were supporting him were too keen to complete the north-south deal to push him hard on the broader issue.

It was clear that the deterioration of the situation in Darfur was a threat to Garang's negotiating strategy, and that it was all the more urgent for him to have a north-south agreement. The war in Darfur was a threat because it challenged the domination of the north by the National Congress Party (NCP), the party of President Bashir and Vice President Taha. It could unravel the deal between the NCP and Garang's SPLM, which essentially divided power between the two dominant actors of the war, at the expense of other political actors. The agreement that was eventually signed on January 9, 2005, would create a "government of national unity" that gave 80 percent of seats in the transitional national assembly to the NCP and the SPLM combined (52 percent and 28 percent respectively) and only 14 percent to northern opposition parties and 6 percent to southern opposition groups. These percentages would have had to be revised if the aspirations of other stakeholders, particularly in Darfur, were to be acknowledged.

In the following years, the people of Sudan would pay a heavy price for their leaders' abandonment of a truly comprehensive solution. Some members of the international community, in particular the United States, encouraged this strategic mistake, which suited the parties themselves. But as 2004 was coming to a close, this was not clear to me, nor was it a major feature of the public debate. The focus was all on the Comprehensive Peace Agreement (CPA), which was signed on January 9, 2005. It was a very complex set of documents, totaling more than 200 pages, the conclusion of a three-year-long detailed negotiation in which a consortium of countries, the east African Inter-Governmental Authority on Development (IGAD) and in particular Kenya through General Lazaro Sumbeiywo, played a key role, as well as the governments of Italy, Norway, the United Kingdom, and the United States, which had done much more than merely "observe" the process.

The strategic compromise was spelled out in the introduction to the agreement. The right of self-determination of Southern Sudan was recognized, and therefore the possibility of a partition was acknowledged, but in the same paragraph, the parties committed "to make unity attractive during the interim period," which would last six years, after which a referendum would take place. In addition, the Western observers insisted, against the views of the NCP and the SPLM, in having elections halfway through the interim period, based on a national census that would determine the distribution of parliamentary seats throughout the country. After the elections, the percentages set in the agreement (80 percent to NCP and SPLM) would be replaced by the actual results of the electoral process. This reflected a profound ambiguity in the agreement, which could be read as a deal between two political movements that would each keep tight control over the part of the country where it was dominant, or as a foundation for a new, more democratic way of running Sudan. Considering the history of the protagonists, the second interpretation was always in doubt, but one could hope that a gradual process would be initiated, one that would not take away power from those who had it but might open political space in which power eventually would be more equitably shared. The influence of international actors was visible in the detailed— probably too detailed—provisions that described the interim arrangements and the process that would lead to an interim constitution; such specificity seemed to ignore the temporary nature of the agreement. It also ignored the great imbalance between the parties: on the Northern Sudan side, there was a strong bureaucracy, with all the resources of a functioning state; on the Southern Sudan side, there was a rebel movement that had waged war while the international community took care of basic support to the civilian population through Operation Lifeline Sudan, run by a group of UN agencies and nongovernmental organizations established in 1989.

The agreement also did not pay enough attention to the political and practical implications of the enormous gap in capacities between the northern part of the country that had always played a dominant role and the southern part that had for all practical purpose been ignored by the colonizers as well as by the postindependence regime and that had borne the brunt of the war. In the south, a government of Southern Sudan was created, while there was no symmetrical arrangement for a government of Northern Sudan. In Northern Sudan, the national institutions would deal directly with states, while in the south, they would have to go through the regional government. The reality was that in the north a functioning state existed, while in the south it had to be created almost from scratch.

Detailed institutional provisions coexisted with great vagueness on some key issues that were at the heart of the conflict. A key provision was that the south would receive 50 percent of the oil revenues generated in the south. The provision was emblematic of the ambiguities of the agreement: Would the government of national unity genuinely allow the south to participate in governing the whole of Sudan, or would the government of national unity become the northern counterpart of the government of South Sudan, with only token participation of the south in it? The question mattered a lot for every aspect of the deal, including the wealth-sharing agreement. On the one hand, it was quite remarkable for the government in Khartoum to accept to share half of the resources collected in the south. On the other hand, it was unclear for whose benefit the asymmetry was created; depending on how the national institutions would function, one could argue that the government of Southern Sudan had obtained full control of half of the revenues generated in its part of the country without surrendering oversight on the resources generated in the other half of the country. Yet it could also be argued that if Bashir's National Congress Party maintained its dominance over national institutions, it had secured continued control over half of the resources of the south, while keeping full control over the resources it generated in the north.

The ambiguity was compounded when one looked into the details. To ensure a fair distribution of revenues, precise figures on the production of each oil well had to be available, but in practice, the Sudanese oil police, controlled through the national government by the National Congress Party, was responsible for the security of and access to the wells, and the government of South Sudan was dependent on the figures provided by technicians and specialists of the north. Even more fundamental, to distribute resources between north and south, one had to know where the north ended and where the south began. The power-sharing agreement included a crucial reference to the January 1, 1956, border. That border was of great importance for several critical issues: the distribution of resources, the apportionment of votes, and the re-deployment of forces. But there was no agreed map of the 1956 border, and the parties had explicit differences on some of the most sensitive areas, which led them to include in the peace agreement protocols that pushed into the future the resolution of the most contentious issues. As for the role of the United Nations, it was not spelled out. The negotiation had been conducted by the IGAD regional organization and the Western "observers," who were interested in the deployment of a peacekeeping operation to monitor the redeployment of forces but who wanted to keep a central role through an assessment and evaluation commission that would most likely not be chaired by the UN. While it was encouraging to see countries truly committed to a negotiation they had supported, I was concerned that there might not be much congruence in the expectations of the various actors. That was not a comfortable situation for the future peacekeeping operation of the United Nations, which would inevitably play a central role but might not have the leverage required to influence the underlying politics.

The detailed provisions were misleading: The agreement signed on January 9, 2005, was actually a very fragile foundation for peace. It provided a roadmap for future engagement, but its eventual success would depend on the continued commitment of those who had negotiated it. No peace agreement has ever guaranteed peace, but the peace agreement that was signed in 2005, through a combination of bad luck and bad decisions, did not put negotiations on the right track.

Throughout the year, in the south as well as in the north, the focus on deployment of troops—the troops of the UN in the south, the troops of the African Union in Darfur—consumed a lot of effort and was in some ways a distraction. Troops could make a difference if a political process was solidly on track, and they could buy space for political agreements to be strengthened, but in a huge country such as Sudan, their impact would inevitably remain quite limited. When on March 24, 2005, the Security Council authorized the deployment of 10,000 troops in Sudan, I was concerned that this apparently high figure would create false expectations. As in Congo, 10,000 troops looked like a big number, but the reality was that those troops would be spread over an immense territory, protecting observers who monitored the cease-fire, while government troops redeployed north of the 1956 border between north and south, and joint integrated units were created to provide security in some of the most sensitive areas. The attention was on the deployment of blue helmets, as the government of South Sudan had initial concerns about the apparently big size of the force and was wary of including in the force troops from Muslim countries such as Bangladesh or Pakistan, or from China. The views of the SPLM would eventually change; they would come to regret not having a bigger force, and would find that the religion of the troops did not matter.

In Darfur, on the other hand, the responsibility for the deployment of troops lay with the African Union, but as early as March 2005, other options were beginning to be considered. In an internal paper at the beginning of March, I had presented four options for an enhanced mission, to be deployed once a peace agreement was reached: an expanded AU force, an AU-UN force, a UN force, or a multinational force (MNF). I had expressed my preference for an MNF and had spoken against an expanded AU or AU-UN force. The initially small force deployed by the African Union was motivated, and it had some impact, but it was clearly much too small to make a lasting difference, even in the best of circumstances. However, enlarging it was not the solution: logistical support as well as command and control for a force of 8,000 would be incomparably more challenging than for a force of 3,000. In discussions at the Pentagon, the professional military understood my caution. But Jendayi Frazer at the State Department and Cindy Courville at the National Security Council, both of whom were close to Condoleezza Rice, were pushing for a bigger AU force. To make things worse, Jan Pronk, who meant well, made a public declaration calling for an 8,000-strong force. The figure came out of nowhere, and I now knew that the African Union was being set up for failure.

Meanwhile, the relationship with the Sudanese authorities was becoming increasingly difficult. Early in the year, the investigation on Darfur, while not formally concluding that genocide had happened, had recommended that the Darfur situation be referred to the International Criminal Court (ICC). Since Sudan was not a party to the Treaty of Rome that created the court, the only way for the court to be presented with the Darfur situation was through a resolution of the Security Council. The council studiously avoided any reference to sanctions or to the ICC in the resolution authorizing the deployment of the UN mission for Sudan, but adopted a resolution a few days later (Resolution 1593) referring Darfur to the ICC. The United States, which was ideologically opposed to the ICC, abstained, as did Algeria, Brazil, and China. I was surprised that China did not veto the resolution, and I am not sure the countries that pushed the resolution in the Security Council had fully thought through the implications of their action. A judiciary process is a punitive one that should never be afraid of clarity, while a peacekeeping operation is all about compromise and ambiguity. In the difficult road to peace, it deals with all shades of gray, a fact that is recognized by the Rome statute, which gives the Security Council the authority to suspend a procedure before the court if it finds it appropriate. But that legal possibility would hardly be a realistic option if it was the council itself that had initiated the process: justice cannot be turned on and off, and once the council had brought the International Criminal Court into the picture, it would have to suffer the consequences. But the resolution was adopted probably because all the members of the council, those who supported the resolution as well as those who abstained, took a very political view of justice. For those who supported it and for the United States, the resolution was, like the investigation before it, a way to put pressure on Khartoum and also to delay hard decisions. And nobody at the time contemplated the possibility that the prosecutor would dare request the indictment of President Bashir himself. They expected the prosecutor to be as political as they were. I myself thought that it was dangerous to use justice as a tactic, and I feared that justice and peace might eventually both suffer. There was a certain amount of carelessness in introducing the rigor of a judicial process into a situation where one of the potential culprits was a government that no state was prepared to challenge seriously. As with the genocide polemic, the gap between the rhetoric of the international community and its reality was once more in evidence. The rhetoric might complicate the work of the peacekeepers, without ensuring that justice would be delivered.

I made my first trip to Sudan in May 2005. In Khartoum and Darfur, I was joined by Lakhdar Brahimi. He had known Sudanese leaders for many years and certainly was, as a man who had fought for the independence of Algeria, the best placed among UN officials to convince our Sudanese interlocutors that the UN mission was not part of a colonialist conspiracy. Six months earlier, Bashir had told the secretary general that the UN and the government of Sudan would have to work together for a long time, and that it was important for the UN not to be manipulated by big powers. It was not clear to me whether that statement reflected a genuine willingness to work with the UN, but it was worth taking it at face value. If there was a possibility to find common ground on the future of Sudan, Brahimi could play an essential role in reaching such a strategic understanding with the Sudanese leadership. As we were flying toward Khartoum, I recalled what Bashir had said in the same meeting: he was ready for a national conference. So maybe there was a possibility to look at Sudan as a whole, maybe the Comprehensive Peace Agreement had opened a window for peace not just between north and south but also in Darfur. According to statistics of the African Union, there were now fewer than ten persons killed per month in Darfur. Could the "earthquake of peace" described by John Garang reach Darfur? Had a window of opportunity opened?

Meetings with Mohamed Osman al-Mirghani, the leader of the Democratic Unionist Party (DUP), and with Sadiq al-Mahdi, the leader of the Umma Party, showed how difficult a broad move toward peace would be. The DUP and the Umma were the two main opposition parties in the north, representing the traditional Nile-based Arab elite of Sudan. They had dominated Sudanese politics from independence until 1989, when they were ousted in a coup organized by Bashir; as an officer at the time, he had allied himself with the Islamists of Tourabi. The last free election was now twenty years in the past, and it was difficult to gauge the present level of support for the two opposition parties. They claimed to have much greater support than the present regime, and the Umma leaders reminded me that in 1986 they were by far the strongest party in Darfur. They were unhappy with the Comprehensive Peace Agreement, which marginalized them for the benefit of the NCP and the SPLM. When I met with al-Mirghani in Cairo, I suggested to him that while it was not realistic to reopen the agreement itself, since the government of Sudan and the SPLM were not ready for an adjustment, its implementation allowed for some flexibility. They could be given a higher representation in the implementation structure that would be put in place. Mirghani was confident that the DUP and the Umma had a much greater following than the National Congress Party and was therefore not prepared for major concessions. But he appeared confident that the agreement he had already secured with Vice President Taha and further discussion could produce results. He invited the UN to attend the next meetings and was keen to gain more international recognition.

In Khartoum, Vice President Taha was certainly among those prepared to enter serious political discussions, and the meeting with him seemed to confirm that a political discussion among the major Sudanese parties was a real possibility, even though it was difficult to have a sense of where he stood. He appeared to me as a very articulate, but very guarded man. He was another illustration of the ambiguities of Sudan: a thoughtful man who understood that politics was the only way to stability, and who was living proof that describing Sudan as a failed state did not make sense. But he also was a man with a very extremist view of Islam and was mentioned in rumors as a possible target for indictment by the ICC. There was much sophistication in the Sudanese leadership, but the history of the country since independence was one of fighting limited wars to suppress political dissent. The raw use of force, along with money and politics, had been in the toolbox of government leaders since 1956, and this was not going to change quickly. The brutal eviction of displaced persons from a camp in the suburb of Khartoum, while we were still in Sudan, was a reminder of the way the regime dealt with challenges to its authority. It also was an indication that the future of Sudan could no longer be decided through cozy arrangements agreed between leaders who had attended the same universities and were often related through marriage.

Most of the leaders we were meeting were in their fifties, sixties, or even seventies. But what was in the minds of the younger Sudanese, whose demonstrations at Khartoum University were brutally repressed? What was in the minds of the many unemployed youths living in the slums, when they saw the nouveau riche lifestyle of the regime elite? A Palestinian who was working with the UN mission drew some parallels with his own country: the younger generation was much more radical, wanted a genuine Muslim democracy, and was fed up with the compromise and coziness of the old ruling elite. The systematic way in which the Sudan regime was fanning the flames of anti-Western sentiment, using the abuse of prisoners in Guantanamo, the U.S. support for Israel, and the wars in Iraq and Afghanistan, was largely a defensive measure. The leadership of the ruling NCP had no worse fear than being challenged from its Islamic right. An alliance of Islamists and the disenfranchised youth was its worst nightmare, and may now be the greatest threat to what remains of Sudan. I would hear similar concerns a week later in Cairo, when I met Mohamed Fayek, a former minister of President Gamal Nasser who had been the Egyptian member of the UN commission of inquiry on Darfur. Seven years before the "Arab Spring," this human rights activist who had spent years in jail under President Anwar Sadat, whose commitment to democratic values was not in doubt, was afraid that Islamists would be the beneficiaries of a growing demand by younger Arabs for more democracy, because of ill-conceived and inconsistent Western policies.

Meanwhile, the broader regional context was deteriorating. It was difficult enough to encourage the Sudanese to find an agreement among themselves; it would be even harder if various regional actors stoked the flames of conflict. Taha had told us that he put much hope in a meeting between President Bashir and President Isaias Afewerki of Eritrea in Tripoli. Afewerki had influence over various rebel groups that he supported, in Darfur as well as in eastern Sudan. But the meeting went badly and left President Bashir with deep distrust of Eritrea. The fact that the archrival of Afewerki, Prime Minister Meles Zenawi of Ethiopia, had done poorly in elections, losing several major cities to the opposition, did not help. The Eritrean leader probably felt emboldened to pursue a regional strategy of supporting spoilers, which would make him an indispensable interlocutor for the resolution of conflicts in Sudan or in Somalia. Muammar Qaddafi in Libya and Idriss Deby in Chad also were playing their own games in Sudan, in pursuit of pan-Arabic dreams for Qaddafi and consolidation of Zaghawa power in the case of Deby.

Contrasting Scenes in Sudan

The trip to Darfur was a study in contrasts. In Al Fasher, the Khartoum-appointed governor threw a big party for us. He wanted to project an image of peace and control, and he was quite successful at it. We were given various artifacts from Darfur and treated to a banquet, with dances and music. But the day before, after receiving the coordinates of a meeting place through satellite phone, we had flown by helicopter to a remote location in the desert to meet with Suleiman Jamous. He was a member of the Zaghawa tribe, and was at the time close to Minni Minnawi, the rebel leader who would sign the Darfur Peace Agreement one year later (Jamous would then break with Minnawi). He spoke in a quiet and firm tone: "We do not trust the government, they have always cheated, and they will continue to cheat." Jan Pronk encouraged him to resist fragmentation, as it was the only way to have an effective negotiation. The rebels should stop travelling from one European capital to another; they had to be in Darfur, to develop a platform that could bring some unity among them. Jamous seemed to agree. For him, the war, the antagonism between so-called "Arab" and "African" tribes, was a manipulation of the government. The sources of tension could easily be defused if the government did not interfere. It was possible to agree with the nomads on corridors through which their herds would be allowed to move when the dry season came. But the government was escalating manageable issues by giving the nomads armed escorts that would inflame the situation. The Janjaweed were an instrument of the government, not a Darfur phenomenon.

The day after the banquet, we saw what violence could mean in Darfur, what Suleiman was referring to. An African Union helicopter flew us to Khor Abeche. The village had been burned to the ground, and as the helicopter was circling above a patch of brown-reddish earth to find a place to land, we felt we were landing on the moon: no house to be seen, no people. But it all changed when the engine of the Russian-made MI-8 eventually stopped. As the dust raised by the rotors began to settle down, we saw two big groups of people approaching. On one side, they were all in white djellabas: they were the men. The other side was all colors, blue, red, green: they were the women. And then, in khakis, a handful of men with guns, the twenty soldiers deployed by the African Union. Because of those twenty soldiers, some 3,000 people out of a total population of 7,000 had returned to their village, which they had fled when the Janjaweed came. They had returned to nothing. A few broken pots, some blackened by fire, were the only remnants left of the "village," and slight undulations on the ground, of a darker color, were the only sign that houses once stood where we were walking. I was both impressed and frightened by the courage of the African Union troops. Their presence had given confidence to the returning population, but they had no capacity to repel any serious attack. Their deployment in this remote place was a brave gamble, which could turn into a tragedy if their bluff was called.

When we met with the governor of Western Darfur (who represented the Khartoum government), Brahimi spoke up. He did not lecture, he did not patronize, he just assumed that every human being would consider what we had seen as an outrage to our common humanity and appealed to the humanity of his interlocutor. How could human beings do to other human beings what we had seen? The governor was a shrewd man, and he responded without passion. He said that the government had suggested a preventative deployment in Khor Abeche, which the African Union had refused (I learned later that the African Union had wanted to deploy observers, but the government procrastinated). He added that the attack on the village had been a reprisal, in response to attacks launched from the village. It was impossible, on the spot, to tell whether he was lying. But there was no question that the thousands of poor men and women we had seen, who had lost almost everything, save a few sheep and goats, and who were huddling next to the African troops, were victims, and that, at a minimum, the government was not protecting them, if it was not responsible for the attack. Brahimi, without being aggressive, but with great clarity, had intimated as much.

What had happened in Khor Abeche convinced me that the force of 12,000 that was being recommended would either be too much or not enough. If the government was genuinely ready to engage in a process of reconciliation, what would be needed was political help, especially with international actors; development aid; and a mobile force that could support efforts of the army as it began to regain control over the militias it had equipped as its proxies. If the government was not ready for a political process, a foreign force would never have the resources and knowledge required to defuse the myriad local conflicts that could so easily be exploited and manipulated. The African Union or the United Nations could never compete with Sudanese military intelligence in understanding the complex local politics of Darfur. In Darfur, as in Afghanistan, foreigners might facilitate the resolution of conflicts if the key national actors wanted to resolve them. It would be naive for foreigners to pretend that they could bring peace and find solutions for which the Sudanese or the Afghans were not yet ready. There was some hubris in pretending otherwise.

Was there a better chance to succeed in the south? I was pondering the question in the white UN Boeing 727 making its way from Khartoum to Juba, the future capital of South Sudan. The proposed 10,000 troops would be a ridiculously small force, but if Garang and Taha kept their agreement on track, it might work. But as the visit to Southern Sudan was progressing, I felt more and more that the challenges were daunting.

There was the very practical issue of deployment. A few hundreds yard from the Juba airport, the UN camp was in a low-lying area, a green field. From a distance, it looked good, but as you cut the high grass, you found it was full of snakes, and it would become a swamp in the rainy season. The troops as well as the civilian personnel lived under tents, which would be soaked when the heavy rains started. And building hard-wall accommodations would be enormously difficult; there was not one machine to make gravel in the whole south, the roads were mined, and almost everything had to be brought in by plane, which also made life quite expensive for internationals, even more than in Khartoum. It was going to be extraordinarily difficult to attract quality civilian peacekeeping personnel to the south, under such circumstances. The humanitarian personnel of UN agencies had a better pay package, and having been around for two decades, they had had ample time to build nice facilities. But they were over 300 kilometers away in Rumbek, where the World Food Program had just completed an expansion of its base. Rumbek was the temporary capital of South Sudan, but the SPLM's plan was for Garang and the government to move to Juba, which would become their capital. This tale of two cities, Rumbek and Juba, was an illustration of the disconnect between the peace operation, which should help the government build its own capacities, and the humanitarian effort of Operation Lifeline Sudan, which had very efficiently provided lifesaving assistance to the civilian population during years of war, essentially substituting for the rebel government, whose priority was the war with the north.

We took a long helicopter ride to Rumbek to meet with Garang. The low-flying helicopter, dodging thunderstorms, allowed me to see how empty the countryside was: savanna, trees, swamps, and greenery everywhere. In Rumbek, a city of approximately 100,000 inhabitants, there was only a dirt runway, used by World Food Program planes. There was no paved road or electricity, except for the generators in the UN compound and a few villas. There were no vehicles, except for the white Toyotas of the UN and a few SUVs of the SPLM. This was only my second meeting with John Garang, and I did not imagine it would be the last. We were sitting on plastic chairs, on a porch, as the tropical night was falling. Garang immediately made clear that he was somewhat disappointed with the UN operation. His reservations during the pre-deployment phase, about its allegedly big size, were gone. He now wanted more troops, not fewer. His expectations were shaped by his experience with the humanitarian operation: he wanted the UN to provide security services in the same way the UN agencies had provided humanitarian services. I promised that we would do our best to open up and secure roads, combining our engineering capacities with the major demining work conducted by the humanitarian community. But I had to explain to him the limitations of the force. He could not expect the UN troops to be able to crush the Lord's Resistance Army (LRA), a vicious group originating in Uganda, which was suspected of having received some support from Khartoum during the war. A peacekeeping force is not a counterinsurgency force. I told him what I had told the Congolese and other countries recovering from conflict. In the end, any country has to count on itself to create its own security. But as we were discussing the transformation of the South Sudan rebel forces into a professional army, it was increasingly clear that there were still many unresolved political issues.

After Garang left, I continued the meeting over dinner with Riek Machar. I knew about Machar because I had read *Emma's War*, a story full of romance about a British aid worker who had joined Machar in the bush, married him, and then died in a mysterious car accident at the age of twenty-nine. This could be read as a beautiful story of love and idealism, but the backdrop had been a vicious war between southern groups. In the early nineties, Machar, a Nuer, had fought a brutal war against Garang, a Dinka. He had then joined the government of Sudan in Khartoum, becoming an assistant to the president. But in 2002 he went back to Garang, and he was again a key player in the south. I had some difficulty reconciling the charismatic rebel leader, with whom Emma had fallen in love, with the calculating and tough operator who was probably responsible for mass killings of civilians and who had already switched sides twice in his political career. When we discussed the modalities of the creation of a new army, he made clear that he wanted his forces to stay together and had no appetite for any form of mixing with other units, or worse, demobilization. Machar controlled a significant force, and he wanted to keep it that way. Between the Nuer and the Dinka, there was a little more trust than between the government of South Sudan and Khartoum, but not much more. That absence of any real trust eventually exploded in a renewed civil war at the end of 2013, when the Dinka president of South Sudan, Salva Kiir, fell out with his Nuer vice president Riek Machar.

Less than three months later, on the last Sunday morning of July, my phone rang in New York, and I received a terse message from the situation center of the Department of Peacekeeping Operations: the Ugandan helicopter in which Garang was returning from Kampala had gone missing in bad weather. Soon after, the peacekeepers, who had launched an extensive search operation, confirmed what we all feared: John Garang was dead, and there were no survivors in the crash. Three weeks earlier, Garang had been in Khartoum for the inauguration of the government of national unity and had become the first vice president of Sudan. People like to think that events that have big consequences have big causes, and after the death of Garang, many conspiracy theories would flourish. But from my own experience of flying in the treacherous climate of equatorial Africa, I would think that bad weather and bad luck were quite enough to explain the tragedy.

With the death of John Garang, the level of engagement between north and south went down, which hurt the influence and power of Taha, who had been seen as having played a critical role in pulling together the north-south deal. Before Garang's death, there already was a high risk that tactics would trump strategy, and that it would be very hard to agree on a joint long-term vision. The death of Garang tipped the balance in a decisive way. The international community had never shown the political and conceptual strength to agree on a comprehensive and coherent strategy in Sudan, but with Garang and Taha as the two principal actors there was still the hope that together they would be able to shape if not one vision, at least two compatible visions of Sudan. The vision of a new Sudan died with John Garang. His successor Salva Kiir did not have the vision and charisma to keep the whole of Sudan together, and it is now uncertain whether he will be able to keep South Sudan together.

eight

DARFUR

Deploying Peacekeepers against All Odds

The strategic consequences of John Garang's death in July 2005 were not immediately apparent, but it was clear that the negotiating calculus had changed. The international community and the government of Sudan embarked on an increasingly fragmented approach, propelled by the government's lack of trust in the international community and the international community's inability to unify its separate policies toward Southern Sudan and Darfur. As a result, engagement between the north and south of Sudan decreased quickly.

To avoid a power vacuum, Salva Kiir, a Dinka like Garang, was swiftly sworn in as first vice president of Sudan. I had seen Kiir at the meeting in Rumbek. He did not speak much and looked almost shy. But I had noted how he had become animated when the question of recruiting civil servants had come up. He was the most adamant in rejecting encroachment from the north, and it was clear that for him there should not be one Sudanese civil service, but a South Sudan civil service quite distinct from that in the north. Kiir was little known in the north, where Garang was the only leader from the south who could realistically claim to have a following. But in the south, Salva Kiir was a less domineering figure than John Garang had been, and initially he seemed more ready to open up to other leaders. He took Riek Machar as his vice president for South Sudan. A few months after his appointment, in a move that demonstrated his ability to unite leaders, he brought the South Sudan Defense Forces, including troops who had reported to Machar, under the fold of the new Sudan Peoples Liberation Army (SPLA). This was an encouraging move that I had initially thought very unlikely, considering my previous conversation with Machar, when Garang was still in power.

The international community's fragmentation also suited the African Union (AU), which was proud to have its own mission. Alpha Oumar Konare, chair of the AU Commission, was impatient to expand it to 12,000 troops, with little consideration for the constraints of force generation, logistics, and command and control. On my way back to New York, I stopped in Addis Ababa to discuss the situation with him. I tried to impress upon him that instead of spending 80 percent of our efforts on troops and logistics and 20 percent on politics, we should do the opposite. Lakhdar Brahimi had already quietly suggested the appointment of Salim Salim, the former Tanzanian secretary general of the now-defunct Organization of African Unity, as a special envoy, and I reiterated the suggestion. Konare did not seem to disagree. I also stressed that it was time to try to put some order in the disjointed efforts of the international community. Libya, Egypt, and Eritrea each had its own policy and favorite allies, and the same applied to Europe and the United States, which cultivated various rebel groups, making the situation ever more unmanageable. Between Khartoum, Washington, Addis Ababa, and Cairo, there was no agreement on a strategy or endstate.

Meanwhile, the rhetoric of protection and solidarity was getting louder. Kofi Annan was under enormous pressure to demonstrate that the UN could make a difference in Darfur because his position as secretary general remained fragile after a scandal over the UN's management of the oil-for-food program in Iraq (including the role played by his son Kojo), but also because Darfur remained the focus of world attention, at the expense of the strategic north-south agreement for Sudan. For the press and for Western public opinion, the priority was the African Union peacekeeping mission in Darfur, and for the UN the challenge was how best to support it. Donors were providing support through an unwieldy and ineffective combination of bilateral agreements. The United States was building camps through a private contractor, Canada was paying for helicopters and providing equipment, various European countries were writing checks or seconding officers, and the European Union was funding troops and observers (for the latter at a rate substantially higher than the UN rate, which made it even more difficult to recruit observers for the UN mission in the south). While the intention may have been a division of labor, the result was confusion, waste, and mistrust. The donors were unhappy with the accounting of the African Union, and the African Union was frustrated with what it saw as micromanagement and continuous interference by donors.

Following the advice of my deputy, Hedi Annabi, I had selected as the UN representative who would work with the African Union a remarkable man who had a personal experience with genocide: Henry Aniydoho was the

Ghanaian general who had been the deputy of Roméo Dallaire, the admirable Canadian general who commanded the small UN force that was in Rwanda when the genocide happened. Aniydoho had then led the Ghanaian contingent with such gallantry that thousands of Rwandans were saved thanks to him. A big man and a straight shooter with integrity and immense energy, he immediately won the respect of his interlocutors in the African Union, among them Said Djinnit, the very professional Algerian diplomat who was my counterpart in the secretariat of the African Union and the commissioner for peace and security of the AU. Both men injected a dose of realism into discussions that too often ignored the practicalities of deploying poorly equipped troops in a harsh environment. The new African Union had no established structure to run an operation and was roughly in the same situation as the UN at the time of the Yugoslav wars of the 1990s, but without the well-equipped European troops that provided the bulk of UN deployments in the former Yugoslavia. The two men nevertheless were determined to make the best of an impossible situation. It was not easy to find a practical course. African leaders too often believed their own rhetoric, while Western countries, against all evidence, wanted to ignore the fundamental flaws of the operation they were supporting and pretended that writing checks was enough to set up a military force. This was like believing you just need to buy four wheels, an engine, and a frame to have a car. The government of Sudan provided at best uneven cooperation, and rebels leaders were more interested in creating facts on the ground than reaching an agreement. All the hard-learned lessons of the 1990s seemed to have been forgotten.

Back in New York, it became increasingly clear to me that the UN role would essentially be confined to military issues, which did not bode well for the future. The north-south track remained distinct from the Darfur track, which meant that nobody was empowered to nurture a political process that would have brought together all Sudanese. The idea of a national conference was no longer mentioned, and there was no international follow-up to the engagement between Vice President Ali Osman Taha and the Arab opposition parties. The Comprehensive Peace Agreement was managed in isolation, and the international community had a purposefully fragmented approach to it. The assessment and evaluation commission overseeing the Comprehensive Peace Agreement had appointed as its chair a Norwegian diplomat, Tom Vraalsen, effectively taking away from Jan Pronk and the UN a key oversight role. I was convinced that such dilution was bad, and that it would have been preferable to give as much political leverage as possible to one single person: Pronk as the special representative of the secretary general in Sudan. But the Western countries that had played a key role in shaping the peace agreement were wary of surrendering too much control. They did not have a good understanding of the political nature of peacekeeping, and their relations with Pronk were bad. Meanwhile, Jasbir Lidder, the Indian commander of the UN force, was chairing the cease-fire committee. He was doing it very well and would build enough credibility with the military leadership of the Sudanese armed forces and of the SPLA to effectively defuse a number of incidents before they escalated, but that could not replace a comprehensive and coherent political strategy.

In Darfur, the UN had even less of a grip on the situation. It had no troops, but we knew that before long, the UN would be asked to take on a greater military role, as the limits of the African Union mission became more visible. I was uncertain whether those who advocated for a much bigger African mission were aware that they were precipitating its failure or its replacement. In November 2005 Kofi Annan formally requested the Department of Peacekeeping Operations to begin planning for a UN operation in Darfur. Work had already started. I had asked General Randhir Mehta, the Indian military adviser of the department, and his able chief of planning, Ian Sinclair, a British colonel, to be as creative as possible, and to trade numbers for mobility. We would never be able to have a credible footprint throughout Darfur, but a very mobile force might have some deterrent impact. I knew that the capabilities required were in short supply, and I wrote in my little notebook: "Without the participation of armies from the North, nothing will be possible." Michael Gaouette, who held the Darfur file in the department, oversaw planning for the mission. He approached his work with patience and was the one who would try to calm me down when the prolonged and circuitous negotiations got the better of me.

Time of Frustration

I now look at the last two-and-a-half years of my tenure as head of peacekeeping with deep frustration. I would have liked to use them to consolidate reforms and give peacekeeping the institutional strength it needed. Instead, a lot of time was wasted in the endless pursuit of false solutions for Darfur, a pursuit that not only did not make enough of a difference for the people of Sudan, but also ran the risk of embroiling the UN in a major failure that would damage whatever credibility UN peacekeeping had regained through persistent effort. Meanwhile, other missions, which had their share of difficulties, did not receive all the attention they deserved.

Kofi Annan understood the risks better than anybody, and at a lunch of the Security Council in January 2006 he gave a warning to its members, stressing that the mission that would replace the African Union mission would have to be very different. In February, Sudan was barely mentioned during a meeting with President George W. Bush at the White House, where the secretary general stressed only the need for a careful management of the transition with the African Union. But these discussions created the impression in Sudan that the UN was pushing the African Union out. The fact that NATO was again mentioned in Washington, while John Bolton, the neoconservative American ambassador to the UN—who seemed more interested in posturing than helping the people of Darfur—had boasted that the Pentagon was sending planners to the UN, did not help. Sudan was increasingly mentioned as a situation where the "responsibility to protect" should be invoked. And although there was no appetite in the governments of developed countries for any kind of intervention, the rhetoric of intervention was gaining ground. I never believed that a unilateral military intervention in Sudan by developed countries—if it had been an option, which it never was—would have had good results, but I was sure that the inflated rhetoric of intervention was creating new obstacles to the more limited operation that was the only realistic course of action.

I do not know if the Sudanese leadership really believed the conspiracy theories that were propagated in Khartoum. But all the talk, in the mosques of Sudan, was now about the third invasion of a Muslim country, after Afghanistan and Iraq, and how the Sudanese people would defeat the crusaders. There were rumors that President Omar al-Bashir, who did not want his Islamic credentials to be challenged, was again getting closer to Hassan Tourabi, the Islamist leader with whom he had organized the 1989 coup. When I met with Rebecca Garang, the widow of John Garang, she did not hide her concerns that the dream of a new Sudan that her husband had promoted was dying, as Khartoum became more and more Islamist. The group of those within the Sudanese leadership who favored diplomatic engagement was getting weaker, and the time when Bashir could say to the secretary general that his country and the UN would have to keep working together seemed far away. The UN was now identified as part of a Western conspiracy to undermine the regime. My French nationality did not help: Bashir knew that France was close to Idriss Deby, the president of Chad, and the relations between the two countries were steadily deteriorating, as each leader suspected the other of giving support to rebels in the other country. For Bashir, Chad was a staging ground of the conspiracy against Sudan. But in the Security Council, Chad was seen as a victim of the war in Sudan, as refugees from Darfur sought a safe haven in Chad, putting an additional burden on one of the poorest parts of an already poor country. The perception of Chad as a victim was confirmed when Deby was almost toppled by a column of Chadian rebels, coming from Darfur, who reached the outskirts of Djamena. (Only months later Chad would play a similar trick on Sudan, when a column of the Justice and Equality Movement rebel movement, coming from Chad, reached Omb-durman, a suburb of Khartoum.)

We would try for the next twenty-four months to convince Sudan that the UN was not an enemy, just a friend of the people of Sudan. Hedi Annabi was the first to travel to Khartoum in April, in what would prove to be a long series of largely fruitless discussions. He was trying to negotiate with the government of Sudan the conditions under which a UN mission could send a planning team—a preliminary but necessary step before any deployment. Our hope was that Bashir, without committing to the deployment itself, might accept a visit of a planning team. But even that was asking too much, and Bashir took the position that Sudan could accept only an African mission in Darfur, and that in any case no planning could take place before a peace agreement for Darfur was signed (a condition that actually would have made a lot of sense to me).

In early May, the efforts of the African Union to mediate between the government of Sudan and the Darfur rebel movements seemed to pay off: the peace agreement that President Bashir had referred to was eventually signed in Abuja. For months, the negotiation in the Nigerian capital had been a kind of circus, as envoys from various Western capitals hovered around, with no agreed strategy and no consistency. The African Union had enlisted the support of some of the best experts on Darfur. But the Darfur Peace Agreement was actually much too elaborate, with its many details hiding a lack of genuine agreement on the end goal. It was modeled on the 2005 Comprehensive Peace Agreement between North and South Sudan, and it included provisions on power sharing and wealth sharing as well as detailed arrangements for the cease-fire.

The rebel demand that the unity of Darfur—which had been broken into three states by a presidential decree—be reinstated was referred to a referendum that would take place after elections in Darfur, several years in the future. But in the meantime a Transitional Darfur Regional Authority would be created, which would be headed by a "senior assistant to the president of Sudan." He would be appointed by the president, who would base his choice on a list presented by the two rebel movements of Darfur, the Sudanese Liberation Army (SLM/A) and the Justice and Equality Movement (JEM). Meanwhile, the Arab tribes of Sudan, some of which had been opposed to the violence of the Janjaweed militias, were assumed to be represented by the government, which had armed and sponsored those militias. The narrative of an Arab-African conflict suited the government of Sudan as well as the international community, but it did not reflect the political realities of Darfur.

The provisions on wealth sharing were adapted to the specific case of Darfur, where there was not all that much wealth to share. The agreement stated that $300 million would be committed as "seed money" to a Darfur Reconstruction and Development Fund, which would be complemented by an additional $200 million in the following years. The agreement was further embellished by numerous references to the Millennium Development Goals. There was, however, a great ambiguity on the source of the funds, whether they would come from donors or from the oil revenues of the national government. That ambiguity was compounded by the vagueness of the commitment of the government of Sudan with respect to return of internally displaced people and refugees. The amount that the government was ready to commit, as a "down-payment" for compensation, was ridiculously small: $30 million. The government of Sudan was not ready to take responsibility for the violence that had devastated Darfur. In a region where "blood money," financial compensation for injuries or death, is an accepted way of settling disputes, this minute amount and the lack of clear provisions on the way compensation would be allocated were serious and possibly fatal flaws.

While the wealth-sharing provisions skirted the key political issue of an effective compensation process, the cease-fire provisions were absurdly unrealistic in their level of complexity, combining excessive details with critical ambiguities. They provided for buffer zones, demilitarized zones, and redeployment zones without any consideration for the nature of the opposing forces and their uncertain command and control. At the same time, they were ambiguous on the most sensitive issue: the Janjaweed were not defined, and the agreement only stated that the government would "neutralize" Janjaweed activities and provide information on their actions to the African Union mission, which was tasked with verifying the government's activities. A provision on the Popular Defense Forces, which were widely seen as Janjaweed militia, called for the government to demobilize the groups, reflecting the fact that the government of Sudan was not ready to take explicit responsibility for the actions of the Janjaweed, while the international community was not ready to have the militias sit at the table. Furthermore, the agreement, as a sop to the Darfur rebel movements, provided that they would receive nonmilitary logistical support from the international community. How that would be implemented was a practical nightmare, as was the implementation of the detailed provisions on disarmament, demobilization, and reintegration.

The one escape hatch that might have allowed the agreement to connect with reality was the announced convening of a Darfur-Darfur Dialogue and Consultation, described as "a mechanism to connect this Agreement to social and political issues in Darfur so that social mechanisms traditionally established to resolve conflicts can play their role in creating and sustaining social peace." But neither the rebel movements present at Abuja nor the government would have any real interest in opening up the discussions, as had been done in Afghanistan with the loya jirga. So the scope of the dialogue was very narrowly defined; it would be "a mechanism for mobilizing support for this Agreement and implementing it," essentially making it a public information tool, not a negotiation forum. In subsequent discussions, I would try, unsuccessfully, to convince the government of Sudan to use the mechanism to adapt the agreement to broaden its support. The Darfur-Darfur Dialogue and Consultation never became the regional conference that might have helped address the genuine grievances of the people of Darfur.

All the flaws of the agreement were not yet apparent, including the absence of any mention of the United Nations (except for an observer role in the cease-fire commission), an omission that later would be used by the government of Sudan to oppose any UN deployment in Darfur. But the fact that only one faction of one rebel movement—the part of the SLM/A that was led by the Zaghawa leader Minni Minnawi—had signed it, while the part of the SLM/A led by the Fur leader Abdul Wahid as well as the Justice and Equality Movement (JEM) led by Khalil Ibrahim had declined to sign, immediately raised doubts. The signing had been dangerously rushed. After months of discussions, and millions of dollars per diem paid to negotiating teams, the international community was tired and impatient and its presence had complicated rather than helped the efforts of the mediator of the African Union, Salim Salim. There often were more international experts than Sudanese in the negotiating sessions, which probably accounts for why the agreement was so long on technicalities. In early May in Abuja, there were not only major African leaders, like Nigeria's President Olusegun Obasanjo, but also Robert Zoellick, the U.S. deputy secretary of state; Hilary Benn, the UK secretary of state for international development; and a plethora of European envoys. They were in a hurry to conclude, and they all decided to assume that Minnawi represented the biggest rebel group and that it was preferable to have an agreement with him now than to run the risk of waiting indefinitely for Khalil Ibrahim and Abdul Wahid to join. Ibrahim, as an Islamist, elicited little sympathy in Washington, and there was hope that Abdul Wahid, who lived in France, would either join or be deserted by his commanders.

All these assumptions would prove to be wrong, but it would take time for those who had been involved in the negotiation to accept that the Darfur Peace Agreement did not bring peace, and may actually have made peace more, rather than less, distant. The African Union, which had invested a lot of energy and talent in the process and was understandably keen to have a political foundation for its deployment in Darfur, saw the agreement as its agreement and was reluctant to admit its limitations. The same was true for international partners, who started chasing Abdul Wahid to convince him to join. A few weeks later, when some commanders decided to join, the news was heralded as a triumph. But on the ground, there would be more commanders of the Minnawi faction defecting, and the JEM, with some support from Chad, proved to be a much more serious force than expected.

The limited support for the agreement raised a moral issue that often confronts the international community when it supports a peace process: When an agreement has been reached, should the international community apply any pressure on nonsignatories? Can the international community decide what compromise is good enough? The questions have practical as well as ethical implications. An agreement that does not have enough support will fail, but in some situations strong support might convince those sitting on the edge to join. In the case of Darfur, the problem was complicated by the rebels and by the government. The moral case of rebel leaders refusing to compromise was weakened by the fact that many of them, living abroad and enjoying the support of international partners, did not have to suffer the consequences of their intransigence. But the government was also clearly abusing its position. It was labeling nonsignatories "terrorists" against whom military action could be legitimately taken, which made the cease-fire problematic considering the weight of nonsignatories. The government also weakened the one rebel who had signed, Minni Minnawi, instead of helping him gain more credibility. Since he was the only rebel signatory, he was easily appointed senior assistant to the president and given a palace in Khartoum, but the personal favors bestowed—which were not accompanied by efforts that would benefit the broader population—isolated him from his base instead of helping him expand it. The transitional Darfur regional authority remained an empty shell, and the elaborate provisions of the agreement would quickly show their irrelevance. This turned the Darfur Peace Agreement into a pyrrhic victory for the government of Sudan, which had won a personal ally but had lost an institutional partner. As I often observed in my engagement with Sudan, great tactical prowess did not lead to strategic gains, as the government bargained masterfully but overplayed its hand.

The Push for a UN Mission

After the signing of the Darfur Peace Agreement, the United States and the United Kingdom were convinced that the time had come for a UN mission to take over from the African Union in Darfur. But the African Union and the Sudanese government needed to be convinced. One of the conditions mentioned by Bashir had now been met: there was a peace agreement. So Annabi once again went to Khartoum, in a delegation led by Lakhdar Brahimi. Together, they managed to extract a concession from the government of Sudan: Khartoum was now willing to accept a joint AU-UN planning team, without prejudice to the nature of the follow-up mission. This might be a real evolution, but it received contradictory interpretations. For some, it was proof that the tough talk of Washington and London was beginning to work. For Brahimi, it confirmed that engagement with the government of Sudan was essential; the position of Khartoum could only harden as the international community discussed a future deployment in Darfur without consulting the government of Sudan. Rumors that the Security Council would visit only after the joint AU-UN mission had deployed were a disappointing confirmation of the council's reliance on more stick than carrot. Brahimi and I would have preferred the council to visit Sudan before the AU-UN mission, thus endorsing the joint mission before it started its work.

I flew to Sudan in early June, to lead with Said Djinnit the joint AU-UN planning mission. Ever since the Baghdad bombing of August 2003, I was painfully aware that a growing number of people no longer saw the United Nations as the protector of principle against power. Dag Hammarskjold, when he was under attack from the Soviet Union, had courageously stated that those who needed the United Nations, and for whom he had a duty to serve, were not the big powers but the weak, those who needed its protection. What would happen to the United Nations if the weak and powerless were to lose their trust in the UN, and if that loss of confidence was exploited by forces that wanted to destroy everything the United Nations stood for? In Kabul, for the first time in the long history of UN engagement in Afghanistan, violent demonstrators had attacked UN installations. And Osama bin Laden was telling jihadists to go to Sudan to fight the crusaders. The multiple crises that were destroying peace from the Mediterranean to the Hindu Kush were now spreading their poison to Africa, and the Horn, with Somalia and the Sudan as the entry point of the virus.

The first stop for the planning mission was in Addis Ababa to agree with the African Union on our approach to the Sudanese authorities. The mounting difficulties of the African mission, which was on the verge of collapse, and the growing pressure of donors had convinced the AU's Konare that a transition to the UN was inevitable. He was obviously unhappy that reality stood in the way of dreams, and he made clear to me that the African Union would remain in charge of the political process. It was not the first time that I witnessed the same lack of understanding of the political nature of peacekeeping, as if the conduct of military operations and the military posture could be divorced from the politics of the situation. But this was not the time to argue, and we tentatively agreed for a transition to the UN on January 1, 2007.

My meetings in Khartoum confirmed that the evolution of the geopolitical context was going to make UN involvement in Darfur much more difficult than in any other African conflict. Foreign Minister Lam Akol, a member of the SPLM who seemed to enjoy taking a tougher line than members of the ruling National Congress Party since he had joined the government, was hiding behind legal arguments to reject a UN presence in Darfur—the UN was not mentioned in the peace agreement. Majzoub al-Khalifa, a hard-line adviser to Bashir who had been one of the government negotiators at Abuja, was more direct: The UN was now associated with the invasion of Iraq, it was not welcome in Sudan, and African issues needed African solutions. He dismissed my reference to the 10,000-strong UN force in the south. The interior minister was just as hard, with a softer voice; he started by reminding me that Sudan was enjoying fast economic growth and was now a strong country. Yet, he added, Sudan was under constant attack from the UN, with no less than nine resolutions targeting Sudan in eleven months. The UN, which ignored the destruction in 2002 of the Palestinian camp in Jenin, was not impartial, and Europe, which was pushing for the UN to enter Darfur, was helping the rebels, providing them with weapons. The UN should limit its role to humanitarian issues and the environment; he mentioned the pressing issue of white rhinoceros, which were an endangered species. We were a long way from discussing genocide.

When I met with opposition leaders Sadiq al-Mahdi, Ali Al Hassanein, Mohamed Ibrahim Nugud, and Hassan Tourabi in the evening—without Djinnit, because African Union officials are not expected to meet with opposition figures—the message was quite different. They all wanted the UN in Darfur because they saw a UN presence as a way to open a political space that they might occupy, precisely the reason why the government did not want the UN. They reiterated their denunciation of the north-south Comprehensive Peace Agreement, which was anything but comprehensive. It was clear that for them a UN presence was a way to reopen the agreement. Tourabi was the most interesting. It was difficult to imagine that this bespectacled man who had studied at the Sorbonne and spoke perfect French was the Islamist ideologue who had helped bring Bashir to power and who had invited bin Laden to Sudan. He obviously liked to provoke. He was dismissive of Sudan, of Darfur, of the Darfurians, of the Darfur agreement, of the AU, and of the UN. Sudan was more a place than a country, the place of the blacks;

Darfur had made the wrong choice during World War I, when it sided with the dying Ottoman empire; the Darfurians were bellicose people; and the comprehensive agreement was no more than a "peace show." The limitations of the Africans were well known. As for the UN, it was welcome, even if Abu Masab al-Zarqawi (the al Qaeda leader) and the government were threatening. He concluded that the UN might eventually become part of the problem. Tourabi explained that he was not interested in sovereignty, he was not thinking in national terms, but unfortunately, "in this part of the world," there were no free elections.

Tourabi was different from the other leaders because he had a much broader agenda, which went beyond Darfur and even beyond Sudan. He was rumored to be close to the Justice and Equality Movement of Khalil Ibrahim, which also had an agenda that went beyond Darfur, which made it more threatening for the government in Khartoum. For Tourabi, the involvement of the international community in Sudan was probably just an episode, and the crisis of the Sudanese state was an opportunity to promote a new Islam that would make states irrelevant. I could see how his gentle universalist Islam was the peaceful side of the murderous Islam of his former friend bin Laden. But I was not too convinced he would be a strategic friend of the United Nations if we ever managed to deploy. The way he mentioned in passing, and with a nice smile, the possible threat of al Qaeda was less than reassuring. I think he was seeing us as well-meaning tourists thrown into a situation we could not understand, in a place we would never really influence. But we could be used, and that was good enough for him.

Our planning team then went to Darfur, and I quickly realized the situation had changed for the worse since my last visit. After the Darfur Peace Agreement, the African Union, because it had taken such a strong stance against the nonsignatories, was rejected in major parts of Darfur. It could hardly enter camps of displaced persons, which were strongholds of the Fur leader, Abdul Wahid. It was now perceived as an ally of the government. Djinnit, in meeting after meeting, had to hear harsh criticism of the AU mission, which had not met the hopes of the population. The representatives of the displaced persons had only insults for the African Union and were begging the United Nations to come quickly. They expected a UN force to protect them against the government, and like the officials in Khartoum, but with opposite conclusions, did not distinguish among the UN, United States, United Kingdom, and NATO. I would have another illustration of the confusion one year later, in my first visit to Darfur with the new secretary general. When we arrived in a huge camp of displaced persons, the crowd was chanting "Abdul Wahid! Ban Ki-moon! USA!" The paranoia of my government interlocutors in Khartoum had no basis, but it was worrying to see that the crowds in the camps had the same illusions. They would be quickly disappointed, and I knew that before long, we would hear the same criticism that Djinnit had to endure. They all had inflated views of what a peacekeeping mission could accomplish. In the absence of a serious peace process, the displaced Darfurians saw us as an ally in their battle against Khartoum, and the government as an invasion force. But we were not going to go to war with the government of Sudan.

The meeting with Minni Minnawi, who would later have the unnecessary honor of a meeting with President George W. Bush at the White House, was disappointing. I suspect that some in the Western world, without openly calling for military action against the nonsignatories, had the secret hope that Minnawi would bring order to Darfur by cracking down effectively on those rebels who had not joined the agreement. So they would do anything to strengthen him. But to me, he looked more like a guerilla leader pumped up by a few international advisers. That did not give me much hope that he would be the man able to craft a political strategy to bring the people of Darfur together.

My fears were confirmed when I flew near Birmaza and Um Rai, in the desert of Darfur, to meet with a group of rebel commanders. We met in the school of the village, if one can call a little shack a "school," with no other floor than sand. As a "distinguished" visitor, I was the only one given a plastic chair. I discovered it had only three legs when I tried to move it away from the wooden pole against which it was propped. Although most of the leaders were Zaghawa, they were vigorously denouncing the betrayal of Minnawi, who claimed to lead the Zaghawa, and announced their readiness to join Abdul Wahid and the Fur. They mentioned that they would have a meeting in Eritrea to unite their forces. They seemed to have quite a bit of military equipment, judging by the column of "technicals" (militarized 4x4 trucks) that had welcomed us when our helicopters landed. I pleaded with them for a ceasefire, and they responded they were ready for it but were under attack—which was often true. The next day, I would hear from a very reliable source that an attack had just taken place, and that humanitarian workers had provided help to twenty wounded people.

I stayed with them longer than initially planned. By mistake, one of the two helicopters that were supposed to bring us back to Al Fasher had left, and I would have had to leave behind half of my party if I had left with the remaining helicopter. That was out of the question, and so we waited, hoping that the second helicopter would arrive before sunset. The technicals had now taken defensive positions around our meeting place and the lonely white MI-8 helicopter of the UN: most technicals were equipped with machine guns, but some also carried anti-aircraft guns, apparently captured during battles with Sudanese armed forces—although I suspected the rebels also benefited from some external help. Fighters with Kalashnikovs took cover behind rocks, technicals in the open, a couple of hundred yards away. If the second helicopter did not come, we would have to spend the night in the desert, in the middle of a combat zone, which my security detail did not like, but our turbaned hosts were quite pleased at the prospect of taking care of us.

Their world was a world of personal connections and loyalties, and it had been shattered by a conflict that was much bigger than anything they had ever dealt with. The gap could not be more extreme with our connected contemporary world of distant but shallow solidarities. Our helicopter, awkward and stranded, was a good symbol of it, and it looked like a big dead bug. What were we doing here? The expectations of our hosts were simple enough: They wanted some education for their children, some minimal health service, too, and water for their camels. Most of all, they wanted security. They had little or no knowledge of the outside world. At one point, I was talking to a man who was speaking in Zaghawa; his words were then translated by another man into Arabic, and then by another in English. I am not sure we understood much of what we were trying to communicate. The humanitarian workers provided a simple answer to those humble expectations. They would work hard to provide food, health services, and education to people in desperate need. My role was different, and I was not sure I could explain it convincingly to my rebel interlocutors. I could not provide them with outright military protection, which is what they really expected from a man who had helicopters and a whole army of peacekeepers. I knew that what we could realistically try to achieve—if we were allowed to deploy in Darfur—would be only a limited show of force, to make it more complicated for those using violence to achieve their goals and to give a chance to politics. It was all about politics. And for people at war, that was not quite enough.

At first the meeting with the leaders of Arab tribes of Darfur looked like a repeat of the meetings I had in Khartoum with the Sudanese authorities. They obviously had been well briefed, and their message echoed, word-for-word, what we had heard in Khartoum. I was looking at these men, thinking of the misery I had seen in Um Rai. One of our interlocutors was the leader of the Beni Alba, who was considered by many a Janjaweed. His people had committed precisely the kind of atrocities that had brought the people in Um Rai to their desperate situation. As I listened to them, I could not ignore that they too had genuine fears. These traditional leaders were losing their grip on the tribes, they were not sure that their alliance with the government would protect them, and they saw the UN as their enemy, the same enemy, they believed, that had invaded Iraq and Afghanistan, supported Israel, and hated the Muslims. I was aware of the great danger of moral relativism in peacekeeping. In Darfur, killers and victims are all Muslims, but the victims are overwhelmingly members of African tribes against whom a government, which had lost confidence in its own army, had unleashed Arab militias, sometimes against the advice of traditional Arab leaders. And these leaders with whom I was now meeting were caught in dynamics that they themselves no longer controlled. The old social structures through which conflicts used to be resolved were crumbling; the abundance of weapons, the brutality of the war, and the massive displacements were shifting power, within Arab as well as African tribes. Old leaders were losing the respect of their people, and young men, who had shown their capacity to fight, were challenging traditional sources of authority, on the Arab as well as the African side.

This analysis would be confirmed a year later, when I met in a modest London flat the former governor of Darfur, Ahmed Diraige, and his German wife. Twenty-four years earlier he had become famous when he had sent then-president Gaafar al-Nimeiry a letter warning of impending famine in Darfur, after which he had to go into exile. Listening to Diraige, I better understood the plight of Darfur, which has been a neglected part of Sudan ever since it was incorporated into that country during World War I, and where the Arab tribes are themselves seen as second-class Arabs, compared to the Arabs of the Nile region. The polarization between Arabs and Africans in Darfur initially was largely a manipulation to ensure Khartoum's control over Darfur, but it has taken on a life of its own. With the war, new leaders, whose legitimacy has been acquired in combat, are now pursuing conflicting agendas, making it more difficult to develop a common Darfurian platform. After Afghanistan and the Democratic Republic of the Congo, this was the third instance where I could observe how traditional structures were destroyed by conflict much faster than new ones could be created. The increasing fragmentation of rebel movements, which the government of Sudan was very adept at encouraging, and the loss of control by the traditional Arab leaders over their own people would make it more and more difficult to have an effective and structured political process. The social fabric was fraying, and the risk was high of fragmentation, chaos, and anarchy.

I left Sudan worried about the future of the country and about the future of peacekeeping. I doubted that Minnawi would be able to assert his authority over the other rebel movements, and I saw no prospect of a genuine normalization of relations between Sudan and its neighbor Chad, which had been caught up in the Darfur conflict. As for the north-south "comprehensive" peace agreement, while it was encouraging to observe the troops from the north withdrawing from the south according to plans, none of the really contentious issues had been resolved. The government of Sudan was keeping a firm grip on the oil-producing areas and oil exports, and the delimitation of the 1956 border between north and south remained an open issue.

Before leaving Khartoum, I had a very difficult meeting with President Bashir, who was categorical in his rejection of a UN mission, saying twice that the "decision was final." A few days earlier, in a fiery speech, he had said that he would personally lead the fight against the crusaders. In the meeting, he went into a long tirade against the UN, which had constantly shown its hostility to Sudan, imposing sanctions and adopting a resolution under Chapter VII soon after a peace agreement was signed. The international community had had no hesitation in branding as "terrorists" the nonsignatories of the recent Burundi peace agreement (the FNL of Agathon Rwasa), but it was cajoling the rebels of Darfur, welcoming them in Europe. This, he observed, was an indication of the real intentions of the international community. Meanwhile, Chad and Eritrea were also plotting against Sudan, he insisted, and Darfur was a diversion. Abdul Wahid was now getting closer to the JEM, and their common agenda was about the whole of Sudan, not Darfur. Actually, if there was an international force in Darfur, it would become a magnet for terrorists, as had happened in Iraq, and it would further complicate the situation. He dismissed the suffering of people living in camps. They live in camps, but they have houses in the city, for which they receive a rent; this is business, he claimed. And you, the international community, you do not want them to leave the camps. He was proffering the most provocative statements with eloquence. He might be a man under siege, but he seemed to have great confidence in his capacity to resist international pressure. The next two years would prove him right.

We were at a complete impasse. What could be done? Some of my Sudanese interlocutors had encouraged me to be patient, and they did not rule out an evolution of the Sudanese position. The main obstacles, according to them, were the International Criminal Court and the possibility that UN troops from Western countries would arrest members of the Sudanese leadership. The pictures of the transfer of former Liberian president Charles Taylor in a UN helicopter had not gone unnoticed in Africa. Tourabi privately told me that this was the main concern of the leadership; it was never mentioned but always present. Two years later, Nigeria's Obasanjo would refer to a conversation with Bashir where the president of Sudan expressed that concern. Deng Alor, the thoughtful SPLM state minister who would later replace Lam Akol as foreign minister in the government of national unity, also recommended patience. He wondered whether one of the joint integrated units created by the Comprehensive Peace Agreement could deploy to Darfur. I did not believe it was a realistic option, but it was a sign that some people in the SPLM were looking for creative solutions that would help the north-south process as well as Darfur. I wished the same had been the case in the entourage of Bashir.

Kofi Annan was entering the last six months of his mandate as a secretary general. He was determined not to be a lame duck, and he would show, during the Israel-Lebanon war and its aftermath, that he was more willing than ever to take political risks to move a political process forward. The Sudanese situation was for him a particularly difficult dilemma, as the Western members of the Security Council were pushing for a UN mission, while Bashir was adamantly opposed to it. If the UN got involved, there was no guarantee of success and a high risk of a joint AU-UN failure that would make the prospect of any future AU-UN venture very unlikely. Alternatively, he could resist the temptation of joining the African Union in a flawed enterprise, but if he pursued that course, the possible collapse of the AU mission would do enormous damage to a nascent institution that represented a great hope for many Africans. Was there an alternative to supporting the AU?

I was convinced there was nothing to be gained in publicity, which just hardened positions, as the international community blasted the government of Sudan, which in return dug in its heels. But quiet diplomacy, for which I was prepared and had the support of the secretary general, would work only if the government of Sudan saw an interest in climbing down from its radical position. This required a minimum of trust between Khartoum and major powers as well as strategic vision, of which there seemed to be very little wherever you looked.

I met with an adviser of the president, the hard-liner al-Khalifa, the day after an Israeli bunker-busting bomb had killed four UN military observers in Lebanon. My Sudanese interlocutor started the meeting with a cruel observation: How did we expect to protect the people of Darfur if we were not even able to protect ourselves? He obviously was not there to negotiate, and he despised the UN, which he saw as a puppet of the West. The meeting was a complete waste of time, but I flew back to New York with a beautiful green leather-bound copy of the government plan to disarm the Janjaweed! The government of Sudan did not seem to have an interest in quiet diplomacy.

Washington and London also were busy posturing. At the end of July, President Bush, who was advised by people more interested in regime change in Khartoum than in peace, met with Minnawi at the White House, raising suspicions among the Sudanese and giving the rebel leader clout that was completely out of proportion with his real following. A month later, the Security

Council adopted Resolution 1706, which expanded to Darfur the mandate of the UN mission in South Sudan and "invited the consent of the Government of National Unity." The mission was given, under chapter VII of the UN Charter, a robust mandate of protection, which included seizing all unauthorized weapons. This was a very confrontational decision that we had hoped would not be taken. The council had boxed itself into a corner and was now gambling that intimidation could work and that consent could be imposed. But the government of Sudan never gave its consent, and its refusal exposed the emptiness of the strategy pursued by the majority of the council. In the end, the unintended consequence would be the humiliation of the Security Council, which would swiftly show weakness after bluster. The council would hide its humiliation by accepting a bad compromise at the expense of the UN: the "hybrid mission."

In October, the situation was even worse than at the beginning of the summer. Political leaders who had never thought through the implications of their policies were beginning to realize that they had a serious problem, and they were panicking. British prime minister Tony Blair was considering a high-level meeting where some kind of ultimatum would be delivered, while African leaders were thinking of going to Khartoum. President Abdoulaye Wade of Senegal even wanted Condoleezza Rice to accompany them. In a telephone conversation with the secretary general, Bashir confirmed that the only possible role for the UN in Darfur would be political, which would have been good news if his definition of a political role had not been so narrow: to convince the rebels who had not signed the Darfur Peace Agreement to join. In any case, there was growing skepticism about what politics could achieve, and for the Security Council as well as the global media, the deployment of a UN mission had become the yardstick of success. The donors who were supporting the mission of the African Union also were aware of the growing strains of the mission, whose finances and logistics were in disarray. Meanwhile, the African Union was pressing for a tripartite meeting between the AU, the UN, and Sudan—a format that Sudan liked because it had influence in the AU and could play up differences between the AU and the UN.

We had to find a way out, and in early November 2006, I convened a technical meeting with some members of the Security Council. The British, who had realized that they had to climb down from Resolution 1706, were very supportive, and the ambassador himself came. Their preferred solution seemed to be a beefed-up African mission with UN support. The Americans were very suspicious; they still wanted a UN mission and were afraid of any dilution. We presented a plan that I did not like. It had three options, which were quickly understood as three phases: a UN package of light support to the

African Union, a UN package of heavy support to the African Union, and a "hybrid mission." Kofi Annan had already spoken to Condoleezza Rice, who seemed to endorse the proposal of a hybrid mission. I had expressed reservations in internal meetings about the hybrid mission. For me the risk of a hybrid mission was not that the force would receive conflicting instructions from the United Nations and the African Union, as some would later argue, but that the structure would further dilute responsibilities. In a UN mission there is already a risk that the UN becomes a shield behind which member states hide to avoid taking responsibility. In a hybrid mission, the risk would be even greater, as member states would have two organizations to hide behind, and each organization could blame the other. Nobody would really carry the political responsibility.

Agreement on a Hybrid Mission

But the die was cast: the African Union leaders agreed to the three-stage approach, which would include funding of African troops by the UN from the outset, and we started planning for a ministerial meeting in Addis Ababa on November 16, which Kofi Annan himself would attend, as well as the five permanent Security Council members, key African countries, Sudan, the AU, and the European Union. I had increasing reservations, and I hardened the "non-paper" that would serve as a basis for the discussion, stressing that the hybrid mission would have to be very robust—which was what Kofi Annan had told the Security Council at the beginning of the year. The negotiation in Addis lasted nine hours, and at the time it was hailed as a diplomatic breakthrough. Lam Akol, foreign minister of Sudan's unity government, could not resist noting that Resolution 1706 was now "off the table," which was a major diplomatic victory for the government of Sudan, but the impression was that Khartoum had made real concessions, prodded by the Chinese ambassador, who wanted the meeting to end well. The government of Sudan had accepted the three phases, including the hybrid mission, opening the door to the United Nations. The devil was in the details, however. Implementation of each phase would be discussed in a tripartite committee (AU-UN-Sudan), the final size of the mission would be referred to President Bashir, and the wording on command and control remained ambiguous on the role of the UN.

As I digested the consequences of the agreement, my skepticism grew. There was a fundamental flaw in a negotiation where the international community was in essence begging a government to accept to be helped. And the government of Sudan had negotiated in such a way that it had ample means to control the pace of the transition, and to decide whether it wanted the mission to be a success or a failure. The crucial issue remained the political strategy of the government of Sudan. Was it interested in a genuine political process that a robust mission could help support by making military options less attractive for spoilers? Or was it pursuing a military strategy, in which case a peacekeeping force was a complication that should be marginalized? A couple of days later, I tried to find out what was the strategic choice of Sudan. I met with Mustafa Osman Ismail, an adviser to the president. He first focused on the international dimensions of Darfur. In the east, bringing Eritrea on board had been a key factor in securing an agreement. In Darfur, it was important to have an agreement with President Deby of Chad, and Mustafa suggested that Chad, Sudan, and France could together monitor the border. As for the Darfur rebels, he believed that the government could make an effort on compensation, as well as on agreeing to a single Darfur region. As always in a meeting with Ismail, one left feeling that no problem was too difficult for a political solution.

But the news coming from Sudan was not encouraging, except for the peace agreement negotiated by Ismail with the rebels from eastern Sudan. Jan Pronk, whose relations with the government had steadily deteriorated after he criticized the flaws of the Darfur Peace Agreement, had finally been declared persona non grata at the end of October; an entry in his personal blog, where he described battles lost by the government side in Darfur and the low morale of the Sudanese armed forces, had tipped the balance. And in South Sudan, violence had suddenly flared up in Malakal. Without the decisive action of General Jasbir Singh Lidder and the Indian troops that were deployed there, the incident could easily have escalated. In Darfur, there were reports of more bombings in the Birmaza area, where I had met rebel leaders in June. And officials in Khartoum were insisting that every detail of UN support would have to be approved through the tripartite mechanism. Two weeks later, at the meeting of the Peace and Security Council of the African Union in Abuja, where I was representing the secretary general, I made one last effort to convince African leaders that a mission would have no chance to make a difference if it was not considerably strengthened (a reinforcement that, if it was accepted Khartoum, would be a test of Sudanese intentions and expectations), but I felt I was fighting a rearguard battle. President Bashir reiterated, with the authority of a head of state talking to other heads of state, that the situation in Darfur was fine, and the African Union had the right forces. Who was I to raise inconvenient issues? I was alone, and Sudan was sending every signal that it did not want the mission to succeed.

The only hope I saw of salvaging a desperate situation was to reenergize the political process. The best solution would have been for the special representative of the secretary general in Sudan to orchestrate a coordinated approach of the international community to the whole of Sudan. But the African Union was keen to keep control over the Darfur peace process. The only option left was to launch a joint AU-UN mediation for the Darfur peace process. Salim Salim had been the African Union mediator in the Darfur peace talks, and in December 2006, the secretary general appointed as the UN joint envoy Jan Eliasson, the Swedish diplomat who had presided over the General Assembly in 2005 and skillfully salvaged the summit declaration that U.S. ambassador Bolton had tried to scupper. It was agreed that they would work as a team, with UN support. But unlike special representatives, they were not based in the region, and a genuine political process never took off. The two of them shuttled inconclusively for a year between various rebel groups that kept fragmenting, as they were sponsored by countries that each had its own agenda.

The envoys were chasing rebels who did not want to join, and after lengthy discussions between the secretary general of the UN and Konare of the AU, it was finally decided to convene another peace conference, this time in Libya—a country that was not acceptable for several key actors—in October 2007. Before the conference I met in a Paris café with Fur leader Abdul Wahid to sound him out, but it was clear that, like the JEM, he had a national project; he was interested in elections and a possible alliance with the Umma party. He was not interested in a conference that the government of Sudan would use to isolate him as the spoiler who prevented an agreement, to legitimize sanctions against him and attacks against his forces.

The mistakes of Abuja were not corrected when the conference took place in Syrte, Libya. The major Sudanese political parties were not at the negotiating table, nor were the Arab tribes. It was therefore not a surprise that the conference was a miserable failure. Bashir, who had been in Libya for a meeting with Chad two days earlier, did not bother to stay for the Darfur conference, and Qaddafi—even though the UN was one of the co-chairs—opened the conference by speaking at length on one of his favorite themes: the uselessness of the international community for the resolution of African conflicts. The strategic picture for the north-south process was hardly more encouraging; the only senior politician who understood it was the new British foreign minister David Milliband, but some of his interlocutors in Washington seemed more intent on building up the military capacities of South Sudan than on supporting political engagement, as if a conventional balance of power was the way to stabilize relations between Khartoum and Juba. The best and most knowledgeable expert of Sudan in the U.S. government, Andrew Natsios, left his post of special envoy of the United States at the end of 2007.

So we were left with no other goal than to deploy a peacekeeping operation in Darfur, even if there was no political base for its deployment. But because the government of Sudan had a great ability to negotiate ad nauseam, more than a year would pass between the meeting in Addis Ababa on November 16, 2006, and the eventual launch of a hybrid mission at the beginning of 2008. And more than three years after the concept of a hybrid mission had been first discussed, the mission would still be struggling to find the capacities that had been identified as a prerequisite to a successful deployment. During those three years, the deployment of a force became a goal in itself, and the technical issues of troops and capabilities overshadowed the more strategic question of what should be the foundations of peace in Darfur and the whole of Sudan.

The first diplomatic struggle was to move from the ambiguous agreement of November 2006 to the actual authorization by the Security Council of a hybrid mission, this time with the consent of the government of Sudan. It took eight months: four months in 2007 to reach agreement on the "heavy package," another three months to reach agreement on the "hybrid mission," and another month for the council to agree on the resolution.

The new secretary general, Ban Ki-moon, had a deep moral commitment to Darfur, and he was impatient to make a difference. On January 24, 2007, barely three weeks after his inauguration, he sent to President Bashir a detailed letter describing the "heavy support package." The first meeting with President Bashir took place a few days later, at the end of January, during the African Union summit. The president of Sudan stressed how good the situation in Darfur was, while the secretary general, who had studied his file, referred to the millions of people who were still displaced. When he was sharply rebuked by Bashir, he quietly said that on factual issues, it was just a question of verification. He then asked pointed questions on pending issues concerning a hybrid force: command and control, composition of the force, and so forth. There were some tense moments in that first meeting. The new secretary general was determined to make every effort to build trust with Bashir and to hear his real concerns, and the Sudanese government interlocutors were probably hoping to win more concessions from Ban Ki-moon by contrasting him with Kofi Annan and celebrating the new spirit of cooperation. But as the exchanges became more specific, the disagreements became more visible, and Bashir's late response in March to Ban's letter was a watershed. His fourteen-page letter sounded like a rejection of the agreement reached in November and suggested we were back to square one.

In another tense meeting of the Security Council, the secretary general put on a brave face and noted that there were "some positive elements." The crisis seemed to end when, in the margins of a summit of the Arab League in Riyadh, Ban Ki-moon, Konare, and Bashir met and reached an agreement with the help of King Abdullah of Saudi Arabia. Two weeks later, Dmitry Titov, the most senior Russian official in the UN's Department of Peacekeeping Operations (he had been chosen because Russia, like China, was seen as more understanding of Sudan's concerns), was in Khartoum, and the Sudanese effectively agreed to the "heavy support package." The package, which was conceived as a precursor to the hybrid mission, included 1,136 civilian personnel, as well as 301 police officers, 3 formed police units, and 2,250 military personnel to provide military transport, engineering, signals and logistics, surveillance, aviation, and medical services. This was hailed as a breakthrough by the more optimistic. I was personally unhappy that we gradually were tying ourselves into a situation from which it would be hard to escape.

President Bashir gave his formal agreement to the hybrid mission in June, and the Security Council in July adopted the resolution authorizing the hybrid force, which would take over from the African Union on January 1, 2008. The negotiations that led to the resolution were almost as difficult as the ones that had just been "successfully" concluded with the Sudan government, except that the negotiation was now with the African Union, which was looking for maximum funding but minimum control by the UN, and with the Western members of the council, who wanted the hybrid mission to be a prelude to a UN mission. In hindsight, a more flexible position than the one I took might have better served the UN as an institution: encouraging funding of the African Union with minimum involvement of the UN might have allowed for a clearer definition of responsibilities. But such a position would have been very cynical, and probably not practical, since the member states that pay the bill would never have accepted an arrangement where the UN had no control. African countries, which were contributing troops, and Western countries, which contributed funds, were both impatient, but for different reasons. Financially strapped African countries were eager to receive funding from the UN budget, while the Western countries wanted the reinforced mission to be deployed very quickly. The first issue could be resolved once the member states had made the momentous decision to finance troops that were not under full UN command. The second issue was much more difficult, and I spent almost half of my time on it during the last twelve months of my tenure at the UN. It required willing troop contributors and a cooperative Sudanese government.

While I never had any illusion that military force could bring peace to Darfur, I hoped against hope that a combination of political engagement and the robustness of a peacekeeping mission could help create a better dynamic on the ground. As I had observed in many peace operations, much depends on perceptions and momentum. If, in the early phase of its deployment, the mission could show some success in a limited engagement of its choosing, that could have a deterrent effect and lower the level of violence. That is why we had developed a plan with an emphasis on what we called "early effect." The objective was to have on the ground on January 1, 2008, a limited number of very high quality forces, including special forces, with military transport helicopters and attack helicopters. They would be able to reinforce at short notice any unit in Darfur. They would be complemented by expert engineering units, which would help facilitate the deployment of additional troops in a region deprived of good infrastructure, and they would also provide significant support to the population: drilling wells, fixing abandoned irrigation ditches, and similar tasks. I soon found out that while many non-African countries were speaking very loudly about the plight of Darfur, very few were willing to put the lives of their own soldiers at risk. After dozens of meetings and calls, only the Nordic countries in Europe were prepared to contribute a very valuable unit of specialized engineers. As for helicopters, no country was willing to deploy any, especially attack helicopters, of which our planners had requested eighteen. We had a tragic reminder of the need to have responsive and highly trained troops when at the end of September 2007 a military camp of the African Union near Haskanita was attacked by rebels who were retaliating against what they saw as a lack of protection by the AU. Several African soldiers died in the attack, without any casualties being inflicted on the assailants, and the camp was eventually rescued by forces of the government of Sudan. This was a great humiliation, which showed that the mission had lost its credibility. It was becoming urgent to have an injection of fresh troops with a good morale, to reenergize the mission.

I was all the more concerned because the European Union, at the instigation of France, was developing plans to deploy an EU mission in Chad. The contrast between well-equipped and self-sustained European troops deploying in Chad and a weak AU-UN hybrid force on the other side of the border would hurt. But a European force in Chad would help contain the Darfur conflict. It would make it more difficult for a force coming from Sudan to remove Chad's leader Deby—and that risk was real, as demonstrated by another attempt in early 2008, before the mission was deployed. The European presence also would make it more difficult for Chad-based rebels to launch operations against Khartoum. A robust international presence would lower the tension between Sudan and Chad, which would be a good thing, as Mustafa Osman Ismail had suggested. I was, however, less convinced that the

UN, which was expected to train a Chadian gendarmerie to police camps in eastern Chad and to replace the European force after a year, had a useful role to play in Chad, whose problems were only in part a consequence of the Darfur conflict.

Meanwhile, the government of Sudan made our already difficult task even more difficult. The smooth deployment of a mission is a complex undertaking that requires the goodwill of all actors, troop contributors, host country, and the UN Secretariat. But every action in Darfur was subject to a painful and lengthy negotiation: the status of forces agreement, the color of berets, the markings on vehicles, even customs clearance of containers in Port-Sudan, 1,000 miles from Darfur. The tripartite mechanism, far from easing difficulties in the vast Sudanese bureaucracy, was used as a bureaucratic tool to block progress. The most difficult issue was the composition of the force. The Sudanese authorities insisted that the hybrid mission have only African troops. The fight over the composition of the force became a symbolic test of the good faith of the Sudanese government. We all knew that there were some capacities, like specialized engineering units, that only armies from rich countries had, and excluding them would hurt the mission. We knew that most African armies were overstretched and had no self-sustainment capacity, which was critical if the deployment was to happen quickly. And we knew that we needed a quick response from the government of Sudan, to make the necessary arrangements with the troop contributors so that they would be ready to deploy in time. This last factor was particularly important for the units that would be part of the "early effect package" and for the engineering units that would facilitate the deployment of the rest of the force.

On all counts we lost. The government remained ambiguous for a long time on several proposals, and when it finally clarified its position on the Nordic engineering unit, it was a resounding no. This was a great embarrassment: the Nordics had worked hard and spent significant amounts of money to prepare the unit, and I had made a great effort to convince them to get involved. We had also hoped to have a significant contribution from South Asian countries, which are traditional, experienced peacekeepers, and we were counting on a Gurkha unit from Nepal. But the Sudanese government, after much prodding, took the position that non-African troops could be accepted—except for the Chinese, with whom it had no difficulties—only once all African offers had been exhausted. This was politically and operationally problematic. We could not have too many troops from Ethiopia, because of its enmity with Eritrea, which was close to some of the rebels, or from Egypt, because of its closeness with Khartoum. Other African countries were making offers of troops with no equipment and no self-sustainment capacity. Absurd negotiations ensued in New

York, Khartoum, Addis Ababa, Lisbon, and Dakar. I traveled several times to Addis to try to negotiate a compromise, agreeing to increase the number of Ethiopian and Egyptian troops on the condition that their deployment would not delay the deployment of other troops that were at the time ready to deploy, in particular an elite Thai battalion. In the margins of an EU-Africa summit, my deputy accompanied a close adviser of the secretary general to discuss again the composition of the force, and the secretary general himself raised it with President Bashir at a summit in Dakar, accepting an additional increase in the participation of Egyptian troops. In Khartoum, at a meeting with President Bashir, I noted that from a military standpoint, troops needed to be familiarized with their equipment before they deployed, and that was why we could not accept troops without proper equipment. The president reminded me that he was a military man, and he insisted that one day of familiarization was more than enough. He later chided me for not being cooperative.

In hindsight, I may have been wrong to put so much effort into a silly negotiation that was lost the day we agreed to a hybrid mission. Deng Alor, for whom I have great respect, later told me, when he had become the foreign minister of the Government of National Unity, that my insistence on a few specific units—the Thai battalion, the Nepalese special forces company—might feed the Sudanese government's paranoia about the intentions of the international community. I could not accept defeat, but I should have known better. The plan for an early-effect package was long gone. As for the test of Sudanese intentions, it was no longer needed, as it had become abundantly clear that the government of Sudan did not want an effective mission, and damage limitation was now the only realistic goal. The mission could probably contribute to a lower level of violence in Darfur, especially with the presence of police in the camps, which made a difference, but the mission would not play a strategic role and was just a costly sideshow. The government of Sudan had won.

In the weeks before the handover date, I spoke in public more and more stridently, asking the Security Council at the end of November: "Do we move ahead with the deployment of the force that will not make a difference, that will not have the capacity to defend itself, and that carries the risk of humiliation of the Security Council and the United Nations, and tragic failure for the people of Darfur?" By then, any hope of changing course was long gone.

I returned to Sudan a few weeks after the hybrid mission had been launched. In Khartoum, Mustafa Osman Ismail asked me why my tone had changed and become more strident. I replied that I had done more than most to find compromise with the government of Sudan, but I had a responsibility to peacekeeping, as he had a responsibility to his people. I had long felt those responsibilities were not in conflict, and that an effective peacekeeping operation in Darfur was in our common interest. But the obstacles that the government of Sudan was continuously putting in our way—the latest was the decision to remove a very capable British general we had appointed as chief of staff to tighten the military headquarters of the mission in Al-Fasher—condemned the mission to failure. I had a duty to peacekeeping, which would suffer badly if the mission in Darfur failed. As I was talking to him, I was thinking of an incident that had happened a few days earlier. A supply convoy of the mission had been under fire from Sudanese government forces in eastern Darfur. The circumstances of the incident were such that there was no doubt, although it would be denied, that this was not a mistake, and the attack had been intentional. The officer in charge of the convoy had decided not to return fire. It was probably the right decision from a tactical standpoint. But I have often wondered whether an escalation of that incident, in the early days of the new mission, would not have forced the Security Council to recognize that it had deployed a mission into a place where there was no business for peacekeeping. Maybe then the council could have changed course.

The provisional conclusion of my engagement with Sudan happened on July 14, 2008. I was in Paris with the secretary general, to attend the Bastille Day celebration, which this year was honoring the blue helmets, who were opening the traditional military parade on the Champs Elysées. On that day, Luis Moreno Ocampo, the prosecutor for the International Criminal Court, made public his request for the indictment of President Omar al-Bashir. This was the outcome of a long process, which had started with the use by Colin Powell, four years earlier, of the word genocide. It had been followed by the UN inquiry, which itself had led to the resolution of the Security Council referring Sudan to the ICC in 2005, and then in the spring of 2007 to the indictment of a government minister, Ahmad Muhammad Harun, of a Janjaweed leader, and of a rebel leader associated with the killing of the African Union soldiers in Haskanita. President Bashir had repeatedly affirmed, publicly and privately, his confidence in Harun. Some members of the Security Council had probably hoped that the indictment of second-tier officials would push the leadership of Sudan to abandon them and change course. Justice as a political tool had not worked. After the announcement of the request for Bashir's indictment, the African Union and the Arab League went to great lengths to try to undo what could not be undone. The members of the Security Council were embarrassed: they knew that it was too late to back off, but they were afraid of the consequences. More than six years later, it is not peace but the credibility of international justice that has suffered. The reaction of the government of Sudan was mild, and there was no retaliation, but nothing has changed. President Bashir is still president. He is more cautious in the choice of countries he visits, but is still defiant, and he appointed Harun to be the governor of the critical state of South Kordofan. After the humiliation of the UN, it was the turn of the International Criminal Court to be humiliated. Of course, it is too early to tell who will have the last word, and depending on how the regime in Khartoum evolves, quite opposite conclusions will be drawn. But there is growing recognition that peace in Sudan requires evolution, not revolution or regime change, which was the implicit goal of many supporters of the indictment of President Bashir.

The story of Sudan in general, and Darfur in particular, says a lot about the present state of the "international community." By chance, I found myself in a remote base in Darfur one evening with Mia Farrow. We had dinner together at the military canteen. I admired her commitment to poor people whose plight would have never been known to the world if it was not for the advocacy and hard work of people like her or George Clooney. At the same time, I sometimes ask myself what this new proximity is achieving. I am reminded of a comment made by Qaddafi that I heard in a vast tent—adorned with a flat-screen TV, a mini-bar, and enormous white leather chairs—where he was receiving Ban. Playing with a fly-swatter, he politely explained to the secretary general of the United Nations how useless the UN is. "Conflicts in Africa escalate if you pay attention to them," he remarked. It is an unacceptable statement, to which the genocide in Rwanda, ignored by the international community, is the most tragic rebuttal, and the courageous Rwandan troops who patrol Darfur are living testimony that Rwanda, based on its own experience, thinks otherwise. But it is true that the gap is enormous between the perception in stable, rich countries of crises in developing countries and the complex realities of conflict. It is becoming ever harder to satisfy domestic audiences while effectively contributing to peace. We like to think of our engagement in the world as a fight of good against evil, and indeed, the search for compromise and common ground should never hide the facts that there are victims and killers and that there is no moral equivalence between them. Ignoring that led to the flawed engagement of the United Nations in Bosnia.

But the peacekeepers are not the SWAT team of the world, assigned to the straightforward task of cleaning up its bad neighborhoods. Most of the time, we are confronted with competing goals, which create moral dilemmas. In 2005 the international community was delighted with the awkward formula of the Comprehensive Peace Agreement, a commitment "to make unity attractive." That was a good illustration of the dilemmas of international engagement. Most observers were convinced that a breakup of Sudan would not be good for Africa or Sudan, but they also accepted that it was for the Sudanese to decide. So we tried—not very hard—to influence and to cajole, appeasing our conscience, and sometimes complicating an already complicated situation. Who are we to decide what is good enough for the Sudanese to stay together? Who are we to decide what is good enough for Darfur? When massive crimes are committed, it is easier to answer, and the international mobilization may actually save lives—although it usually comes after the worst has happened. But when the situation has settled in the gray area of a low-intensity conflict, the answer is much more difficult.

After more than a decade of international engagement in Sudan, the results are at best mixed. On one hand, the referendum of 2011 that decided the partition between north and south happened without major violence, a success for which the United Nations can take some credit. The referendum paved the way for what then looked as the peaceful birth of the world's newest country, South Sudan. While it was inspiring to see the will of the South Sudanese people fulfilled, the young country faces the daunting task of building a state from scratch as long-dormant intertribal tensions now spill out in overt conflict. The reality is that what united the disparate tribes in South Sudan was their opposition to Khartoum, and that there was a lot of ideological prejudice, encouraged by evangelical missionaries, in the creation of South Sudan. The hundreds of thousands of displaced persons who took refuge in UN compounds when the civil war started in 2013 are unlikely to return to their homes any time soon, and South Sudan may turn into a failed state even before it has consolidated as a state. Meanwhile, negotiations between Sudan and South Sudan continue at the same slow pace established before independence, and the threat of renewed conflict between the two states still exists.

In Darfur, the picture is just as unclear. There is unquestionably less violence now than a decade ago, and the humanitarian effort has saved hundreds of thousands of lives. But Darfur has changed forever. Darfur rebel groups, including the JEM and factions of the SLM and SPLM-N (former SPLM rebels who remained in the north), have united with ambitions that extend beyond Darfur, though Khalil Ibrahim of JEM was killed in an operation advancing toward Khartoum in 2011. Most of the poor people who fled when the Janjaweed attacked will never come back to their villages. They will stay in camps, which are becoming new cities. Whether these cities will be dysfunctional hotbeds of despair and violence or evolve into the foundation of a new economy will depend on the resolution of broader problems, which neither the humanitarian community nor the peacekeepers can resolve. We have had, sometimes unwittingly, an enormous impact, but with all our goodwill, we remain outsiders.

A number of ominous signs in Sudan point to possible further deterioration. President Bashir continues to manipulate Arab identity in Darfur but also more broadly throughout Sudan as he faces ongoing challenges to his authority from Islamists. This artificial polarization—between the Africans of the south and Arabs of the north, and between Sudan and Darfur—points to much deeper challenges facing Sudan, and the question of Sudanese identity remains, in many ways, unanswered. One of the most difficult challenges may be yet to come, as Sudan is confronted by the demographic and economic pressures that have come to characterize the Arab Spring. Indeed, Arab Spring–inspired stirrings have already been witnessed; should these isolated protests expand to organized demands for change, it could prove disastrous for Khartoum. Are we ready for that? As outsiders, for more than ten years we have sought an end to the multiple conflicts and crises in Sudan. But in Sudan as in other crises, our engagement has been half-hearted, as if we were not quite sure of what we wanted. As "crusaders," we seem to be full of doubts.

nine

LEBANON

How to End a War

On July 12, 2006, Hezbollah fired a series of rockets against Israeli Defense Forces and villages in northern Israel; crossing the cease-fire line, Hezbollah fighters attacked an Israeli army patrol. Three Israeli soldiers were killed, and two were abducted. Israel's response was immediate. It launched a massive air operation, which was gradually extended from south Lebanon to the whole country and supported by artillery shelling and small incursions. Finally, several weeks later, in the last days of the operation, the Israeli Defense Forces launched major ground operations in south Lebanon. The war lasted thirty-three days, during which Hezbollah fired some 4,000 katyusha rockets into Israel. Forty-three Israeli civilians and more than 1,000 Lebanese civilians were killed. The number of Hezbollah fighters killed cannot be ascertained, but was certainly in the hundreds. The Lebanese army lost 28 soldiers and the Israeli army 118, mostly during the ground operation at the end of the war.

In the week before the war began, I had been focusing on Sudan and the increased fighting in Darfur. On the day the Hezbollah attack took place, I had briefed the Security Council on Darfur, highlighting the dangers of ignoring those who had not signed the peace agreement, and of forging ahead. There was an overload of crises, as the Middle East seemed to be descending into chaos. Israeli military operations were ongoing in Gaza; the situation was deteriorating in Iraq; and there was no progress with Iran on the nuclear issue. The Hezbollah attack, coming after the abduction of an Israeli soldier in Gaza, seemed to suggest that all sides were now agreed that a policy of confrontation, which would further polarize the Middle East, was the preferred course. There was speculation that Hezbollah, which was supported by Iran's Revolutionary Guards via Syria, might be creating a diversion to help Iran at a time when the international pressure was increasing on Tehran over its stance on nuclear issues. Meanwhile, Arab countries allied with the United States were increasingly concerned that Iran would be the great beneficiary of the deterioration of the situation in Iraq. The Hezbollah attack had opened a new front in the "global war on terror."

For UN peacekeeping, the war raised major political issues and soon created operational dilemmas. The political challenge resulted from the fact that the UN mission in Lebanon (UNIFIL), although it had been deployed for twenty-eight years, and was as such one of the oldest peacekeeping operations, was also one of the most awkward. In one sense, it was peacekeeping at its most traditional: The first task defined by Security Council Resolution 425 in 1978 was to confirm the withdrawal of Israeli forces, which had invaded Lebanon to establish a "security zone" to keep Palestinian guerrillas away from the border. Israel did not withdraw until 2000, at which point the UN mission declared that its first task had been completed. Even that was not without controversy, because there was no agreement on how to define the Lebanese territory from which Israel had to withdraw. The UN resolved the issue by asserting its own definition of Lebanese territory for the implementation of Resolution 425.

The criteria for the completion of the UN mission's two other tasks were even more difficult to define. The second task was "to restore international peace and security," a goal that would be achieved only once Israel and Lebanon had signed a peace treaty. While Egypt and Jordan eventually signed their own peace treaties with Israel, Lebanon was a much harder case, and the existence of the mission was therefore dependent on fundamental strategic issues over which it had no influence. The third task was to "assist the government of Lebanon in ensuring the return of its effective authority in the area." What was "effective authority?" When the Israeli army finally withdrew from south Lebanon in 2000, the vacuum was not filled by the Lebanese army, which stayed north of the Litani, a small river that marks the northern limits of south Lebanon. Instead, Hezbollah, which had been founded in 1982 as a response to the second major Israeli operation in Lebanon, consolidated itself as the only effective authority south of the Litani. This created a very difficult situation for an organization of states like the United Nations. On one side of the cease-fire line, there was the state of Israel; on the other side, there was a heavily armed nonstate actor, Hezbollah, and to make things worse, Hezbollah was formally considered a terrorist organization by Israel and the United States. Nevertheless, the UN mission, in its daily management of a precarious cease-fire, could not ignore the de facto authority on the ground, Hezbollah, which made the UN an easy target for criticism, especially by Israel: the UN was an organization that condoned terrorism and whose officials could sometimes be seen meeting with terrorists.

All this did not represent a very attractive mission statement, and between the Israeli withdrawal in 2000 and the summer of 2005 the mission had hobbled along, defusing incidents. The mission was in an increasingly weaker position, as the long-standing political crisis in Beirut deepened between the pro-Syrian (and pro-Hezbollah) factions and the anti-Syrian groups. The Security Council, led by France and the United States, weighed in, pressing for the departure of Syrian troops from Lebanon and for free and fair elections. In September 2004 France and the United States managed to pass a tough resolution (Resolution 1559) demanding the withdrawal of Syrian troops, the disarmament of militias, and free and fair elections. China and Russia abstained, as did four other members of the council. A showdown between Syria and a Western camp led by France and the United States had started. A series of assassinations followed, the most important of which was a February 2005 car-bombing that killed former prime minister Rafiq Hariri. A billionaire businessman, Hariri had initially become prime minister with the support of Syria but eventually had become the head of the "anti-Syrian" camp.

The pro-Western camp in Lebanon seemed to have won the following month when parliamentary elections brought to power an anti-Syrian majority, and after lengthy negotiations, a new prime minister who had worked with Hariri, Fouad Siniora, could finally be appointed. Syria withdrew its troops from Lebanon in April 2005. At the same time, Siniora was able to bring Hezbollah into the government. A fragile national unity appeared to be emerging, which we at the UN believed should also make life less difficult for our peacekeeping mission deployed in the south. Although Lebanese government armed forces had continued to refuse to deploy south of the Litani, there was hope that since Hezbollah was now a part of the government, the gap between the de facto interlocutor on the ground and the de jure partner at the state level would narrow.

This was naive, and I should have known better. I had a first flavor of the difficult UN peacekeeping role in Lebanon in October 2000, almost immediately after I became head of peacekeeping, but the violence of the political storm hit me only a few months later. I had been barely a week on the job when Hezbollah ambushed and abducted three Israeli soldiers near the ceasefire line. The next day, as UN peacekeepers were in the process of recovering vehicles that had apparently been used to transport the abducted soldiers, operatives from Hezbollah forced the UN peacekeepers to surrender the vehicles. In the following months Israeli authorities and the aggrieved families of the abducted soldiers asked for any information we might have. We responded we had none. I was therefore surprised when, during my first visit to Israel in May 2001, my Israeli interlocutors informed me that the peacekeeping mission had a videotape of the event. I promised to check and found out, upon returning to New York, that indeed, a few weeks before, unbeknownst to me, the force commander had brought a tape to headquarters. And to make things worse, as the tape was being examined in New York, a representative of the secretary general in the region denied the existence of the tape, of which he had not yet been informed. I immediately called the Israeli ambassador to inform him officially of the by now famous tape, and I believe he understood that I was acting in good faith. Even so, a lot of damage had been done, and soon there was a media storm. The talk was now of UN "cover-up," as the Israelis demanded that the UN surrender the tape. Made by Indian troops, the tape was actually not of the abduction itself, but of the recovery of vehicles the next day and of their subsequent takeover by Hezbollah operatives. There was nothing in the tape of humanitarian value, but it illustrated the impossible situation in which the UN found itself. It showed the UN at its weakest and was a clear illustration of the awkward position of the mission. The UN was unable to accede to Israeli requests and unable to resist demands of Hezbollah: we could not surrender the tape to the Israelis because Hezbollah operatives could have been identified, allowing Israeli forces to launch targeted operations, making the UN an auxiliary of Israel and an immediate and easy target for Hezbollah retaliation. And it was the same weakness that had prevented the peacekeepers on the ground from resisting Hezbollah's demands to surrender the vehicles. The weakness was to be expected, as Israel, after twenty-two years as an occupying force, had itself been unable to defeat Hezbollah. The UN mission certainly was not in a better position to pick a fight with a de facto interlocutor in the maintenance of a cease-fire; it could only report on violations.

The Secretariat and the Security Council had long been aware of that situation, and we knew that nothing would be more dangerous for the UN peacekeeping mission than to give the appearance of strength when it was actually in a very weak position. That was the reason why, over recent years, there had been agreement in the Security Council to gradually reduce the size of the mission to 2,000 troops, after a temporary reinforcement at the time of the Israeli withdrawal. As I read the reports that I approved and that the Security Council was happy to endorse, I think we should have been more direct with the Council. In early 2001, I approved a report by the secretary general that stated:

Of the three parts of its mandate, UNIFIL has essentially completed two. It has confirmed the withdrawal of Israeli forces and assisted, to the extent it could, the Lebanese authorities as they returned to the area vacated by Israel. UNIFIL functions in close cooperation with those authorities and no longer exercises any control over the area of operation. UNIFIL cannot, of course, compel the Lebanese Government to take the last step and deploy its personnel down to the Blue Line [the UN-designated boundary between Israel and Lebanon].

It was all true, insofar as one accepted that the tasks that the mission could "complete" were actually very limited: the mission had done all it could within its limited means, but the "effective authority" of the government of Lebanon had certainly not returned to South Lebanon. The gradual downsizing of the force was more a recognition of the limits of a peacekeeping force that has to deal with a nonstate actor than the conclusion of a successful process. Israel, which never had much consideration for UNIFIL but appreciated its liaison role and the way it could help diffuse some incidents, had no illusion in that respect, but it did not oppose the downsizing.

By the summer of 2006, troop contributors who had long been symbols of UNIFIL, like Finland—which had even brought saunas to South Lebanon—had left. So had the Fijians, and so had the Irish, except for a few officers. But the mission, under the command of a shrewd French general, Alain Pellegrini, who understood the politics of Lebanon very well, retained an interesting mix of troops. It had Indian troops in the east, where Israel, Syria, and Lebanon meet. It had a Ghanaian battalion, Chinese engineers, a French company, and an Italian air unit. It was one of those increasingly rare peacekeeping operations that genuinely represented the international community, as troops from Europe were deployed side by side with troops from the developing world. But international symbolism was not enough to maintain a fragile cease-fire. It had not deterred Hezbollah from launching attacks on Israel, and it did not deter Israel from launching a massive retaliatory operation.

What was to be done? As a symbolic interposition force, the peacekeeping mission had failed, and it now found itself in the most dangerous situation since the Israeli operation of 1982. In the summer of 2006 a full-blown war was raging, and 2,000 peacekeepers were caught right in the middle of it. Before any solid assessment could be made, the instinct of Secretary General Kofi Annan, of the UNIFIL force commander, and of myself was not to pull out. For the Lebanese who were now under intense shelling, the mission, as limited in its capacities as it was, was a clear signal that the international community had not abandoned them at a time of great peril. But staying created pressing dilemmas. As bombing intensified, terrified Lebanese civilians wanted to enter UN compounds. If the UN opened the gates, it might quickly be overwhelmed, not having enough rations to feed thousands, and there was a risk that Hezbollah operatives would enter with the civilians, turning the UN compounds into targets for the Israeli air force. If the UN kept its gates shut, it would be abandoning civilians in distress. The peacekeepers performed with great bravery, but their task was immensely difficult. When Israeli rockets were fired at two cars in which villagers from Marwahin were fleeing, and sixteen were killed, UNIFIL could only collect the bodies, and Lebanese media immediately blasted a mission that was refusing to give refuge to people who were then killed by Israelis. The next day, UNIFIL managed to organize and safely accompany a convoy from the same village to Tyre, but Tyre itself was being bombed. A few days later, a UN civilian member of the mission would be killed in an aerial bombing of Tyre. Our instinctive preference for not evacuating also had a political rationale. Without at the time having any idea of the scenario that would end the war, we also believed that the UN peacekeepers would most likely have a role to play. If the mission pulled out, it would be much harder to contribute to the termination of the war.

But staying was difficult and dangerous. Early in the conflict, the Israeli Defense Forces declared the area contiguous to the cease-fire line to be a "security zone" in which no vehicle would be authorized. If we accepted the Israeli decision, the presence of UNIFIL would quickly become unsustainable because we would not be able to bring supplies to most of our positions, which were in the security zone. On Saturday, July 15, three days after the start of the war, Kofi Annan called Ehud Olmert, the Israeli prime minister, who reassured him that UNIFIL's freedom of movement would be safeguarded. I rushed to the Security Council to make the commitment public, to consolidate the Israeli concession. But on the ground, the situation remained difficult, and General Pellegrini had to send resupply convoys without waiting for Israeli authorization. The convoys were moving when there was a lull in the fighting. As for Hezbollah, it had deliberately established many of its firing positions right next to UN positions, which heightened the risk that a UN position would be hit by Israeli fire.

No Rush to End the Fighting

Meanwhile, many in the international community were not in a hurry to stop the conflict. Kofi Annan was the only one honestly trying to put an end to the devastation. He dispatched a mission to the Middle East, led by Vijay Nambiar. Nambiar was the former Indian ambassador to the UN, and he was now a close political adviser of the secretary general, known for his integrity and commitment to the values of the United Nations. He was accompanied by two other experienced UN diplomats: Terje Roed-Larsen, who was the UN official responsible for the implementation of Resolution 1559 and for that reason was perceived as anti-Hezbollah, and Alvaro de Soto, who was UN special envoy for the Middle East—a position that had previously been occupied by Roed-Larsen. But they could achieve nothing. On the contrary, when attempts were made in the Security Council to issue a declaration calling for a cease-fire, they were blocked—most notably by the United States, which was widely seen as supporting Israel—as was an innocuous press statement. Somewhat perversely, the Security Council now used the Nambiar mission to delay action. An ambassador argued that the council should wait for the mission to return and report, and wait also for the decisions of the Group of 8, which was meeting in St. Petersburg. Little came out of the St. Petersburg meeting, although the idea of an international force was discussed for the first time. That idea would later become a key element in the negotiations to end the war. The G-8 communiqué was weak, and for good reason: during the meeting, U.S. president George W. Bush and British prime minister Tony Blair had made no secret that the war should not end quickly and that they wanted to give Israel more time. They were not the only ones: the European Union issued a communiqué that was also weak, because a stronger message would have divided the Union. Jose Manuel Barroso, the president of the European Commission, referring to Gaza and Lebanon, drily noted that the business of the EU was now more and more to rebuild what others were destroying.

Ten days later, the war was still raging. The bombing of Lebanon continued unabated, while millions of Israelis living in northern Israel were terrified by Hezbollah's rockets that were raining down on them. I flew with the secretary general to Rome, where Bush's national security adviser, Condoleezza Rice, and Massimo d'Alema, the Italian foreign minister, had organized an international conference on Lebanon. It started tragically. The day before the conference, I was informed in the early evening that we had lost contact with four military observers who were under intense artillery and aerial bombardment in their bunker near Khiam, a village in the east of the UNIFIL area of operations. And as I was having dinner, I received a telephone call informing me that a party of Indian troops had finally reached the observer post; it had been destroyed by a powerful bunker-busting bomb, and the four military observers were dead. The repeated attempts by General Pellegrini to stop the Israeli bombing had failed, although the bunker, which was one of UNIFIL's oldest posts, was clearly marked as a UN position. Kofi Annan was informed of the loss during a meeting he was having with Condoleezza Rice, and we convened later in the evening in his hotel room. It was too late to reach Olmert in Israel, and the secretary general spoke with General Pellegrini and General Clive Lilley, the chief of the observers. The circumstances of the bombing were troubling, and a communiqué in which it was characterized as "apparently deliberate" was issued. The Israelis were furious at the choice of words, and the next morning, when the secretary general and Prime Minister Olmert eventually spoke, Olmert apologized for the Israeli action, which he characterized as a mistake. The secretary general accepted the apology. In September a formal UN report on the death of the four military observers would only conclude:

> UN Patrol Base at Khiam was struck by a 500 kilogram precision-guided aerial bomb and destroyed at 1925 hours on 25 July 2006. The Board of Inquiry notes that the Israeli authorities have accepted full responsibility for the incident and apologized to the United Nations for what they say was an "operational level" mistake. The Board did not have access to operational or tactical level IDF commanders involved in the incident, and was, therefore, unable to determine why the attacks on the UN position were not halted, despite repeated demarches to the Israeli authorities from UN personnel, both in the field and at Headquarters.

The day after the bombing, the only statement of substance at the Rome conference was made by Fouad Siniora, the embattled prime minister of Lebanon. He was able to attend thanks to UNIFIL. Beirut airport was closed, but a UNIFIL helicopter had flown him to nearby Cyprus, from where he flew to Rome. He presented a seven-point plan to end the war. It included the deployment of a reinforced UN force, an exchange of prisoners, and an immediate cease-fire. The plan did not mention the disarmament of militias, meaning Hezbollah. It soon became clear that agreement on a negotiated text would be impossible, and that the lack of a result suited many, including some Sunni Arab countries like Egypt for whom the war provided an opportunity to decisively weaken Hezbollah, a pro-Iranian Shia force. In the end, a bland "chairman's statement" did not even call for a cease-fire. The conference was a show attended by fifteen nations that were keen to be seen doing something, because public sentiment against the war was growing, but they had no intention of changing the situation on the ground. Unsurprisingly, it had achieved nothing.

However, the Rome conference provided a first opportunity for me to discuss with Siniora how to terminate the war. The prime minister was by training a financier and had no knowledge of peacekeeping, but he was remarkably aware of the political constraints that any military deployment would have to integrate. He understood that the deployment of a "force" was becoming a necessary element of any war-termination strategy. But the force should not be seen as an extension of the Israeli action, deployed to "finish the job" started by Israeli Defense Forces. It should deploy at the request of the Lebanese authorities, of which Hezbollah was a part. It should be perceived in Lebanon as a "protection force of Lebanon." This was a long way from the international force suggested in St. Petersburg by Tony Blair, and I wondered what would be the equilibrium point between the expectations of Israel and its Western friends on the one hand, and the opposite demands of Lebanon. I broached the idea of a multidimensional UN mission whose military component would be reduced to UN military observers, while the troops would be an EU force.

The war would last two more weeks. As the danger to our troops increased, I was more and more inclined to ask the secretary general to order their withdrawal. One morning, we had a dramatic teleconference. General Pellegrini, who was opposed to a withdrawal, argued from his headquarters in Naqura that withdrawing would be a very complex operation, as fraught with dangers as staying. Actually, the only practical way to withdraw would be through Israeli territory, since most of our positions were very close to the cease-fire line, and that would be politically devastating. Kofi Annan decided against the withdrawal, but in a lunch meeting with the Security Council he astutely used the threat of a UNIFIL withdrawal to put pressure on the council to reach agreement on a resolution that would end the war. He was right not to evacuate, and his decision, which carried serious risks, paved the way for the critical role that UNIFIL eventually played in the agreement that allowed for the end of the war.

The pressure to end the war kept mounting, as pictures of devastation in Lebanon were broadcast around the world. Jean-Marc de la Sablière, the French ambassador, and John Bolton, the U.S. ambassador, slowly began to negotiate, since the United States and France were traditionally the two countries that sponsored Security Council resolutions related to Lebanon. A proper cease-fire seemed too ambitious since fundamental political issues needed to be resolved between Israel and Lebanon, and the two ambassadors decided to proceed in two steps. A first resolution would sanction a cessation of hostilities, which would give time to resolve complex pending political issues. Once they had been resolved, a second resolution would endorse a cease-fire agreement. I was doubtful about this approach: There might never be a second resolution, since pending political issues would certainly prove difficult to resolve. But if the first resolution was adopted while Israeli ground troops were deployed in South Lebanon, it might well become the legal basis for an indefinite reoccupation of south Lebanon by Israeli troops. This would not be good for Israel, which would find itself in the same situation it had painfully extricated itself from in 2000. And it would not be good for Lebanon, which would again have an occupying army on its territory. Once the Israeli ground troops had established themselves in south Lebanon, it was obvious to me that this approach would be disastrous. But the United States and my French compatriots did not seem ready to change tack. Meanwhile, the Lebanese desperately wanted to kill the two-step approach and have only one resolution that would simultaneously end the war and trigger an Israeli withdrawal. They did not have much clout in New York, however, and they did not know how to influence a discussion that was going against their fundamental interests. Diplomatic demarches were not going to have any serious influence; the only way to change the dynamics was to create new facts on the ground.

Finally, during the first weekend of August we came up with an idea; a new "fact on the ground" could be created that could transform the negotiation. The Lebanese government should solemnly announce that it was reversing its position of many decades and was now ready to deploy its army to the Blue Line, acceding to a demand of Resolution 425 in 1978 that had never been fulfilled. That would make it possible to create a link between the cessation of hostilities and the Israeli withdrawal, and it would obviate the need for a second resolution. This was a simple idea, but it would have a chance to fly only if it was conveyed quickly to the highest levels of the Lebanese government. The idea had emerged in discussions with Ghassan Salame: Ghassan was an old friend, from the time when we taught together at Sciences Po in Paris, and he knew the UN well. He had been with Sergio de Mello in Baghdad, where he had miraculously survived the bombing in 2003. Most important, he had personal access to Prime Minister Siniora. The other channel was Geir Pedersen, the Norwegian diplomat who represented the secretary general in Lebanon; his integrity and finesse had won the respect of Lebanese and Israeli interlocutors alike. He was immediately supportive and undertook to pass the message informally. I was not too hopeful that the government of Lebanon would be ready for such a bold step, which would in effect mean that for the first time in many years it was taking responsibility for south Lebanon, but it was worth trying.

To my surprise, the Lebanese cabinet, which included Hezbollah, announced the following Monday, after several hours of deliberation, that it was ready to deploy the Lebanese army to the south. Hassan Nasrallah, the leader of Hezbollah who had until then been the true master of the south, lent his support to the decision. This was a strategic turning point, and the negotiation in New York immediately changed. The Lebanese had acquired a say that they did not have before. But there were still many complicated issues to resolve. In particular, the synchronization of the Israeli withdrawal with the deployment of the reinforced UN force and of some 15,000 Lebanese troops was a very complex operation. The United States wanted the Israelis to control the pace, while the Lebanese and the French wanted to put some constraints on the Israelis. Another key issue was the control of borders. As one would expect, Israel did not want Hezbollah to rearm and to be in a position to start another war a few years later.

The most difficult issue was the nature of the interposition force that would be deployed. The United States and Israel wanted NATO, but that was totally unacceptable to the Lebanese government and never really had a chance. Remarkably, when Washington realized that the NATO option would not work, it actually put pressure on Israel to compromise. Solana was wondering whether this might open an opportunity for a force of the European Union. But the perception of the European Union in the Middle East was not what the Europeans had hoped for, and the EU did not have the legitimacy it thought it had. The only forces acceptable to the Lebanese were UN blue helmets. The Israelis and the United States could agree to that demand only if the force was strong, and they insisted on a Chapter VII resolution, thus authorizing the UN force to take military action to restore peace.

As the negotiations developed, Hezbollah—without which there would be no Lebanese government position—hardened its position, categorically rejecting a Chapter VII force. Once again, I found that the discussion in the Security Council showed a surprising lack of understanding of what Chapter VII entails; Chapter VII is designed for situations where force needs to be used without the consent of the state concerned. The drafters of the UN Charter had in mind situations comparable to the one that existed in Europe before World War II: the objections of a new Hitler should not stop the use of force against him. The best example is the U.S.-led multinational force that expelled Iraq from Kuwait in 1991. In the case of Lebanon, Chapter VII would have been warranted if the Security Council was willing to deploy a force in south Lebanon without the consent of Lebanon, or was prepared to maintain its deployment even if that consent was withdrawn. This was obviously not the case: almost three decades of difficulties for the Israeli army in south Lebanon were a strong warning to any outsider that might consider deploying its troops without the consent of the Lebanese. But the absence of a reference to Chapter VII did not mean that an interposition force had to be weak. We explained that to the French and other potential troop contributors who did not want their troops to go to war with Lebanon but who demanded enough "robustness" to ensure that their troops would be capable of defending themselves and would not be humiliated.

In the end, we were asked to draft a paragraph that would be acceptable to the Lebanese while addressing the concerns of the Western powers. Salman Ahmed—my special assistant, who had been the main drafter of the 2000 Brahimi report on UN peacekeeping reforms and who had the best political mind in the department—drafted it quickly, and the Americans and the French immediately accepted it. The text was a delicate balancing act. It stated that the Security Council, "acting in support of a request from the Government of Lebanon to deploy an international force to assist it to exercise its authority throughout the territory, authorizes UNIFIL to take all necessary action in areas of deployment of its forces and as it deems within its capabilities, to ensure that its area of operations is not utilized for hostile activities of any kind, to resist attempts by forceful means to prevent it from discharging its duties under the mandate of the Security Council." The reference to the request of the Lebanese government, and the definition of the role of UNIFIL as "assistance" to that government, put an implicit ceiling on the initiatives UNIFIL could take on its own. But at the same time, the reference to the request for assistance was general, so that the question whether UNIFIL could take action and "assist" on its own, or only if it was requested to do so by the government, was not clearly answered. The use of the expression "to use all necessary action" was close to the expression "all necessary means," which in UN parlance traditionally refers to Chapter VII. Likewise, the expression "hostile activities of any kind" was purposefully vague.

An agreement was reached to have one resolution in which all the key elements of the compromise would be included. A central element of the deal was that three military forces would have to coordinate their movements simultaneously: the Israeli army would withdraw as the deployment of Lebanese and additional UN forces began. The resolution outlined the principles of a permanent cease-fire, which included agreement on the delineation of the Blue Line, as the cease-fire line was called; the disarmament of armed groups, which was coded language for the transformation of Hezbollah from an armed militia to a political party; effective control of the borders to prevent entry of unauthorized weapons; and the recognition of the government of Lebanon as the sole authority in South Lebanon. The government of Lebanon would receive the assistance of a considerably reinforced UNIFIL: from a force of 2,000 personnel before the war, UNIFIL would be augmented to 15,000. The figure was very high, considering that the area of operation of UNIFIL was quite small: its east-west dimension was roughly

80 kilometers from the Mediterranean to the Syrian border, and its depth was never more than 20 kilometers, from the cease-fire line with Israel to the Litani River. The figure was not the result of any thorough troops-to-task planning but the outcome of a political deal: some had mentioned 20,000, some 10,000. The number 15,000 looked good because it was a sufficiently high number to reassure the Israelis, and there were doubts that 20,000 troops could have been accommodated in this tiny piece of land. Actually, UNIFIL never reached 15,000, and nobody ever complained that there were not enough troops. South Lebanon is probably, along with the frontline between the two Koreas, one of the most densely militarized areas in the world.

Need for a Rapid Deployment

The challenge was now for the United Nations to rapidly deploy a reinforced UNIFIL. While there was an understanding with Israel that its troops would withdraw before the deployment was completed—a delayed withdrawal carried a high risk of resumption of war—the United Nations had a political obligation to deploy quickly. I was very worried because I knew that UN deployments usually take several months. The only way to have a rapid deployment was to rely on troops that had the capability to sustain themselves and came from countries that had a national capacity to project force. Since U.S. troops were out of the question for many reasons, the only possible sources for a rapid initial deployment were European countries, which had been keen to end the war ever since the Rome conference. Now was the time for the Europeans to put their money—actually their troops—where their mouths were. And since France had played a major role in drafting the resolution, every other European country was watching what France would do before taking a decision. Initially France was ready to deploy only an additional 200 troops. We were a long way from what was needed, and if that ridiculously low figure was confirmed, there would be no reinforced UNIFIL in the foreseeable future; the prospects for success of the UN resolution would end in a debacle.

The military establishment in France had very bad memories of its participation in UN peacekeeping during the Balkan wars. The French military remembered the hostage-taking, the white flags, and they were committed to never again endure such humiliations. I had tried, with little success, to explain that the abject failures of the early 1990s were the result of a fatally flawed strategy rather than the consequence of bad command-and-control arrangements. President Jacques Chirac himself, who had played a decisive and positive role in restoring the credibility of the international community at the end of the Balkan wars and who was, according to the French constitution, the supreme commander, had a lot of sympathy for the concerns of his military, and was less than enthusiastic about a major increase of the participation of French troops in UN peacekeeping. I was later told that the headline that a French regional daily had extracted from an interview I gave in the middle of August had irritated him because it put France too much on the spot: I was quoted as saying that "France has to provide the backbone of the force." Eventually France, Italy, and Spain did indeed provide the backbone, but it did not happen without some effort.

A competition between Italy and France helped. The two countries had excellent relations, their militaries worked well together, but neither wanted to be outdone by the other. Spain, which has a tradition of political engagement in the Middle East, did not want to be left behind. But the top brass of France and Italy had to be convinced that the UN of 2006 was not the UN of Bosnia in 1995. We invited a team of French officers to work with our own staff to develop the rules of engagement for the force and see with their own eyes that the UN had changed. They were half-convinced, but when the chief of staff of the Italian army, Admiral Giampaolo Di Paola, arrived in New York and heard that the UN was not interested in his request for a strategic headquarters, the worst fears of defense establishments used to the many layers of the NATO chain of command were confirmed: The UN was not serious and could not be trusted. It operated on a shoestring and was dominated by civilians who did not understand military affairs.

I was not in total agreement with my own staff. I believed the French and the Italians were right to criticize the excessively light headquarters of the UN, which did not have the resources to develop contingency plans and enter into a strategic dialogue with theater commanders. But their fear of civilian interference and their request to have NATO-type structures for a peacekeeping operation were misplaced. In Lebanon as in most peacekeeping missions, politics mattered enormously, and the force commander would need solid political guidance. I would have preferred to have a civilian head of mission who would help the Lebanese develop a national consensus, which is vital for the mission to be successful. But this was not a battle I could win, and I did not even try. I was also convinced that while it was good to allow the troop contributors to a specific mission to be more closely involved at the strategic level, it was important that the United Nations not surrender the strategic direction to the troop contributors. A balance had to be found between the need, on the one hand, to make the troop contributors comfortable and the need, on the other, to protect the universality of the United

Nations and to benefit at the strategic level from the experience of other peacekeeping operations. I was in a weak negotiating position because there was no alternative to European troops.

I accepted the creation of a strategic military cell in the Department of Peacekeeping Operations whose structure was similar to a traditional military headquarters, and whose officers were seconded by participating countries. It reported directly to me rather than to the military adviser and was at the start somewhat isolated in the department; there was initially no structured inter-action with the political and logistics parts of the department. But most of the officers who had been seconded were first class, and they made it work. They quickly understood that they would benefit from more interaction with their political and support colleagues, the latter supporting both civilians as well as military personnel. The strategic military cell, which had initially been the fruit of expediency, evolved over the following years as it was integrated in the Office of Military Affairs, which it helped strengthen and transform. The tra-ditional non-European troop contributors at first had been wary of the new structure, which seemed tailor-made to accommodate the Europeans, and they resented the special treatment given to those new troops. But they were part of it, since some of them, like India, contributed troops and at my insis-tence a deputy force commander. Eventually they saw the benefits of the new arrangements and helped correct the initial mistakes.

Once the structures were agreed, other delicate issues had to be resolved. In NATO, the troop-contributing countries have much more influence than in the UN—often for the worse, as they impose national constraints, called "caveats," on the use of their troops and divvy up the key appointments. I tried as best as I could to protect some space for the UN in the appointments process. I had to accept that the nationality of key commanders would be decided by the troop-contributing countries. I had always tried to resist this practice in peacekeeping operations because it weakens the loyalty of com-manders to the UN and leads to a dangerous system of rotations, limiting the pool of applicants, with the risk that the wrong commander may sometimes have to be appointed. But I forced nations to propose several candidates, which could mitigate the risks if the contributing nations played by the book and put forward a credible slate of candidates.

The other delicate issue was the nature of the capacities to be deployed. The perennial problem of a UN peacekeeping force is to lack capacities, and there were many instances in which I was desperately looking for capacities that no state was willing to provide, like the helicopters in Darfur. For once, I had the opposite problem. General Jean-Louis Georgelin, who had just been appointed chief of staff of the French army, made clear to me that the French troops sent to Lebanon would deploy with antiaircraft weapons systems, heavy artillery, and thirteen Leclerc heavy tanks.

I was happy that the troops would have sophisticated radar systems that would make it less difficult to quickly identify the origin of rocket fire. I was less convinced that antiaircraft systems were a good idea, because the only planes flying over the UNIFIL area of operation were Israeli planes violating the Lebanese airspace. It was good to have the capacity to precisely identify them and report violations, but what about the antiaircraft missiles? No peacekeeping force would ever fire even warning shots at the planes, although the Lebanese would consider such overflights as "hostile activities." The non-use of an existing capacity might make the force look partial, and I thought it is sometimes better not to have a particular capacity when it is obvious that you are never going to use it. As for the tanks, there had been a lot of controversy on the performance of the Israeli Merkava tank during the war, and I had doubts about the usefulness of heavy tanks in Lebanon. UNIFIL was not going to fight the Israeli army, and I was not sure that a heavy tank was the optimal deterrent against nimble guerilla fighters, nor was it the best signal that could be conveyed to the civilian population on the narrow roads of South Lebanon. But I was not a general, and I was grateful to my country for having made the strategic decision to deploy. All these new weapons systems were deployed, and two years later I saw the squadron of Leclerc tanks, as well as impressive howitzers, by then all painted white, parked at a UN base in South Lebanon. They have since been quietly withdrawn.

I flew to the Middle East with the secretary general in late August. The cease-fire was holding, but the situation was tense. Israel, concerned that Hezbollah was going to quickly rearm, was maintaining a tight blockade on Lebanon. Lebanese prime minister Siniora was requesting the United Nations to deploy a naval task force, as part of the UN "assistance" to the government of Lebanon. The deployment of a naval task force along the coast of Lebanon was an unprecedented type of activity for a UN force. It proved easier to put together than I had thought it would be, simply because several countries were happy to support Lebanon at sea rather than on land, and it was a kind of real-life naval exercise. It eventually proved less revolutionary than initially anticipated, as lawyers from various contributing navies agreed that the force did not have the authority to forcefully board suspicious ships and inspect their cargo on the high seas. It systematically hailed ships—some 28,000 of them in four years—but could only refer the suspicious ones to the Lebanese authorities. A total of 400 ships were referred, but to this day there is no report that any unauthorized cargo was ever found. Siniora was less forthcoming on the assistance to control the land borders and the airport. He wanted equipment, which Germany undertook to provide, rather than people. I did not think that the UN had much experience and credibility in border control. The most we could do probably would be to monitor the efforts of the Lebanese, who were on very sensitive ground, considering the close relations of Hezbollah with Syria.

I had a first glimpse of the impact of the war when we walked in south Beirut: this was the stronghold of Hezbollah, and the whole neighborhood had been destroyed by Israeli bombing. The UN was not popular among a largely pro-Hezbollah crowd, and the crowd quickly became hostile when it recognized some members of the delegation who it considered pro-Israel. In south Lebanon, the organizers of the secretary general's visit were more cautious, and there was little contact with the population. But we could see the extent of the devastation from our low-flying helicopters. In some villages that Israel deemed pro-Hezbollah, few houses were left standing. In others, the destruction had been more selective as houses belonging to Lebanese unconnected with Hezbollah had been spared. I stayed behind, after the secretary general had left, to welcome the San Marco battalion landing on a beach near Tyre. This elite unit was the first from the Italian army to reinforce the mission, which until then only had a helicopter squadron from Italy. The soldiers were impeccable, and I felt that the efforts of the summer to bolster the UN mission had not been made in vain.

Earlier in the day, I had attended a religious ceremony with the Sikh battalion, in the eastern part of the area of operation. I had surrendered my belt, because it was made of leather, and put on a kind of yellow turban. After the ceremony, on the banks of the Wazzani—a small tributary of the Jordan River that had once caused serious tensions when Israel protested the installation of a pump by the Lebanese authorities—it was easy to forget that Sikhs initially were Hindu warriors fighting Muslims. The Indians had brought their rites and their food to this quiet corner of Lebanon, and under the shade of old trees we were enjoying a moment of tranquility, silence broken only by the soothing sound of running water. The bells, the muezzin, the mysterious mumbling of a Sikh priest, and the water that had run since biblical times— it all made the convulsions of war seem rather absurd.

The rapid deployment of UNIFIL and of its naval task force was a major success for the United Nations, and for European nations, which for the first time in many years were playing a truly strategic role in the Middle East. It was argued that if UNIFIL made the northern border of Israel secure, the precedent might lead to further engagement in the Israel-Palestine conflict. If a reinforced UNIFIL delivered security, it would change the perception in Israel of the UN and of Europe. The United States, the Europeans, and Israel itself had high expectations in the late summer of 2006. Up to a point, those expectations were met: In the first five years following the war, there were relatively few incidents along the Blue Line. But as protests turned to civil war in Syria in 2011, the chaotic convulsions of the region once again have put the stability of Lebanon at risk.

There was always a certain naiveté in the expectation that a UN military force would achieve in south Lebanon what decades of Israeli occupation could not. The massive deployments and the continuous patrols certainly made life more difficult for any group that would want to launch "hostile activities" from south Lebanon. Did they prevent Hezbollah from rearming? Certainly not, and now there are clear signals that conflict in Syria has led to further rearming of that nonstate group, which now also exercises de facto veto power over the Lebanese government. The Israelis complain that UNIFIL does not search houses that are, according to them, Hezbollah bases. And indeed, UNIFIL cannot forcefully enter a house just because it has suspicions. Likewise, the UNIFIL observation posts along the Litani River are established at a certain distance from the Lebanese checkpoints. I visited them in the summer of 2008 and was struck to see that Lebanese soldiers were waving through heavily loaded vehicles without any control. Fifty yards away, UNIFIL troops with binoculars were observing them.

Could it have been different? Lawyers will regret that the mandate includes the word "assist," making UNIFIL an auxiliary of the Lebanese government. But if UNIFIL had more authority, it could quickly find itself in a collision course with the Lebanese government and Hezbollah. When Spanish units of UNIFIL courageously started expanding their interpretation of the mandate, taking photographs of potentially hostile activities, a Spanish armored personnel carrier was blown up on a road near Khiam. Six Spanish soldiers died. No responsibility was established, but this was a tragic reminder that nonstate actors are operating in the area and that UNIFIL operates in an environment where it could quickly become a target.

Lebanese politics continue to be the single most important factor in the success or failure of UNIFIL, but Lebanese politics are themselves greatly influenced by regional politics. The international community, by increasing the pressure on Syria through Resolution 1559, succeeded in obtaining the withdrawal from Lebanon of Syrian troops, but the period was also marked by a wave of killings, culminating in the assassination of former prime minister Rafiq Hariri in 2005. After the war, the investigations of the political assassinations, notably the international tribunal that had been created specifically for

Lebanon, and the unresolved issue of the election of the president of Lebanon led to increased domestic tensions, culminating in the withdrawal of Hezbollah from the government. This was the most difficult period for UNIFIL, which could no longer turn to the government to control Hezbollah. Lebanon was increasingly becoming a victim of the regional polarization, which pitted Iran and Syria against the Western camp. Whether intended or not, Resolution 1559 had reinforced the link between Lebanese domestic politics and regional politics and created risks for UNIFIL and for Lebanon. The resolution weakened the one interlocutor that had emerged in the south as a result of the war: the Lebanese state and its army, which was the anchor of Lebanon and its best hope of stability.

I paid one last visit to Lebanon in the spring of 2008. The Qatari government, which shares a huge gas field with Iran and has, more than any country in the region, a lot to lose in a confrontation of Iran, had just engineered a breakthrough in Lebanese politics. An agreement had been reached in Doha on the election of the president and the participation of the opposition in the government. General Michel Suleiman, who as chief of staff of the Lebanese army had been the main interlocutor of UNIFIL, was to be the next president of Lebanon. I had a long conversation with him on May 23, a few hours before his formal election by the parliament. Clearly, UNIFIL played an important role in helping Lebanon find a balance. But it was not the role that the Israelis, the Americans, or the French had hoped for. UNIFIL's presence was not going to lead to the disarmament of Hezbollah, but it lowered the level of tensions in the south, it diffused local conflicts, and that, more than any forceful action, strengthened the hand of those Lebanese who wanted to move their country away from the destructive politics of polarization and violence. It was an essentially political role: UNIFIL had an impact on the political dynamics of Lebanon. General Suleiman, who had had the difficult role of leading the Lebanese army and avoiding confrontation with Syria while maintaining Lebanese sovereignty, knew better than anybody else that battalions sometimes have an important operational role to play, but that in the end what mattered was politics. The operations that the Lebanese army launched to take control of Palestinian camps were a good illustration of that role. Those operations had helped rebuild the credibility of the Lebanese state. A strong UNIFIL in the south would not prevent a resumption of war by Hezbollah or by the Israelis if they so decided, but it certainly complicated their strategic calculations—and that was the best a peacekeeping operation could achieve in Lebanon. With the invasion of Iraq and the fall of Saddam Hussein, the precarious Lebanese compromise that had been negotiated at Taef, Saudi Arabia, in 1989 after a devastating civil war was again under threat: The conquest of power by the Shia in Iraq—after centuries of domination by the Sunni—was a watershed event for the whole Middle East. In the three Arab countries where the Shia have a significant presence but do not rule—Lebanon, Bahrain, and Saudi Arabia—the victory of their brothers in Iraq has for the first time given hope and self-confidence to the Shia.

The escalation of the civil war in Syria (the conflict and my role in the UN's response is covered in chapter 12) has thrown regional politics into a period of unprecedented uncertainty and risk. As action by the Security Council has been stalled by differences between Russia and the United States over the role of President Bashar al-Assad in any transition government, regional actors have moved in to support either pro- or anti-government forces. Many called attention to the risks to Lebanon early on in the conflict. But Lebanon—which has followed a policy of "disassociation" from the Syrian conflict—has managed to maintain a surprising degree of stability, even as hundreds of thousands of refugees have fled Syria across its borders. However, as Hezbollah takes an increasingly active role in supporting Assad's government, it will risk pulling Lebanon further into what increasingly resembles a regional sectarian war.

ten
KOSOVO
The Long Goodbye

The peacekeeping mission in Kosovo was the first one I visited, and it would be the most pressing issue in my last months in office. For many Europeans and North Americans, Kosovo is a moral cause. The region suffered terribly under Slobodan Milošević's rule, and supporting Kosovo nationalism is seen by many as a duty, a reaction against the ethical blindness of the international community during the Balkan wars of the 1990s, when little distinction was made between victims and killers under the assumption that a peacekeeping mission should be "neutral." I never accepted that moral equivalence and always believed that the United Nations should be on the side of the victims. But I never felt compelled, as so many western diplomats seem to have been, to side with one form of Balkan nationalism against another. That lack of passion helped me when it came to managing the endgame of the UN presence in Kosovo, but it did not endear me to some of my Western interlocutors who thought I was betraying their cause.

Kosovo is the smallest and poorest of the fragments to emerge from the former Yugoslavia. It is barely a quarter the size of Estonia or the Netherlands—smaller even than Fiji or tiny Montenegro. It is entirely land-locked. Wedged between the backyards of Serbia and Albania, its location is not strategic. It has few natural resources, apart from lignite—the dirtiest and most polluting form of coal. Its economy is weak, other than a lively engagement in various forms of organized crime, including the trafficking of drugs and women for prostitution. Pristina, its capital city, is an unhappy child of socialist town planning and often sits under a pall of smog belched out from the smokestacks of a decrepit Yugoslav-era power plant.

The great majority of Kosovo's population is ethnic Albanian, a non-Slav people forcibly absorbed by Slav Serbia during the First Balkan War in 1912.

Relations between the Serbs and Albanians were bad even before the two Balkan wars that preceded World War I, and then got worse. During World War II, Kosovo's minority Serbs sided either with the royalist Chetniks or with Tito's Partisans. In 1944 the Albanians raised a Waffen SS division to support Nazi Germany—the 21st SS Division Skanderbeg. Under communism, Kosovo's Albanian majority was never really integrated into Yugoslavia and pushed, noisily but with only limited success, for ever wider autonomy.

But there is another Kosovo: a Kosovo of the Serb imagination—"the Serb Jerusalem," as John Zametica calls it. Kosovo is remembered by many Serbs as the cradle of their medieval kingdom and for its monasteries—the holiest sites of the Serbian Orthodox Church. And for the battle that ended it all. The word Kosovo, in fact, derives from the Serbian word *kos*, meaning blackbird. And it was on the Field of Blackbirds, now in the peri-urban sprawl of Pristina, that the Kingdom of Serbia was defeated in the Battle of Kosovo by the Ottoman Empire and effectively extinguished on St. Vitus Day, June 28 of 1389.

Despite this, Kosovo might have remained a quiet, depressed corner of eastern Europe, but for three additional factors: the rise of Slobodan Milošević, the Western response to the collapse of Yugoslavia, and the fall and rise of Russia. Together, over time, these three factors managed to ensure that a small conflict in a small place would become big enough to absorb the energies not only of Europe, but also of the United States, Russia, and the United Nations.

Nationalism—angry, xenophobic, autocratic nationalism—has been the exit strategy of choice for many communist leaders. The genius of Slobodan Milošević, if it can be called that, was that he saw this earlier than most. Milošević himself seems not to have been particularly nationalistic—his nationalism was more opportunistic than visceral. But Kosovo seems to have given Milošević a sense of the power and potential of Serbian nationalism. Sent by the Yugoslav government to the Field of Blackbirds in the spring of 1987, he was speaking with local leaders when a crowd of several thousand Serb demonstrators clashed outside with the mainly Albanian police force. Television footage shows Milošević, then still relatively unknown, emerging from a building to listen to complaints from the demonstrators, and then saying, "You will not be beaten."

From relatively mild comments in support of Serb demonstrators in Kosovo, Milošević's rhetoric and power grew. In 1989, with Milošević's support, the Serbian constitution was amended to give Belgrade greater direct control of law enforcement in Kosovo and greater leeway in dealing with ethnic Albanian unrest. The Kosovo Albanians responded with a boycott of Serbian elections and institutions. Before long, a sort of primitive apartheid existed in Kosovo—with state institutions and the Serbian language for the dominant Serb minority and parallel Albanian institutions and language for the Albanian majority.

In another country, it might all have ended with an easy divorce, as eventually happened in Czechoslovakia. Even without the aggressive behavior of Milošević, however, Yugoslavia presented several problems. One was demography. Emerging from the ruins of two multinational states—the Hapsburg and Ottoman empires—Yugoslavia had no common language or national identity.

Yugoslavia's borders, both international and internal, also posed particular problems. Having been relatively successful in struggles with its neighbors, Yugoslavia's international borders enfolded large populations not only of Serbs, Bosnian Muslims, Croats, Slovenes, Macedonians, Montenegrins, and Kosovar Albanians, but also of Hungarians and, at one point, of Italians and Germans. In an age of growing nationalism, each of these communities was touched by divided loyalties.

The internal borders were even more complicated. With the exception of the Slovenes, the peoples of the former Yugoslavia tended not to live in homogeneous areas that could be separated by lines on a map. Croatia had a Croat majority, but also a large Serb minority. Bosnia, the most mixed of all of Yugoslavia's six republics, had three main communities, none of which comprised an absolute majority and all of which, to some degree, lived intermingled with the others. Macedonia had a Slav Macedonian majority, but also a large and fast-growing Albanian minority. And Serbia had Kosovo, with its Albanian population, along with various other kaleidoscopic complexities: the Sanjak with its Bosniacs (that is, Bosnian Muslims), the Vojvodina with its Hungarians, and others. Yugoslavia was almost uniquely unsuited for being carved into smaller national units: dismembering the country could not be done without alarming—or moving, or killing—large numbers of people from the "wrong" group.

Yet it was done, and it was done with active Western support.

As Yugoslavia broke up, the European Community, soon to morph into the European Union, took the lead. Europe's response was largely defined by the Badinter Arbitration Committee, which in 1991 determined that "Yugoslavia is in the process of dissolution" and that the internal boundaries of Yugoslavia's constituent republics could become international borders, and "except where otherwise agreed, the former boundaries become frontiers protected by international law."

This opinion seemed to produce, or at least recognize, two effects. First, due to the demography of the country, multiethnic Yugoslavia was going to be broken up into several smaller multiethnic states—which would not obviously resolve the nationalistic tensions that were driving the problem in the first place. And second, it meant that some parts of the former Yugoslavia, like Montenegro, could ultimately become independent, with frontiers protected by international law (because Montenegro was one of the six constituent "republics"), whereas other parts of the former Yugoslavia, like Kosovo, which has three times as many people as Montenegro, could *not* become independent (because Kosovo was not a republic of the former Yugoslavia in its own right, but just an "autonomous province" of the Republic of Serbia).

If the goal of the exercise was to stabilize the situation, or to protect lives, it was not conspicuously successful. Pandora's box was open, and everyone wanted to be in the majority. Wherever the new countries resulted in some groups being new minorities, those minorities took up arms to try to create even newer entities in which *they* would be the majority: the Serbs in Croatia; the Serbs and Croats in Bosnia; the Albanians in Serbia and Macedonia.

Ten thousand were killed in Croatia. A hundred thousand were killed in Bosnia, mostly by the Serbs, who had inherited much of Yugoslavia's old military and police capacity. The world dithered. In his poem *Kolo*, Joseph Brodsky captured some of the disconnect between the brutality on the ground—much of it instigated or enabled by Milošević—and the emptiness of the international response.

> In March the soldiers
> with rifles on their shoulders
> Out run through brambles
> the locals with their bundles.
>
> Off fly the envoys
> contemplating new ways
> of creating symmetry
> in a future cemetery
>
> Up go the pundits
> explicating bandits.
> Clearly outworded,
> down go the murdered.

At the United Nations, Secretary General Boutros Boutros-Ghali was opposed to the deployment of peacekeepers in the former Yugoslavia. Reflecting on a request to send peacekeepers to Sarajevo, in May 1992 the secretary general wrote to the Security Council as follows:

The situation is tragic, dangerous, violent and confused. I do not believe that in its present phase this conflict is susceptible to the United Nations peacekeeping treatment. Any successful peacekeeping operation has to be based on some agreement between the hostile parties. Such an agreement can range from a simple ceasefire to a comprehensive settlement of their dispute. Without an agreement of some sort, a workable mandate cannot be defined and peacekeeping is impossible.

Yet the Security Council, not for the last time, chose to overrule the secretary general and deployed the United Nations Protection Force (UNPROFOR).

Successes and Failures of UNPROFOR

The UN's peacekeeping efforts in the former Yugoslavia covered almost the full spectrum of what peacekeepers are asked to do with almost the whole spectrum of results.

The UNPROFOR operation in Croatia, and then in Bosnia, was the largest of these adventures. At its height, more than 20,000 UNPROFOR troops were deployed in Bosnia, mainly from Western countries. Around the lightly armed blue helmets raged a war fought by some 400,000 armed men from six main armies—by far the largest war in Europe for almost half a century. Over a hundred UNPROFOR soldiers were killed, some by Serbs, some by Croats, some by Bosniac Muslims.

UNPROFOR achieved its basic mandate to ensure the delivery of humanitarian assistance to war-torn Bosnia. Almost for the first time in the history of European warfare, a large-scale protracted war took place with almost no one dying of hunger or cold. Almost a thousand tons of food was delivered daily, for over three years, to more than 2 million beneficiaries. UNPROFOR troops, often against extraordinary odds, escorted convoys of assistance from the UN's High Commissioner for Refugees (UNHCR) to Bosnia's remotest valleys. Almost every family in Bosnia ate food hauled by UNHCR and covered its homes' shell-blasted windows with ubiquitous UN plastic insulation sheets.

UNPROFOR's basic military task was also achieved. Once a peace agreement was reached, it marked the cease-fire lines, separated the main armies, monitored compliance with the agreement, and held the line until peace was fixed. When UNPROFOR was finally replaced by a much larger NATO-led force in December 1995, the war had been over for months.

Yet, for much of the world, UNPROFOR was not only a failure, but a humiliation. UNPROFOR was the world's response to Bosnia, but Bosnia required much more than the delivery of humanitarian assistance, or the monitoring of agreements. It needed the political and military engagement that would end fighting and enforce peace. For much of the world, the image of UNPROFOR is the image of Dutch troops standing by and watching as Bosnian Muslims are taken away from Srebrenica, under the smiling supervision of Bosnian Serb general Ratko Mladić, for execution.

So deep was the sense that UNPROFOR was the wrong tool for the wrong job—and so deep, I often suspected, was the need to find someone else to blame for the inadequacy of the international response—that the Western countries largely withdrew from peacekeeping after UNPROFOR, rewriting history to forget their policy failures, of which they had been warned by the secretary general himself. Prior to Bosnia, almost half of UN peacekeepers had been from Western countries. Though they slowly trickled back during my time, when I left office the West provided fewer than one in ten of our blue helmets.

The other UN missions in the former Yugoslavia were all better fits between problem and solutions. In Macedonia, a small preventive mission monitored the country's sensitive borders and helped keep at bay a simmering dispute between the Slav Macedonian majority and the Albanian minority. The UN mission was later followed by NATO and European Union missions, one of which was led by my successor at the United Nations, Alain le Roy. It was the first time that the United Nations had deployed peacekeepers in a preventive role and represented, in its way, a growing international awareness that once a conflict has begun—once blood has been spilled—a return to true peace becomes exponentially harder.

In eastern Slavonia a UN transitional administration ran the territory as it prepared for integration into postwar Croatia. The mission was led by Jacques Paul Klein, a cigar-smoking, gun-toting, war-criminal-arresting American ambassador and general. A postwar mission in Bosnia also was a success, defanging and rebuilding the local police forces and reestablishing freedom of movement between the Bosniac-, Croat- and Serb-controlled zones of the country. An almost unimaginably pleasant mission on the Dalmatian coast monitored a thorny territorial dispute between Croatia and Montenegro, until it, too, could be quietly resolved.

Intervention in Kosovo

During the early and mid-1990s, Kosovo Albanian resistance to Serbian rule was mainly peaceful, broken only by the killing of the occasional police officer and the elimination of some internal enemies. The standoff continued until 1997 when neighboring Albania was convulsed by a bizarre financial scandal involving the collapse of pyramid investment schemes in which huge numbers of Albanians lost their life savings. In the resulting mayhem, armories were opened and weapons began to flow freely, including into Kosovo.

The number of clashes rose, with increasing casualties on both sides. On March 5, 1998, Serbian security forces cornered Adem Jashari, one of the commanders of the new Kosovo Liberation Army, sparking an incident that was to mark a new phase of radicalization in the conflict. Fifty-eight people were killed in the Jashari family compound, including the guerilla leader himself, but also including many who were unarmed. By the end of summer, a full-scale insurgency was under way, as was a full-scale, often brutal, Serbian counterinsurgency.

The United Nations envisaged no operational role for itself in managing the Kosovo conflict. In September 1998 the Security Council called for the withdrawal from Kosovo of Yugoslav forces "used for civilian repression," but did not deploy a mission. Instead, U.S. envoy Richard Holbrooke negotiated with Milošević the deployment of a Kosovo Verification Mission (KVM) formed by the Organization for Security and Cooperation in Europe. Neither side respected it much, and Kofi Annan's report to the Security Council noted only that "Kosovo Albanian militias have taken advantage of the lull in fighting" to consolidate their position, and that heavy-handed Serb retaliation was taking place.

When Serbian forces killed forty-five Kosovo Albanian civilians in Račak in January 1999, the West, led by the United States, prepared an ultimatum. It was delivered, after inconclusive negotiations, at the Chateau de Rambouillet, near Paris: either a proposed settlement would be accepted or force would be used. Milošević refused. The KVM was withdrawn, and on March 24, NATO bombers attacked Serbian targets across Kosovo, and later in Serbia proper. Without authorization from the United Nations, NATO was for the first time in its history at war.

The immediate response on the ground was for the Serbs to step up their wholesale "ethnic cleansing" of Kosovo, with some 800,000 Kosovo Albanians being forced to flee. But Milošević, as ever, had overplayed his hand. As the bombing continued, and as preparations for a NATO ground attack grew, Milošević finally capitulated on June 3 and Yugoslav forces began to withdraw from Kosovo.

On the ground, the roles were now reversed. As Kosovo Albanian refugees returned, it was the turn of the Kosovo Serbs to be ethnically cleansed: More than half of the Serb population was forced to flee, never to return. Many of those who chose to stay were killed. For a while, Kosovo became almost a free-for-all of burning and looting and killing.

In the Security Council, a compromise was reached on June 10, 1999, with the passage of Resolution 1244. A NATO-led force, known as Kosovo Force (KFOR), would be deployed to provide security. The United Nations, instead of slowly handing over its Balkan operations to the rising power of the European Union, would be asked to take on its most ambitious project yet, an "interim administration" of Kosovo—in effect, a government—for some unknown period of time, with some unknown outcome. From the outset, there was a fundamental difference between Washington, which expected Kosovo to become an independent country, and Moscow, which was determined to uphold the sovereignty of Serbia over Kosovo.

For the West, the Security Council resolution had the advantage of providing some legal basis for an intervention that sorely needed one. For Russia, it provided a role and an excuse to put behind it the divisions of the Security Council—as Russia had strongly opposed the NATO campaign. For all parties, it deferred the problem. The resolution said little about how or when the issue of Kosovo's final status would be resolved, however. The United Nations would govern Kosovo, the resolution seemed to imply, until the world could decide what to do with it.

At first, the United Nations Interim Administration Mission in Kosovo (UNMIK) was comprised of no more than Sergio Vieira de Mello, the special representative of the secretary general, and a dozen aides. Since UNMIK had no real authority, power largely lay where it fell. In the Albanian areas the hard men of the Kosovo Liberation Army established a "provisional government" under their commander Hashim Thaci. The remaining Serbs set up a phantom administration of their own centered on the northern city of Mitrovica, funded and supported by Belgrade and protected, on the ground, by a gang known as the Bridge Watchers (named after a bridge over the River Ibar that separates the city's Albanian and Serbian communities).

Throughout the summer of 1999, despite the presence of KFOR and the gradual buildup of the United Nations mission, the killing and looting continued. UNMIK did not have the means, and KFOR did not have the will, to confront the new Albanian power brokers. Little action was taken to prevent or punish the violence.

Initially, given the chaos on the ground, the United Nations chose to administer Kosovo directly. Not only would international police patrol the streets, and international judges preside over courts, but all the regular functions of a government administration—from customs collection to air traffic control—would be directed and managed by international personnel. For several months, Pristina was the scene of European policemen, American judicial officials, Indian civil administrators—all of them unpacking boxes, connecting computers, and confronting the realities of starting a government from scratch.

The UN is not particularly well-suited to the role of colonial administrator. Its operations are mandated and governed by resolutions passed in New York. These resolutions are heavily negotiated, and often so opaque as to defy even quite determined exegesis. Administratively, the United Nations is designed, like many organizations, but somewhat more cumbersomely, to administer itself rather than others. It has none of the systems, controls, and traditions— or even the staff—to write laws, control the money supply, collect taxes, run education and health systems, determine the appropriate level of fines for running red lights, or any of the other things that keep a normal government running. Yet it was done in Kosovo, not with great elegance, but more successfully than one might have imagined. Some areas, like the generation of electricity, never worked well and suffered from UNMIK's short-term time horizon. Other areas, from policing to customs, worked much better.

During my first visit to Pristina in the summer of 2000, Bernard Kouchner, who had replaced de Mello as the head of the UN mission, warned me— before I had even taken up my new position—that I had better let the mission start giving responsibilities to the Kosovars, and that he was not going to let lawyers and bureaucrats in New York tie his hands because of a Security Council resolution. Kouchner had assembled an improbable team of driven young men and women. There was a Moroccan prince, a French judge, and a doctor who had followed him since the founding of Doctors without Borders. There were also some more traditional UN staff, who had initially been suspicious of Kouchner's unorthodox ways but were all carried by his empathetic style. Kouchner's constant need to be liked could be exasperating, but it certainly helped him build a human rapport with whoever he had as an interlocutor, and that was an important part of his job. I believe that Albanian Kosovars, after five minutes of discussion with him, were convinced that they could not have a better friend. The same applied, at least at the beginning, to Serb Kosovars. Partly the result of strategic vision and partly the tactical need to handle a difficult situation where the UN was under pressure not to challenge the emerging de facto Kosovar Albanian government structures, Kouchner had decided that the UN's best way out of Kosovo would be to build up local government structures, and then to move, as quickly as possible, from direct administration to political oversight. The policy had the strong support of Holbrooke, who had become the U.S. ambassador to the UN, and the Western members of the Security Council. During 2000 and

2001, UNMIK oversaw the adoption of a "constitutional framework" and established a local government-in-waiting known as the Provisional Institutions of Self-Government (PISG). As the capacity of the ministries of the PISG grew, UNMIK passed on to it more and more of its authority.

Two problems were seen from the beginning, but grew over time. The first was the participation of the Serbs in the PISG. Relations between the Albanian majority and the Serb minority were bad: worse even than intercommunal relations in other post-Yugoslav conflicts. Many Serbs actively resisted participating in the PISG, which they saw—rightly, as it turned out—as the embryo of a future government of an independent Kosovo. As a result, the PISG, despite UNMIK's best efforts, grew up as an overwhelmingly Albanian-dominated institution. When Hans Haekerrup, Kouchner's successor, intensified efforts to woo the Serbs into the institutions, the Albanian majority reacted badly, so much so that he was threatened with death for trying and quietly left.

The second problem, related to the first, was that of the future. Security Council Resolution 1244 spoke in vague terms about "a final stage" in which UNMIK would oversee "the transfer of authority from Kosovo's provisional institutions to institutions established under a political settlement." But what that political settlement would be, or how it would be arrived at, was left unexplained by the Security Council, for the simple reason that the council itself had no idea—or, at least, no single idea its members could agree on.

Unguided by the Security Council, UNMIK played for time. The mission's next special representative, Michael Steiner, presented the Security Council with a list of eight "standards" that UNMIK would work with to help Kosovo become a functional society in harmony with contemporary European values. Steiner coined a marvelously dilatory phrase, "standards before status." Without ever quite saying it, Steiner created the impression that if Kosovo could just use its time well by building up clean and effective democratic institutions, the status issue might somehow be resolved. For a while it worked: tensions were calmed, institutions were strengthened, and progress was made. Steiner, a wiry German of extraordinary intensity and energy, made it all seem possible.

The problem was that, to a large extent, it was a bluff, and the Albanians quickly understood that UNMIK, Penelope-like, had an interest in endlessly spinning out the standards process, to put off the day of reckoning.

Violence Forces a Rethink by the Security Council

A spasm of violence convulsed Kosovo in March 2004, just after a visit I had made to the territory. Nobody in the UN mission or in NATO had seen it coming, and I had not heard a word of warning during my trip. The trigger of the violence was the death of three Albanian boys who drowned in the River Ibar, which divides the Serb-dominated north from the rest of Kosovo. Whipped into a frenzy by the Albanian media, which blamed Serbs for the boys' deaths, angry mobs turned on Kosovo's remaining Serb communities. The isolated Serb enclaves south of the Ibar were the most exposed; some 700 homes were torched, and several thousand Serbs—most of them elderly—were forced to flee the new wave of ethnic cleansing. Even the Serb stronghold of Mitrovica was not spared. One group of rioters, held back at the main bridge over the Ibar, succeeded in crossing a smaller pedestrian bridge before being pushed back. Two of the Serb dead in Mitrovica were killed by snipers shooting across the river from the Albanian-dominated south.

Serb holy sites were singled out for attention. Thirty-six of the Serbian churches and monasteries that dot Kosovo's landscape were damaged or destroyed. A particularly melancholy photograph shows members of one mob, having torched an ancient church in Prizren, urinating on the embers, while KFOR troops look on.

Before long, however, it was UNMIK—now, even more than Serbia, seen by Albanians as the principal obstacle to independence—that was the object of violence. Rocks and molotov cocktails were thrown at UNMIK offices; UN flags were burned; more than a hundred UN vehicles were destroyed. Neither UNMIK nor KFOR performed particularly well. There were some honorable exceptions, such as the Norwegian soldiers who successfully defended the ancient cathedral of Gračanica, and the Italians, who protected the incomparable Dečani monastery, a UNESCO World Heritage site and one of the pearls of European culture.

Having briefed the Security Council on the unfolding events, I spoke with Kofi Annan about the need for a review of our options, all of which were awful. We could continue to play for time on the ground, hoping that the council eventually would find a compromise on Kosovo's status, but meanwhile risking an even greater eruption of Albanian frustration and violence. Or we could "give in to violence" by giving the Kosovo Albanians a timetable for independence, even without having met the "standards" they had agreed to. Annan agreed that the review should be made by Kai Eide, an unsentimental and clear-sighted Norwegian diplomat.

Eide tried to reconcile the realities on the ground, which called for a quick exit of the UN, and the realities in the council, where no quick consensus on a future status was possible. He recommended that a "future status process" be launched, and that the UN interim administration of Kosovo be brought to an end before there was a complete meltdown. In a sense, Eide's solution was also playing for time, in that it assumed that the future status process would arrive at some end state minimally acceptable either to the parties, or to the Security Council, or both.

Just for a moment, it all did seem possible. In late 2005 the Contact Group of countries working on Kosovo issues—including Russia—agreed on a number of principles that would guide the status process: no return of Kosovo to the pre-1999 situation, no partition of Kosovo, and no union of Kosovo with any or part of another country. Kofi Annan asked former Finnish president Martti Ahtisaari to serve as his envoy to oversee the process. Ahtisaari had played a decisive role in the early 1990s in ensuring the success of the UN mission that oversaw the independence of Namibia, and he had successfully negotiated with Russian prime minister Viktor Chernomyrdin the agreement that ended the war in Kosovo. I traveled to London at the end of January 2006 for a further meeting with the Contact Group ministers, and a paper was produced with the text of some "private messages" that would be passed to Belgrade. These messages went beyond the principles agreed in November, saying that "a return of Kosovo to Belgrade rule is not a viable option." Russian foreign minister Sergei Lavrov was mostly silent. Rather optimistically, it turned out, this was understood to represent some form of Russian acquiescence.

Operating out of a small suite of offices in the elegant historic center of Vienna, Ahtisaari and his staff produced a range of position papers on everything from decentralization to the preservation of religious heritage. These were discussed in more than a dozen rounds of technical talks. What was very rarely discussed was Kosovo's future status, the ostensible purpose of the process. The Serbs were suspicious that the entire effort was a way of associating them with arrangements that would ultimately lead to Kosovo's independence. This was, indeed, the result: the Comprehensive Proposal for the Kosovo Status Settlement was submitted in 2007 to the Security Council with a recommendation, not seen in advance by either party, that Kosovo be granted "supervised independence."

The process suffered from two related flaws. First, it lacked an essential ingredient of any negotiation: good faith. The Serbs were first given the private messages, which told them, in general terms, what the outcome of the process would be, and then they were invited to participate in talks that would reach that outcome. When the Serbs pointed out that there was no reason for them to go through a sham process, they were roundly scolded for not cooperating. Second, the process was not really independent, despite its UN imprimatur. The text of the Comprehensive Proposal for the Kosovo Status Settlement was not based on an agreement between the parties, or even on texts or ideas agreed within the Contact Group; it was largely drafted by a young U.S. State Department lawyer "on loan" to Ahtisaari's office and faithfully reflecting U.S. policy.

Neither of these flaws was fatal—the real problem was more specific. The process rested almost entirely on the assumption that the Comprehensive Proposal would be accepted by the Security Council, which would then pass a new resolution superseding Resolution 1244, to end the UN interim administration and to authorize the new EU and ad hoc operations that would be required to oversee the implementation of the proposal.

In what became one of the more spectacular acts of group think, Ahtisaari and the major Western powers were all convinced, right up to the end, that Russia would not block the Comprehensive Proposal in the Security Council, despite increasingly loud and high-level Russian pronouncements to the contrary. When I met with Ahtisaari in September, he told me that he had been in touch with Lavrov and that he was confident that Russia would abstain in the council, allowing a new resolution to pass. He predicted "twelve or thirteen" positive votes and "two or three abstentions," with none openly opposed, and no vetoes from any of the Permanent Five. I did not contradict him because I had the same illusions.

When it finally came to the council, the result could not have been more different. Not only was it clear that Russia would cast its veto, but so would China. In addition, several major nonpermanent members of the Council—led by Indonesia and South Africa—came out against Kosovo's independence. Despite Ahtisaari's insistence that Kosovo's independence would not be an encouragement for ethnic secessionist movements in other parts of the world, there was a fear in many countries that if the council supported Kosovo's independence, it would set a dangerous precedent for other regions with similar aspirations. The draft resolution produced by the United States and its friends had even less support than the ill-fated 2003 draft resolution on Iraq. Rather than put it to a vote, and fail, it was quietly withdrawn in July 2007.

More than eight years after the Security Council had asked the UN to establish an interim administration in Kosovo, an agreed way forward seemed as remote as ever. Joachim Rücker, the latest UN special representative, felt that the Kosovo Albanians were on the brink of another explosion. "I don't think," he said in June, "that we can hold it beyond July."

Once it became clear that the council would not approve the Ahtisaari plan, a group of Western countries began to develop a plan that would lead to Kosovo's independence without a new resolution in the Security Council. This plan became known as the "Script"—the set of steps and legal justifications that would move Kosovo from UN interim administration to independence. At the heart of the Script was the idea that if looked at generously enough, Security Council Resolution 1244 could provide the legal basis for Kosovo's independence and for the deployment of the new international missions foreseen in the Ahtisaari plan.

Mainly to mollify skeptical European countries, the Americans agreed that they would hold off from recognizing Kosovo for 120 days, while an EU-U.S.-Russian Troika made a further effort to find common ground between the parties. Again, however, the effort was in bad faith, with the Americans saying that they wanted the Troika process to fail so that the Europeans would be convinced that there was no alternative to recognition. In the end, Wolfgang Ischinger, one of the best German diplomats and the European representative on the Troika, advanced a proposal for Serbia and Kosovo to deal with each other in a "good neighborly" way, much as East and West Germany had agreed under the *Grundlagenvertrag* of 1972. As foretold, the Troika process expired without result and attention turned again to the Script.

The Script also had a number of weaknesses. First, it required a truly imaginative interpretation of Resolution 1244. Nicolas Michel, legal adviser to the secretary general, was not at all convinced. He was willing to remain silent, since the Security Council is the interpreter of its own resolutions, but he was not willing to say that a declaration of independence by Kosovo would be consistent with 1244. Quietly, a number of Western legal advisors shared his view. A second problem with the Script was that it required the active cooperation of the United Nations secretary general because if new missions were to be deployed under 1244, then the original mission—UNMIK—would have to make way.

Ban Ki-moon met with me, the legal adviser, and others in his private conference room on the thirty-eighth floor of the UN Secretariat building—a wood-paneled room much improved by a very restful Marquet river scene painted in 1914. I argued that, given where we were, Kosovo should be independent. I acknowledged that the arguments against it had real merit. One could argue about whether the West had been right, in 1991, to start recognizing smaller and smaller pieces of the former Yugoslavia—it didn't seem to have saved many lives, and it didn't seem to have resolved many of the underlying problems. One could also argue that the Ahtisaari plan had not included any face-saver that could have made its passage easier in the council: some nominal qualification to independence, at least for a while; some delay, followed by a referendum that would have allowed the Serbian and Russian governments a degree of "plausible deniability."

There were also arguments here and now against independence. It would not be consistent with Resolution 1244; there was a risk that the Kosovo precedent would exacerbate ethnic secessionist problems elsewhere; and so on.

But, on balance, independence was compelling. The Albanians absolutely did not want to be a part of Serbia. And for Serbia it made little sense to try to govern 2 million angry, armed, internationally supported, and fast-increasing Albanians. I also thought that it would be a mistake for the United Nations, with the council blocked from action, to just do nothing while waiting until the situation blew up. What I proposed, therefore, was that the UN acquiesce to Kosovo's emergence as an independent state, while working with the Serbs and Russians to see if some of their basic concerns could not be accommodated. There was, I felt, a solution that, although it could never be agreed on, met the minimum political needs of all.

The secretary general decided, after several such debates, that the United Nations would stand aside and, in his phrase, "let the river of history flow." I recommended that he not speak out against the declaration of independence—despite the misgivings of the lawyers—and that the UN see if the Kosovo Albanians, the Americans, and others could create a fait accompli. If they could, and if there was a sudden cascade of recognitions from around the world, then the UN would "evolve according to the emerging realities." This position was quietly conveyed to those in favor of Kosovo's independence, who were delighted, and supremely confident. With the door thus opened by the United Nations, they were predicting upwards of a hundred recognitions.

The reality, however, again turned out to be quite different. As I was meeting with Ban Ki-moon in New York, a very different meeting was taking place in the vast—and generally deserted—office complex that once housed Tito's Yugoslav government in Belgrade. Richard Wilcox and David Harland, two of my closest colleagues on the Kosovo file, were meeting with Slobodan Samardžić, a truly quixotic figure who had the unfortunate job of being Serbia's "minister for Kosovo and Metohija." Samardžić, a soft-spoken law professor much detested by those promoting Kosovo's independence, was laying out Serbia's vision of the coming months. "We expect," Samardžić said slowly, "a sort of parallelism to emerge. Some countries will recognize Kosovo—we estimate 55 or 60. Kosovo will be able to enter some international organizations and agreements, but not all. On the ground, we expect that the Kosovars will be able to control much of the territory, but not all."

Kosovo declared independence on February 17, 2008. In Kosovo, and in many European cities, the streets were lined with young Kosovo Albanians waving the red and black flag of Albania, and as I was leaving the UN building in New York, I saw a Mercedes drive by, honking in celebration, with its passengers triumphantly waving the red and black flag. The new Kosovo authorities, in a gesture to multiethnicity, had designed a more neutral blue and yellow flag. But as well as being ugly, it had the disadvantage of having a map on it. Putting a map on your flag—like Cyprus, or, more abstractly, Bosnia—is invariably a sign that there is a problem with the map. The flag closest to the hearts of the Kosovo Albanian people remained that of Albania.

The Serbs responded by burning down two customs posts on the boundary between Serbia proper and the Serb-controlled northern Kosovo. Their point seemed to be that if the Kosovo Albanians were going to be independent, then the Kosovo Serbs would throw in their lot with Serbia, with no borders standing between them. Apart from this, things were relatively quiet.

There was no immediate cascade of separatist groups around the world claiming independence. Nor was there a cascade of countries lining up to recognize Kosovo's independence. Despite considerable effort by the United States and several of the world's other leading diplomatic services, the recognitions of Kosovo trickled in only slowly. The worst problem was close to home. By early summer, only nineteen of the twenty-seven members of the European Union had recognized Kosovo. Facing a tight election, Spain's foreign minister Miguel Ángel Moratinos flummoxed some of his counterparts by denouncing Kosovo's declaration of independence as "illegal"—an obvious expression of concern about the potential impact on secessionist sentiment in Catalonia. As predicted by Samardžić, Kosovo was recognized by about a quarter of the UN membership and was able to get into some international organizations—including the Miss Universe competition—but not immediately able to get into the International Civil Aviation Organization, the International Telecommunications Union, or some other more useful bodies.

The United Nations—like the European Union and NATO—declared itself to be "status neutral." By the spring, Kosovo seemed to be entering into a sort of limbo: not quite a state, not really a part of Serbia, and not truly under UN administration. The United States and the United Kingdom urged the United Nations to try to force the issue on the ground—to use force to impose Kosovo's independence on the reluctant Serbs. The secretary general was opposed, but UNMIK's leadership—Joachim Rücker of Germany and Larry Rossin of the United States—was supportive. I cautioned against the use of force, to the point of being accused of micromanaging the mission. In the end, when a group of Serb protestors occupied the courthouse in Northern Mitrovica, Rossin saw his chance. Early in the morning of March 17, he ordered UN police, backed by KFOR troops, to storm the building and to arrest the protestors. In the melee that followed, one UN police officer was killed, several dozen were injured, and the UN was forced to evacuate its personnel from the north. More perfectly than the Serbs themselves could have done, UNMIK had shown that the Serbs could not be forced to accept Kosovo's independence—not, at any rate, with the level of force that the international community was willing to use.

I came to believe that there might be a better way forward. I started from the assumption that UNMIK could not continue to govern Kosovo. If we stayed, UNMIK would, sooner or later, be thrown out, and its legacy would be lost. The goal, therefore, was to find a way—even with the world divided, the Security Council blocked, and Kosovo partitioned—to hand over to someone who could "lock in" whatever we had achieved and manage the situation in its next phase. That "someone" had to be the European Union. The UN had lost any lingering political leverage, since it could no longer dangle the prospect of a future status, but the European Union had leverage. Although the Serbs suspected it of promoting Kosovo independence, they shared the common Balkan aspiration to join the Union. My goal, therefore, came to be to end the UN interim administration, and to get the EU in.

The problem was how to make it happen. I gave the secretary general several options, and the one he liked was the idea that the EU would come in to Kosovo "under the UN umbrella." The general idea was that the secretary general, recognizing the new facts on the ground, would use his authority to "reconfigure" UNMIK—ceding the police role to the EU-led police mission known as EULEX. This option, I hoped, played to a certain asymmetry of goals. The Serbs didn't want EULEX, but what they most cared about was "status neutrality" and the continuation of Resolution 1244 and UN authority. The Kosovo Albanians, on the other hand, wanted the UN out, but above all they wanted the EU in, as confirmation, in their eyes, of their new status. The "umbrella formula," if properly developed and presented, should allow both communities to have what they most wanted, while only conceding on their second-order objectives.

In April the secretary general traveled to Moscow to pitch the proposal. David Harland, who had been instrumental in putting together the UN plan, accompanied the secretary general. His report of the trip was encouraging. President Vladimir Putin and Prime Minister Dmitry Medvedev were in the first steps of a delicate dance that would result in them switching jobs, if only temporarily. The secretary general had called on them both. Putin was confident but watchful, cocking his head and smiling wryly at almost everything the secretary general said. He was completely fluent on the Kosovo issue, disconcertingly familiar with Resolution 1244, making references to various paragraphs without consulting his notes. As well as plunging into the specifics of 1244, Putin clearly enjoyed the general issues arising from the Kosovo situation. He treated the secretary general to a stern little lecture about how the West, by recognizing Kosovo's independence the way it had—without a clear legal basis, without the consent of the country from which it was seceding, and without the approval of the UN Security Council—was fundamentally undermining the principle of the territorial integrity of states, which for 150 years, he said, had been at the heart of an evolving system of international law. Where, he asked, would the world be without that system, weak as it is? And why would the West want to undermine in it in this way?

Putin seemed skeptical of Ban's proposal but agreed, in principle, to support an EU role in Kosovo provided that it was clearly status neutral. Medvedev seemed a little less skeptical but also a little less well versed in the issue. It was Foreign Minister Lavrov who seemed the most forthcoming when they met for dinner. Also looking confident, Lavrov listened to the secretary general's proposal as he lit up one cigarette after another. In the end, he agreed that Russia could support EULEX's deployment in Kosovo, on three conditions: that it would be status neutral; that its mandate would be Resolution 1244, not the implementation of the Ahtisaari plan, even the name of which was now anathema to the Russians; and that it would operate under UN authority.

Kosovo was the ideal issue for Russia. It was an issue on which Russia could be on the legal high ground, an issue that not only played well domestically but also allowed Russians to lecture the West, much as the West had often lectured Russia. It also provided a useful point of leverage for Moscow on the Abkhazia conflict in Georgia. The more the West pushed for Kosovo's separation from Serbia, the more Russia would press for Abkhazia's separation from Georgia. And when the secretary general tried to put Kosovo aside for a brief moment—to talk about Iran and North Korea—Lavrov insisted that "there is no issue more important than Kosovo," for Russia, "and for the international system."

With Russia apparently on board with the "umbrella formula"—or at least not completely off-board—the EU, in the person of foreign policy high representative Javier Solana, quickly added its support to the UN proposal. The EU, in fact, was in an awful position, given that it wanted very much to play the leading international role in Kosovo. First, it was just as divided on Kosovo as the Security Council, with a group led by Spain and Cyprus loudly insisting that any EU mission in Kosovo be, like the UN, status neutral. Second, having announced that it was going to Kosovo under Resolution 1244, it wouldn't be able to deploy, at all, if the UN was still there and still implementing the same resolution. Some accommodation with the UN had to be found. The United States, with somewhat less enthusiasm than the Europeans, also supported the UN proposal. The Kosovo Albanians, although not at all confident about what was happening, seemed content to leave the international arrangements to the internationals themselves.

The Serbs were a problem. Boris Tadić, Serbia's pro-Western president, was suspected by some Serbian nationalists of not caring very much about

Kosovo. But the suspicion that he was soft on Kosovo made him politically vulnerable, particularly since, as seemed constantly to be the case, Serbia was in electoral mode.

Richard Wilcox, head of the UN office in Belgrade, came up with a plan to try to secure a degree of Serb acquiescence to the UN reconfiguration proposal—an acquiescence that, we hoped, would also draw the poison from the issue in the Security Council. Wilcox, who the UN had received as flotsam from the Clinton White House, was a large and entrepreneurial young man, with a PhD from MIT and a background in military intelligence, much given to giggling. The Serbs liked him immensely, which caused him some trouble with his own government. His idea was that we would take an earlier Serb proposal to "co-govern" Kosovo with the United Nations and turn it into a short list of areas in which, after the reconfiguration of UNMIK, the UN would acknowledge a degree of Serb autonomy in Kosovo.

The list covered six areas—police, courts, customs, boundaries, transportation, and the status of the Serbian Orthodox Church in Kosovo. Under the Wilcox proposal, there would be no co-governance from Belgrade, but there would be talks aimed at formalizing, for a certain period, the sweeping local autonomy the Kosovo Serbs had already secured for themselves. It would also leave internationals in certain positions that would normally have been filled by government officials.

The gambit had something in it for all sides. For Belgrade, it confirmed that President Tadić was serious about Kosovo, which was what Tadić needed for domestic political reasons, and that Serbia, having salvaged something, had not been completely humiliated. For the Kosovo Serbs, still deeply unsettled by the declaration of independence, it confirmed their autonomy and offered the prospect of giving that status the sanction of international blessing. For Pristina and the Kosovo Albanians, who anyway had no control at all over the Kosovo Serb areas, it confirmed that the local Serbs were still a part of Kosovo, however autonomous they might be for the time being.

In fact, it was almost impossible to get the protagonists in Kosovo to agree. We decided from the outset, therefore, that we would not even try to get the sides to agree formally. We would talk to the Albanian leadership in Pristina, and to the Serbs in Belgrade, listen to their concerns, and then present the proposal in what we thought might be its least objectionable form. From there, we would proceed to implement it. The Security Council, which itself had become distinctly Balkanized by the long-running problems of the Balkans, was similarly gridlocked and would get the same treatment: full transparency, full consultation, a genuine effort to accommodate the concerns of all, and then an executive decision from the secretary general.

It was far from ideal, but it did seem to hold the promise of some deescalation of the international crisis over Kosovo, as well as reducing the possibility of renewed fighting on the ground. Besides, the alternative seemed to be paralysis, followed by the collapse of UNMIK. The United States, the United Kingdom, Germany, and to some extent my own country were unhappy with the UN plan. They did not want the Secretariat to take the initiative on a file that they had closely managed, and they were worried that we were taking excessive risk and conceding too much to Belgrade. Their political directors gave me an unpleasant dressing-down in a conference call to ensure that the UN would fall in line, and the United States openly warned my colleagues that they "wouldn't be able to control" the Kosovo Albanians if things didn't go their way.

In early May 2008, the secretary general decided it was time for me to go to the region. I met with Fatmir Sejdiu, Kosovo's weary-looking president, and with his prime minister, Hashim Thaci, a much more chipper former guerilla commander. On the wall was a photo of Kosovo's former leader, Ibrahim Rugova (who had died two years earlier), and another of Mother Teresa, who was not from Kosovo but was nevertheless Albanian. The Kosovo Albanian leaders weren't enthusiastic about our reconfiguration plan. They were, like the United States, particularly suspicious of our dialogue with Belgrade, but they reluctantly agreed to go along with the plan, provided that we didn't agree to Serbian co-governance and provided that it really did lead to the arrival of EULEX. This was about as good as it was going to get.

Nor were things much easier in Belgrade. Tadić took me into a small room that smelled of paint. I must have turned up my nose, because the president apologized profusely and said he was getting it redone "to get rid of the smell of the former occupant," Slobodan Milošević. This was perhaps an ill-chosen joke, given that the election result threw him into coalition with the late strongman's party. On my way out, Tadić asked me if I was going to see Prime Minister Vojislav Koštunica, with whom he was sparring in the run-up to elections the following weekend. When I said I was, he gave me a rather anemic smile and said, "Lucky you: I don't get to meet with my prime minister."

On June 20 we took the plunge. For the first time in UN history, the secretary general simply informed the Security Council that, in the absence of any agreed guidance to the contrary, he was going to take drastic action on his own initiative. He was going to reconfigure UNMIK to provide a role for the European Union.

President Tadić, who had come to the UN for the occasion, spoke against the proposal, as did the Russian ambassador, Vitaly Churkin. The preparatory groundwork, however, seemed to have paid off. Almost all members of the council—including those opposed to Kosovo's independence—acknowledged that we had engaged the parties in good faith and were presenting a plan that really did seem to be the least objectionable way forward. China, to the surprise of many, joined the majority in acquiescing to the initiative, gently sidestepping the issue that we were acting without a mandate from the council. Even Tadić and Churkin, aware that they were isolated, spoke in quite moderate terms.

Five days later, in another first for the United Nations, the secretary general signed instructions to his new special representative, Lamberto Zannier, directing him to implement the plan, and largely ending nine years of UN administration.

It was not the end of the Kosovo problem, however. Kosovo lay too squarely on the fault lines of the international system to have an easy end. But it was a good outcome, given the circumstances. It avoided a hard partition between the northern, Serb-populated part of Kosovo and the rest of the country. It clarified that Kosovo's independence was slowly crystallizing, which is what the Albanians most wanted. It made it possible for the EU to deploy, to achieve some unity among its members on the Kosovo issue, and to engage with Serbia and Kosovo using EU membership as an incentive that, years later, continues to motivate both parties. And it allowed the Serbs to save face by holding onto their holy sites and by exercising an almost total autonomy in their own communities. For the Serbs, this would be a good-enough result to protect the Serbian government from a nationalist backlash that would stall its progress toward joining the European Union. And it would link Kosovo to the European Union, which is where it needed to be. A gradual de-escalation had started, which would eventually make it possible for Serbia and Kosovo to begin to overcome their fractured history.

eleven

HAITI
The Difficulty of Helping Others

I heard news of the earthquake in Haiti on January 12, 2010, almost as it happened. My immediate reaction was to write a short e-mail of support to the head of the UN mission in Port-au-Prince, Hedi Annabi. Six months earlier, I had proposed his name for the job to the secretary general, who knew Hedi's qualities and had immediately decided to appoint him. There was no question that Hedi Annabi was the most experienced and respected peacekeeper in the United Nations. His engagement in peacekeeping had started with the negotiations in Cambodia that led to the end of the Khmer Rouge regime and the deployment of a peacekeeping mission in 1991–92. He had been the director of the Africa division of the Department of Peacekeeping Operations (DPKO), when Kofi Annan was the head of the department. After Annan was elected secretary general in 1996, he was the obvious choice for assistant secretary general for peacekeeping, the number two in a department where the number one is traditionally a political appointee—like me. When I arrived in 2000, some had suggested to me that I should appoint a new assistant secretary, hinting that I would not control the department until I had my own deputy.

How wrong they were. I had indeed my share of disagreements with Hedi. He had been deeply scarred by the tragedies of the 1990s, when he felt that the UN was cynically abandoned by its member states, and he was skeptical about my efforts to establish a relationship of trust with member states. I sometimes felt that he was too focused on the Security Council, as if he was playing a game of chess with a partner that would be quick to exploit any vulnerability of the Secretariat. But he was intensely loyal to the institution of the United Nations, and his battles with the Security Council were always waged on behalf of the people we were meant to help. He did not want to promise them more than he could deliver. He reviewed every report that was issued by the department on behalf of the secretary general with admirable thoroughness. He was famous for the red-and-blue pen with which he edited the reports that were submitted to him, weighing each word, each sentence, like a chemist preparing a potentially explosive mix. But his caution should not be confused with indifference. I remember how furious he was the day when a well-meaning ambassador from the P5 (the five permanent members of the council) had criticized his recommendations on Chad, suggesting that DPKO did not see the urgency of taking bold action. He took it very personally, because his engagement in peacekeeping was intensely personal. Although he lived outside New York, he was always the first to arrive in the office, around 8 a.m., and often the last to leave, at 9 and sometimes 10 p.m. There were evenings when he would be so tired that he would fall asleep on the train and miss the station near the Hudson River from which he would drive home. Although he could have continued to pursue a brilliant career in his native Tunisia, he had found in the United Nations the ethical home he was longing for, and he was more at ease serving the United Nations than a national government. From discreet comments he sometimes made on Tunisian politics, I know he probably would have been happy with the Arab Spring in his country.

Hedi never received my message of support. He had died when the earthquake hit, collapsing the former hotel housing the UN mission (MINUSTAH). And with him died another 100 UN colleagues. I knew many of them, including Luis da Costa, a Brazilian who was the ultimate operator, the man who knew how to make things happen. When I first heard of da Costa after I had joined the UN, he had the reputation of being a headquarters man, and I encouraged him to go to the field, making clear that his future career would benefit from it. He had several children, and it was a sacrifice for him, but he did it, first in Kosovo, then in Liberia. In both missions, he had succeeded brilliantly, and Hedi had been eager to convince him to come to Haiti. When I saw him on my last visit to Haiti, in July 2008, he was a man who was totally comfortable and happy with his new life as a field person. Another fatality was Andrew Grene, a young American, quiet and so perfectly well-behaved and respectful that you could easily take him for granted, but Hedi, to whom he had been a close aide in New York, had not, recognizing in Andrew not only someone with similar work habits, but also a thoughtful man who cared, and did not make a show of it. Renée Carrier, the very private French Canadian assistant of my predecessor, who had generously stayed a few months with me to help my entry in the UN, also died. Another was Gerard Le Chevallier, a Salvadoran who had joined the UN when a mission had deployed in his country and had an acute sense of politics, nurtured by years of engagement in his own country.

These lives were just a few in the quarter of a million lives lost in the earthquake, but they made the immensity of the tragedy of Haiti more personal.

It is true that in Haiti in 2010 and the Baghdad bombing seven years earlier, the UN lost some of its best and brightest, and for the same reason. As different as were Sergio de Mello and Hedi Annabi—the first a sparkling charismatic leader, the second almost masochistically disciplined and low-key—they were both totally committed to the United Nations. Their reward was a capacity to attract the best people, throughout the UN system, and to enjoy the fierce loyalty of their staff.

The Haiti mission was known as a "good mission," because it had been lucky enough to be led by a succession of good mission heads, or special representatives of the secretary general (SRSGs), starting with Juan Gabriel Valdes, a former foreign minister of Chile, who had been the ambassador of his country to the Security Council during the Iraq crisis and had launched the mission. Edmond Mulet had succeeded him; he would replace Annabi in New York as the second in command of DPKO when Hedi left for Haiti. Mulet's great success—which he shared with an outstanding force commander from Brazil, General Carlos Alberto dos Santos Cruz—had been to radically transform the security situation in Port-au-Prince through joint police-military operations targeting the gangs who terrorized the population in the slums of Bel Air, Martissant, or Cité Soleil. For some, this was an improbable achievement, coming from a diplomat known for his great courtesy and soft-spoken manners. There was nothing soft-spoken in Edmond when the lives of poor Haitians were at stake, however, and those who worked for him in the mission told me how he relentlessly pushed his staff, the police, and the military, often accompanying patrols and asking hard questions, until he was satisfied that the mission was really doing its very best within its limited means. When Hedi died, Edmond went back to Haiti to lead a traumatized mission, sleeping in a container for months. I saw him again when he returned to New York a year later, in 2011. He was giving a talk on his Haitian experience, and what he said was devastating, as he described the lack of commitment and cynicism of the Haitian elite. The Haitian ambassador was sitting in the front row, and I was afraid that he would walk out of the room, offended by the brutal report that he was hearing. He did not; on the contrary, he commended him, acknowledging that Edmond, because he had become so close to the Haitians and had shown genuine empathy and commitment, had earned the right to speak the unvarnished truth, which would have been offensive and unacceptable coming from any other foreigner.

I could not think of a greater compliment, but I left the meeting worried. The frustration of Edmond Mulet was evident, and it raised difficult questions for Haiti and for the whole enterprise of peacekeeping. Haiti is a small country, with a population of less than 10 million people. It has had several outstanding special representatives of the secretary general. It has benefited from the advocacy of no less than Bill Clinton himself, who hosted a conference to attract foreign investment to the island. This is a remarkably positive combination of circumstances that should normally give success a much greater chance than in huge countries like Congo or Sudan. And yet, many today are losing hope.

Haiti is one of the peacekeeping missions in which I was the most invested, and from the day the UN mission deployed in June 2004, I was determined to make sure that this time, we would succeed. If I had not been a Frenchman, given my country's unfortunate history in Haiti, it is the mission where I would have been most happy to be appointed as the special representative of the secretary general. I knew one Haitian very well, my executive assistant, Yanick Saint-Victor, who had been the assistant of Perez de Cuellar and Boutros-Ghali. She exemplified the extraordinary resilience of the Haitian people, their remarkable work ethic, and their commitment to education. All those qualities have made the Haitian diaspora, important in Canada and the United States, quite successful. And the creativity of Haitians is well known: how many countries with a population of less than 10 million have such a lively art scene? Imagination in Haiti sometimes seems to be the revenge against abject poverty!

How is it, then, that Haiti is still by far the poorest country in the Americas? How is it that it has one of the worst inequality ratios (as calculated by the Gini coefficient, which measures the distribution of income in a society) in the world, ranking as the eighth most unequal country out of the 134 countries for which a comparison is made? And how is it that several successive missions of the United Nations have failed to make a break with the past? Today, Haiti is not significantly better than it was twenty years ago.

Of course, the immense tragedy of the earthquake undid much of the limited progress that had been achieved. Thousands of criminals—including many who had been arrested by MINUSTAH—took advantage of the earthquake to escape from the jail where they were held. They are back in the slums, and the devastation of the earthquake, combined with the flow of international money, has given them new opportunities to develop their criminal activities. But the earthquake could also have provided an opportunity for the country to come together and move beyond the deep social divide that separates extreme poverty from considerable wealth, the miserable people living in the slums while the bourgeoisie are ensconced in the luxurious villas of Petionville, in the hills above Port-au-Prince. It was an opportunity to begin fixing a dysfunctional and corrupt judiciary system. It was an opportunity that Bill Clinton tried to exploit, to focus international attention and mobilize foreign capital. But as Edmond Mulet pointed out in his 2011 talk, the judiciary remains as corrupt as ever, and of the hundreds of investors who came to the conference organized by Clinton, very few decided to invest in Haiti. The election of the singer Michel Martelly to the presidency of Haiti in 2011 signaled the deep disenchantment of Haitians with decades of politics that have brought nothing. One is at pains, however, to identify the political project that will make a real break with the past. The legitimacy of the president has been steadily eroded as municipal and senate elections have been postponed for years, and elections to the national assembly have also been delayed. Once again, the Haitians feel cheated. There are no jobs for the expanding number of young people, and more than 100,000 Haitians are still living under tents five years after the earthquake.

I fear that more than the earthquake is to blame. It was unfortunate, when the earthquake struck, to see how the international community focused almost exclusively on the "hardware" of reconstruction, which was important, but maybe not the most important. Of course, clearing the rubble and rebuilding homes for the homeless was absolutely necessary, but focusing on the "hardware" without fixing the "software"—the political institutions, the judiciary system, and, most important, the Haitian society itself, whose commitment is essential if institutions are not to remain empty shells—is wrong.

Haiti is a frightening example of the immensely difficult task outsiders face in helping another country. Some of the difficulties are specific to Haiti. The Haitians are rightly proud of having been, after the United States, the second independent country in the Americas. This small half of an island, where slavery was abolished sixty years before the United States ended its own slavery, defeated the armies of Napoleon to gain its independence in 1804. And yet, its arid hills, destroyed by soil erosion, make a striking contrast with its neighbor the Dominican Republic, lush with green vegetation. Part of the blame lays with France: After the defeat of Napoleon in Europe, the restored French monarchy forced Haiti to agree to the payment of some 90 million gold francs—roughly $13 billion today—in reparation for the damage caused to French slave-owners by its independence. This colossal amount was not fully paid until 1947. Meanwhile, the United States did not recognize Haiti as an independent country until 1862 and imposed highly unfavorable trade conditions. The Haitians have not forgotten that, nor have they forgotten the U.S. military occupation of Haiti from 1915 to 1934, which had a mixed impact. Infrastructure was considerably improved, but a significant part of the national income was channelled to foreign banks to pay off loans made during the previous period.

This long history of exploitation of Haiti's weakness by powerful foreigners explains why Haitians are deeply suspicious of any foreign engagement; many believe that foreigners have never really forgiven Haiti for having led the way to the freedom of slaves and the freedom of Latin America. And as people who have been the underdogs for a long time, they have developed great techniques to dodge power and go their own way, bending but not breaking. They even have a word for it: *marronnage*, which initially referred to fugitive ("maroon") slaves but now describes a way of avoiding reality through ambiguity, as if the whole of Haiti had become a fugitive nation.

This history also makes it very difficult for foreigners to engage with Haitians. Softness will be interpreted as weakness and will be abused; a stronger posture will quickly conjure memories of a colonial past and will trigger an immediate backlash. Such a reaction is certainly not unique to Haiti, but I have not seen any other country where that feeling is more acute. That is why the acceptance by some Haitians of the harsh words of Edmond Mulet was so remarkable. Haiti is weak, but Haitians know very well that the narrative of Haiti versus foreigners can also become *marronnage*, a way to escape another reality: the divide between the very rich and the very poor, the exploitation of Haitians by Haitians. And they knew that Mulet knew this and could not be fooled.

When Jean-Bertrand Aristide was forced to flee the country in 2004, under strong U.S. pressure and amid a wave of armed conflict, his departure was, like most recent Haitian history, full of ambiguity. He had destroyed the hopes initially put in him by increasingly abusive methods of power, appointing cronies to run the police and using thugs called the "chimeres" to consolidate his power. But it was a very narrow constituency that ousted him. The relentless populist campaign by Aristide to raise Haiti's very low minimum wage had made him strong enemies in the business community. Low wages are one of the few competitive advantages of Haiti if it wants to attract foreign investment, and the business community had some reasons to be wary. But the balance between business interests and the welfare of the population should not be decided by coups.

It was in that extremely polarized environment that the UN mission was launched. A multinational force made up of U.S., Canadian, and French troops had deployed in February 2004 to quell the violence during the transition period after the ousting of Aristide. The force stayed in Haiti until the summer, but the three countries were eager to be quickly replaced by a UN mission. It was operationally and politically tricky. The initial request for the deployment of a UN force in two months was wildly unrealistic, and a three-month timetable was finally agreed. This was not much better, and the full deployment of the UN, as expected, took much longer; there were only 3,000 troops in September 2004, which was not enough for a mission confronted by demonstrations of former soldiers and a deteriorating security situation. The political context was even more difficult. The sub-regional organization, the Caribbean Community or CARICOM, was very unhappy with a UN deployment that it saw as interference by a few big powers in the Caribbean. Kofi Annan, aware of the sensitivities, had appointed a diplomat from Trinidad to be his special adviser on Haiti, so the UN role would find more acceptance in the Caribbean region. But Haiti also had to be more open to its Caribbean neighbors, and that was not easy. Fellow Caribbean states elicit mixed feelings among Haitians, who resent the sometimes patronizing attitudes of some of the more successful Caribbean islands.

In Haiti, as in other crisis zones, I found that proximity is not always an asset. The appointment of Juan Gabriel Valdes as special representative was an intelligent compromise. As an ambassador, he had been known to be among those Chileans who had opposed the Iraq war, and therefore could not be suspected of being a stooge of Washington. (We actually had some concern that the United States might oppose his appointment.) He was from the region, but not from the sub-region, and his appointment signaled a strong commitment by Latin America to Haiti. It is remarkable how Haiti became an opportunity for many Latin American countries, including all the major ones (except, unfortunately, Mexico, which continues to have doctrinal objections to participation in peacekeeping), to rally around the UN flag. Brazil claimed the military leadership of the mission, and has kept it to this day.

First Visit to Haiti

My first visit to Haiti took place a year later, in June 2005, when a new government cabinet was formally installed. The ceremony that took place on June 22 in the impressive Palais National (later destroyed by the earthquake) was a study in contrasts. Inside, there was the formality of a ritual that reminded me of my days as a judge at the French Court of Audit. Boniface Alexandre, the president of the Cour de cassation—the Haitian Supreme Court—was in charge, and I listened to a litany of laws and decrees. The president of the court then saluted a long list of "constitutional bodies," a poor translation of the French *corps constitués*, which describes the various components of a state: parliament, judges, but also governors, district administrators, ambassadors, and so on. At the end of the list, like the red lantern of the last wagon of the train, he saluted the *peuple haitien*, the Haitian people. The *peuple haitien* were outside, and you could hear them. Coming down from the hill of Bel Air, the slum that overlooks the Palais, people were shooting, and we had to wait for a lull in the shooting to leave the Palais National. The next day, in bulletproof jacket and blue helmet, I toured the neighborhood with Valdes. I was later told we had been shot at, but the engine of the Brazilian armed personnel carrier in which we were riding was too noisy for me to have noticed. And we did not even try to enter the bigger slum of Cité Soleil, which was too violent for a visit. Three years later, I would walk around, stopping to talk to the people, after the joint operations led by General Santos Cruz.

Valdes's priority was to organize elections that would not trigger another round of violence. It was an immensely difficult task, considering the violence that already existed without an election; gangs were organizing kidnappings as a regular source of income, a kind of tax on both the rich and not-so-rich. At a dinner in an elegant restaurant of Petionville, "La Souvenance," where I met with key figures of *la bourgeoisie* and had one of the best meals I ever had in a crisis zone—although the chef had warned us it would be a *menu de crise* (a crisis menu!)—the message I heard was loud and clear: the UN mission has to do whatever it takes to purge Haiti of its dangerous elements; it has to rein in the dangerous class, the poor. Valdes, a Social Democrat from a country that had escaped a ruthless military dictatorship, knew that it was not so simple. He was well aware of the need to accommodate the bourgeoisie, without which there would be no investments and no jobs. He also knew of the summary executions conducted by the police, and he had difficulty getting the full backing of Western powers to act at the highest levels and clean up a corrupt internal security that often was complicit in the crimes it was supposed to stop. He made sure that I would meet the whole range of Haitian society, including those who were still supporters of Aristide, who was now in exile thousands of miles away, in South Africa. I met with leaders still close to Aristide, including Father Gérard Jean-Juste and Leslie Voltaire. I listened to their populist rant but also to their valid complaints about the high number of prisoners kept in jail without judgment because of an enormous backlog of cases, in a dysfunctional justice system of absentee and corrupt judges. The gap between what I had heard in Petionville and what I was hearing from Jean-Juste was very wide.

Throughout 2005, Valdes made immense efforts to bridge it and defuse political tensions. The security situation remained bad, but his constant cajoling of all the political forces paid off, and the election was relatively peaceful. There were long lines, and voting stations stayed open well into the tropical night, lit by candles in the many places where there was no electricity. One last problem had to be tackled; as votes were counted, it appeared that René Preval was less than two percentage points shy of the majority in the first round of voting, and close to 5 percent of the ballots were blank. The purist electoral observers of the European Union wanted a second round, although there was no doubt that Preval would be the winner. There were demonstrations by Preval supporters, and the tension was mounting. Valdes knew that a second round would just be an opportunity for an explosion of the violence he had managed to avoid. With the support of the Organization of American States and of the UN, wisdom prevailed, and a legal solution was found to avoid a second round of voting. Preval was proclaimed president.

Preval was definitely not the candidate that the "group of 184," which had been created to oppose Aristide and had played a large part in his downfall, wanted as the elected president of Haiti at the end of the transition. Preval had been close to Aristide, and without being identified with him, he was seen as a representative of those supposedly dangerous classes that could threaten the interests of the bourgeoisie. I do not think that Valdes had a preferred candidate. At some point, wary of the reactions of the right, he had mentioned to me that a Spanish solution—referring to the period that followed the end of dictatorship in Spain—based on an alliance of the right and of the center-left might be the best for Haiti. But he was certainly convinced that there could be no genuine stability in Haiti if a large fraction of the population was excluded. From that standpoint the election of Preval was a good thing. It put the UN in a position to help as it was no longer seen as an adjunct of big-power politics, and there was hope that a Preval presidency, while avoiding the dangerous populism of Aristide, would demonstrate that power in Haiti could genuinely serve the people.

It did not happen, however, and five years later the landslide victory of Michel Martelly and the elimination, in the first round of the ballot, of the weak candidate who had the support of Preval showed the extent of the rejection of the Preval years. And yet, the UN did many things right, and there were real moments of hope, starting with the appointment of General Santos Cruz as force commander of the UN force in 2007. Preval's September 2008 appointment as prime minister of Michele Pierre-Louis, the energetic president of FOCAL—a Haitian NGO that is part of the Open Society network of George Soros—gave another chance to Haiti. What went wrong?

The joint operations led by Santos Cruz, combining the military and police components of the UN mission, are, with the operations led by General Patrick Cammaert in eastern Congo, the best examples of so-called robust peace-keeping, at least until the creation in 2013 of the intervention brigade in Congo.

The gangs that had controlled the slums of Port-au-Prince lost their grip, and although the UN was at one point blamed for civilian casualties—the gangs operated in the middle of a city, and they sometimes used human shields—there is little doubt that the people of Haiti who were directly affected by these operations had for a while a better image of the mission. Their daily lives improved, all the more so as the operations were combined with a few innovative disarmament and reintegration programs that provided opportunities for former young gang members to find a legitimate occupation. In many ways, the operations conducted by the UN transformed robust peacekeeping to an approximation of counterinsurgency as defined by General David Petraeus and the U.S. doctrine: it was all about loosening the grip of gangs on a population that was both "protected" and terrorized by them. It was exceptional in the history of peacekeeping and could hardly become the normal posture of peacekeeping troops. The operation required very well-trained troops, prepared for a very difficult environment close to urban warfare, and a first-class general, two requirements that could be met only if a troop-contributing country was prepared to make an exceptionally strong commitment to the UN. The troops would incur serious physical risk, and the troop-contributing country would be exposed to political risk, if the operations went wrong and the troops were blamed for war crimes—which would be bad news in any situation, but would be particularly shocking in a UN context. Brazil deepened its engagement and sent some of its best troops and one of its best generals, when it realized that, like other troop-contributing countries, it had initially underestimated the security situation, assuming that stability could be quickly achieved through development. But that courageous decision paid off, and the UN for a while acquired an unprecedented credibility with the Haitian people—at least in Port-au-Prince—and with the Haitian authorities.

The fact that, in the end, the operations did not achieve the political breakthrough that would put Haiti on a sustainable path to peace and development raises serious questions not only for "robust peacekeeping"—questions that are increasingly relevant for more recent peacekeeping activities in eastern Congo and Mali—but also for the now-fashionable counterinsurgency doctrine. Both doctrines gloss over the fact that gangs, insurgents, and "spoilers" of all kinds are always present for a reason: they fill a vacuum in the fabric of society, and if that fabric is not repaired, they will reappear, with or without an earthquake. The decisive use of force may help prevent marginal actors from derailing a peace process, and may contribute to the credibility of an international deployment by creating leverage that can then be used to influence and even shape a political process. But in the end, the critical element is the political foundation of peace.

An Attempt to Avoid Past Mistakes

When the United Nations deployed in Haiti in 2004, the memory of the previous deployments was very present, and there was a genuine determination not to repeat past mistakes. The Security Council gave a strong mandate to the mission with regard to the police, including the authority to vet personnel, and it gradually expanded the role of the mission in "the rule of law," adding judiciary and correction officers so that the reform of the police would be complemented by parallel reforms of the judiciary and the corrections system. The lesson learned from past experience was that training and equipping the police were useless if an effective process to eliminate corrupt or criminal elements was not put in place. In the past, initial progress in the reform of the police had been quickly reversed when Aristide eventually appointed corrupt or ineffective leaders. This time, a good relationship with the Haitian chief of police, Mario Andresol, did help build a police force that was more credible. After the earthquake, which destroyed many police stations, many Haitian police officers spontaneously reported for duty, earning some respect from a population that had grown accustomed to a corrupt and inefficient police. Undoubtedly, some limited progress was made.

Unfortunately, the same cannot be said of the broader rule-of-law effort. Justice is at the core of sovereignty, and the Haitian judicial authorities have so far resisted very effectively all the efforts to build a more accountable and more effective judiciary. The police may arrest criminals. But depending on their financial means, they either will be quickly released or will wait indefinitely for a trial. This failure is not unique to Haiti. In most places where it has tried, from Afghanistan to the Democratic Republic of the Congo, the international community has been incapable of fundamentally reforming the justice system. The exception may be Kosovo, where mixed courts and an intrusive posture of the international community for several years did achieve some genuine progress, which, however, now seems quite reversible. The "rule of law" that appears more and more often in Security Council mandates is an ambiguous concept that papers over fundamental differences dividing the members of the council. For Western countries, it is a way to introduce a democratization agenda without using the word democracy, and to assert a normative agenda that will allow for the promotion of a set of international norms and human rights. Other countries have a more limited understanding and equate rule of law with a law-and-order agenda, which at best would constrain the actions of security forces with effective rules.

Our Western vision of the rule of law, with its emphasis on process and form, is shaped by our own historical experience. It comes directly from the

Age of Enlightenment, and I should not have been surprised by the formalistic pomp of the ceremony I attended at the Palais National: it is only natural that the Haitian people, whose first encounter with freedom was the result of the French Revolution, would embrace it. But the failure of Haiti to link form and process to substance should give us pause. The political problem that the philosophers of the Enlightenment wanted to solve was very different from the one that Haiti and other fragile states have to address. Theirs was a world of absolute monarchies that had concentrated enormous power, and their political objective was to limit the extent of that power so that the emerging class of merchants and traders could prosper. The concept of separation of power was invented to achieve a balance that would create more space for enterprising individuals. And they started with the assumption that the new institutions they were advocating—parliament and independent judiciary—would develop in a society whose fabric was solid, woven together by the connections of morality and common social purpose between individuals. Adam Smith wrote of the "fellow feelings" that bind us together. The institutional constructions that those philosophers envisioned were not built on abstractions; they were shaped by the informal links of culture and history. Montesquieu produced a whole theory of how different climates produced different societies. Their vision was very different from our mechanistic understanding of the rule of law, which has lost the subtlety and texture of its eighteenth-century inventors, as if societies could be managed by rules in the same way computers are run by programs. Contrary to computer programs, rules require the positive adherence of human beings, and they acquire real authority not through force, but through trust, which is the fragile result of complex historical, social, and political processes. The mortar that keeps a society intact and at peace is much more than a set of laws.

Most of the desiccated "rule of law packages" now peddled by national and international bureaucracies are too often ignorant of local circumstances and of history, and therefore unlikely to meet the needs of the fragile societies for which they are designed. The problem of Haiti is not to limit the powers of an all-powerful state, but rather to create some power and authority in a country where the state is extremely weak and has little enforcement capacity. And indeed, law can be a power multiplier, and modern states eventually have become infinitely more powerful than the states that existed in the eighteenth century. However, the "merchants" of the twenty-first century, in a fragile state like Haiti, have a perspective that is very different from the "merchants" who launched the American and French revolutions.

I learned that lesson of political science at a dinner in Port-au-Prince during my last visit to the country in 2008. The fifteen or so businessmen who control most of the wealth of Haiti were present. They made their money importing consumer goods, producing textiles, and managing the harbor of Port-au-Prince. The discussion was about the future of the country, and their role in it. It quickly appeared that they were roughly divided into two camps and that some of them were of two minds. Some were quite happy with a state of affairs that ensured that they would continue to have full control of the Haitian economy, with little competition from outsiders. They welcomed the absence of reliable courts as a formidable obstacle to foreign investors, who would never have the familiarity with corrupt judges that old Haitian dynasties of businessmen had. They did not see improving the performance of the judiciary system as being in their interest, and they had all the means to prevent it, buying senators so that the "wrong" laws would not be passed, and judges, so that the "wrong" sentences would not be issued. They could also buy a demonstration, if some political drama was required to influence politics.

Another group of the businessmen saw benefits in a state that would improve its enforcement capacity through an effective police and judiciary. Foreign investors would enter the Haitian economy, and Haitian businessmen would no longer have full control of the economic pie, but the pie would grow so much that in the end they would all be wealthier. They also believed that improved law and order would have some benefits for their own private lives. Although all of them had the means to pay for private security and were safe in their well-protected residences of Petionville, they were concerned about the increased violence brought to Haiti by drug lords from Latin America who were using the country as a platform from which to introduce cocaine to the United States and Canada. They feared that in the jungle of Haiti, these new predators might eventually eliminate them.

For some of them, there was also a kind of patriotism. They were born in Haiti, they had grown up on the island, and they experienced the "fellow feelings" described by Adam Smith. They were proud of Haiti, of its culture, and of its extraordinary human texture, and at the same time they were ashamed of its dire poverty. They would not have sacrificed their considerable assets to help their miserable compatriots, but I could sense that some of them—a minority—were uncomfortable enjoying so much wealth in the midst of so much poverty, and would be willing to consider different ways of doing politics in Haiti if only their key economic interests could be safeguarded.

We were far from the technocratic discussion on a "rule of law" strategy. The conversation could have been almost the same in Congo, Sierra Leone, or even Afghanistan. It was about gambling on the future of one's own country, taking the risk of change, with the possibility of losing everything, or managing a fragility that delivered great benefits to a few. There was no obvious answer, and the political calculations of the elite would be affected by many factors, including the level of its patriotism, which in a globalized world was generally low, since its members always had the option to hedge their bets and leave the country. The conversation was about interests but also emotions, and it was clear to me that interests alone would not be enough to tip the balance toward positive change.

Many of us in the developed countries of the West naively assume that the path of history is linear and that the fragile states of today have to follow the same path we took two centuries ago, and that their leaders naturally aspire to emulate our model. They will not and they do not. The coexistence of highly developed countries and extremely fragile ones is a phenomenon without precedent, and we do not yet fully understand how the interface between the world of stability and law and the world of fragility functions. In one sense, this disparity carries a lot of hope as remittances from diasporas bring fresh money to countries that badly need it—now close to $2 billion every year in Haiti. It can also undermine any prospect of development, as corrupt elites benefit from our laws by putting their money in our banks and benefit of their own absence of laws to collect monopolistic rent. And it drains fragile countries of many of their best and brightest, who will get richer with a good diploma if they settle in Europe, Canada, or the United States than in their own country.

All of these considerations were present in that last conversation in Haiti. How could the international community influence its outcome? Building effective institutions, assisting a government to set priorities, a ministry of finance to collect taxes equitably, a judiciary system to deliver justice in a timely manner would indeed help. I created in DPKO an office of rule of law and security institutions precisely because I had observed firsthand that the international community, when asked, was incapable of delivering the most basic services, and the frustration and disappointment of the countries we were meant to help could only tip the balance toward more violence.

We are still a long way from being able to provide credible responses on these technical issues. But even if we had all the resources, and were better organized, the most difficult challenge, one that we have not really overcome, is: how can we influence the conversation so that we will be asked to help, so that a constituency for change will gain real political traction in a weak country? That is the real question, and we have to admit that we do not have solid answers, because we do not fully understand the social forces at play. The very expression "fragile country" is misleading because it refers to the rest of us as "strong countries" representing the model, while the reality is that "fragility" and "weakness" are the consequences of our interaction as much as of the internal dynamics of the countries themselves.

I learned in Haiti that we should be modest. No force will produce peace, and no technocratic plan, as carefully considered and well-resourced as it might be, will deliver a functioning state—although both force and technical plans may be necessary, and we should not give up trying to improve our performance. But these technical efforts must be complemented by a personal engagement with the people of the country and a deep understanding of their politics. That understanding may help devise strategies that will nudge a country in the right direction. All the tools in the toolbox—military, economic, and political—should be used, but one should be under no illusion that they can by themselves deliver success. In the end, the "fellow feelings" among the people may well be more important determinants than any of our actions, and we do not know how to influence them; the only ones who can deliver success are the people of the country we are trying to help. Without their patriotism, a patriotism that looks increasingly quaint in a globalized world, failure is likely.

twelve

SYRIA

A World out of Control

Of all peacekeeping missions, the observer mission deployed on the Golan Heights, in the buffer zone separating Israeli-occupied territory from Syrian troops, was for decades one of the safest and most quiet. Despite the rhetoric, Israel and Syria had reached a modus vivendi that they had agreed not to disrupt. In a troubled Middle East, the Austrian troops deployed on Mount Hermon, enduring a sometimes bitter winter but enjoying the snow, could have easily forgotten that a war had been fought on the slopes of the mountain, except for the posts alongside desolate fields signaling the presence of mines. Every once in a while, a sheep would step on a rusting tank mine from the early 1970s, and be blown up. There also was the ghost town of Quneitra, frozen in the destruction inflicted by the withdrawing Israeli army in 1974. The Syrian government had decided not to rebuild it, to make a political point, but it was a restricted zone, and the only witnesses were UN peacekeepers caught in their routine. Who cared anymore? The weeds were growing between slabs of concrete and torn iron, and in the distance, one could see through the haze Israeli settlements and Druze villages on the Israeli-controlled side. Israeli settlers were growing vineyards, and Druze villagers tended to their orchards producing excellent apples.

Over the thirty years of peacekeeping, the Syrian government had perfected the art of managing relations with the UN. It never missed an opportunity to remind the UN that it scrupulously abided by the terms of the disengagement agreement that was the basis for the peacekeeping mission, while at the same time lacing our meetings with vicious anti-Israel remarks. The government wanted to make clear that it had everything under strict control, embracing visitors with an almost suffocating hospitality. This was the nice facade of a regime that had the tightest of grips on its country. Each of my movements and conversations was probably monitored, but in the midst of banquets it was difficult to imagine that while the regime closely monitored visitors like me, it intimidated and sometimes terrorized its own people. There was the torture, the secret jails, the disappearances: "internal" matters that were not the responsibility of the peacekeepers.

When the Arab Spring started in December 2010, sparked by the self-immolation of a poor Tunisian who had suffered more than his share of humiliations and could not take it anymore, Syria seemed at first immune to the tremors that were felt throughout the Arab world. It had the appearance of stability. The well-maintained roads, the low-cost housing projects, the nascent tourist boom, the juxtaposition of mosques and churches, the secular outlook of a large part of the elite had encouraged international investors as well as tourists to pay more attention to Syria. After the death of Hafiz al-Assad in 2000, there had been hope that his son Bashar, who had studied in London and married a British-Syrian banker, would usher in reforms and open up the country. That had been the recommendation to him of the king of Jordan, who had come to power the year before. Little was left of those early hopes a few years later. The economy had indeed become less statist, and private investors were busy building hotels or acquiring cellular phone franchises. But the veneer of progress was very thin. Power failures attested to the decrepit state of key infrastructures. Close to a third of the population lived in poverty and one-tenth in extreme poverty.

All these facts were well-documented, and one could have concluded that Syria, among Arab countries, was at a particularly high risk of upheaval. And yet it took more than a year after the beginning of the Arab Spring for Syria to be affected by the revolutionary wave. That may not be so surprising, considering the ruthless efficiency of the many security services protecting the regime. When demonstrations eventually began, the brutal reaction of the security forces confirmed that there are few countries where challenging the regime, even peacefully, was as dangerous. What is more surprising and significant is that so little was done to support a peaceful transformation of Syria. Maybe it was not possible, but the contrast between international activism once violence began in Syria and the passivity and indifference beforehand is striking. It says a lot about the limits of the idea of an international community, and how little the rest of the world really cares. And it has not gone unnoticed among Syrians and other Arabs. Despite all the nice talk about prevention, there is very little appetite in today's world for serious engagement in countries that have not yet reached the stage of full-blown crisis. The reasons for that reluctance vary. For the majority of national leaders, it reflects a vision of sovereignty that remains wary of any interference in the internal affairs of another country. There is a natural solidarity among many rulers of the world, who assume that they know better how to run their respective countries than foreigners whose intentions can be questioned. For the Western powers, which claim to support the emerging norm of the responsibility to protect, and which often make—rightly—the case that prevention is the best and cheapest option, the practical reality is that the immediate political and financial costs of prevention always trump the longer-term benefits. Why engage in a risky and complicated venture when there is no domestic political pressure to do so?

By 2012 the Syrian crisis had become sufficiently intractable to force the world to pay attention. Suddenly the major powers were in a hurry to be seen to be doing something, and the appointment of a UN special envoy was the easiest and most logical move. What was not expected was that the envoy would be the former secretary general himself, Kofi Annan. It was a bold move on the part of his successor to make such an appointment, and it was a bold move for Kofi Annan to quickly accept to take on the responsibility. And it was a complete and wonderful surprise for me when, on his first trip to New York as a special envoy, Kofi, after a dinner with my wife and me, called the next morning and asked whether I would join him in Geneva as his deputy. He then called the president of Columbia University, Lee Bollinger, where I was a professor, to convince him to lend me to the United Nations.

Kofi Annan, as soon as he was appointed, had developed a comprehensive plan, which addressed all five key issues of the conflict: an inclusive Syrian-led political process; a United Nations–supervised cessation of violence in all its forms; the timely provision of humanitarian assistance; the release of arbitrarily detained persons; and the freedom of movement of journalists. Because it was already clear that it would be very difficult to have direct talks between Assad and the opposition, the proposal was for an "empowered interlocutor" to be appointed by the Syrian authorities when invited to do so by the envoy. The principle of a "Syrian-led" process was firmly established, in deference to the sovereignty of Syria, but the future would show that the principle was open to many interpretations. Who were the Syrians who would lead the process? A government seen by the opposition as an illegitimate dictatorship? An opposition characterized by the government as a group of "terrorists"? In a conflict where the parties deny any legitimacy to the other side, "national ownership," another cliché of the international community, can result in paralysis and stall any peace process. For the supporters of the Assad regime, a Syrian-led process meant that the envoy should only have an accompanying role, and that the Syrian government would determine the steps to be taken.

For the opposition, a Syrian-led process meant that the envoy had to create the political space that would make it possible for a repressed people to freely express its ambitions and chart the path of change. Indeed, in many peace negotiations, an envoy has to find a delicate balance between duly recognizing the formal authorities and allowing for the expression of other actors, as the old institutional order unravels.

Kofi Annan had two deputies, Nasser al-Kidwa, a nephew of Yasir Arafat and a former Palestinian ambassador at the UN, and myself. This was part of a complicated arrangement, whereby Kofi Annan was not only the special envoy of the United Nations but also of the Arab League. Initially, Kofi Annan was to be the envoy only of the United Nations, but political pressure built up quickly for him to be appointed joint special envoy of the United Nations and the Arab League. The Arab League had already identified Nasser al-Kidwa when I was appointed. It was agreed that he would deal with the peace process, while I would deal with the rest (cessation of violence, human rights, humanitarian affairs, and so on), and especially with all peacekeeping issues related to a "cessation of violence." This was an awkward arrangement, because peacekeeping essentially is a political undertaking, and Syria was no exception. It was made even more awkward by the fact that the Syrian authorities refused to meet with al-Kidwa, so that the person dealing with the political process could only talk to one side. These difficulties reflected a more fundamental problem that would poison the efforts of Annan and his successor, Lakhdar Brahimi. There was no uniform view on Syria in the Arab League, but the growing influence of Saudi Arabia and Qatar and the evolution of Egypt under President Mohamed Morsi meant that the league took an increasingly strident anti-Assad stance, calling for the removal of the regime. How could a mediator mediate if one of the organizations on behalf of which he is working has clearly sided with one of the parties? When I joined the Annan team, these questions were still blurred in ambiguities, and there was hope that the international community could genuinely come together in support of a political process. The deepening crisis would show that it was an illusion. The international community was divided, and for some countries, the fall of Assad would prove to be a much more important goal than a quick end of the war.

Could the result have been different? In the early spring of 2012, the priority was to stop the violence before it destroyed the country. Government tanks had moved into cities. Artillery rounds had destroyed a whole neighborhood of Homs, an important city halfway between Damascus and Aleppo, and smaller operations were reported throughout the country. That is why a "cessation of violence" figured prominently in the Annan plan and became a priority of the envoy. My immediate role, upon arrival at Annan's offices in

Geneva, was to work for the deployment of an observer mission that would monitor a cessation of violence. We made a big push to quickly achieve a cessation of violence that would lead to a genuine peace process. Kofi Annan was gambling that a momentum for peace could be created if guns could be silenced. There was also a hope that if the Security Council members could agree on the limited goal of stopping the violence, that agreement could gradually be broadened. Annan was keen to have a "big bang," a dramatic moment that would alter the dynamics that were beginning to destroy Syria. He had decided to dare the combatants to challenge his call for a cessation of violence.

At the end of March 2012, the Syrian government gave its acceptance of Annan's plan. An assessment team led by a Norwegian general, Robert Mood, was quickly dispatched to Damascus to negotiate with Syrian authorities the conditions for deployment of a mission and to obtain the guarantees that would allow it to do its work efficiently. The negotiations were difficult, as the Syrians, who had several decades of experience in managing their relations with a UN mission, wanted to make sure that they would control every aspect of it from communications to nationality of staff and freedom of movement. The signals sent by the Syrian authorities were mixed, to say the least. On the legal front, Foreign Minister Walid al-Moallem and his team wanted to negotiate every detail of a possible UN presence. He also claimed that since there was no formal structure that could authoritatively speak for the opposition, it was for the envoy to give written guarantees of compliance on behalf of the various opposition groups. This was obviously something that we could never agree to, and the Syrian government would pointedly remind us of this asymmetry, thus keeping open the possibility for it to get out of its commitment at any time. Meanwhile, military operations conducted by government troops were continuing unabated. A Human Rights Watch report would later confirm that several operations early in April targeted villages in Idlib province and resulted in the deaths of civilians. That report, based on oral testimony of witnesses, was corroborated by satellite imagery showing armored vehicles and trucks deploying in the villages on the same days mentioned by the people who had spoken to Human Rights Watch.

Annan was well aware of the dangers, but he was convinced that there was no way forward other than to create new facts on the ground so as to build momentum. In the end, he won, and the Security Council reluctantly went along with his recommendations. In less than three weeks, a divided council, which had for months been incapable of agreeing on anything on Syria, completely changed its posture. On April 5 it endorsed a timeline that required a cessation of violence by the government on April 10 and a full cessation of violence within forty-eight hours. That forty-eight-hour delay between the actions expected from the government and the follow-up by the opposition was important for all those who wanted to make clear that the government had the primary responsibility for stopping the violence. There was a widespread expectation among many members of the international community that Assad's forces should take the initiative and be the first to stop the violence. The insurgency, responding to the new posture of the government, would then desist from using violence. However, the interval between the cessation of violence by the government forces and the response of the insurgency had to be extremely short to be workable, and in practice, there would be a much greater chance of success if the insurgency changed its own posture almost simultaneously. As one would expect, the Syrian authorities had the opposite view. In last-minute discussions, they imposed their own timeline, which Annan accepted because, as he noted, it would be much harder for the government to reject a deadline that it had itself selected.

The gamble worked, and on April 12, there was a palpable improvement. The guns had seemingly fallen silent. Annan briefed the Security Council from Geneva by video-link in the afternoon. "Early today," he said, "the cessation of violence appeared to be observed. However, after initial reports of calm this morning, there are some unconfirmed reports of violence in some cities. And I must stress this is not unusual. Usually when you achieve a cessation of violence the parties can continue to test each other." Two days later, the Security Council authorized the deployment of an advance team of thirty observers, and the Department of Peacekeeping Operations swiftly dispatched observers pulled from headquarters and other missions, which were led by a Moroccan colonel. One could immediately feel how much in demand UN observers were, and how difficult and dangerous their work would be. On several occasions, the observers were surrounded by crowds, which could quickly turn hostile. They wanted observers to stay with them in their villages, fearing that harsh repression would come as soon as the observers had left. In the village of Arbeen, Syrian troops opened fire on the crowd while observers were speeding away. But as Annan had anticipated, once a cessation of violence—whatever its limitations—was in place, and observers were on the ground, it was politically impossible for the Security Council not to move ahead and authorize a full mission.

Continuing at the fast pace that had made the initial success of the cessation of violence possible, Secretary General Ban Ki-moon sent to the council the letter it had requested, outlining what an observer mission would look like. At the same time, negotiations were continuing with the Syrian government on the practical arrangements for the mission to deploy, and on April 19, "preliminary understandings" were reached with the Syrian authorities. These understandings did not replace a status of forces agreement, but they were sufficiently specific to alleviate some of the concerns within the council regarding the cooperation of Syrian authorities. On the same day, I briefed the council, mentioning all the risks, but stressing that "a United Nations monitoring mission deployed quickly with a clear mandate, the requisite capacities, and the appropriate conditions of operation would greatly contribute to observing and upholding the commitment of the parties to a cessation of armed violence in all its forms and to supporting the implementation of the six-point plan."

On April 21 the Security Council adopted Resolution 2043 authorizing, for ninety days, a UN Supervision Mission in Syria (UNSMIS). This was a remarkable turn of events, considering where the council had been a few weeks before. I myself had deep doubts about the possibility of achieving a genuine cease-fire. As a former head of peacekeeping who always fought for clear and achievable mandates, I was concerned that the conditions under which we were deploying observers would be extremely dangerous. Many members of the council had the same doubts, and in particular Susan Rice, the American ambassador, who was chairing the Security Council in April and whose key adviser was Salman Ahmed, my own former special assistant at the UN. In that new capacity, he could share his UN experience and give good advice to a government that was now supportive of the UN and did not want to recklessly put at risk the credibility of the organization. For him, good advice meant great caution on a possible observer mission in Syria. That is why the resolution authorized the deployment for only three months and gave the secretary general the unusual authority to slow down, stop, or accelerate deployments according to the situation on the ground.

Kofi Annan knew as well as any of us the risks involved. But his sunny personality has allowed him on several occasions to defy the odds by creating a dynamic situation that so radically transforms perceptions that an irresistible momentum is generated. On April 21 the odds of success were low, but the possibility of success was better than the certainty of disaster, and that is probably what led him to push so hard for the deployment of observers, and to gain the support of the Security Council.

The language of the resolution that described the "cessation of violence" referred to the Annan plan, and it was very ambiguous. It requested the Syrian government to "cease troop movements towards, and end the use of heavy weapons in population centers, and to complete pullback of military concentrations in and around population centers." While ending the use of heavy weapons in population centers was a clear and verifiable commitment, the cessation of troop movements toward populations centers and their eventual pullback would be a much more difficult undertaking, in part because military facilities were often located in cities. The plan had implicitly acknowledged that this could only be gradual, and it had to be part of a much broader effort that would include the end of human rights violations. That language allowed the UN mission to have a human rights and a political component, which was unusual for an observer mission led by a general. It meant that the work of the mission would have many more facets than a traditional observer mission.

On the military side, an important part of the work of observers would be to check whether armored vehicles and tanks were still present in cities. Their work would be complemented by satellite intelligence provided by several member states. For the first time in its history, the UN would be in a position to compare information collected by observers on the ground with satellite images and, crucially, to guide observers by helping them go to the right place at the right time. Without satellite help and use of multiple sources of information, there was a risk that the observers would be engaged in a wild goose chase, while satellite technology could considerably increase their efficiency. But for that complementarity to work, there was a need for secure communications between New York, where the headquarters of peacekeeping was located, Geneva, where Annan was based, and Damascus, where the headquarters of the mission would be deployed. In the three months that the observer mission was deployed, significant efforts were made, but I had a confirmation of the difficulty of ensuring confidentiality in a UN context. The UN bureaucracy had its own views on what was "secure," which did not coincide with the views of member states that were in a position to provide intelligence. We nevertheless owed it to the Syrians who would confide in us not to jeopardize their security. This was an almost impossible task when confronted with a regime that has an extensive network of security services.

The difficulty of putting in place a secure system of communications was just one aspect of the fundamental flaw of a mission that could do its work only if all sides wanted it to work and be successful. In the case of an observer mission, the traditional principle of consent was an absolute political and operational necessity. That applied even more to the civilian responsibilities of the mission, which would be almost impossible to discharge if the Syrian authorities were uncooperative. Annan's plan had rightly identified human rights as a core issue. There was no doubt that tens of thousands of people were detained, but there was no figure that could reliably be quoted. Likewise, the right to demonstrate peacefully was regularly denied, and there were countless instances of violent dispersion of crowds after Friday prayers. Meanwhile, journalists and humanitarian workers employed by foreign organizations were often denied visas. There was a need to investigate the detentions, working closely with the Red Cross, to monitor demonstrations, and to relentlessly press for more access given to humanitarian workers and journalists. Since the Annan plan provided a roadmap for the work of the mission, we were determined to regularly report on all those issues, which we considered as part and parcel of "cessation of violence *in all its forms*."

From the outset, we knew that the cooperation of the Syrian government would be limited at best. An unusual arrangement was therefore put in place, with a small—too small, unfortunately—but very strong human rights component in Damascus, led by Georgette Gagnon, whose work in Afghanistan had won the respect of all, backed by a senior human rights officer in Geneva with intimate knowledge of Syria, Hania Mufti, who would be able to connect with various sources of information more freely, not being in the country. Under difficult circumstances, the human rights officers deployed in Syria would team up with military observers, courageously going to places that a purely civilian team would never have been able to access. We were hoping that additional information collected by Hania would help guide their work, in the same way military observers could benefit from satellite imagery.

The pullback of troops and armor, the release of detainees, and peaceful demonstrations would be important milestones if they happened, but they all depended on a credible political process. While I knew that there was little chance of peace if the divisions of the region and of the world could not be overcome, it was clear to me that the mission needed to be in close contact with the Syrian protagonists, to win their trust, which would be needed when the time came for a settlement. Trust also was needed to have influence on the big powers. But in the cafés of Paris—where much of the secular opposition in exile lived—and along the peaceful shores of Lake Geneva, or in the conference halls of Cairo or Istanbul, the screaming violence of a civil war was somewhat muffled. The gap between the outside and the inside opposition was wide, and it has hurt the Syrian opposition from the outset. I was not in charge of the peace process, but I was not barred from entering Syria. The physical and human distance between the solemn corridors of the Palais de Nations in Geneva and the dust of Syria made me uncomfortable. When you engage in diplomacy on behalf of your own country, you can find a justification and an anchor in the national interests that you defend. But when you work on behalf of the United Nations, your intrusion in the life of others has to stand on stronger ground than what diplomats gently call "good offices." It is a difficult balancing act. You need to keep a distance and avoid being drawn into the passions that you are expected to overcome; but that distance must not become indifference, and I do not think that the principles of the UN

Charter can be well-served without real empathy for the people on whose behalf it was written.

I was therefore very grateful to Kofi Annan when he encouraged me to go to Syria to check on the observer mission that was deploying. In Paris and Geneva, I had already met some of the leaders of the secular opposition. I knew as a friend the spokesperson of the Syrian National Council, which was at the time still new and hoping to acquire a central role. Bassma Kodmani would later be marginalized and would eventually have to resign, but she is a shining example of a Western-educated Arab woman, at the same time thoughtful and passionate, who was willing to make considerable personal sacrifice to transform her country. She put a lot of hope in the capacity of the mission to stop the violence. She would call me, sometimes late at night, to convey demands coming from Syria; someone had called from a remote village or a suburb of Damascus, to request the immediate deployment of observers to stop an impending military operation. We would relay the message to the mission, which eventually established its own direct channels of communication with the opposition. Since it could not attend to all emergencies, it would have to make difficult judgment calls when prioritizing patrols. I had also met Michel Kilo, who was from an older generation, a Christian Nasserite who had grown up with the ideals of Arab nationalism only to see them betrayed by corrupt leaders.

A Range of Rebels

It was only when I arrived in Syria that I took the full measure of the gap that needed to be bridged. Thanks to Riad Seif, a courageous businessman, also from an older generation, who wanted me to gain a good understanding of his country, I was introduced in his modest apartment in the periphery of Damascus to a number of opposition actors of all ages and professions. One was a doctor who was assassinated a few days later in front of his office because he took care of patients wounded in combat. Another was a young dentist from Deir Ezzor. They all made it clear to me that this was a revolution that was led by young revolutionaries. They did not believe in the old political parties, which were led by old men; they were deeply suspicious of any party tolerated by the regime, which made it very difficult to have an organized political opposition within Syria, and present in Damascus. Some, like the dentist from Deir Ezzor, were from religious families and were close to the Muslim Brotherhood. As a respected imam told me in Damascus, the rejection of the Assad regime was at its core a moral rejection. The older Assad had run a ruthless dictatorship, but there was never any suspicion that private interests motivated him. On the contrary, since his death in 2000, the much celebrated (in Western media) opening of the economy, including to Sunni businessmen, had benefited cronies of the president's family rather than the Syrian people. Syria was ranked as the second-most corrupt country (after Iraq) in the Middle East and North Africa. No business deal could be completed if the family of Assad's wife did not benefit. That sense of deep injustice and immorality, more than the absence of democracy, had triggered the revolution, and part of the appeal of the Muslim Brotherhood was its ethical stance. People were not looking for the program of a political party, but for the guidance of just leaders. That was a far cry from the political debates of old Marxists and secular intellectuals in Western capitals. Young Syrians, not so different from the youth of rich democratic countries, were not interested in the politics of the older generation. They were interested in issues that affected them, and the gap between them and the older generation was not just a gap in years but also a gap in vision. That gap widened even more when I traveled to rebel-held areas in Homs and Ar Rastan.

I had known Syria as one of the most controlled states in the world. Wherever you went, you had to assume that some secret police was monitoring you, and it was almost impossible to meet anybody incognito. I had had a hint of that when I made some visits in the past to Damascus; I was always followed, and the people I met were always identified unless they had come to the meeting point much earlier and left much later. And when someone had come to see me at the hotel, because he looked Syrian, he had been stopped on the way out and was let go only after showing his American passport. This continuous harassment made it very difficult for any legal opposition to organize itself and contributed to the gap between officially recognized movements and the opposition in exile. On this trip, I went to Homs in a UN convoy, but the government, because it had a "responsibility to ensure our security," surrounded me with a heavy military presence. It was therefore all the more striking, after a meeting with the governor of Homs province, to drive to the rebel-held area of the city; our security escort abandoned us at the last checkpoint manned by Syrian troops, and we drove through a kind of no-man's-land, amid destroyed houses and uncollected garbage. At a street corner, we were met by a vehicle of the Free Syrian Army, which we followed to a house where the Homs Revolutionary Committee was assembled. Men in black uniforms, equipped with modern automatic weapons and sniper rifles, were now protecting us. The all-powerful Syrian state had lost control over a part of its territory. Back in Damascus, officials would stress that they could at any time regain control of any part of Syria, which was probably true at the time, but at least temporarily, they had obviously given up. And this was a watershed.

The discussion with the Revolutionary Committee was sobering. There was continuous shooting in the background, and the sense of urgency was anything but fake. The men—there were few women at the meeting—represented a wide spectrum of society: teachers, businessmen, doctors, and civil servants. They very much looked like the members of a town council in any peaceful country. They had well-prepared and clear messages. They wanted a reinforced presence of observers to deter government offensives, and more important, they wanted the international community to bring down the regime, in the same way it had brought down Muammar Qaddafi in Libya. I then went to a smaller town further north, Ar Rastan. The procedure to move from a government-controlled to a rebel-held area was the same, but the dynamics were different. There had been intense military battles, and we drove past several abandoned tanks and armored personnel carriers. Our interlocutors were no longer civilians. Ar Rastan is a largely Sunni town, and it is the birthplace of many of the Sunni officers of the Syrian army. They were enrolled in the army because of the influence of the then minister of defense, General Mustafa Tlass, himself a Sunni and a native of Ar Rastan, who was part of a small Sunni elite allied with the regime. The loyalty of the Sunni officers to the regime had broken down, and the city was now under the control of troops commanded by commissioned officers who had defected. I had an illustration of their good organization in the briefing they presented. Each city in the province of Homs had sent an officer to describe the situation. There was not one civilian among them, but the message was not very different from the one I had heard in Homs, except that it was expressed more dramatically. I tried to explain that a quick NATO intervention was unlikely, and that the UN mission was there to create conditions for a negotiated outcome. I was brutally rebuffed. One officer stood up and said, looking me in the eyes: "If what you say is true, it just confirms that the international community cannot be trusted, it is the ally of Israel and the regime, it has no interest in Syria. If that is true, then I will have no other option than to join those who put on a suicide vest!" There was a lot of rhetoric in this outburst, but I could sense how our Western rhetoric, which creates high hopes and often delivers little, is extremely dangerous and can only feed despair. In 2012, when there were still "moderates" among the groups fighting Assad, almost nothing was done to help them. The world may now be paying the price of that indifference, and the recent rise of the Islamic State has been in part a direct result of the gap between Western rhetoric and action.

I was in Syria in the spring of 2012, and my interlocutors were at least willing to engage and give me the benefit of the doubt. The first signs of the unraveling of the cessation of violence came in May. On May 25 pro-government militias entered the village of Houleh, in Homs province, and massacred whole families. This was clearly a sectarian killing, in a mostly Sunni village surrounded by Alawite villages. The village had been a continuous irritant for the regime, since it was on a main road to an Alawite part of the country, and tensions run high between Houleh and neighboring villages. The May 25 massacre followed a pattern that has been repeated many times. Regular Syrian troops would establish a security perimeter around a village, shell it, and then pro-government militias known as *shabiha* would enter the village and commit atrocities. It was unclear whether the militias were just tolerated by the Syrian authorities or actually coordinated by them. In Houleh, the monitors, supported by the human rights officers of the mission, had been able to enter the village the next day and document the massacre. They had seen the bodies and had interviewed witnesses, although in a war zone with no witness protection program and the constant risk of violent intimidation, no testimony could ever be completely trusted, and pro-government media would use that uncertainty to cast doubt on UN reports.

Two weeks later, government troops did not even allow the observers to reach a village. When they were eventually allowed, it was too late to conduct a proper investigation. The work of the monitors was becoming more dangerous by the day, and they were increasingly criticized for not being able to report effectively and deter violence by their presence. On June 16 the media-savvy Norwegian general who commanded the mission announced that he was "suspending operations." The rationale was the security of observers, but he had a political goal: by making this announcement, which had not been reviewed by Kofi Annan, but that Annan supported because he never second-guessed the commanders on the ground, General Mood was hoping to create a political shock and send a clear message to the parties, putting the responsibility for a breakdown of the cessation of violence squarely on them. I was in agreement with Mood, because I believed that it is always wrong for a peacekeeping operation to have to beg the parties to be accepted. If it does so, it loses its authority and reverses roles in a perverse way. I had observed the dangerous consequences of that reversal of roles in Darfur. It is not the parties who are doing the UN a favor by allowing it to deploy peacekeepers; it is the international community that is doing a great favor to the parties by expending blood and treasure to bring peace. Mood's gambit did not work, and it marked the beginning of a process that eventually would lead to the pullout of the mission in August, after a conditional one-month extension in July.

The failure of the observer mission, after a brief moment of hope in April, was to be expected. Without a credible political process, any de-escalation of violence was bound to be temporary. Annan's plan had acknowledged that fact, as it referred to "a Syrian-led political transition leading to a democratic, plural political system, in which citizens are equal regardless of their affiliations, ethnicities or beliefs, including through commencing a comprehensive political dialogue between the Syrian government and the whole spectrum of the Syrian opposition." How could the envoy help bring about such a transformation? Part of the effort required a deep engagement with a wide spectrum of Syrian society: the government, the security services, the army, the armed opposition, the unarmed opposition both inside and outside the country, and also all the Syrians who were bystanders in the unfolding tragedy and who could help build a critical mass for a negotiated process. I got a sense of the immensity of the task when I was in Syria. So many obstacles needed to be overcome: the gap between generations, the gap between the internal and external opposition, the gap between those who fight and the silent majority that can only dream of a return to peace—as well as the practical difficulties of contacting people in Syria. Clearly, creating the conditions in Syria itself for a negotiated settlement was always going to be hard, after years of a ruthless dictatorship that has done immense damage to the fabric of society.

Annan, as a former secretary general, was less focused on the internal dynamics of Syria than on the global and regional dimensions of the conflict. If the regional and global actors could be shepherded in a direction that would foster reconciliation, then maybe the fragmentation that was increasingly apparent in Syria could be contained and eventually reversed. He was looking for a course that could unite the Security Council; the adoption of resolutions 2042 and 2043 had been the first steps in that direction. He was regularly on the phone with key foreign ministers, especially Sergei Lavrov and Hillary Clinton. He had some leverage with them because neither Russia nor the United States wanted a dramatic failure of the political process, which would expose the limits of their policies and might force them to consider alternative policies. Both had an interest in keeping the mediation show going.

However, in June, as the situation on the ground kept deteriorating, the contrast between the leisurely pace of a mediation that was not delivering progress and the accelerating pace of killings in Syria was becoming unbearable. After the Annan plan and the rapid launch of the observer mission, a new initiative was needed to regain political momentum and salvage the observer mission. Annan took a third bold initiative. He decided to convene in Geneva an "action group" that would include all the key international players and would try to chart a course that the international community would support. Several weeks of intensive diplomatic engagement followed. Annan knew that without a Russian-U.S. agreement there was little chance of a successful meeting. He therefore convinced the American and Russian senior officials in charge of the Syria file to come to Geneva to quietly try to develop a common position. The meetings were a complete failure, confirming that the respective positions remained far apart. There was no agreement on the participation in the meeting, or on process.

The United States, and even more so France, was adamantly opposed to the participation of Iran in the meeting. It feared that if Iran was included, some linkage would inevitably be made with the Iranian nuclear issue, and that would weaken the pressure applied on Iran to unequivocally abandon any program that could lead to a nuclear weapon. In taking this position, it had the strong support of Gulf states, especially Saudi Arabia. The fall of Saddam Hussein had given a considerable strategic advantage to Iran, and Saudi Arabia and the other Gulf monarchies were keen to regain the lost ground. The fall of Assad, an Alawite leader allied with Iran and Hezbollah, would indeed be a strategic defeat for Iran, and they were not prepared for any concession. On the other hand, Annan, who had undertaken several trips to the region, meeting not only with the leaders of Turkey, Qatar, and Saudi Arabia—all of which had played a major role in putting the Syrian crisis on the international agenda—but also with the leaders of Iraq and Iran, was convinced, and we all agreed, that Iran should be included. If we wanted to make sure that Syria would not become the battleground for a proxy war between the Sunni monarchies and Iran, it was important in our view to discuss upfront the interests of the regional players. Some regional actors could indeed play the role of spoilers in the conference if they were included, but they also could spoil any prospect of implementation if they were excluded. It became clear that the participation of Iran would be a deal breaker, and in the end neither Iran nor Saudi Arabia was present. But Iraq, which was perceived as close to Iran, was invited as the chair of the summit of the Arab League. And Qatar, as the chair of the follow-up committee on Syria of the league of Arab states, also attended.

The difficulties on participation were ominous. But agreeing on a communiqué proved even more difficult. The Western powers wanted to make clear that a transition to a post-Assad regime would be initiated, while Russia was adamant that nothing should be prejudged in a "Syrian-led process." The discussions had gone so badly that on the day of the conference, contrary to normal diplomatic practice, there was no agreed draft of a communiqué. I became convinced, as the negotiation was unraveling, that it would be better for the mediation and for Kofi Annan, who had published an op ed column in which he outlined the key parameters of a solution, to call off the meeting and suspend his own mediation, at least at his level. I believed that a statement of principles would be better than an acrimonious negotiation that would badly damage relations between key players. Annan thought he had to force the issue in a meeting. He was convinced that, in the end, the protagonists would blink and a document would be agreed that incorporated most if not all the key points of the roadmap he wanted. In the end, that is what happened. On June 30 Hillary Clinton, who had met with Sergei Lavrov the night before, signaled early in the meeting that she was committed to an agreed outcome, and Lavrov was ostentatiously relaxed, leaving the room to smoke cigarettes. The other members of the group had almost no role in the outcome.

The document that was agreed on June 30, 2012, was more a set of principles than an action plan. It spoke of a "transitional governing body"—a formula that was vague enough to allow, in the eyes of the Russians, for the participation of Assad—but qualified that concession by adding that this new body would be formed "on the basis of mutual consent," which was reassuring for the opposition. It was not a bad roadmap, but there was no agreed understanding on its implementation. Minutes after the communiqué had been agreed, Lavrov and Clinton were busy giving opposite and incompatible interpretations of it to an understandably skeptical press. Clinton was stressing that Assad would never pass the "mutual consent test," while Lavrov noted that nowhere in the text was the exclusion of Assad mentioned. It would be up to the Syrians to decide those issues. That was exactly what I had feared. The show had been kept on the road, but there was no prospect of any concrete progress. The mediation had become a convenient diversion for big powers unable to agree on a viable strategy. After an initial flurry of efforts to get the "action group" to act—Russia was only too happy to be the host—it became clear that the efforts were going nowhere.

Reaching a Dead End

By coincidence, I was asked by President François Hollande to chair a French commission on national security, at the very moment when Annan had decided to resign. The Geneva office closed; the observer mission, which had been tentatively extended for thirty days, was pulled out; and a few weeks later, Lakhdar Brahimi courageously accepted to restart the effort. The Annan mediation had provided a temporary lull in an escalating spiral of violence, and Syria had entered a new phase in its worsening civil war.

One year later, Brahimi would again try to convene a meeting in Geneva, and his efforts would take as a starting point the document that had been agreed on June 30, 2012. Annan seemed vindicated in his efforts, as everybody seemed to accept—maybe wrongly—that there was no basis possible other than the one he had provided. The dynamics were eerily similar. The participation of Iran continued to be a bone of contention as was the nature of the process. The opposition—supported by Western powers, Turkey, and the Gulf states—continued to make the departure of Assad a precondition, and Russia continued to hide behind a "Syrian-led process." But there were some important differences. Assad had recently made some military gains, and he was no longer the embattled leader whose rapid collapse was expected. The Syrian parties were now invited to the meeting, and the Syrian government had quickly accepted, exposing the deep divisions of the opposition. After 70,000 more people were killed, the question of arming the rebels had taken a new urgency. But the increasingly dominant influence of Islamist groups in the opposition, resulting in fragmentation and internecine warfare, raised new doubts about the wisdom of military support for the opposition. The Sunni officers that I had met in Ar Rastan in 2012 had not received the support that could have transformed them into a significant force, and the groups that were now dominant in the opposition were dubious partners. The European Union, unable to muster the required unanimity, had not extended an embargo imposed in 2011 on arms exports to Syria, while Russia very publicly had confirmed that it would deliver ground-to-air missiles and other weapons systems to the Syrian regime. This was but one aspect of the growing internationalization of the conflict. The Lebanese Hezbollah was now very publicly engaged in battle to support the regime, while the Syria/Israel front was heating up. Israeli airstrikes had sent a clear signal to the Syrian regime that no strategic weapons, missiles, or chemical weapons, should be transferred to Hezbollah. And the traditionally quiet Golan had become a source of tensions, as the demilitarized zone could become a safe haven for rebels. After some shelling and hostage-taking, UN peacekeepers had begun to leave what had been one of the safest missions in the world.

A potential turning point was passed in August 2013 when chemical weapons were used, in all likelihood by the Syrian army, in a suburb of Damascus. They probably had been used before, on a very limited scale, but the international community had looked the other way. This time, several hundred people were killed, and President Barack Obama, who had said publicly that their use would be a "red line" for the United States, was pushed into threatening military action. Israel, which had been ambivalent about the Assad regime, was seriously concerned about chemical weapons, which could one day be used against its people. This was an awkward situation for Western powers, which had to reconcile their rhetoric with reality. They now had a real strategic concern that had little to do with the welfare of the Syrians, who were killed in much greater numbers by conventional weapons. But the U.S. military had deep doubts about what limited airstrikes could achieve and no appetite for another war in the Middle East, especially when the strategic priority was Iran; U.S. public opinion was even more skeptical. Obama never-theless called for airstrikes, but decided to share these dilemmas with Congress by requesting its support, at the risk of appearing weak. After a decade of U.S. military adventures, Obama was trying to find the right balance between reck-less interventionism and strategic retreat, acknowledging that intervening in the lives of others had proven much more difficult than his predecessor had anticipated.

The United States and its Western allies eventually did not have to face their strategic dilemma because Russia, cleverly taking at face value the Western outrage over the use of chemical weapons, proposed to make the elimination of those weapons in Syria a priority and convinced the Syrian regime to go along with the proposal. This was a brilliant tactical move on the part of Rus-sia, which relieved the pressure on its ally Assad and allowed the Security Coun-cil to regain its unity for the first time since it had authorized the deployment of an observer mission in April 2012. Inspectors were quickly deployed in Syria to prepare the process of dismantling chemical weapons, and there was again hope that the newfound unity of the Security Council on chemical weapons could gradually lead to an agreement on a political solution.

The hope was that while exiled opposition leaders continued to clamor that they would never negotiate until Assad had left the country, in Syria the hor-rors of war might push a growing number of Syrians not to reject a negotia-tion out of hand, provided that cease-fires were not capitulations in disguise. On the regime side, there were also signs that the leadership, while it was increasingly confident that it would not be defeated, understood that com-plete victory was out of reach. In Alawite villages, many "martyrs" had been killed in action, and the fatigue of a cruel war might begin to be felt. There had been a stalemate for more than a year, but no awareness of it among the pro-tagonists; that awareness might now begin to sink in. That did not mean that Syrians were ready for a direct negotiation, but the exhaustion of civil war might make it less difficult for them to accept a solution if the international community—through the Security Council—took a leading role in shaping it. It was therefore all the more important that the region and the major powers agree on a way forward. In the region, the signals were mixed. Saudi Arabia appeared more determined than ever to continue to fight a proxy war against Iran in Syria, but it now saw the Muslim Brotherhood as an even greater threat than Iran, which could create some common ground with Russia. Iran under President Hassan Rouhani was sending some positive signals that deserved to be tested, but the Revolutionary Guards, under Qasem Suleimani, were the leading Iranian actors on Syria, and their support to Assad was unwavering. As for the West, it was beginning reluctantly to accept that the rhetoric of "Assad must go" had led nowhere. But these evolutions may have come too late, as the "Islamic State" and other extreme jihadist groups linked to al Qaeda became dominant in some towns, in the eastern and northern part of the country, making the prospect of a political process remote.

Who, then, is to blame for the utter failure of the international community to end the most violent crisis so far in the twenty-first century? Russia and Iran, and to a lesser extent China, are usually seen in the West as the key culprits. Russia has economic, military, and political interests in Syria. It has signed major armament contracts, it uses a small facility for its navy—the only one in the Mediterranean—and Syria is its last ally in the region. At a more general level, the way Western countries tried to turn the surprisingly long bombing campaign that eventually brought down Libya's Qaddafi into a shining example of the "responsibility to protect" has perversely encouraged Russia and China to make sure that no precedent was established. Regime change, they argue, should never result from a decision by the international community, and the Syrian crisis provided a good opportunity to make that point. After years during which Russia was taken for granted, its persistent support for the Assad regime was the first powerful signal that this era is over, that Russian interests must be taken into account, and that the global agenda cannot be dictated solely by Western powers. Russia pays no price for that stance, and on the contrary gains an international clout that puts it back on center stage.

The above narrative has become common wisdom in most Western capitals. The perspective from Moscow is quite different. A number of Russian officials admit that they might not be able "to deliver" Assad, even if they decided to try. Indeed, Russia is a key ally of Syria, providing critical weapons systems, but Syria also has Iran as an ally, and for Iran, because of its confrontation with Saudi Arabia, Syria is a vital interest. If the Russians were to significantly change course—and why would they at a time when the departure of Assad looks increasingly less likely?—they might well expose the limits of their influence, which is the last thing a power keen on building its aura of influence would want to do. The initial and unrealistic assumption of Western powers that Assad could be brought down like Ben Ali in Tunisia or Hosni Mubarak in Egypt made the search for a political solution much more problematic at a time when it was less difficult to achieve than it is now.

Annan, Brahimi, and all those who have tried to build bridges with Russia stress that the Russian and Western interests in Syria now should be converging rather than diverging. They have been proven right when they said that continued violence would provide a fertile ground for more radical brands of Islam that both Russia and the West want to avoid. But until now, Western and Russian analysts have drawn opposite conclusions from the same set of facts.

For Western analysts it shows that continued support to Assad can only lead to a catastrophic ending. On the contrary, Assad and his supporters may believe that Western powers will gradually come to the conclusion that the Syrian regime is the least bad option in a Middle East where the control of traditional state structures is under threat.

Syria today has thus become a magnifying glass of the strategic quandaries of the twenty-first century. An unholy alliance of great powers to support the status quo at any cost—which is what the Syrian regime may be counting on—is likely to lead to more instability and terrorism. But there are few credible partners in Syria and in the region to manage change. At the heart of our dilemmas is the diminishing capacity of great powers to shape events, which has been accelerated by the breakdown of their relations and their incapacity to chart a convincing course toward a peaceful Syria. The two issues are linked.

Syria exposes in a dramatic way the international community's limited capacity to influence events in individual countries. The potential veto in the Security Council of Russia and China has conveniently allowed us to assume that a political solution would be quickly found if the threat of a veto did not exist. It is indeed possible that the common and immediate threat of the Islamic State in Iraq and the Levant (known as ISIS) could bring about a long-awaited rapprochement between conflicting powers. If it happened, that could lead to de-escalation, and eventually to some broad-based agreement that would include the various components of Syria who would agree on hard security guarantees. But it is also possible that the fractured opposition would actually be incapable of delivering, and that Saudi Arabia and the region—through the action of states but also of private individuals—would prevent a political solution. It would thus be confirmed that the Syrian revolution has been another element of a transformation of states in the Middle East that cannot be controlled. That may be one of the reasons why Russia and China continue to support the Assad regime: their deep historical pessimism is rooted in their own past, which has convinced them that revolutions cannot be "fine-tuned." The confidence of Western powers, and in particular the United States, that they can change the world for good strikes them as naive at best.

Between the conservatism of former revolutionary powers and the shallow activism of democracies, is there some intermediate course that could be taken? The public debate in the West seems to be designed to appease our consciences rather than to provide real solutions. Recommendations to lift the arms embargo, to establish no-fly zones, or to launch limited strikes would not decisively break the stalemate; they would just prolong and deepen the agony. Russian leaders know it, and that is one of the reasons why they do not take the West very seriously. They also know that a moral interest in Syria will always have less impact than the strategic interests of regional powers, and that fact limits dramatically the capacity to escalate.

In the end, there may be no alternative to a frustratingly modest policy of diplomatic engagement that does not pretend that tactical use of force can be a substitute for a real strategy. The mistake in the first meeting in Geneva may have been, contrary to what I thought at the time, to be too ambitious, and too specific in our ambitions. In a world where solidarities and commitments are shallow, lofty goals are not only unrealistic, they can be dangerous, as they create false expectations that harden positions and make the prospect of peace less, rather than more, likely. Russians may be right when they caution that the changes set in motion by the Arab Spring may be much bigger and much less controllable than we think. This is not a reason to abandon the principles that have guided democratic societies. It would be wrong—strategically and ethically—to support an oppressive status quo as the best defense against the Islamic State and transnational terrorism. We should, however, be more humble, recognizing that it is the Syrians, and not us, who are sacrificing their lives for those principles. We are not yet used to the new state of affairs, but the future of the Middle East will be determined first and foremost by the people of the Middle East, not by Americans, Russians, or Europeans.

thirteen

MAKING THE UNITED NATIONS RELEVANT IN TODAY'S WORLD

I served the United Nations as the head of peacekeeping for eight years, the longest commitment of my career, and returned to support Kofi Annan's work on Syria in 2012, but I still remember my first day as a UN international civil servant. It was October 1, 2000, a Sunday, and I was not at the office, but at a spectacular estate near New York, the former residence of the Whitney family, Greentree. At the request of Kofi Annan, a retreat had been organized to discuss the new roles that the United Nations had just been given in Kosovo and East Timor. The UN had never before faced such a daunting task: for the first time in its history, it was being asked to effectively take over all the responsibilities of a sovereign government in not one but two locations. That discussion at Greentree was the beginning of a conversation that has not yet found a satisfactory conclusion, as the UN continues its search for new ways to adapt itself to the twenty-first century.

The beginning of new responsibilities, the patrician beauty of the place where we were meeting: one could only be humbled, and slightly disturbed by the contrast between the peaceful and harmonious environment of our retreat and the trouble spots of the planet that we were discussing. As a student of twentieth-century history, I had heard of Dumbarton Oaks, of Bretton Woods, and I had kept with me the mental image of the wise men who had shaped the post–World War II order. The splendid American settings in which they met had been like an illustration, beyond the devastation of Europe, that the spirit of enlightenment was alive and well, and that the "United Nations" of 1945 were willing and ready to build a new order that would preserve the best of European traditions and open the way to a rejuvenated world. And here in Greentree most of the top leadership of the United Nations had assembled. The group reflected the evolution of the world and was a much more diverse group than those who created global institutions in 1945. There was Louise Fréchette, the Canadian deputy secretary general; Iqbal Riza, the Pakistani chef de cabinet; Shashi Tharoor, the Indian under secretary general for public information; and Kieran Prendergast, the British under secretary general for political affairs. The old Western world was—belatedly—beginning to mix with the world of emerging nations in the twenty-first century. Some of them had interviewed me before I took my job, and I still felt a bit like the student who is being allowed in a meeting of the faculty. Sergio Vieira de Mello, who was running East Timor after a brief stint in Kosovo, and Bernard Kouchner, who was now running Kosovo, also attended, as did Lakhdar Brahimi, who had just completed a landmark report on the reform of UN peacekeeping—a report I would have the responsibility of implementing. I felt I was present at the creation of something new and big. There was a spirit of optimism and entrepreneurial confidence.

Everyone in the room was aware that UN peacekeeping was at a critical juncture after the hopes and the failures of the 1990s. When the cold war ended, there was a sense that the Security Council of the United Nations, which had been paralyzed by the divisions among its permanent members—especially between the Soviet Union and the Western powers (United States, United Kingdom, and France)—would now be in a position to take decisive action. The early successes in Cambodia, Namibia, Mozambique, and El Salvador, where UN blue helmets effectively helped usher in peace and stability, seemed to vindicate that assessment. But those successes were later overshadowed by the tragedies of the former Yugoslavia, Somalia, and Rwanda, where UN peacekeepers were bystanders to horrible atrocities. UN peacekeeping, which had expanded rapidly in the first half of the 1990s, shrank just as rapidly in the second half of the decade. In early 1999 the common wisdom was that UN peacekeeping was a thing of the past, and that from now on, regional organizations would take charge.

But there were conflicting signals. After its failure to agree to authorize the NATO bombing campaign in Kosovo, the Security Council had come together on the follow-up to it, and a UN mission with a mandate of unprecedented ambition was deployed in the second half of 1999. Likewise, in East Timor, the violence following a referendum that put an end to Indonesian rule, and the subsequent withdrawal of Indonesian forces, led to the deployment of another UN mission, with a similar broad executive mandate. Lastly, a United Nations mission was deployed in the Democratic Republic of the Congo, which had seen in the 1960s the most ambitious peacekeeping mission of the United Nations. These three deployments, authorized in quick succession in the course of one year, showed that the United Nations was still a player. In terms of legitimacy, as well as force-generation, it had comparative advantages that no other organization had. But would that be enough to revive UN peace-keeping, and to rebuild confidence in the world organization? Would that be enough to recreate a sense that a new world order was not empty rhetoric?

The discussion at Greentree ranged from mundane issues to grand visions. Sergio de Mello and Bernard Kouchner were like two swash-buckling musketeers on a mission. They both raised issues that would prove fundamental but hard to fix, and they were passionate, but in very different ways. Sergio de Mello had spent over two decades in the UN system, and he was polished even when he was provocative. To convey the gap between what we were doing and what needed to be done, he would quote the Timorese: "You were full of promises!" "We let them down," he soberly commented. But he had all sorts of practical recommendations for how to make things better. Most important, the budget of the UN mission should fund not just the mission—that is, pay for the troops and the civilians deployed—but should also support the mandate. This was, and still is, a revolutionary recommendation; it means supporting development and the country itself with obligatory contributions of the member states, instead of voluntary contributions, as is normally the case for development aid. He also wanted more flexibility for the mission to recruit personnel and more mobility between headquarters and the field. All these were issues on which I would later fight, to make the UN a more field-oriented organization.

Bernard Kouchner brought to the room a fresh breeze of passion: "All humanitarian interventions are political interventions. . . . When injustice is the law of the land, of course we become outlaws, as we fight injustice. . . . In Kosovo, we came ten years too late. . . . War stops when it stops in the hearts and minds of the people. . . . Peace is a long-term effort: it took nine months to have Rugova and Thaci [two Kosovo Albanian leaders] in the same room. . . . The United Nations has to involve local partners early on, and it has to be independent from them, to maintain its credibility." Kouchner, contrary to some French who consider speaking in English as close to an act of high treason, has never shied away from speaking English. As a born communicator, he used the fact that he was not a native speaker, that his English had nothing smooth, to convey that reality itself—especially after a conflict—is not smooth. He juxtaposed short sentences, like irreconcilable realities that would nevertheless have to be reconciled. The way he spoke reflected the way I would see him operate in Kosovo, where his unlimited capacity for empathy helped him manage difficult tactical situations. At Greentree, he was building a bridge between his humanitarian past and his full engagement in the politics of Kosovo. I hope I am not distorting his views when I say that he had come to recognize that the most humanitarian act is to fix the politics, but fixing politics does not mean forgetting the reason why you are there in the first place—to fight injustice.

There was some irony that it was left to a man who had built his reputation on humanitarian action to remind all of us of the centrality of politics. The person who could have most eloquently spoken on this issue was Lakhdar Brahimi. At the beginning of the meeting, he had given an update on the reaction of member states to his report, but he did not intervene much in the debate. I would later learn that he had expressed reservations about the East Timor mandate, and when the time came, more than a year later, for the United Nations to get involved in Afghanistan, he convinced the secretary general and the Security Council not to give the UN the responsibilities of a sovereign power, but rather to establish a process that would quickly restore Afghan sovereignty.

At the Greentree retreat, while the difficulties and challenges of such wide-ranging mandates were considered, we did not ask whether there was a consensus among member states about how to implement these mandates. And yet, without their support there is no hope of success. The greatest challenges for peacekeeping are not technical but political. This is not just because the most critical element for the success of a peacekeeping operation is the political process that must underpin it—and it is an illusion to think that there is some technocratic fix to the challenge of state-building—but also because the instrument of peacekeeping is itself a political endeavor, as different countries have different and often conflicting views of what they expect from peacekeeping and of the United Nations itself. Addressing these questions would require important reforms of the UN, difficult in any environment but all the more so in the poisonous context introduced by the storms over Afghanistan and Iraq in the years after the Greentree retreat. I learned the hard way that managerial reforms, like the reform of peacekeeping or the fight against sexual abuse, and institutional challenges, like the changing nature of conflict or the composition of the Security Council, couldn't be easily separated. They are all part of a political context and cannot be successfully tackled when there is no genuine agreement among member states on what they expect from the United Nations.

Matching Capabilities with Responsibilities

By 2003 the optimism of the Greentree retreat had dissipated. Many in the United Nations felt under siege, faced with a deeply divided and bitter Security Council, an indifferent American president, and a hostile right wing of the

U.S. Republican Party. Kofi Annan, pressed by a journalist, had called the Iraq war "illegal," but he had desperately tried to make the UN relevant once the war had ended because Iraq mattered to Washington and he knew that the United Nations would wither away without the support of the United States. The UN had paid a high price in that attempt: Sergio de Mello and twenty-two of the best and the brightest in the United Nations had died in Baghdad, and many believed that they had died for nothing.

When the General Assembly reconvened for its annual meeting in September 2003, the bombing of the UN compound in Baghdad was just a month in the past. Kofi Annan gave one of his best speeches: "We have come to a fork in the road," he said. "This may be a moment no less decisive than 1945 itself, when the United Nations was founded." He had decided during the summer that the response to the Iraq crisis and the growing estrangement between the United Nations and the United States should be to launch a reform of the United Nations. He therefore went on to announce that he would establish a High-Level Panel to examine the peace and security challenges the UN faced and recommend reforms to strengthen its capacity to respond.[1] He added that "the Panel will focus primarily on threats to peace and security. But it will also need to examine other global challenges, in so far as these may influence or connect with those threats."

This was an extremely ambitious enterprise, which reflected the fundamentally optimistic vision of Kofi Annan. From the outset, as a European pessimist, I doubted that a bold reform of the United Nations could succeed when a president who seemed to have little or no interest in multilateral organizations occupied the White House. At the end of 2003, there was little doubt about American supremacy, and Kofi Annan was trying to convince his American audience that the UN was a natural ally. At the same time, the Security Council was expanding the role of peacekeeping just as the UN faced a series of scandals that added fuel to the fire of its critics.

As the head of peacekeeping, which had the unenviable privilege of being at once the flagship of the United Nations and its riskiest activity, I was acutely aware that any new peacekeeping failure would further weaken an organization already under siege. And 2004 turned out to be not a good year

---

1. Specifically, Annan assigned the panel four tasks: "First, to examine the current challenges to peace and security; second, to consider the contribution which collective action can make in addressing these challenges; third, to review the functioning of the major organs of the United Nations and the relationship between them; and fourth, to recommend ways of strengthening the United Nations, through reform of its institutions and processes."

for peacekeeping. The Security Council seemed to have forgotten one important assumption of the Brahimi report: that no more than one mission would be deployed in any given year. Instead, it was authorizing new missions or radically altering old ones in rapid succession. The mission in the Democratic Republic of the Congo had been transformed, but after the improvement that followed Operation Artemis in Ituri, crisis had struck again in Bukavu, and this time the peacekeeping mission had not reacted well. It now had to regain its credibility. A new mission had been deployed in Haiti, and it was struggling against the gangs of Port-au-Prince. And another mission was now being deployed in Côte d'Ivoire. UN peacekeeping was clearly overstretched. This provided a convenient argument in support of outsourcing UN peacekeeping to regional organizations. The stance was advocated by some permanent members of the Security Council, who wanted the UN to move away from peacekeeping, with the Security Council becoming the ultimate legitimizing body that outsourced its operational tasks to more effective organizations, such as NATO.

Although I agreed that the UN's operational role was ahead of its real capabilities, I did not believe that systematic outsourcing could be the solution. The world was becoming too fractured for that, and it was unlikely that outsourcing operations of real strategic significance to NATO or the European Union would ever become the response of choice. The UN-authorized multinational operations in Iraq and Afghanistan had already begun to discredit such arrangements. In 2006 the rejection by the Lebanese government of a NATO or EU operation confirmed my suspicions. Outsourcing to the African Union might become more frequent—and happened in Darfur in 2004—but it would be more a sign of the lack of interest in Africa among powerful countries than a way to enhance operational effectiveness, since the African Union had significantly less operational capabilities than the United Nations. The other reason why I did not believe in outsourcing was that the distinction between strategic direction and operational implementation that the model implied did not work for peace operations, the success of which is all in the art of implementation. Once the Security Council had authorized a force that was not under UN command, it had, for all practical purposes, lost control over it. This would represent a dramatic weakening of the concept of the United Nations.

However, if the United Nations were to keep an operational role, it had to demonstrate that it could be a capable and competent operator. And that required not only the support of its member states but determined action by the Secretariat itself. Kofi Annan, who had been head of peacekeeping before becoming secretary general, knew very well that the UN Secretariat is almost powerless if it does not have the strong backing of member states. He had experienced firsthand during the crises of the 1990s how member states were happy to blame the United Nations when things went wrong, even when they had a direct responsibility in the failure. But contrary to many UN civil servants, who themselves have a symmetrical tendency to blame member states for their own failures, he knew that there was much room for improvement in the way the Secretariat of the United Nations works. He had commissioned the Brahimi report on reforming peacekeeping not only to confront member states with their responsibilities, but also to spur the UN Secretariat into action.

In 2000 I had been appointed head of peacekeeping precisely to professionalize peacekeeping. It was not enough to respond to the crisis of the day. My job was to build a Department of Peacekeeping that would be more than the sum of its parts, an organization that could perform exceptional tasks with sometimes unexceptional people. And what I had found at the UN was the exact opposite. While there were some very mediocre staff whose only professional ambition seemed to be bureaucratic survival, I had been impressed by the exceptional quality of many others. What was frustrating was that success was generally achieved in spite of the system rather than thanks to it. Stifling rules that only seasoned bureaucrats could understand, and a bureaucratic culture that rewarded passivity and punished risk-taking, meant that strong personalities rarely lasted very long in the UN. And those who had not become discouraged and stayed often completely disregarded the rules, which was also dangerous.

Early on, I had told my staff that the managerial challenge of the Department of Peacekeeping was to nurture the entrepreneurial spirit that had made its reputation while institutionalizing procedures to reflect the enormous growth of peacekeeping. In the jargon of management consultants, the Department of Peacekeeping had to become a learning organization. It needed to become responsible for lessons learned and best practices, instead of remaining isolated and cut off from operational activities. It had to acquire a new authority and become instrumental in developing new processes. To achieve this, we established communities of practice and gradually built a coherent set of procedures through a consultative approach, so that the mass of experience and knowledge of UN peacekeepers could be more effectively captured and shared. One could not rely on the memories of a few talented individuals. At the same time, I felt it was very important to mobilize the energy of individuals. Kofi Annan had established the practice of town hall meetings for the staff, which I amplified and systematized because no reform could be sustained without the full engagement of the staff. Old bureaucracies have a natural "esprit de corps," but the United Nations is a comparatively young organization, and it does not have traditions to carry it forward. I felt the most important dimension of my managerial responsibilities was to make every staff member proud of being a peacekeeper. With pride and self-confidence, the natural tendency to see change as threatening could be overcome. In New York, as in every peacekeeping mission in the world, I worked hard to convince every peacekeeper that he or she was part of an enterprise much bigger than himself or herself. At the same time, I had to win as much support as I could from member states; the UN needed their money, their troops, and their political support. I learned from Kofi Annan that there was no option other than to develop a cooperative relationship, based on the simple idea that we should all be united by the common goal of making peacekeeping successful, even if different countries had different interests. The rich countries that provide more than 80 percent of the budget want their money to be well spent; the developing countries that provide most of the troops want their soldiers to be well-commanded and well-supported; and the members of the Security Council want peacekeeping missions to succeed.

The Nadir of Peacekeeping?

The scandals of sexual abuse that almost brought down the Department of Peacekeeping became the acid test of those simple goals. The worst moment during my time as the head of UN peacekeeping came in 2004 when I learned that peacekeepers were abusing women and girls in the Democratic Republic of the Congo. Not only was peacekeeping accused of failing to do good, it was now accused of doing real harm. There was, sadly, no doubt that the information reaching headquarters was true; it was, if anything, incomplete. This was not an isolated problem, and the more I asked, the more I understood that this was a dirty secret that everybody knew, but nobody was willing to address because it meant challenging the dominant culture of many armies. Even before the Congo reports, instances of abuse had been reported to me, and they had involved armies and police forces from the developed as well as the developing world. I had been shocked to see how countries that claimed to have an impeccable human rights record were usually less than transparent about the behavior of their own nationals, and were quick to exfiltrate them when needed. At the time, I had naively believed such cases were isolated. I was obviously wrong. But to effectively address sexual abuse in peacekeeping, it was necessary to go beyond the hypocritical outrage of states that were only too happy to let the public relations disaster engulf the Secretariat of the United Nations while they were doing very little to enforce discipline in their contingents, for which they had full responsibility. Progress would be made only if member states were ready to accept that the problem was their problem as much as the UN's.

Kofi Annan immediately understood the magnitude of the crisis, and he asked the Jordanian ambassador to the UN to present recommendations. Prince Zeid Ra'ad Zeid al-Hussein, who later became the first UN high commissioner for human rights from a developing country, was the best possible choice. He came from a country that was a major troop contributor; he knew peacekeeping from within, having served in Yugoslavia; and his integrity and thoughtfulness made him one of the most respected ambassadors at the United Nations. It would be hard to dismiss his recommendations. The report he issued in March 2005 provided a roadmap that has only been partly implemented and that still represents, ten years later, the best hope of effectively stopping abuse. But in 2005 some member states were not prepared to take the issue seriously, and the usual cohort of UN-bashers was more interested in using the problem to attack the UN than to actually address it.

When pictures of sexual abuse found their way onto the Internet, the anti-UN campaign intensified, and it was alleged that the UN was now facing its own "Abu Ghraib," similar to the scandal that resulted from the abuses by U.S. soldiers at a prison in Iraq. The comparison was disingenuous, but effective. The unrelenting attacks were doubly painful. They were a reminder of the abominable behavior of some peacekeepers, and that made me angry with those who were a disgrace to the enterprise of peacekeeping. The criticism also confirmed that the UN had some very strong enemies who would never give up and were very systematic in their attacks. I agreed with Jane Lute, my then deputy for management who later joined the Obama administration to become the deputy head of homeland security, that we would continue to be totally transparent, and that building on the excellent recommendations of Ambassador Zeid's report, we would go on the offensive, pledging to take all necessary action to eradicate sexual abuse from UN peacekeeping. I was under no illusion that this would be anything but a long and arduous road, but I was determined not to be intimidated. I believe that in the subsequent years the United Nations did more to stop sexual abuse than it had done in the previous fifty. There would be many setbacks, and when in the middle of the broader UN crisis I gave another press conference where I had to speak about the shameful acts of some of our peacekeepers, the *New York Times* described the situation as the "nadir of peacekeeping." But we gradually turned the crisis into an opportunity to achieve long-overdue reforms. I had far-from-total success, and there actually has been some rollback by member states that are wary of a proactive Secretariat, but the issue is no longer a taboo, and I believe that with political will more progress can be made.

Fighting sexual abuse and professionalizing peacekeeping are essential parts of reforming the United Nations because results and delivery are a foundation of legitimacy. However, as difficult as this enterprise is, it is only a small part of the much bigger undertaking of adapting the UN to the twenty-first century. Managerial and political reforms raise similar questions: Are the member states of the United Nations ready to consider the organization as their organization, as an instrument for achieving bigger ambitions than their national ambitions? Or is the UN just a convenient facade behind which they can hide? Of course, the United Nations will always be both, but in 2004 and 2005 the ambitious reform agenda launched by Kofi Annan became a test of how much states really cared about the organization they had created in 1945. Would they let it wither away into irrelevance through lack of ambition? Would they let it collapse under the weight of operational responsibilities that required a much stronger commitment than what they were prepared to make? As I watched the discussions on reforms—the reform of peacekeeping and then the revision of the UN Charter—unfold in 2004 and 2005, I was increasingly concerned that real commitment was in short supply.

Despite efforts to focus member states on the multiple issues that needed to be addressed, including how the UN approaches so-called "preventive war" and failed states, it was unfortunately not possible to disentangle those new issues from the reform of the Security Council. These issues posed a challenge to the basic initial compromise of the UN Charter. In 1945 the authors of the Charter, drawing on lessons of the failure of the League of Nations, had agreed to give extraordinary powers to a small group of countries, which would form the Security Council, and among those countries to the five permanent members: the principal victors of World War II who would continue their wartime alliance and retain special responsibilities in the maintenance of peace and security. This bold arrangement was made possible by the reaffirmation of the right of self-defense and the principles of sovereignty and noninterference in the internal affairs of a state, which put clear limits on the scope of the Security Council's responsibilities.

Sixty years later, that clarity is blurred by the transformation of the concept of security. Self-defense was a clear criterion when wars were started by armies crossing international borders. But with the threat of weapons of mass destruction and the possibility of state-sponsored terrorism, it would be irresponsible to wait for the clarity of a hostile act. After 9/11, as already noted (see chapter 1 on Afghanistan), the Bush administration had reached the simple conclusion that it should radically expand the concept of self-defense for the benefit of states, thus destroying the precarious balance agreed in 1945 between the sovereignty of states and the authority of the Security Council. A majority of countries were not ready for such a change, but if they were to be consistent, the alternative should be a much-expanded role for the Security Council, which would have to pronounce itself on ambiguous situations that require passing judgment on the conduct of states before their consequences become obvious. Some member states were not ready for that, either, and the implication was that unilateral action by states was unacceptable, but collective action by the Security Council was unlikely. The basic compromise of 1945 was being undermined by the transformation of security.

Likewise, because international security had traditionally focused on the management of power, and on constraining actions of states that might abuse their power, state weakness had not been seen as a threat to peace and security and therefore was not an area requiring the Security Council to act. But the possibility that weak states might become safe havens for terrorist organizations and the destabilizing consequences of civil wars on neighboring countries—massive flows of refugees and proliferation of small arms—have made fragile states a genuine security threat. In an international system based on the sovereignty of states, states are the first line of defense of a stable order. If some of them lose the capacity to exercise their sovereignty, the whole system is at risk. There again, the implications were wide-ranging, and they were reflected in the ever-expanding responsibilities of peacekeeping operations, which were increasingly engaged in helping shore up the fragile sovereignty of states in distress. This put an additional burden on the Security Council because it had to decide on the scope of such ambitious undertakings, which by definition encroached on traditional concepts of sovereignty. In fact, for the new generation of peace operations, as well as for prevention—from intrusive inspections to preemptive action—the maintenance of a rule-based international order required that the Security Council fill the gap that had opened with a shifting concept of international security. It was unrealistic to expect the broader community of nations to accept such an expanded role if the composition of the Security Council did not evolve. However, the reform of the composition of the council was an extremely difficult undertaking, and efforts in Kofi Annan's high-level panel on reform to propose a creative solution for semi-permanent seats failed to garner the support of Germany, which was not represented on the panel and remained steadfast in its desire for a permanent seat.

These fundamental issues could hardly be addressed effectively as storm clouds were gathering over the UN. The real storm came in November and December 2004. There were growing rumors that the panel appointed by Kofi Annan, and chaired by Paul Volcker, to investigate the UN-administered oil-for-food program in Iraq would issue a damning indictment of the UN

Secretariat. And it did, even though the responsibility of member states was no less engaged than in the case of sexual abuse. Actually, all Iraq contracts— for exports of oil as well as imports of goods—had been authorized by the Security Council, and they were scrutinized by the council's five permanent members. The strategic goal had been to maintain sanctions against the Iraq of Saddam Hussein, while trying to minimize the impact on the civilian population. The Security Council's approval was requested to ensure that revenues from oil exports were controlled, and that no imports with a potential military use were authorized. Such administered trade with a dictatorial regime was bound to create opportunities for corruption, as companies importing oil from Iraq would compete for oil quotas while companies trying to export their goods to Iraq would try to increase their market share. Members of the Security Council with knowledge of markets and intelligence assets were in the best position to uncover corruption, but they wanted to protect their own companies, and their goal was to deprive Iraq of military capabilities, not to fight corruption.

The Volcker commission uncovered many such instances of corruption, but found only one instance of possible corruption involving the UN Secretariat, and it was based on circumstantial evidence.[2] In any case, it should have been reassuring that an inquiry that cost some $30 million and examined a $60 billion program, would incriminate the UN Secretariat only for the possibility of a $160,000 bribe. The real blow, one that almost toppled the secretary general, was the revelation by Fox News that the son of Kofi Annan had worked for a firm involved in the oil-for-food program and might have used his father's name to further his business interests. The revelations hurt Kofi Annan, though we would later learn more details about the conduct of his son, who had not committed any crime, and had not taken any bribe, but who had not told the whole truth to his father, including the fact that he had continued to be paid by the firm involved in the oil-for-food program until 2004. This revelation put Kofi Annan in the worst possible position. To defend his integrity and the reputation of the United Nations, he would have to admit not only the improprieties of his son, but also that his son had been less than truthful with him.

---

2. Benon Sevan, a larger-than-life Cypriot who had been the head of the program, had deposited $160,000 in cash in his bank account, which gave the appearance of a bribe. To this day, I, like many others who knew him, find it hard to believe that a man who had been known throughout his career for his total commitment to the UN, and who was managing billions of dollars, accepted a bribe of $160,000. He has always denied any guilt.

I had reminded the secretary general of the speech that Dag Hammarskjöld had given before the General Assembly after Soviet leader Nikita Khrushchev had called for his resignation as secretary general in October 1960. I learned afterwards from Lakhdar Brahimi that he had had the same thought, bringing a copy of the speech to the secretary general as the scandal around his son threatened his position. Dag Hammarskjöld, as quoted by Brian Urquhart, said:

> It is not the Soviet Union or, indeed any other big powers who need the United Nations for their protection; it is all the others. In this sense, the Organization is first of all *their* Organization and I deeply believe in the wisdom with which they will be able to use it and guide it. I shall remain in my post during the term of my office as a servant of the Organization in the interest of all those other nations, as long as *they* wish me to do so.

We were all agreed that the secretary general should not resign, but Kofi was determined to do what was good for the institution. Many of us were left with the impression that he was not willing to fight, and I was surprised in December 2004 to read a *New York Times* op-ed column on Kofi Annan with the title "America's man at the United Nations." Its author, the great journalist William Shawcross, meant well and wanted to help, but I did not think that the position of the secretary general should be saved by pandering to a big power, as powerful as it was. Of course, the situation had changed since 1960: Dag Hammarskjöld could call on smaller powers because the East-West confrontation had neutralized the big powers, while at the end of 2004 the United States looked like the only remaining superpower. By early 2005 the secretary general had recovered his balance, partially as the result of the UN's prominent role in the international response to the Asian tsunami in late 2004, and there were clear signs that the worst of the confrontation between the United States and the UN was over. Kofi Annan had just completed a European tour during which British prime minister Tony Blair, who during that period was always a good barometer of sentiment in Washington, had warmly welcomed him.

Searching for the UN's Role

Meanwhile, the structural issues affecting the future of the UN had not gone away, and the steady expansion of peacekeeping was a source of growing worries. At the end of January 2005, I solemnly and publicly expressed my concerns. Not only was peacekeeping growing much too quickly, but the member states were repeating the mistakes that had almost killed UN peacekeeping in the 1990s, adding new tasks without giving the resources. The rapid expansion of mandates had begun to expose the lack of conceptual clarity about what needed to be accomplished in these countries, and one of the consequences was a lack of resources for additional tasks. I had a difficult exchange with my compatriots in January when they tabled a resolution requesting our mission in Côte d'Ivoire to enforce a weapons embargo but without giving it any additional capacities.

At the same time, as the head of peacekeeping, I strongly believed that the unique contribution of the United Nations was political: It is that place where conflicting views of the world clash and where compromise can be reached. The irreplaceable and immensely difficult role of the secretary general is to facilitate such compromise while remaining anchored on principles. I admired the critical roles played by the High Commissioner for Refugees or UNICEF, but I did not think the UN could survive if it abandoned its political role. And while in 2004 some NATO advocates continued to argue for a leading role for NATO in peace operations, there was no real consensus, including among NATO members, on a new relationship between NATO and the UN. Without a defining threat, NATO's strategic rationale had been weakened, and it could not transform itself into an alliance of democracies. Some of its members had very different views on what promoting democracy meant, and some major democracies would never want to be associated with NATO. But the United States was uncomfortable asserting its global influence through power alone, and even with an administration that appeared very skeptical of multilateral organizations, Washington was looking for structures through which it could exercise its leadership. Among Democrats as well as Republicans, the dream of a United Nations that would play the role of an alliance of democracies, subcontracting its operational tasks to a Western organization, was never abandoned. I was convinced that such a course would lead to a dead end: the divisions of its membership would quickly paralyze the UN if it simply became the rubber stamp of Western powers. For me, the real challenge was never to lose sight of the principles that make the United Nations more than a practical arrangement among major powers, and yet, without giving up, to work with countries that do not really agree with the inspiration of the Charter. The risk, of course, was always that accommodation is habit-forming, and the UN can lose its moral compass as it compromises on tactics to salvage lofty but controversial goals.

By 2005 the position of the secretary general at the helm of the United Nations was no longer under threat, as it had been at the end of 2004, but a year of damaging reports on the management of the oil-for-food program had taken its toll. The Volcker commission had not uncovered significant corruption inside the UN, but it had exposed a poorly run organization, incapable of professionally managing a huge program like oil-for-food. The momentum that existed in 2001, when Kofi Annan and the UN had won the Nobel Prize, was long gone. The 2003 bombing in Baghdad, the sexual abuse and oil-for-food scandals had left the United Nations wounded, physically and morally, and there was not much political momentum, in the Secretariat or among member states. Kofi Annan issued his own report, "In Larger Freedom," in March 2005, inspired by the report of the high-level panel, which had been issued in the middle of the oil-for-food crisis. "In Larger Freedom" was an attempt at compromise between the expectations of the United States and the expectations of less-powerful countries. Loosely drawing on the famous 1941 speech of President Franklin Roosevelt on the "four freedoms" (freedom of speech, freedom of religion, freedom from want, freedom from fear), it tried to offer something to every constituency. The elegant construction had the merit of providing a coherent framework of reform, but it was a vision that owed more to a moderate American liberalism based on enlightened self-interest than to cogent principles around which the entire world could rally. And, indeed, the world was now much too divided for a principled approach to provide a rallying point. I had deep doubts that the liberal pragmatic approach had a greater chance of success. I was afraid that the UN might lose its moral standing without gaining genuine American support, even if the Bush administration now seemed to have reconciled itself to the idea that the United Nations might not be completely useless. In my first meeting with Steve Hadley, who replaced Condoleezza Rice as the national security adviser in early 2005, I was struck by his genuine interest in peacekeeping. The triumphalism of "mission accomplished" in Iraq was gone, and it was clear that the U.S. administration was looking to the United Nations for help in the many crises that were not a primary interest of Washington but could not be ignored.

Despite these promising signs, the relationship between the UN and United States was dealt a blow in August 2005 when John Bolton was appointed U.S. ambassador to the United Nations. Bolton did not hide his total opposition to the very idea of the United Nations. He lost no time in making his best effort to wreck the reform process that was under way and undermine the 2005 World Summit that was intended to be the culmination of these efforts. As the summit declaration was in the process of being finalized, he introduced hundreds of amendments to the final declaration, which infuriated diplomats who saw it as an act of sabotage. For a few days, there were doubts that the summit would agree on a declaration, and the whole effort could have ended in disaster if Kofi Annan had not reached out to Condoleezza

Rice, then the secretary of state, going around a U.S. ambassador who had a very sharp intellect but no interest in finding solutions unless they were his solutions.

The summit declaration that was finally agreed was surprisingly ambitious. It reflected the overall architecture of the reform promoted by the secretary general, acknowledging that the three "pillars" of the United Nations were development, peace and security, and human rights. It endorsed several proposals made by the secretary general, notably the creation of a peace-building commission and a peace-building fund, which would focus on post-conflict recovery, thus creating a bridge between development and peace and security; and the creation of a Human Rights Council, which would replace the widely discredited Human Rights Commission. The acknowledgment, in a document agreed by the General Assembly, of the "responsibility to protect populations from genocide, war crimes, ethnic cleansing and crimes against humanity" was one of the most remarkable features of the declaration. It was hailed at the time as a major breakthrough: never before had the international community taken on such a responsibility. The language reflected the difficult negotiations that had been necessary; the primary responsibility to protect lay with each individual state, and the international community should as a priority help states exercise their responsibility. If the international community were to take action, it should do it "through the United Nations" and by peaceful means. It is only if states were "manifestly failing to protect their population" that the international community might consider, "on a case-by-case basis," taking collective action through the Security Council, "including chapter VII" (enforcement). It appeared, at least for a moment, that the members of the United Nations managed to overcome the toxic environment to identify urgent changes to the UN's structure and aims in response to changes in the nature of conflict.

Yet more than nine years later, it is becoming clear that the declaration of 2005 was ahead of the international consensus, as was—and still is—the universal declaration of human rights of 1948. I have often been asked if another Rwanda genocide would be possible today. Probably yes, because moral clarity generally comes too late, and in the confusion of a rapidly deteriorating situation, unless the interests of great powers are directly affected there is little appetite for action, although early action might save hundreds of thousands, and possibly millions, of lives. It has been said that a decisive action against Hitler—whose plans had been clearly outlined in *Mein Kampf*—when he reoccupied the Rhine region in 1936 would have prevented the holocaust and World War II. And in Rwanda, according to General Roméo Dallaire, who commanded the tiny peacekeeping force there in 1994, a limited reinforcement of a few thousand soldiers might also have prevented the genocide.

The reluctance of nations to take action reflects the lack of domestic support for foreign engagements, but also a genuine uncertainty about what needs to be done. I witnessed several situations that could spiral into extreme violence. In the Ituri Province of the Democratic Republic of the Congo, an international deployment was agreed, which may well have prevented massive killings. In Côte d'Ivoire, the ethnic hatred propagated by the media was reminiscent of the pre-genocide incitement by *Radio Mille Collines* in Rwanda, and no emergency deployment took place. Violence occurred, but it remained limited, and no genocidal violence happened. In Darfur, the reference to genocide focused the international debate on military action, for which no resources were available, while political negotiations became less of a priority. In Libya, the growing chaos has cast a doubt on the wisdom of the intervention. In Syria, the paralysis of the international community reflects its divisions but also the difficulty of identifying an effective political response that will consolidate a legitimate center of power around which all, or even most, Syrians can rally. And in the many situations that fall short of the extreme violence envisaged by the 2005 World Summit declaration, but where civilians have nevertheless become the main targets of warring parties, the loose reference to the "responsibility to protect" has often raised the suspicion of governments. There is a certain tragic irony in the fact that the countries in which the debate about the responsibility to protect is most active are those least likely to actually deploy troops in conflicts that may not correspond to the definition of the summit declaration but where the civilian population nevertheless needs some protection. Meanwhile, the countries that actually provide the troops and offer a modicum of protection are often those that are the most suspicious of the concept of responsibility to protect.

The gap between rhetoric and action will reinforce the view of those who believe that the United Nations is nothing more than a useless talking shop. And indeed, some of the reforms that were enacted in 2006, the last year of Kofi Annan's second term, have shown their limits. The Human Rights Council, in particular, has not had much impact, and in many countries human rights have regressed rather than progressed in recent years.

Actually, the most powerful countries, while they may agree on some universal principles, are moving away from the vision they endorsed in 1945 and now seem less and less prepared to voluntarily limit their own power. After the Second World War, the United States, although it was at its highest relative power—producing half of the world's wealth, extending its credit to an industrialized world destroyed by war, and enjoying a monopoly of nuclear weapons—nevertheless decided to bind itself through an international treaty, and was the most influential actor behind the creation of the United Nations.

A few years later, the Europeans, who had invented the modern nation state, invented a new political form: the European Community, later transformed into the European Union. Today the United Nations as well as the European Union are both facing institutional crises as they find it increasingly difficult to reform and adjust to new realities. There is no realistic prospect of a reform of the Security Council in the foreseeable future; the countries that have long been candidates for a permanent seat are gradually losing hope. But for most of them it is less a priority today than it was in 2005. As for the "middle countries," those whose size precludes any possibility of joining the Security Council as permanent members but who have traditionally been active at the United Nations, they may be satisfied to have a seat at the table of the G-20, even if it is an informal arrangement. Powerful countries can live with gentlemen's agreements and informal arrangements.

The consequence is that formal institutions have a diminishing base of support. There clearly is much less ambition and confidence in institutions than there was in 1945, and the relevance of states as the building blocks of an international order is weakening. Twenty years ago I wrote about "the end of the nation-state." Certainly, a growing number of issues cannot be dealt with at the level of the state: states are either too big to relate to their people, or too small—even the biggest and most powerful—to provide answers to challenges that have become global. And yet, national sovereignty is a concept that continues to elicit deep emotions and attachment, and each new state that joins the United Nations is a confirmation of that. The concept of national sovereignty is a great equalizer, and in a world of enormous imbalances, it is not just the dictators who are attached to sovereignty. The people of poor and powerless countries are also attached to it, because they see sovereignty as their ultimate protection against the rich and powerful, who could otherwise de facto recolonize them.

The political space that the UN is allowed to occupy is thus shrinking as the challenges it faces move further away from those its creators had in mind in 1945. The UN must fight on several fronts to maintain its relevance and credibility. It faces the disappointment of those who would like it to be a value-driven organization rather than one that seems to seek awkward compromises, and it must counter the hostility of Americans who resent an organization whose accountability to foreign states—many of which are not democratic—can be seen as a challenge to the sovereignty of the American people. The UN also generates resentment among emerging powers that believe it is freezing an outdated status quo, and it has to suffer the wary indifference of the many countries that suspect the UN Secretariat is a convenient cover behind which a small set of countries can exercise their waning power. As a Frenchman, I was always aware that many countries would have great difficulty believing that my loyalty was to the UN, and not to France, a permanent member of the Security Council whose influence and power were so enormously—and in the view of many, unfairly—boosted by that status. Dag Hammarskjöld's vision of a Secretariat that would acknowledge the realities of power, but would stand up for those who have no power, now has little support. Twenty-five years after the end of the cold war, the spirit that inspired the grand visions of 1945, and that Boutros-Ghali's 1992 Agenda for Peace tried to revive, is gone. Even the more cautious approach of Kofi Annan seems overambitious now.

Moreover, the United Nations does not have the institutional and cultural foundations of a nation state. Its institutional memory lies with the international civil servants who carry forward the dream of the founders. From Ralph Bunche and Brian Urquhart, who were both in San Francisco, to Sergio de Mello or Lakhdar Brahimi, the UN has been shaped by individuals who make the best of imperfect arrangements. They are more important in the United Nations than in a national bureaucracy, because they are the ones who carry the flame.

It is quite revealing that the flagship reform of Ban Ki-moon has been a management reform: the breakup of the department of peacekeeping operations, which by 2007 was considered too big and possibly too powerful. Ban Ki-moon knows that legitimacy depends on effectiveness as much as on process. By putting the emphasis on a UN that delivers, he may hope to regain some of the ground lost by the UN. He has been blessed with a U.S. administration that genuinely wants the UN to work. But like his predecessor, he still has to manage the considerable gap that exists between the vision that the United States and Western democracies have of the world and the vision of most other countries. That gap has not narrowed in recent years, and emerging powers, even when they are democratic, are wary of being associated with a Western world that is still perceived as exploitative, if not colonial. Can the secretary general bridge that gap? Could he help create a coalition of diverse countries championing the UN, as was the case in the 1950s when Dag Hammarskjöld could claim the support of Sweden, India, Canada, and Yugoslavia? The enterprise is difficult. The lower the profile of the secretary general, the greater the risk that he will be seen as irrelevant; but the higher the public profile, the greater the risk that he will be seen as inconsistent and that expectations will not be met after having been unduly raised. Every secretary general has to grapple with that dilemma, and the diversity of styles is just another illustration of the conflicting signals sent by the international community: a secretary general is expected to lead the way, but he will be quickly reminded of his limitations when disagreement occurs.

My eight years at the UN almost perfectly overlapped with the two terms of President George W. Bush, and that overlap may taint my vision of the UN and its ability to adapt to face new challenges. A genuine reform, which would adapt the creaky machinery of 1945 to the twenty-first century, would require not just the acquiescence of the United States but its active engagement, as well as a joint effort by China and the United States to build common ground. The Europeans, who are proud of their willingness to constrain national power through the rule of law, who together pay some 40 percent of the budget of the United Nations, and who are by far the most generous among rich countries in providing development aid, could in theory also play a major role in promoting a reform of the United Nations. But to be able to bridge the divide of mistrust that blocks reform, they would have to be more open and reach out more effectively to a world that is increasingly un-European if not anti-European. They would also have to sort out their own divisions on the reform of the Security Council. Today there is no enduring alliance of the big powers as in 1945, and no solid coalition for reform among middle-income countries. And yet, I believe that institutional reform remains necessary. Informal arrangements are fine for the powerful, who can rely on their power, but the weak and powerless will always depend on the equalizing authority of the law and of formal arrangements. Gentlemen's agreements are just not enough when it comes to issues of life and death. Institutions still matter, but there is no agreement on how to reform them.

A world in which the United Nations would gradually be marginalized, even if it could count on the informal leadership of twenty or so countries, would be a throwback to the time of the concert of powers. It is a system that has been tried repeatedly, and that has repeatedly failed and ended in war. True institutional reform should not be abandoned.

But for a true reform of the United Nations to succeed, states themselves will have to adjust to new forms of conflict and new threats. At the heart of this issue is the fact that the UN, an organization of states designed to prevent war between states, is poorly equipped to respond to the much deeper problem that exists in states where power is elusive, as is the case in many countries currently on the agenda of the Security Council. Here the main challenge is to build state institutions, to create state power rather than constrain it. This is a much more challenging and long-term task, and despite important efforts—such as the civilian capacities review, which I led in 2011—the UN has enormous difficulties filling that vacuum and providing real help to fragile states. Even the most powerful states are struggling with how to respond to the global fragmentation of power that pits state-based institutions against the threats of small groups or even individuals operating on their own. We see this clearly in the evolution of the nature of terrorism and in the efforts of strong states to counter it.

The global challenge is no longer only about managing centers of power but also in building them in fragile states. We see this manifested clearly in the work of peacekeepers deployed throughout some of the world's most insecure territories. In its earliest form peacekeeping sought to manage states' power, but now its task is to help build it from scratch. This is a profoundly new and ambiguous task that the UN and its member states must address together. There is a continuing lack of clarity about how to go about such ambitious work, and while the international community's inability to act in Syria stems in part from divisions among the great powers, the much deeper issue is the inability to identify the political response to underpin an end to the conflict. An enormous responsibility comes with intervening in the lives of others, but ethically we can no longer engage half-heartedly, nor do we have the luxury of washing our hands of problems that occur in seemingly far-off lands.

EPILOGUE

As I am writing an epilogue to this book, the crisis in Syria continues unabated. Despite the loss of more than 150,000 civilian lives, the displacement of nearly 8 million people, and the use of chemical weapons, the international community has difficulty agreeing on how to achieve peace and support a political process to bring the bloody war to an end.

The inability of the international community to come to an agreement on the path forward is influenced by, and stands in contrast to, the 2011 intervention in Libya. Then, after agreement in the Security Council, NATO planes bombed forces loyal to Muammar Qaddafi. Contrary to the environment in Syria or even to 1999, when there was no agreement in the Security Council to authorize NATO to bomb Serbia to stop Slobodan Milošević's ethnic cleansing in Kosovo, this time the Security Council authorized use of force "to protect civilians." The authorization was broader than the establishment of a no-fly zone because it legitimized use of force to support a strategic goal—protecting civilians—and not just a tactical goal—preventing use of aircraft to harm civilians. Supporters of liberal interventionism celebrated the decision as the first concrete implementation of the "responsibility to protect," which was endorsed at the 2005 summit of the United Nations. Yet the strong stance taken by NATO countries prompted backlash from other members of the Security Council who believed that NATO activities extended beyond their expectations. The rapid crumbling of international consensus on Libya has left a lasting impact on international negotiations around the response to Syria.

The example of Libya shows how the initial moral clarity of a decision may vanish as a crisis unfolds, and we know only in hindsight what was the right decision. The prospect of massive killings in Benghazi if Qaddafi's forces had overrun it, and the potential chilling impact on the Arab Spring of a Qaddafi victory, provided strong reasons to intervene. Yet in Syria, even more massive civilian killings and the negative impact on regional stability and the Arab Spring have not proven compelling enough for a UN intervention. The decision to use force also yields a high degree of uncertainty about the results. The action to save lives in Benghazi has not been followed immediately by a protracted and inconclusive civil war on the scale of the one in Syria, but the deteriorating situation in Libya raises questions about the legitimacy of the decision to intervene. Likewise, had a swift intervention in Syria led to an even more intense conflict and greater loss of lives, the decision would have lost its initial moral clarity.

Such uncertainty raises hard questions: While the international community may be able to reach a consensus on what it does not accept—another genocide, for example—it finds it much more difficult to agree on what it wants. The international community does not have the cohesiveness of a national community. The word community is actually a misnomer when applied to that motley group formed by 193 very diverse nations. And although the Security Council remains an arena where the game of power is played, adopting twice as many resolutions in the twenty years since the end of the cold war as it had in the preceding forty-five years, this new activism does not reflect a genuine emerging consensus, even after the momentous resolutions on Libya. Actually, most of the national powers that are expected to shape tomorrow's world did not embrace, although they did not prevent, the council's activism on Libya. Brazil, Germany, and India joined China and Russia in abstaining on the resolution that authorized the broad use of force in Libya. Although there are considerable differences in the cases of the "preventive war" against Iraq launched by the Bush administration without the Security Council's authorization, the "humanitarian" intervention authorized by the Security Council against Libya, and the forceful action to uphold the result of elections in Côte d'Ivoire in 2011, the caution of Brazil, Germany, and India reflects deep and widely shared concerns about the use of force and intervention. If those concerns were to be vindicated by ultimately disappointing outcomes in Libya or Côte d'Ivoire, and if the Security Council continues to be paralyzed on Syria, its activism in the spring of 2011 could then mark a peak of collective action rather than the beginning of a new trend. National views would assert themselves more bluntly, confirming that when it comes to the politics of intervention, the international community has no common vision, and the Security Council reflects that ambivalence.

In fact, the more ambitious the tasks, the more politically ambiguous are the resolutions of the Security Council. At the beginning of the decade, the

Brahimi report had called for "clear and achievable" mandates for peace-keeping missions. As the person who would have responsibility for implementing those mandates, that was a recommendation I could only applaud. But I also knew that Brahimi had put an impossible demand on the council, since in the absence of an international community capable of forging a genuine consensus any agreement in the council would either be minimal or unclear. Security Council resolutions are ambiguous for a reason: There is rarely in the Security Council a genuine strategic agreement on policy, and the talent of diplomats is to find words that will cover up the differences but do not really provide clear operational answers. The member states of the United Nations are satisfied with that state of affairs, since it shifts the responsibility away from them.

What to do then? Should an international civil servant take the easiest route, and have a minimalist interpretation of the ambiguous directions given by the Security Council? This may be the safest course bureaucratically because the lack of interest of major powers in some situations means that the Secretariat will have little support if things go wrong, and can easily become a scapegoat. The old hands in the Secretariat knew that very well; they remembered how lonely they had been when the Rwandan genocide happened. Their instinct was to reinforce the natural tendency of any bureaucracy to be risk-averse.

My inclination was the opposite. I did not think the Secretariat should hide behind the authority of the Security Council and be a passive implementer, all the more so as I was given considerable space to act by the two secretary generals I served. I dutifully informed them of all my decisions, but I do not recall that we ever had any significant difference on an issue for which I was responsible. I always felt a moral duty to occupy all the political space that I was given. The divisions of the council, and sometimes the indifference of major powers, open a political space for the Secretariat of the United Nations. It actually has much more power than is generally assumed, and except for the few crises where a major power has a strategic interest, the Secretariat can often be in the driver's seat, like a sixth permanent member of the council. Although I knew that the most common sin of an international bureaucracy is self-righteousness, and that it is easy to wrap the natural appetite of any bureaucracy for self-aggrandizement in the lofty flag of grand ideals, I felt my duty was to make choices where they had been studiously avoided, and to bring clarity where there was none. Otherwise, lives might be lost, and confusion could lead to debacle. Not making choices is a choice by default.

But who was I to make choices that would impact the lives of others? On what basis would I make them? The framework in which national civil servants operate makes such choices less difficult. The reference to a national interest—perceived or real—is a solid foundation, and even when the law is ambiguous, even when the margin for appreciation of a national civil servant is broad, he has the comfort of being answerable to his nation and its legitimate authorities. There is no such reassurance when the ultimate authority is an ambiguous and divided Security Council. As an international civil servant, I often felt I was on my own, which had its advantages, but was also a heavy moral burden.

In most situations in which I was involved, much less force was used than in Libya or Côte d'Ivoire, but the "ethical gamble" was the same: I was never sure that the moral clarity of the initial engagement would still be there at the end, and I was always aware of the ethical uncertainty of international intervention in support of peace. The fog of peace is as difficult to navigate as the fog of war. I took Satan's warning in Lesek Kolakowski's short story "King Herod, or the Misery of the Moralist" as a cautionary tale: "Whether it is your actions or your intentions, they can be judged only once everything is really over. The moral dimension of any action is—contrary to its technical aspect— totally unpredictable, and can be well understood and assessed only after the fact."[1] Of course, the fact that the ethical value of the decisions we make will be known only once their ultimate consequences have unfolded is not unique to peacekeeping. All political leaders who make strategic decisions have to confront the fact that their outcomes will be greatly influenced by the decisions of other intelligent—or not so intelligent—human beings, whose intentions we may try to predict but about which we can never have certainty. That is what differentiates the world of human actions, including politics, from the laws of nature. That also is why strategy is such an important and difficult part of politics. Indeed, any position of responsibility, in whatever context, has moral implications. The general who puts the lives of his troops at risk in an operation, the regulator who authorizes a particular product, the judge who determines a sentence—all face moral choices.

International intervention is, however, of a different nature. Our actions in other countries will affect the lives of other human communities much more than they will affect our own. We are not the ones who will have to live with the consequences. This is a dangerous situation, which carries great moral hazard. We are not as bad as the gods of Shakespeare, in the words of the duke of Gloucester:

1. *Tales from the Kingdom of Lailonia and the Key to Heaven*, translated by Agnieszka Kolakowska and Salvator Attanasio (University of Chicago Press, 1989).

"As flies to wanton boys are we to the gods,
　　They kill us for their sport."

— *King Lear*, act IV, scene 1

We do not want to kill, and as UN peacekeepers, we seldom kill. We want peace. But we sometimes act like the gods of Greek tragedies, unable to let the humans take charge, and yet incapable of steadily holding their hands. We intervene in the affairs of humanity, but only at a distance, whether it is with bombs expected to tip the balance against a Libyan dictator, or through more benign engagements in fragile countries, where we often oscillate between arrogance and weakness. When one looks at some of the biggest investments of the international community in the last ten years—Afghanistan and Congo, for example—one cannot but be distressed by its fickleness. Grand plans were elaborated and immense hopes were generated among the people we had suddenly decided to help. But hope was often dashed, and we then faced resentment if not outright hostility, while on the home front, ambition has been replaced by a pressing desire to pack up and leave.

That fickleness is a symptom of the very particular moment in the history of the world we have reached and explains why the decisions and questions I faced as an international civil servant are really the questions and dilemmas for all concerned citizens. The circulation of people and ideas has sufficiently unified our planet that there is an emerging awareness of our common destiny, but that awareness does not really translate into shared values, let alone shared emotions. Contrary to our ancestors, we hear about distant catastrophes almost as they happen, and images of foreign wars penetrate our peaceful households through television and the Internet. Just as our ancestors, however, we are more concerned by what happens to our families than to people we do not know, by what happens to our fellow countrymen than to foreigners. There is nothing wrong with that very human feeling. Kinship, proximity, and emotions matter, although we sometimes pretend otherwise. But that simple fact has serious implications for the politics of intervention, and international civil servants have to be aware of the fragile political base on which their actions are based.

Politicians are buffeted by opposing winds. They know that the spectacle of people in distress generates sympathy, but they also know that sympathy to be shallow, and that their domestic constituencies have little patience for distant ventures unless they can be convinced that nonintervention might have bad consequences for their own lives. Troop contributors from developing countries, which today provide the bulk of peacekeeping troops, are reluctant to take the increasing risks that the rich countries, which pay for peacekeeping, would want them to carry, while the experience of Afghanistan and Iraq has further eroded the willingness of developed countries to engage ground troops in foreign interventions. Most Western powers now doubt the wisdom of putting troops on the ground to shape the future of another country, and from Congo to Haiti, the enterprise of state-building appears more difficult than was ever anticipated. There is little appetite today for so-called multidimensional peacekeeping operations, and there are growing doubts about the realism of ambitious agendas—skeptically described as "social engineering"—in fragile countries. The world is confused, and its ambiguous stance reflects those contradictory impulses: a growing awareness of our global condition, but increasing caution in global engagements.

Where then is the compass that will guide an international civil servant, or for that matter an informed citizen engaged in international affairs? I knew very well that my own appointment was a consequence of the status of France as a permanent member of the Security Council, and that I had been chosen because of my nationality more than my values. But I also knew that the UN Charter instructed me not to "seek or receive instructions from any government or from any other authority external to the Organization." I was grateful to France that it generally respected the Charter, which requests member states "not to seek to influence" staff. But would the Charter of the United Nations be enough of a guide? The inspiration of the Charter was the Second World War, and the chain of events that led to it.

Today's world is very different. Moments of absolute moral clarity, like the fight against Hitler, are a historical exception, and even in such moments many decisions that need to be taken at the strategic level—the alliance with Stalin, the choice of priorities in targeting or opening fronts—had little or no moral clarity. Today, not only is the world all the shades of grey, but assessing the ultimate consequences of our actions is becoming even more difficult because the world is more interconnected than ever. What limited actions we take in a particular place are quickly known worldwide, but that universal exposure produces different interpretations and reactions in different lands, and we have little influence over those responses, which enormously complicates the ethics of an already difficult strategic calculus. As the world becomes more aware of the strategic and moral uncertainties of a global stance, the temptation grows to give up, or withdraw into the cocoon that we know, or to lash out in the vain hope that we can decisively shape the world.

We are at the end of a long cycle: Over the last 500 years, the world gradually became a single strategic space, and that unification was brought first by Europe, and then by its creation, the United States. The European colonial enterprise came to an end after the Second World War. But the United States replaced

Europe as the great strategic unifier, and when the Soviet Union collapsed, it seemed briefly that the universalist agenda had finally won. That was the time when the American political scientist Francis Fukuyama could claim that history—understood as a battle of ideas—had ended. "The end of History" that he described did not mean that the world had entered into a lethargic peace and that there would be no more wars. But there seemed to be no viable alternative vision to the dominant narrative of the triumph of markets and democracy. I was always uneasy with that triumphalist vision,[2] but I was willing to espouse it in 1989, as I was listening to Lech Walesa. In the following two decades, activists have tried to maintain that confidence, and the democratization agenda of liberal interventionists reflects that optimism. But the reality I observed at the United Nations and in the many crises I was involved with is very different. The limits of national power make national politics less relevant, but global issues do not produce global politics, because the world is just too heterogeneous to be unified by a single conversation.

That absence of a global perspective is what makes the debate about international intervention so important. At the very moment when the world is less and less unified by ideas, it faces more and more global challenges, and sometimes threats that the traditional order cannot cope with. An international system based on the sovereignty of states cannot be sustained if some states are too weak to assert their sovereignty and be the trusted custodians of their own people. And when that trust is lost a vicious circle sets in, which further erodes the capacity of the state to serve its people. The multiplication of "interventions," from Congo to Libya, should therefore not come as a surprise. Nor should it be a surprise that these interventions have generated contradictory interpretations. Do the interventions reflect mounting national fears on the part of those who inhabit islands of peace and stability, or an emerging global responsibility? The United Nations, as an organization based on the old order of states, has no option other than to try to reconcile the two interpretations and harness national sentiments and interests for the service of global goals.

As a servant of the United Nations, I found myself in the middle of that battle. I could not realistically pretend to ignore states, but my ethical duty was always to think first of the people for whom the Charter was written. I felt that in the never-ending tension between the rights of the people and the sovereignty of states, the Secretariat of the United Nations should always be on the side of the people. Even so, it can be only a few short steps ahead of the prevailing consensus of states, taking initiatives that will rally support if they end

2. Jean-Marie Guéhenno, *The End of the Nation-State* (University of Minnesota Press, 2000), translated from the French, *La Fin de la Démocratie* (Flammarion, 1993).

up being successful. It should not push its luck. Any failure may trigger a backlash beyond the specific circumstances of the crisis and destroy the fragile achievements of the first decade of the new millennium.

The world is indeed evolving, and the United Nations should do more than accompany that evolution. But there is nothing preordained in that evolution; it is slow, and can be easily reversed. Often lost in the fog of an elusive peace, I thus struggled to reconcile a sense of global responsibility with the recognition that there is no such thing as an international community. I also had to manage the moral ambiguity of the increasingly assertive, and sometimes reckless, engagement of the international community in the "life of others." I often thought of the humanitarian principle: do no harm.

And yet, amidst so many tragic situations, I never thought we had the right to stay away, and I refuse to accept that we stand still in the face of mass atrocities. I believe that we have to choose engagement, and engagement comes with high risks: for the troops, for the reputations of the institutions, and most of all for the citizens on whose behalf we intervene. Between the extremes of isolationist denial and unrealistic universalism lies a very narrow path for the UN, but also for all concerned and informed citizens. It is doubtful that an elusive "international community" will have the will, sophistication, and capacity to reshape human communities, and the tasks at hand—building or rebuilding centers of power in fragile states—are more difficult than we initially believed. Our universalism must therefore be tempered by caution: we should approach our responsibilities with humility and set clear limits to our agenda. We must be modest, but not defeatist.

That is why I led peacekeepers into actions whose ultimate consequences would remain beyond their control, and I accept the moral hazard of such actions. When I have doubts, I can whisper a poem by T. S. Eliot read in a booming voice by Kishore Mandyan, an Indian who had worked in the UN mission in Yugoslavia, in Zagreb, the day when Kofi Annan inaugurated a monument to the many peacekeepers who died in the Yugoslav wars:

A man's destination is his own village,
His own fire, and his wife's cooking;
To sit in front of his own door at sunset
And see his grandson, and his neighbours's grandson
Playing in the dust together.

Scarred but secure, he has many memories
Which return at the hour of conversation,
(The warm or the cool hour, according to the climate)

Of foreign men, who fought in foreign places,
Foreign to each other.

A man's destination is not his destiny,
Every country is home to one man
And exile to another. Where a man dies bravely
At one with his destiny, that soil is his.
Let his village remember.

This was not your land, or ours: but a village in the Midlands,
And one in the Five Rivers, may have the same graveyard.
Let those who go home tell the same story of you:
Of action with a common purpose, action
None the less fruitful if neither you nor we
Know, until the moment after death,
What is the fruit of action.

— T. S. Eliot, *Collected Poems 1909–1962*

ACKNOWLEDGMENTS

When I started writing *The Fog of Peace*, I decided that I should write it as a memoir, to convey the uncertainties and confusion of action and avoid the misleading clarity of hindsight. At the same time, I wanted the book to contribute to a broader discussion on the imperfect art of crisis management. When I took my position at the United Nations in 2000, I knew that the events that I would witness might be of interest in the future, but I was also aware that memory tends to reinterpret and reorganize the past. That is why I decided to record in small notebooks events, meetings, conversations, and thoughts that I had at the time. The eighteen notebooks that I filled are the primary source of this memoir. They have been complemented by my own archives and by publicly available documents.

Writing a book is a lonely enterprise, but I have been fortunate to have the support of remarkable institutions and individuals. As the director of the Center for International Conflict Resolution and a professor of practice at the Arnold A. Saltzman Institute of War and Peace Studies at Columbia University, I have benefited from the intellectual stimulation of a great academic institution, and my students have been a constant source of inspiration. I owe thanks in particular to Richard Betts, the director of the institute, and Robert Jervis, who read the whole manuscript.

After I left the United Nations in 2008, the Brookings Institution welcomed me as a senior fellow, associated with the Center for International Cooperation at New York University. I am especially grateful to Strobe Talbott, Martin Indyk, and Bruce Jones for their encouragement and support. Bruce Jones reviewed the entire book and gave me helpful advice on how to balance a personal memoir with analytical research. I also benefited from the review of eminent specialists for individual chapters. I would like to express my gratitude to David

Malone, now the rector of the United Nations University and a keen observer of the works of the Security Council, who read the chapter on Iraq; Herbert Weiss, the uncontested dean of Congolese studies in the United States, for his helpful insights on the Democratic Republic of the Congo; Ghassan Salamé, a close friend and dean of the Paris School of International Affairs, who read the chapter on his country, Lebanon; and David Harland, the executive director of the Centre for Humanitarian Dialogue in Geneva, who worked with me on the Kosovo file at the UN and helped me better understand the Balkans. Needless to say, while I have tried to heed their advice, I take full responsibility for the final product, which reflects my own thoughts, uncertainties, and maybe errors!

Throughout this long process, I have been privileged to have the support of exceptionally dedicated and thoughtful research assistants. As I was slowly retracing the years I spent at the United Nations, Nealin Parker and then Megan M. Gleason accompanied me on that journey, fact checking, reviewing, asking hard questions, and most important, encouraging me.

Last, I want to thank my wife Michele and my daughter Claire. I did not see enough of them during my years at the UN, but they understood that having the possibility of making a small positive difference in the life of others was an opportunity that I could not ignore. I have written this book for Claire, with the hope that it will help the world in which she will live become less violent and more humane.

This book is part of the Brookings Foreign Policy Program project on Order from Chaos.

INDEX